Sasha Graham

365 TAROT SPELLS

About the Author

Sasha Graham teaches tarot classes and produces tarot events at New York City's premier cultural institutions, including the Metropolitan Museum of Art. She has shared her love of tarot on film, television, radio, and print. She resides in New York City. Visit her online at sashagraham.com.

Sasha Graham

365
TAROT
SPELLS

CREATING THE MAGIC IN EACH DAY

Llewellyn Publications
WOODBURY, MINNESOTA

SIXTH PRINTING, 2023
First Edition

Author photo by Karl Giant
Book design and edit by Rebecca Zins
Cover design by Ellen Lawson
Interior images: *Llewellyn's Classic Tarot* © Eugene Smith
Cover images: iStockphoto.com/6524824 © Chapman and Smith; tarot cards from
  So Below Deck, Book of Shadows Tarot, Volume 2, courtesy of Lo Scarabeo

Llewellyn is a registered trademark of Llewellyn Worldwide Ltd.

LIBRARY OF CONGRESS CATALOGING-IN-PUBLICATION DATA
Names: Graham, Sasha, author.
Title: 365 tarot spells : creating the magic in each day / Sasha Graham.
Other titles: Three hundred sixty-five tarot spells | Three hundred and
  sixty-five tarot spells
Description: Woodbury : Llewellyn Worldwide, Ltd, 2016. | Includes index.
Identifiers: LCCN 2016000928 (print) | LCCN 2016001757 (ebook) | ISBN
  9780738746241 | ISBN 9780738748795 ()
Subjects: LCSH: Tarot. | Magic.
Classification: LCC BF1879.T2 G6564 2016 (print) | LCC BF1879.T2 (ebook) |
  DDC 133.3/2424—dc23
LC record available at http://lccn.loc.gov/2016000928

Llewellyn Publications
A Division of Llewellyn Worldwide Ltd.
2143 Wooddale Drive
Woodbury MN 55125-2989
www.llewellyn.com
Printed in the United States of America

FOR
Izzy, Mac, and Sky

Contents

Introduction 1

How to Use This Book 5

January • 8

February • 39

March • 68

April • 99

May • 129

June • 160

July • 190

August • 221

September • 252

October • 282

November • 313

December • 343

Index of Spells 375

Index of Cards 395

3*65 Tarot Spells* is a direct result of my passion for Janina Renée's *Tarot Spells*. I began working with Janina's book over a decade ago. Back in those days I held very different ideas about magical practice, witchcraft, and tarot. The first night I cast from *Tarot Spells*, two profound experiences occurred.

My desired goal was money manifestation. Nerves racked my belly as I sat at my kitchen table. The candles flickered; the tarot cards were spread out. About halfway through the process, I stopped. The air was different. The space looked different. I felt different. The environment I had created with my focused intention was so beguiling, so strong, and so remarkably different from the normal world that I sat inside it like a sun worshipper, soaking it in.

My original goal of manifesting money was tossed aside. I had discerned something more important than obtaining a future outcome or material gain. I sat inside the space where my interior and exterior met. It was the electric nature of sacred space. My actions had created the space. It did not stem from religious dogma, a Sunday church service, or a New Age bookstore. It blossomed from my intention. It was spectacular.

The second impactful lesson I learned that fateful evening was that Janina Renée brings the practitioner inside the tarot cards. She created an immersive experience in which you could converse with archetypes, explore the environment of the card, touch them, feel them, and see them moving about. This simple adjustment rapidly expanded my tarot experience beyond the practice of magic or divination. She brought the entire deck to life. It is my sincere hope that *365 Tarot Spells* will offer you the same rich tarot experience.

Eventually, I took my magic practice outside. Why confine yourself to the kitchen table? Why sketch a pentacle on a sheet of paper when you can trace one across a snow-covered field? Why settle for a little pine incense when an army of pine trees await your call? Why stay indoors when you can see your magical intention crystallized as you whisper it into winter's eastern wind?

Nature spirits soared above, reminding me of spiritual height. Fast, furry animals burrowed below the ground, reminding me of the underworld, darkness, and growth. Weeping willows demonstrated how strong and delicate the human spirit can be. A great buck's white bones, plucked clean by scavengers, offered meaningful meditations on the nature of death. Vegetable and flower gardens offered valuable guidance on how to nurture my young daughter. Lessons appeared everywhere. The more I observed, the more I learned. You can move your consciousness inside of a tree or an herb the same way you can enter a tarot card: through observation and intention. You can align with the energy of anything. And you can work in tandem with the energy, be it the property of an herb or the collective resonance of an archetype.

Magic is based on the tapestry of interconnectivity between you and the natural world. It is a majestic interplay. Magic is best understood as a threefold process:

1. Desire (Thought, Idea)

An idea dawns on you. You realize you want something. You discover a truth inside yourself that must be made reality. You are ready to experience it. You realize you would like to live close to the sea. You want to change career paths. You desire more fun in life. You are ready to experience love. From desire you form a concise intention for your magical goal, i.e., "I will live next to the ocean" or "I am attracting an amazing romantic partner."

2. Feeling (Align Yourself, Visualize)

You have stated your desire. Now it is time to align your energy with your desire. See it. Feel it. Smell it. Taste it. Bring it into focus. Act as if you have it already. If you want to live near the beach, smell the salt air, taste the fish tacos, and see the moonlight rippling across the ocean waves. This is also where magical accessories are selected—items whose natural energy align with your goal: roses and chocolate for love, caffeine for action, mint for money. Tarot cards are chosen: Queen of Wands for charisma, the Sun for health, King of Pentacles for money, and so on.

3. Action (Spell)

The fastest way to bring something into your life is to take action on it. Performing a spell is that action. It makes your desire known, your intention clear. It is your call and response with the universe.

Making magic is like making love. No two souls perform or experience magical practice in the same way. The magical act can be an intimate experience enjoyed by the solo practitioner or a shared experience with a friend, lover, or coven. The choice is yours. Some people achieve seemingly magical results without ever performing spells, but spellcasting is sensual, emotional, and always a discovery process.

Each of us has a unique magical fingerprint. Some of us are built for natural magic, finding that our talents and results soar in the rustling forest or amidst the wild winds of seascapes. Others may excel using the precise nature of ceremonial magic. Some of us are naturally drawn to gemstones and crystals while others prefer candle or crafting magic. Discovering and cultivating personal magic is one of the most exciting things you will ever do. It is the absolute delight and right of every person to find out where their magical ability lies.

Tarot is the perfect magical tool. Tarot cards operate at a different energetic level than herbs, food, candles, or incense. Tarot does not grow from the ground nor does it have a season in which it thrives. Tarot is a metaphysical machine that has sprung from human consciousness. It communicates through symbol. Archetypes of tarot are strong and embedded in our psyche. We may enter the card as if through a gate. We move into an altered state—the subtle world that exists between nature and imagination, where all things become possible. This is where true change occurs. This is where we alter the shape of the psyche. We are able to access and unlock hidden parts and pieces of ourself that might have otherwise lain dormant. This unlocks new possibility.

Magical practice will teach you that you are not separate from the natural world; you are part of it. It teaches that you are not separate from other people; we are all connected. Magic will teach you that the gateway to the supernatural and your imagination is found through the pleasurable cultivation of your five senses. Magic teaches that what you put out in the world via spells, words, or day-to-day interactions will come back to you. A magical practice will teach the value of living in the moment, engaging the present, and releasing the ego.

Magic doesn't teach you how to "get" things from life. It teaches you how to embrace and experience it. It teaches you how to interface and play with your reality in order to make your soul's intention/manifestation real, and the manifestation of your true self just happens to be why we are all here to begin with.

Venture out into the world. Break out of the conventions of those who have come before. Don't be defined by books of magic. Discover your own archetypes. Make your own magical associations. Find out what resonates for you. Become your own guru. Let experimentation become your teacher. Magic is experiential. Experience it!

Magical practice offers everyone the opportunity to reinvent themselves from the inside out. Why? Because you are a sorceress who has already created the world you inhabit, whether you realize it or not. Magical practice and tarot give you the tools and opportunities to cultivate, explore, and expand that world, and its boundaries are infinite.

Just like you.

Sasha Graham
NEW YORK CITY, 2015

365 Tarot Spreads, a book I wrote in 2014, contains a tarot spread for every day of the year. As I crafted *365 Tarot Spreads* it dawned on me that the structure would make an excellent premise for a spell book. You may notice that interesting historical factoids are cross-referenced between the two books. This was done intentionally. Feel free to use the books in conjunction, first performing a tarot spread for clarity, then performing the spell to manifest your desired outcome.

You need not perform the spell on the date it is listed. The calendar simply supplied an excellent framework for a collection of spells I hope you will find useful for a lifetime.

Anyone Can Use This Book

You do not need to know anything about tarot or have magical training to use this book.

Choose Your Deck

Llewellyn's Classic Tarot was selected to illustrate this book. Its vivid, colorful images will bring the viewer straight into the heart of the arcana.

You should use any tarot deck you feel a strong magical connection to for spellwork. It is a good idea to select a separate tarot deck, one used only for the purpose of magic. There are two reasons for this. First, you will foster a specific energetic connection with the magical deck. Second, it will free you to carry your magical or charmed tarot cards with you and keep your spell mandalas in sight (as is often advised), while a separate deck will be available for readings and other uses.

Read Each Spell All the Way Through and Gather All Tools

Mise en place is a French cooking expression meaning "everything in its place." Preparing recipes and casting spells retain similar principles. You should be thoroughly familiar with each spell before preparing and crafting it. Have all required tools at your fingertips. Read each spell all the way through. Visualize yourself performing each step as you read the spell. It will pave the way for improvisations and additional elements you might add to provide a personal touch.

Every spell in the book requires a tarot card. If an item suggested is challenging to find, either discard its use, find a substitute, or let the procuring of that item become part of the spell.

Pick, Choose, and Improvise

Magic is an art form, not a science. Each spell offers different ingredients, incantations, and cards. Some spells are simple and use only the tarot; others are more complicated and use accessories.

Just because I wrote it doesn't mean it is right for you. Change and adapt the spells as wildly as you see fit. The more emotionally intuitive your connection with your tools and accessories, the stronger your magic will be. Consider each spell a base, a guideline. Let it inspire your own interpretations. Built upon what I wrote. Make it your own.

Create Sacred Space

It is assumed that each practitioner will open their personal sacred space before casting any spell in this book. That may be as simple as lighting a single dedicated candle or as complex as invoking the elements or guardian angels, burning incense, and working with lunar cycles, astrological timing, etc. The opening and closing of the space in the spell is left for you to determine as you see fit.

Responsible Magic

1. Magic is not a substitute or a replacement for medical treatment, financial responsibility, or psychotherapy.

2. You are required to do the work to back up your spell. Magic is never a quick fix.

3. Remember the magical rule of three: what you send out to the world will come back to you three times as strong. Never, ever, *ever* cast harmful or negative magic on another person, place, or thing.

Enter the Card

Many guided meditations and spells will ask you to enter the card. Entering the card means literally bringing your consciousness inside of the arcana. Due to the wide variety of deck availability, some elements I describe may differ from the image you are using.

Become the Figure on the Card

Tarot is seventy-eight reflections of you. There are many instances when I suggest you become the figure—the Empress, the Queen of Cups, the Hierophant, and so on. Inhabiting the figures of tarot and looking through their eyes is a unique way to experience their lessons and the higher and lower, outer and inner aspects of yourself. Embrace this process, then try this practice in your regular life. Look at your boyfriend through the Knight of Wand's eyes or sip tea with your mother and look at her through the Hierophant's eyes.

Connection Rituals

Scattered throughout the book are seventy-eight connection rituals to each and every arcana of tarot. These rituals are to foster a deep connection between yourself and the arcana. It will expand your tarot practice and your experience of the cards. This is your opportunity to climb smack-dab into the heart of the arcana.

It's the first day of the new year! Perform this spell when you are turning over a new leaf, replacing an old habit with a new one, and marking a new cycle in your life.

INCANTATION

Goodbye old

Embrace the new

Fresh cycles bring

Surprises too

This moment marks

My soul and heart

As I make

A brand-new start

The Fool's Fresh Start Spell

Ingredients
1. Death
2. The Fool
- White rose

Method, Visualization, and Meditation

The Death card represents endings and marks the moment of transformation. The Fool reflects fearlessly leaping forward toward new realities and possibilities. White roses represent purity. The color white represents a fresh start and a blank page.

Place the Death card. Enter the card. Listen carefully. What do you hear: music, wind, voices? Can you hear the clip-clop of the horses' hooves? A lifeless king lays upon the ground. He represents what has passed, what is finished and done. A girl in white turns from the skeleton in fear, who marches forward like time. Like the child in blue, you look up in amazement at Death and its gifts. The sun rises between two towers. You usher in a new dawn, release the past, and discard what no longer serves you.

Place the Fool card. Enter the card. Morning sunlight spills over from Death's arcana and fills the Fool's arcana with a vibrant midday lemon-yellow light. Drag the Fool card over the Death card so the Fool sits atop Death. Hear the wind of opportunity blowing across the mountain peaks.

Take your white rose in hand. It is the Fool's symbol. Smell the flower and contemplate its petals and beauty. Leave it on your table to remind you of the fresh possibilities your new year brings.

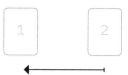

8

Honor Your Ancestors Spell

Ingredients
- Ancestral altar, shelf, or table
- Fresh flowers
- Candle
1. Nine of Pentacles
2. Six of Cups
3. Four of Wands

Method, Visualization, and Meditation

Ancestral alters can be combined into the decoration of a home. The Nine of Pentacles represents our physical connection to our family tree. The Six of Cups represents emotional qualities and the stories we inherit from our family (positive and negative). The Four of Wands reflects happiness and stability in the hearth and home.

Create a space for ancestral photos, items, and keepsakes. Place a bowl of fresh flowers and light a candle. Place the Nine of Pentacles. Enter the card. Stand inside the vineyard and consider how you are the fruit and blossom of your family. Every garden has its season and its day; this moment in time is yours. Consider those spirits who lived before; they stand in the castle, observing. You are the living connection to the past, the result of millions of years of evolution.

Place the Six of Cups and consider how you embody certain family traits. How do you experience your birthright? What have you been given? What are you grateful for? Acknowledging the positive, begin to feel an emotional swell of gratitude for the good you have been given.

Place the Four of Wands. How has stability been passed to you? Where do you draw your strength? How does happiness bloom and thrive?

The cards should be left out for twenty-four hours.

Haitians celebrate Ancestors' Day (Jour des Aieux) today. Relatives celebrate and pay special homage to those family members who have passed to the other side.

INCANTATION

House of spirits
Ghosts of mine
Thank you for
Your gifts divine
You lived your truth
Now's my time
Thank you for
Your gifts sublime

Paris celebrated the Feast of Saint Genevieve today. Genevieve's protection, clairvoyance, and miracles were widely believed to have saved Paris from both the plague and the fearsome Attila the Hun.

INCANTATION

Swords and silver

Blades and steel

Thoughts have power

They are real

Seal myself

Inside safe space

Protective shield

Is now in place

Personal Protection Spell

Ingredients

1. Two of Swords
2. Queen of Swords
3. King of Swords
4. Knight of Swords
5. Ace of Swords
- 2 pinches of sea salt

Method, Visualization, and Meditation

Swords are the suit of the mind. Perform this spell sitting on the floor and facing north. Focus on yourself, not the negativity you wish to avoid. Remember, Swords are the suit of the mind.

Place the Two of Swords before you. Mirror her posture from your waist up: settle into your hips, straighten your spine, and cross your arms before your chest. Close your eyes. Nothing can hurt you. See and feel two long swords in your hands.

Place the Queen of Swords. Turn to face her. She protects you from the east. Your new beginnings are safe. Place the King of Swords. Turn to face him. He protects you from the south. Your passions are safe. Place the Knight of Swords. Turn to face him. He protects you from the west. All you manifest is safe. Place the Ace of Swords above the Two of Swords. Turn to face it. It protects your true north. Your truth and inspiration belong to no one but you.

Resume your Two of Swords posture for as long as you like, imagining a protective lattice of swords around you. Imagine this lattice of protection when you need to summon protectiveness in the world.

Throw two pinches of salt out your front door.

5

1

4   you   2

3

Fairy-Tale Magic Spell

Ingredients
1. Card representing your desire
2. Item representing your tale of choice (an apple for Snow White, a fancy shoe for Cinderella, a feather for the fairy godmother, etc.)
3. Nine of Cups

Method, Visualization, and Meditation

What is your favorite fairy tale? This creative spell asks you to invent a personal spell woven from childhood enchantments and dreams.

How can we invoke fairy-tale magic into our life? Think of your favorite fairy tale and what element you would like to access. Would you like to transform like Cinderella at the ball? Choose a pumpkin. Wake up to the gentle lips of a prince like Sleeping Beauty? Choose a needle. Communicate with animals like Snow White? Choose a song. Perhaps you are in need of a fairy god-mother's service? Find a feather.

Select a card representing your desire and place it before you. Enter the card with your mind's eye and imagine yourself embodying your desire. Take your time and enjoy.

Place the item you have chosen next to the card while repeating the incantation to the right.

Place the Nine of Cups. Your wish has been granted.

1   2   3

Jacob Grimm, of Grimm's Fairy Tales, was born on this day in 1785. The Grimm brothers' dark and evocative stories have been weaving magic for multiple generations of avid readers.

INCANTATION

Fairy tales
Bewitching spells
Enchanted forest
Sorcery dwells
"Once upon a time" is said
Familiar line sticks in the head
Focus on the power of you
[said to item]
As I'm done
my dream comes true

Three of Pentacles Connection Ritual

The Three of Pentacles was called the Lord of Material Works by the magicians of the Golden Dawn, who assigned it the time period of December 31–January 9.

INCANTATION

Three of Pentacles
Creative mind
Magic with others
You will find
Work together
Open, inspire
Success comes quick
Hearts afire

Three of Pentacles Connection Ritual

Ingredient
• Three of Pentacles

Method, Visualization, and Meditation
Enter the arcana of the Three of Pentacles.

You are standing on cool slabs of cement on an oppressively hot day. You have found shelter in an ancient cathedral. Its Gothic ramparts twist, turning into the far reaches of the ceiling and disappearing into dim shadows. You are at the spiritual center of a centuries-old town.

The stone walls crumble with age. Bricks and rocks whisper to you. The gravelly voice of the masons who set them into place beg your attention with their muttering. These artisans call out from the rising walls of the church. The shadows of villagers who have lived their lives inside and amongst these walls call to you. Centuries of prayers and song rise in your ears as the emotions of those who have come to worship, pray, and weep sweep across the dim chamber. It is a truly sacred space.

A murmured conversation brings your attention to a small alcove. Three people stand, absorbed in collaboration. A Freemason is identified by his white apron, masonic instrument, and ceremonial bench. Two people hold architectural plans and discuss what is being built.

Three pentacles adorn the archway above them. The people stand like the holy trinity represented above. Trinities—be they father, son, ghost or maiden, mother, crone or conscious, super conscious, or subconscious—always represent creativity and the exponent of ideas.

Pentacles are the material world. These three have come together in collaboration that will lead to something physical. Like cells generating new growth, three minds create a new solid and enduring structure.

Spell to Reconnect with Personal Magic

Ingredients

- Vacuum
1. The Magician
2. King of Wands
3. Queen of Wands
4. Knight of Wands
5. Page of Wands

```
          [ 2 ]
   [ 4 ] [ 1 ] [ 5 ]
          [ 3 ]
```

Method, Visualization, and Meditation

Have you ever suffered a crisis of personal power? The feeling can be disheartening at best, depressing at worst. Losing touch with personal power can feel like falling out of love with your life; sometimes we just forget how to plug in. Use your vacuum like Befana to remove this problem.

Housecleaning is powerful magic because as you bring order to your home, you literally rearrange the world around you. Spacial energy changes as you clean, dust, and organize. The Magician, your electrical outlet card and personal power source, channels electricity into the four passionate Wand court cards.

Place the Magician card. Standing as the Magician, feel energy flowing through you, entering from the top of your head and going through the bottom of your feet. Assume his posture with hand raised skyward and point down with the vacuum hose. Turn the machine on and feel the power of the vacuum. Clean mindfully and return to the cards.

Place the King of Wands. Activate the powerful side of your personality. Your actions are done with the least amount of resistance.

Place the Queen of Wands. Activate the feminine side of your magical power. Consider how you nurture others and where you create change in the world.

Place the Knight of Wands. Feel passion radiate, exploding from your body in every conceivable direction.

Place the Page of Wands. Contemplate the joy and fun you feel when engaging your magical talents. Your imagination is the map; your talent is the tool.

Italy associates tonight with Befana, an old woman who flies through the night on a broomstick leaving gifts for children, like Santa. She is said to sweep away the problems of the previous year as she leaves.

• • • • •

INCANTATION

Invoke my power
Raise it high
Wands' passion
Fire's sigh
Blood races fast
Heart beats quick
This cleaning spell
Does the trick

January • 7

Weight-Loss Spell

We are what we eat!
The Fanny Farmer Cookbook, *kitchen classic and harbinger of good food and quality ingredients, was published on this day in 1896.*

INCANTATION
Cells grow small
Fat release
Negative habits
Now will cease
Feed myself
With health and wealth
My body becomes
Swift and stealth

Ingredients
1. The Sun
2. The Magician
3. The Star
• Apple

Method, Visualization, and Meditation
Weight-loss spells are best cast during the waning moon. As the moon shrinks, so does your waistline.

Ruled by Venus, apples are the most magical fruit, a symbol of the witch. The Sun card represents ultimate health, the Magician is assertive energy, and the Star is your weight-loss goal.

Place the Sun card. Place your attention on the sun's face. Feel the heat radiating out of the sphere, sinking into your skin, warming your body. It pumps and powers everything you do. Place one hand on your hearth and the other on your belly. Spread the warmth through your entire body. Envision the healthiest version of you possible. Your body is the perfect physical machine to house your soul. Decide at once that you will feed your body healthy and life-sustaining foods.

Place the Magician card. See him channeling the healthy energy of the sun. He is the conduit of this powerful electrical current. Place the Star card. Feel yourself standing naked under the night sky. Peace and calm fill you. You know who you are. You know you are perfect. You achieve your goal effortlessly.

Eat your apple. Linger on the tart, sweet flavor. Imagine the mix of sun, seed, and organic matter that created this apple. You are energy consuming energy. Know you have already achieved your goal.

If health and taste permit, eat an apple every single day, mindfully recalling your spell, until you hit your goal weight.

1

2

3

14

Get Out of Debt Spell

Ingredients
1. Ten of Wands
2. Knight of Pentacles
3. King of Pentacles

Method, Visualization, and Meditation

The Ten of Wands represents debt. The Knight of Pentacles is the allocation of money. The King of Pentacles represents wealth and the result of the spell.

Place the Ten of Wands. The wands in his arms are like the debt you have accumulated. His head is drawn toward the ground, his back bent. You are about to relieve him, and yourself, of this stress.

Place the Knight of Pentacles to his right. This knight holds a pentacle in his hand. Focus on this pentacle. It represents the energy of money and your ability to make and spend it. The horse snorts and snuffs impatiently. His pentacle is the very first payment you will make. You are going to toss this pentacle like a baseball from the knight into the Ten of Wands card. Doing so, you're knocking out one of his wands and paying down the debt.

Focus all your mental energy; when you are ready, throw.

Place the King of Pentacles immediately on top of the Ten of Wands. The king represents your future. You are solid and secure. You have paid down your debts and enjoy savings and holdings that offer protection and freedom. Dwell in this space, feeling the prosperity all around you. Keep the king in sight to remind you of this.

The United States became debt free on this day in 1835 and stayed debt free for one year. Perform this spell after you have formulated a plan to rid or pay down your debt.

• • • • •

INCANTATION
Debt, begone
Be paid away
I make my first
Payment today
You disappear
Do not return
You are a lesson
I have learned

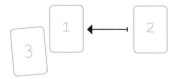

On this day in 1493, Christopher Columbus reported spying three mermaids off the coast of the Dominican Republic. They were actually manatees.

INCANTATION

Queen of Cups

Mysteries deep

Watery depths

Secrets keep

The deeper I dive

The further I go

A mermaid's heart

Is what I know

Mermaid Magic Bath Spell

Ingredients

- 1 cup kosher salt
- Shells and ocean accessories
- Queen of Cups

Method, Visualization, and Meditation

Mermaids—the witches, sirens, and goddesses of sea foam—exist in cross-cultural mythology. Prepare this mermaid magic bath spell and let the mermaid express the hidden and sacred feminine aspects of yourself.

Kosher salt is used because it has been blessed. The Queen of Cups is the mermaid of the tarot deck.

Run the water and add the salt. Place your shells and ocean accessories around the tub. Remove your clothing. While your bath is filling, focus on your Queen of Cups card. Look at the shiny stones that scatter the sand beneath her feet. The water laps over the stones. Each smooth ocean undulation caresses the shiny rocks, who glisten in the sun. They are remnants of the force of water crushing granules of sand, compressing and compacting them. Memory is trapped inside these ancient stones. Which stone calls to you? Is it the blue, yellow, or deep ruby-red stone? In your mind's eye, pick it up and hold it in your hand. This stone contains an answer you have been seeking.

Enter the bathtub. As you allow the water to wash over you, allow memories to wash over you as well. Mermaids live in duality, both above and below the water. How do you do the same? Consider the mysteries you unravel and weave around yourself. Mermaids swim to the darkest depths—to the repository of your secrets and talents. Let your inner mermaid journey down and bring something back for you.

Activate the Muse Spell

Ingredients
- Three of Cups
- Object representing your work
- The Star
- Chocolate offering

Method, Visualization, and Meditation

Ancient Greeks credited muses and geniuses as co-creators in their creative process. A muse may be present in the form of spiritual energy, like a guide or an angel, or a muse can be an actual person who inspires your work.

The Three of Cups represents muse energy. The Star card represents you channeling your muse's inspiration.

Select an object representing the work you do. For example, to summon a writing muse, select a pen; for a performing muse, an eyeliner wand; for a painting muse, select a paint brush.

The power to invoke occurs when you repeat a word or phrase three times.

Place the Three of Cups above your line of sight but where you can see it. Look up at the card and consider the work at hand and the muse who would help. Pick up the object you have selected, point it toward the card, and repeat the incantation.

Place the Star card before you. Feel creative energy pouring into your soul from above. Feel the pathway opening—the highway of creative inspiration. Feel inspiration fill you like water in the Star's jug. Feel it from the soles of your feet, moving through your body to your waist, up your spine, and all the way to the top of your scalp. Call forth your greatest work from the very fabric of the universe. Be the channel.

Place the chocolate in front of the Three of Cups as a thank you to your muse.

Painter Georgia O'Keefe was awarded the Presidential Medal of Freedom on this day in 1977. Tap into your own creative powers, call for guidance, and summon your own personal muse for any project at hand.

• • • • •

INCANTATION
Brilliant inspiration
Come to me
To your terms
I do agree
Pluck me like fruit
Upon the tree
I call for you with
The magic of three
Te invovo, meditatus sum
Te invovo, meditatus sum
Te invovo, meditatus sum!

Postpartum Ritual for Peace

Have you or a close friend become a new mother? Today Carmenta—goddess of childbirth and prophecy, protector of midwives, mothers, and children—was celebrated by a Roman feast day.

Ingredients
- Music you love
- Lavender in multiple forms
- Organic white cannellini beans, garlic, and olive oil
- The Star

Method, Visualization, and Meditation

New mothers are busy caring for their new arrivals and healing from childbirth. They have little energy to devote to other things. If you plan to perform this ritual for yourself, be sure to have all items ready ahead of time.

Carmenta is often depicted with a flute; play your favorite music to honor her. Lavender is sacred to Hecate, a guardian of midwives, and is the most restorative of herbs. Garlic, olive oil, and beans contain sacred health-protecting properties and are also derived from ancient Roman cuisine.

Clean the home or arrange to have it cleaned when the new mom arrives home with baby.

Place fresh lavender around the home. Have spritz bottles of lavender available to freshen rooms daily. Tuck lavender sachets into pillows to deepen restorative sleep.

Play your favorite music. Bring about instant peace and nurturing by sautéing a little chopped garlic in olive oil. Add a can of drained and rinsed organic white cannellini beans. As the beans are cooking, focus on the Star card. Just as the Star channels inspiration from above, you have channeled life. Honor your body and its waters for its miracle. You are the embodiment of true magic. You are the gateway to life. You must rest and restore yourself while keeping a piece of you open to that connection. Let the Star card remind you of this every time you glance upon it.

Enjoy the garlic and beans with some salt and pepper. Continue to contemplate your health, energy, and sense of well-being.

INCANTATION

Light of life
And peace of home
Healing food
And garlic foam
Restore the body
Sleep in, maybe
Nurture my soul
And love my baby

X-Ray Vision Spell

Ingredients
1. Eight of Swords
2. The Sun
3. The Hanged Man reversed

Method, Visualization, and Meditation

Want to look deeper or uncover hidden truths? The bound Eight of Swords represents personal blind spots. The Sun reflects illuminating energy. A reversed Hanged Man depicts an altered point of view.

Place the Eight of Swords. Enter the card. Feel yourself wrapped inside tight white cotton bands. You hover above the ground, bare feet inches above the sand.

It is time to come to earth. Feel yourself dropping, the sand beneath your feet, your bonds releasing. Using newly freed hands, lift the blindfold from your eyes.

Place the Sun card. Enter the card. The light is blinding: so bright, you must keep your eyes tightly clenched shut. Eventually, the blackness behind your eyes fades to brown and then yellow, and you know it is safe to look around. As if waking from a nap and into a new reality, the light of the sun helps you to see further than before. Look at the wall in front of you. Allow your mind's eye to look through the wall. Look at your cupboards, your closets. What rests behind closed doors?

Look outside into nature. What resides at the base of a tree, in the innards of a plant, or on the other side of that mountain? What hides in the forest? Really "see" it.

Place the reversed Hanged Man. The illumination glowing around his scalp glows around yours. Your light has been officially switched on. From this moment forth, you permanently see further, wider, and greater.

[1]   [2]   [3]

The world's first X-ray image experiments were successfully conducted on this night in 1896. Perhaps our own lack of perception or insistence of our particular point of view keeps greater secrets from being revealed to us.

• • • • • •

INCANTATION

My gifts unwrapped
Are on display
Invoke the power
Of X-ray
Peer through all
See every sign
X-ray vision
You are mine

The Knights Templar gained papal sanction on this day in 1128.

Knight of Pentacles Connection Ritual

Ingredient
- Knight of Pentacles

Method, Visualization, and Meditation

Tarot knights are often messengers heralding news. They represent actual people or qualities of your personality. A knight's appearance always brings movement, action, and exchange of energy.

Enter the arcana of the Knight of Pentacles. A warm clover-scented breeze caresses your face. The knight's stallion smells of sweet hay and his coat is the color of fertile, upturned earth. The horse snorts out his nose and you sense the latent power residing in his strong legs. Green sprigs of tender growth decorate his bridle.

Silver armor ensconces the knight. Reach out to feel the smooth metal; your finger leaves a short trail across the gleam. Your eyes, hair, and reflection look back at you from the knight's armor. His soft flesh lies beneath his armor, and you consider the risk he puts himself at when he moves toward an adventure. His red cloak carries with it the power of the sun, which blesses this knight.

INCANTATION

Knight of Pentacles

Helps life to grow

His power's within me

This I know

Action creates

Cause and effect

Take my time

Pause and reflect

A golden pentacle rests in his hand. Inside the pentacle resides something that looks like the illuminated gears of a clock, all miniature movement and light.

He hands you the pentacle, pulls his leg up and over his saddle, and lands on the ground next to you. The pentacle is heavy, like a crystal ball in your hands. His brown eyes take you in, and you have the uncanny sense he can see all of you. He takes the pentacle back, kneels to the ground, pushes loamy dirt aside, and plants the pentacle in the earth. He dusts the dirt off his gloves and hops back into his leather saddle. It creaks beneath his weight. He nods at you, shoots you a wink, and is off.

He rides, slow and steady, into the distance. You look back to his seed. It has already begun to sprout, a tiny green shoot quivering through the earth, reaching up and toward the sun in the blue sky above.

Four of Pentacles Connection Ritual

Ingredient
- Four of Pentacles

Method, Visualization, and Meditation
Enter the arcana of the Four of Pentacles.

Fours represent stability. The arcana of three burst forth creatively and has evolved to the next stage. A fourth appears: stability is reached. A square. A home. A haven. The structure is complete. Four seasons. Four directions. Four elements. Four suits of tarot. Reality in the physical world has been achieved.

You stand at the foot of a stage about neck high. Lean forward, cross your arms, and rest your chin on your forearm in front of you. The stage's backdrop is painted with a bustling medieval city, towers reaching toward the sky. Colorful flags wave in the breeze. The thriving town is cheerful in its architecture and landscaping.

An actor adorned in royal clothing sits on a concrete block, center stage. He balances a pentacle on his forehead crown chakra and another at his chest's heart chakra. His hands and arms wind strangely around this disk as if they were rubber. Each foot rests lightly on two more pentacles. They look like circles on the ground. His direct gaze rests upon you.

It is impossible to interpret his intent. Is he hiding behind his money or is he protecting himself with it? Has the merchant's wealth built the town behind him? What does financial security bring us in the end? Is he the Merchant of Venice?

The merchant is so grounded, he does not move. He continues staring at you. From his protective stance, a structure grows. It is the home you live in. The reality you inhabit. It is the manipulation of material wealth. Humankind's invention of money contains an energy all its own, but it echoes the energy of the natural world.

The Four of Pentacles was called the Lord of Earthly Power by the magicians of the Golden Dawn, who assigned it the time period of January 10–19.

INCANTATION
Four of Pentacles
Stability of cash
Solid structure
Protect my stash
Slow and steady
Does the trick
Enjoy financial
Arithmetic

Healthy Pregnancy Spell

Today is the second feast day of Carmenta, the Roman goddess of childbirth and divination and the patron of midwives. This spell is cast to ensure a healthy pregnancy for both mother and child.

Ingredients
1. The Sun
2. The Empress
- Pomegranate

Method, Visualization, and Meditation

The Empress is the Mother archetype. The Sun card signifies a healthy pregnancy for both mother and child. Pomegranates are symbols of fertility and eternal life. The Berber women of North Africa prophesize their family's future with a pomegranate. Drawing a circle on the ground, they drop a ripe pomegranate inside. The number of seeds breaking the circle is the number of children they will have.

Place the Sun card diagonally above the Empress card. Look for a moment at the spirit of the child hovering over the mother. This echoes the child soul's selection of parent prior to pregnancy. The Empress's wand points toward the sky. Like the Magician, she has manifested the greatest magic. The Empress is a life giver and gateway to life. Notice the pomegranates decorating her gown.

Contemplate the sacred nature of what is happening inside your body. Bring attention to your physical needs so that, like the Empress, you have all things needed at your fingertips: healthy foods, comfortable sleeping, a loving environment. The Empress has everything she requires surrounding her, and so do you.

Slice the pomegranate in half. Divide the seeds from one half into three servings. Eat a single serving of seeds for the next three days, echoing the number of the Empress. Bury the other half of the pomegranate in the earth. Eat every seed of the other half.

INCANTATION

Healthy, healthy

Pregnant glow

Precious life

Inside me grow

Healthy, healthy

Nice and slow

Precious gifts

I do bestow

1

2

Boost Your Business Spell

Ingredients
- ½ cup fresh basil leaves
- Mason jar
1. Queen of Wands
2. Ten of Pentacles
3. King of Wands

On this date in 1412, the Medici family was chosen to be the official banker of the papacy. Use legendary Medici luck to boost your business, no matter what you do for a living.

Method, Visualization, and Meditation

New Orleans business spells often include the use of basil. The Queen and King of Wands carry an intense and passionate combined power. The Ten of Pentacles reflects expansive financial abundance.

Shred the basil leaves while visualizing incoming money. Place leaves in a Mason jar. Pour two cups of boiling water over the shredded green leaves. When cool enough to handle, place the jar on your table. You will place the cards in a row before it.

The Queen of Wands is placed on the left side, representing the feminine pillar of the Tree of Life. Feel the contractive power of feminine fire welling within you. Imagine heat radiating from the bottom of your feet up to your scalp. When the energy is high, send it toward the basil water. Now place the King of Wands on the right side. Feel the masculine expansion of fire. It too grows in your feet and moves through your body. When it reaches its threshold, send the energy toward the water.

Place the Ten of Pentacles between the King and Queen. Enjoy the abundance and wealth pictured on the card. See the pentacles falling like rain through the card. The coins clink like winnings from a slot machine. The multiple figures on the card are people eager to throw money your way.

Let the basil water steep for three days. Sprinkle at thresholds of your business, shop, mailbox, and places where you receive payments and conduct business.

INCANTATION
One, two, three
Wealth comes to me
Like falling leaves from a tree
Abundance pouring over me
Every direction I see
Wealth it comes
Quickly to me

1   2   3

January • 17

*The Feast of St. Anthony
is celebrated today in Spain.
Revelers dress in scarlet devil
costumes to leap and dance
through the licking flames
of bonfires until dawn*

INCANTATION

The Devil
Called by many names
Holds his hostage
Ensconced in flames
We are the ones
Who place those chains
When power and addiction
Race through our veins

Devil Card Connection Ritual

Ingredient
• The Devil

Method, Visualization, and Meditation
Enter the arcana of the Devil.

Sour smoke and sulphur fill the back of your throat. The air is sweltering, liquid with humidity as lava bubbles and flames leap and lick at the walls around you. The Devil perches above you with clawed feet. He gestures with his hand, making a secret signal. You are safe to explore this card. There is no danger.

He is a gruesome feast for the eyes and his piercing gaze holds you in his grip. Curling ram horns sprout from his scalp; furry goat ears perk and twitch. Giant bat wings protrude from his back. They undulate back and forth hypnotically. A black ratlike tail flicks like an agitated cat behind him. He carries the intelligence of man and wildness of beast in one body. His upper body and arms are a thick human shape. Beneath his belly button he becomes wild animal once again, thick curled hair matted and hiding his genitals.

Nude figures like Adam and Eve statues stand beneath the Beast, their skin slick with sweat. They have sprouted small horns upon their heads as if to imitate their master. The man is consumed with the heat of desire, his burning tail stoked by the Devil's torch. The ripe and lush female stands with grapes sprouting on her tail. The man extends his hand to the female, begging her to join him and reaching for her. She refuses him. Instead, she slips the chain from around her neck. She disappears into thin air. The chain falls to the ground with a heavy clank.

The Devil looks on in dismay and disappointment. He throws his head back and peals into hysterical laughter. It echoes through his cavernlike underground dwelling as a realization hits you.

The Devil wields only the power that is given to him...

Open Kundalini Root Chakra Energy

Ingredient
- Queen of Wands

Sir John George Woodroffe, the gentleman who brought tantric philosophy to the West, passed away today in 1936.

Method, Visualization, and Meditation

The root chakra is located at the base of your spine. It is said to be the center of our energetic body and the seat of our kundalini, which is described as an energetic force like a coiled snake. Once unlocked, kundalini rises through the body, creating profound mystical experiences. The root chakra is associated with earth, the sense of smell, and excretion. It is the very seed of who we are and where our essence emerges. On the most basic level it is our primal survival and safety center.

The root chakra connects to the charismatic Queen of Wands due to her energetic stance. Note how she sits on her throne. The root chakra is also associated with the color red, this queen's signature color.

Sit in a chair with your feet flat on the floor or sit in yogi position, legs crossed, on the floor. Place the Queen of Wands before you. Focus on the very base of your spine. Feel it from the front of you and from the back. Tighten your anus. If you are a female, it will feel exactly like a Kegel exercise. Sit straight and adjust your spine. Your root is now locked.

From this position, take a few long, conscious breaths. Imagine a red, glowing circular light at the root of your spine. Spin it. Hear it, smell it, perhaps even taste it. Now gaze at the queen. See how she sits, her spine in perfect alignment, her energy under her deft control. She knows what she wants and how to get it. Survival is guaranteed. She commands her energy. She retains control of her thoughts and actions.

Feel the energy rise through your spine as you fill your vision with light. Send the energy out through your heart in a wave of love.

INCANTATION

Root center

Root of me

Feel my power

Hold the key

Call it forth

Help it rise

Purpose unfolds

Before my eyes

Cast this "moth to a flame" spell on the anniversary of the 1942 film release of Keeper of the Flame, *starring legendary lovers Katharine Hepburn and Spencer Tracy. They met during the making of the film.*

INCANTATION

Lover, lover
Come to me
Light your flame
Feel my plea
See me, love me
Want me more
Than anything
You've wanted before

Spell to Attract a Lover

Ingredients
- Red rose petals
- Two red candles
1. The Empress
2. Ace of Cups
3. Ace of Wands
4. Card representing lover

Method, Visualization, and Meditation

Red roses signify passionate love. Red candles are associated with sex, desire, and Scorpio energy. The Empress card is aspected by Venus, representing beauty and radiance. The Ace of Cups reflects an outpouring of emotion. The Ace of Wands represents passion, fire, and attraction. Select a significator card representing the person you want to attract to you.

Fix a bath. Toss in a handful of rose petals as the water runs. Soak to your heart's content and envision how you attract your lover, why you want them, what you will do with them. Air dry your body, using no towel, then light a single red candle. Cast your cards.

Place the Empress; ponder your inner beauty. See a beautiful summer field in your mind's eye. Imagine yourself reclining on a chaise made of the softest velvet. Your beauty and charisma literally spill out of your body like a waterfall at your feet. The water flows and transforms as you place the Ace of Cups sideways. The water contains the power of your feelings and emotions for the person you desire.

Place the Ace of Wands sideways after the Ace of Cups. Feel a magic wand in your hand, reverberating with explosive energy. Internalize every ounce of energy in your body and collect it in a ball at your tummy. When it feels right, flip over the significator card, point toward it, and send all your desire and magnetism toward the person the card signifies. Feel the energy flowing, creating a bond between the two of you. When you are certain the bond has been created, light the second red candle and repeat the incantation.

1   2   3   4

Aquarius Outside-the-Box Originality Spell

Ingredients
1. The Star
2. Ace of Swords
3. The Tower

Method, Visualization, and Meditation
Cast this spell when you need to embrace a new way of thinking.

The Star card represents Aquarius, the water bearer. The Ace of Swords is the source of pure communication. The Tower card is explosive energy.

Place the Star card and note the figure's nudity. Rather than releasing your clothes, release all the previous ideas you have held about the subject at hand. Starlight twinkles above you. One particular star shines brighter than all others. Illuminate yourself with its light. Allow the glowing light to fill your body as if it were a lantern. The light fills you with new thoughts and new perceptions with which to examine your current situation.

Place the Ace of Swords sideways; it is the conduit of communication. Channel the light within you through the base of the sword. You will use the light to destroy your old thought patterns.

Place the Tower card as the receptacle of your brilliance. Send the light through the sword and into the Tower. It explodes all previous notions into a million tiny pieces. It dislodges and removes all obstacles toward clean, clear thinking.

Place the Star card over the Tower card to replace the darkness of destruction with light.

As you bring your mind's eye back to current reality, keep the light of the star shining from your third eye. Facing any issue, shine the star's light through your third eye to allow it to illuminate all possibilities for you.

Today marks the first day of the astrological sign of Aquarius. Originality graces Aquarius, whose symbol is the water bearer. Aquarians move ideas, communicate, and circulate like freshwater mountain springs. Aquarius energy brings a rush of pioneering energy to any project or effort.

INCANTATION

Star of night
Empower sight
Sword of steel
New thoughts will heal
Tower destroys
Old blocks are gone
New thoughts create
A golden dawn

1   2   3

27

*Today is
National Hug Day.*

Rejuvenate Love and Tender Feelings Spell

Ingredients
1. Two of Cups
2. Ace of Cups

Method, Visualization, and Meditation

This spell was created to provoke, rekindle, and cultivate love inside any relationship, be it romantic, familial, or platonic. This is an especially powerful spell to use when you need to activate the power of forgiveness.

The Two of Cups represents finding your heart's delight in another. The Ace of Cups reflects an outpouring of emotion.

Place the Two of Cups. Enter the card. Facing the person with whom you are involved, see them as they were on the first day you met them. They are looking into your eyes. Look deeply back at them. What is your favorite quality about this person? Hear their voice tell your favorite inside joke. Smile at them.

Place the Ace of Cups above the Two of Cups. What has been bottled up is now open. Flowing feelings and emotional health spills across the two of you. The fountain flows into the two cups.

Once again, you are standing across from this person and you are each holding a cup. At the same time, drink from this cup's healing, clear, sparkling waters of rejuvenation. When you are done drinking, embrace them with a hug.

INCANTATION

Two of cups

Elixir of life

The two of us

Are clear of strife

We'll walk upon

The path anew

As I invoke

My love for you

2

1

Cleopatra's Power Spell

Ingredients
- The Tower
- Card representing your desire
- Cleansing bath or shower
- Fresh bar of soap
- Chopstick
- Coconut oil

Method, Visualization, and Meditation

Cleopatra was famous for her political and erotic powers. Draw anything you desire to you by invoking her intense power. The Tower card represents Cleopatra's Needle and the conduit of magical energy you can use to manifest your desire. Decide specifically what you want. Choose the tarot card that best represents it. You will create a magic amulet with a bar of soap.

Prepare a hot bath with your favorite indulgent bath oils and bubbles, matched to your intention if possible (rose oils for passion, salt and lemon for clarity, etc). As the tub fills, remove your clothing. Hold the Tower card before you. See the tower right before the lightning strikes. It is a monument of power pointing to the sky. Feel the barometer drop as the clouds roll in, electricity filling the air. See lightning striking the tower and recite the incantation.

Place the card representing your desire where you can see it from the tub. Enter the bath. Embrace this new reality filling your life. Enjoy how delicious it feels. Select one symbol from the card.

Take your fresh bar of soap. Using the chopstick, engrave the symbol into the soap. You have created a magical bathing amulet. Wash your entire body with the soap, making sure to cover every inch of your skin with the silky suds. Exit the bath and moisturize your body with coconut oil, which embodies female, lunar power, covering every inch of skin with its nourishment. Wash your hands at least once a day with your amulet soap.

Cleopatra's Needle, an Egyptian obelisk, was erected today in NYC's Central Park in 1881. Visitors have found offerings and the traces of rituals around the needle ever since its erection.

• • • • •

INCANTATION
Tower card
Cleopatra's might
Grant my desire
True tonight
Wish be granted
With strength and speed
Fullfill my every
Want and need

The Five of Swords was called the Lord of Defeat by the magicians of the Golden Dawn, who assigned it the time period of January 20–29.

INCANTATION

Five of Swords

Blades of steel

Will you have

The strength to heal

Language carries

A life of its own

Words malicious

Slice to the bone

Five of Swords Connection Ritual

Ingredient
- Five of Swords

Method, Visualization, and Meditation

Enter the arcana of the Five of Swords.

Fives imply challenge. Fives are the halfway point, the turning point. What has manifested up until now begins to build on itself. The required challenge provides perspective for the ultimate outcome in the finality of the ten. Inside every challenge lies a gift.

You stand on a large wooden stage. A theater is packed to the rafters with people. Hundreds of audience members share a look of shock upon their faces, their mouths shaped like little Os. Something disastrous, graphic, and upsetting has just occurred.

The stage floor is smeared with puddles of blood. Bodies of the slain lie scattered. The audience waits to see what will happen next. You could hear a pin drop. A nasty laugh breaks the silence. The actor closest to you, his hair in spiky chunks, holds two swords and picks up a third. He laughs into the wind as if the air itself were under his command.

A second actor makes his way to a distressed figure near the water. Moving with the air of an ambassador or seductor, it looks as if he means to soothe the situation. The small, distraught figure in the distance keeps his face hidden in his hands. He has lost.

He turns. "How could you destroy everything? Do you think your actions have no consequence? Do you think your words cannot pierce like a knife? Why must you feel good at the expense of another's defeat? Why would you hurt someone else to feel good about yourself?"

The lights go dark.

There is no clapping, no bows. The audience disperses. The show is over. Time to go home.

Release Obsessive Thoughts Spell

Ingredients
- Eight of Swords
- Small spool of thread
- The Fool

Method, Visualization, and Meditation

Use this spell to rid yourself of a negative or harmful thought or idea that refuses to leave.

The Eight of Swords represents being caught in a negative thought pattern. The Fool represents ultimate intellectual freedom. Magical practices use thread as a binding agent. Thread will also work in the opposite direction, releasing you from bonds as you unspool it.

Write down the plaguing thought or idea clearly on a piece of paper. Clearly articulate it before you release it.

Place the Eight of Swords before you. Enter the card. Feel the mental binds that hold you and recall how you feel as the thought consumes you. Note how the feet of the figure on the card do not touch the ground. Place your own feet firmly on the ground. Feel the earth connection.

Pick up the spool of thread. Recite the incantation as you unspool the entirety of the thread.

Place the Fool card over the Eight of Swords. Look at the Fool's upturned face. You have released yourself. The knowledge of what you have done stays with you inside the Fool's bag. Walk forward, freely, like the Fool. Bury the thread in the earth to dispel its energy.

Today in 1915, Ernest Shackleton's ship Endurance *became frozen in Arctic ice. It remained lodged for ten months until it was crushed and sank. Just like Shackleton's ship, our minds can seize hold of a thought or idea and refuse to let go.*

INCANTATION

Obsessive thought
Begone, goodbye
Served your purpose
Now you fly
I release you now
With love and light
Free of your bonds
Free of blight

31

Brighten Winter Doldrums Spell

Ingredients

1. Strength
2. The Sun
• Yellow flowers

Suffering from a case of the winter doldrums? Scotland and the UK celebrate Burns Night today, where suppers are held to celebrate the life and work of Romantic poet Robert Burns. This feast lifts all spirits burdened by the long, dark winter.

INCANTATION

Sun of suns
Moonlight at night
I seek your warmth
I feel your light
Fill me with
Sustaining grace
And bring a smile
To my face

Method, Visualization, and Meditation

If you have a case of seasonal blues and spring feels too far away, perform this spell to lift your spirits.

The Strength card reflects the courage to beat any plaguing issue. The Sun card represents the full glory of summer energy.

Place yellow flowers in a vase of water. Inhale their scent deeply. Place them on the table before you.

Place the Strength card. Enter the card. Hold the great, powerful lion by the mouth. Feel the bone and muscle beneath his fur, his hot breath in your hands, the moistness of his tongue. You are unafraid. Hold him like a kitten. You know how strong you are. Personal strength has brought you to this exact moment. You are strong, capable, and have the power to override any emotion that drags you down.

Place the Sun card against the base of the vase. Focus on the radiant, life-giving sun. This yellow star holds the power of all life on earth. Should you require rejuvenation, look above. See it everywhere. It is expansive, all-encompassing. The energy of the sun warms your body. Feel the heat on your face, on your hair. Life-giving energy—making flowers bloom, babies grow, and love possible—is around and inside you.

Take a single flower from your bouquet. Thank it for its gift of beauty. Remove all petals and place in your palm.

Whisper the incantation and scatter the petals in the wind.

2

1

Face Your Fears Spell

Ingredient
- Eight of Cups

Method, Visualization, and Meditation

Use fear as an agent of transformation. Moving through the fear, a person is initiated and reborn to the other side. You can do the same.

The Eight of Cups takes a cue from the soundtrack of *The Sound of Music* as the "Climb Every Mountain" card. It represents the march onward and upward.

Place the Eight of Cups card. Enter the card. Step into the dim light and stand before the stacked cups. Choose the cup closest to you. Using both hands, pick it up. The cup is heavy. It is filled with liquid. Do not spill it. Gaze into the liquid.

Your fear reflects on the surface. Allow the vision to become clear. What does it look like? Is it a person, an obstacle, a goal, a behavior? Set it down.

Pick up the next cup with both hands. Inside this cup is the same liquid, but the reflection is different. You see the direct opposite of your fear. What is the polar opposite of your fear? How does it look? How does it change?

What gifts await when your fear is faced? Gaze at the reflection as if it were a scrying glass. See your life once you move through your fear. How is it affected? How does it look? How does it feel? When you see the polar opposite of your fear as a specific vision in the cup, set it down.

You now have a choice.

Will you remain frozen in fear at the bottom of the mountain or will you move forward? If you choose to face your fear and accept all of the challenges and rewards that come with it, embrace the cup with that vision. Drink the sweet liquid long and heavy until it has run dry. Make your way up the mountain.

It is Maria von Trapp's birthday today. Generations have enjoyed watching The Sound of Music *as Maria learns to face her fears about her true calling, her fear of true love, and her fear of the devastation of war.*

INCANTATION

Eight of Cups
Faced my fear
Strength and courage
Are always near
Transform myself
Move past the gate
Unlock myself
From fear and hate
I am not afraid

Enchanting Dream Spell

Lewis Carroll, author of Alice's Adventures in Wonderland, was born on this day in 1832. Alice's adventures unwind like a lucid dream. Incredible landscapes and immersive experiences await the dreamer who decides they will have an active hand in their sleeping self.

INCANTATION

Four of swords
And cup of dreams
Shadows dark
Streams of moonbeams
Close my eyes
Take my flight
Journey through darkness
Dance on light

Ingredients
- Candles
- Almonds, Cheddar cheese, and a teaspoon of mustard
- Four of Swords
- Seven of Cups

Method, Visualization, and Meditation

Almonds are sacred to Artemis, goddess of the night. Almonds, cheeses, and grainy mustards contain high levels of melatonin, which increases the vividness of dreams. The Four of Swords represents a solid night's sleep and a canvas for your dreams. The Seven of Cups allows us to choose our dreams and can even induce a lucid dream, in which you control the events of the dream.

Perform this enchantment while you are preparing for bed. Turn off all electric lights and machines. Light your candles. As the flickering light caresses your skin, lay the four of Swords before you. Enter the card. Stand before the sleeping knight effigy. Feel the solemnness of the cathedral around you. Sense the dark space behind and above you. Look up and note the soaring buttresses and arched ceilings of this ancient Gothic church. Otherworldly light streams through the stained glass. The knight's effigy is carved from heavy stone. Feel the weight of this stone. It is the weight that captures you as you sleep.

Place the Seven of Cups card. Enter the card. Allow your eyes to glaze over. Observe the seven floating cups. Each cup is an experience, a landscape awaiting your footsteps. But wait, there are more than seven cups—the cups and clouds expand far beyond the perimeters of the card. Find a cup that contains something you would like to explore.

Nibble on your bedtime snacks while reciting the incantation.

Spell for Peace in the Home

Ingredients
- Bell
- Ten of Cups

Method, Visualization, and Meditation
Bells can be rung to dispel negative energy. To clear space, ring the bell in each corner of the house. The Ten of Cups represents a happy and positive home.

Place the Ten of Cups. Enter the card. Picture yourself standing beneath a glorious rainbow. A fine spray of mist plays across your cheeks as you look into the sky and see the glorious spectrum of rainbow colors. Children dance around you, their giggles like chimes filling the air.

Imagine the most important person in your life. The individual (alive or dead) fills you with calm and peace. See them standing under the rainbow with the warm white light of peace coming from their heart center and moving into you. It spreads through your body from your feet to your head. It radiates out through your legs and arms.

Beginning in the east, the direction of new beginnings, ring the bell three times in each corner. Move clockwise around your home until you have cleared the space.

Henry VII was born on this day in 1457. His marriage to Elizabeth of York officially ended the War of the Roses. Embrace his royal energy today to inspire a spell for gentle peace in the home.

INCANTATION
House of cards
House of love
Peace of light
Wings of dove
Darkness gone
Prevailing light
Space is clear
As is my sight

Sound Sleep Spell

In need of a deep sleep? Cast this spell to find the peace that only a sound night's sleep can restore. The film Sleeping Beauty *was released on this day in 1959.*

INCANTATION

Blissful sleep, come to me
Overcome and protect me
Twice this card
Means eight solid hours
I summon slumber
With all my powers
I drift on night's tides
Till morning's dew
Then I'll wake up
And feel like new

Ingredients
- Four of Swords
- Sandalwood or myrrh oil
- Black candle
- Bath

Method, Visualization, and Meditation

The Four of Swords represents a sound, solid sleep that puts plaguing thoughts to rest. Sandalwood or myrrh oil aids in sleeping. A black candle represents unconscious slumber and the landscape of dreaming, darkness, and sleep. A hot bath before bed will relax and unwind you.

Prep your sleeping area before performing this spell. Turn off all electronic devices and unplug from technology thirty minutes prior. Set up your white noise machine, draw the curtains, and bless your sleeping space the same way you would cultivate sacred space.

Place the Four of Swords. Enter the card. Note the absence of sound. This knight's crypt is buried far below the earth, under a painted window. He is locked inside the place you go to when in your deepest state of sleep. Behind the knight's head is an alter with a single black candle. Light this candle. You will be regifted with the ability to sleep deeply.

Bring your attention back to your room. Massage your oil onto the candle, working it upward. Contemplate the darkness of sleep as expressed by the candle's color. Focus your intention of sleep inside the candle. Light it and focus on the flame. Capture this flame in your mind's eye.

Prepare a warm bath, adding a few drops of your sandalwood or myrrh to its comforting waters. Bathe, dry, and extinguish your candle. Retire to your bed for a good night's sleep.

As you close your eyes, visualize your candle.

Invoke Internal Peace Spell

Ingredients
- Two of Swords
- Marshmallow

Method, Visualization, and Meditation

People seem to use "happiness" as a catchphrase and appear pre-occupied with searching for it. Perhaps we'd be better off if we sought peace instead of happiness.

The Two of Swords represents a self-created and cultivated inner peace. Marshmallows contain lunar energy.

Place the Two of Swords. Enter the card. The figure has placed the blindfold on herself voluntarily. She wishes to sink away from the outer world and into inner realms of peace. The water's ripples echo distant trouble or disturbances, but she is not bothered.

What part of you remains untouched by anything from the outside world? Can you find that place? Can you let all your troubles sink away and be washed by tidal waters? Can moonlight cleanse you? Think of a moment where you found peace in the midst of stress. You have the capacity to do this.

Gaze upon the Two of Swords daily to invoke a practice of peace and acceptance in your life.

Eat a marshmallow and remember that life is sweet. Buoyancy is key.

Bounce back better than ever.

Spain celebrates a day of nonviolence today. This observance carries the message of universal love and peace and was created by poet Llorenç Vidal Vidal.

INCANTATION

Two of Swords
Calm and peace
Stress and pain
they do decrease
Find my center
In the storm
Nothing does me
Any harm

Creative Project Spell

Today is sacred to Saraswati, Hindu goddess of the arts, music, science, and knowledge. She is known as the free-flowing waters of consciousness. As this, she is considered the place of all creative birth.

INCANTATION

Create, create
Sweat brings joy
Create again
And do deploy
The best of my ability
Dazzling possibility
Sky's the limit
Brilliance shines
See the way
Follow the signs

Ingredients
- 4 pennies (copper is ruled by Venus/Empress)
- 4 dimes
1. Ace of Pentacles
2. The Empress
3. The Emperor
4. The World

Method, Visualization, and Meditation

Cast this spell at the beginning of a new project or to gain momentum when you are underway with a project and you need a boost. Use for any creative project like writing a book, creating a garden, or renovating a house. It is one of my favorite and most powerful spells in the book.

Pennies represent beginnings; dimes represent endings. The Ace of Pentacles reflects the beginning of your idea. The pentacle is the packet containing the DNA of your project. It even contains a mini version of your final product. The Empress reflects a wanton expression of creativity and ideas. She thinks outside the box, exuding originality and flair. The Emperor is the counterpoint to the Empress. He creates the order for her expansive creative explosion and ensures the project stays on track. The World card represents the final stage of completion.

Place the Ace of Pentacles. Pile four pennies on top of the pentacle. Step inside the garden of creativity, feeling the expansion, blossom, and bloom of your plan. Place the Empress. She gives you permission to go wild, pushing yourself to the brink of your creative abilities.

Place the Emperor. Feel yourself pulling back, editing where you need to. Become ruthless with your project so it shines like no other. Place the World card. Place one dime at each edge. See the finished project. Imagine how you will feel when it's complete.

1

2   3

4

School Admission Spell

Ingredients
1. Page of Pentacles
2. Ten of Pentacles
• Red apple

Method, Visualization, and Meditation

No spell can replace excellent grades, required letters, and financial documents. However, this spell will pack an extra power punch for your application process.

The Page of Pentacles is the student card. The Ten of Pentacles represents the institution you seek along with the people who populate it, its history, and what lies inside. Apples are ripe with magic, symbolic of knowledge, and have a history as the educator's gift.

Place the Page of Pentacles. Enter the card. See yourself in the process of learning. What do you want to learn? Where do you want to be? What kind of environment do you crave? What about learning excites you?

Like the Page of Pentacles, see the pentacle on your fingertips. It is the application form to the school you desire.

Place the Ten of Pentacles. Look at this card and see it as the very place you seek admission. This card is a doorway. It offers secret inside information. You and you alone see this.

What do you see? What advantage can you gain? What should you include in your essay and admission packet?

The wise man with white hair turns to face you. He whispers the secret of admission to you. What does he say? What must you do? Once you firmly understand, thank him.

Slice and eat the apple. As you eat the apple, consider how to implement the new information you have gathered.

The Tarot School opened its doors in New York City today in 1995.

INCANTATION

School of my dreams
Fling wide your doors
Desire my presence
I'll walk on your floors
Give me a spot
Grant me a space
Smile of success
Upon my face

1   2

Tarot Candle Spell

Candlemas, the ancient British festival marking the midpoint of winter, is celebrated today. Charge a candle with the energy of a tarot card and enjoy that card's energy as the candle burns.

INCANTATION

Tarot candle

Flicker burn

My desire

It does yearn

To come alive

And come to light

Fill me, embrace me

On this night

Ingredients
- Tarot card of choice
- Seven-day pullout candle
- Oil (olive or scented)
- Carving tool
- Glitter
- Loose incense
- Pennies

Method, Visualization, and Meditation

Cast this spell to invoke the energy of a tarot card for seven days.

Enter your chosen card in your mind's eye. Consider the reasons you chose it. What does it mean to you? How does it empower you?

Pull the candle from the glass container. Warm the candle with your hands. Connect to the energy of the wax. Using a carving tool, write your name and astrological sign on the top of the candle. Carve symbols of the card and your magical goal on the candle. Anoint the candle with oil and rub the oil upward, pushing the energy up and out, in the same direction the flame will burn.

Sprinkle the candle with colored glitter. Fill in the lines you have carved with glitter. It will adhere to the oil.

"Feed" your candle by placing pennies in the bottom of the candle's glass holder. Place a tablespoon of incense in a spoon. Ignite the incense. Drop it to the bottom of the vase once the incense is nice and smoky. Quickly cover the top of the holder with the palm of your hand. Watch the smoke swirl as your desire is made clear to the universe.

Drop the candle inside.

Your tarot candle is now ready to be lit. Place the card next to the candle. Repeat as often as necessary.

Banish Negativity from the Home

Ingredients
- The Star
- Broom
- Sage smudge stick

Method, Visualization, and Meditation

The Star card reflects opening and cleansing. Brooms are a witch's symbol and the essential tool of spacial clearing. The burning of dried sage not only clears space but offers clarity, wisdom, and an increased spiritual awareness.

Place the Star card before you. Enter the card. Feel peace entering your body from above as your body begins to release from the tip of your head down to your feet. Hear the gentle sound of water being poured. The crickets of the night chirp gently as the sky opens in a blanket of stars above you. Move within the card until you have cultivated so much peace that it begins to move through the boundaries of your physical body and fill the room.

Open your windows, allowing the wind to cleanse your space. Take your broom to the highest room in your house and sweep backwards through the door. Move systematically through each room of your home, sweeping the negativity out and allowing peace and inspiration to fill it. End at the front door. Sweep nine times. Recite the incantation and place the Star card on or near your door for twenty-four hours. Burn some sage in your kitchen (or any room you consider the heart of your home) for additional cleansing.

Japan celebrates Setsubun today. The word literally translates into "seasonal division" and is part of a spring celebration. Cleansing rituals are performed to drive away evil from the previous year.

INCANTATION
Broom and air
Air and broom
Cleanse and clean
Each single room
Negative spirits
Begone and disappear
With my broom
I sweep and clear
Out the door
Away with you
I will not stop
Till I am through

Snow White *was released on this day in 1938. The evil queen, jealous over Snow White's youth and beauty, set out on a path ultimately leading to her own destruction*

INCANTATION

Fire of passion

Raging heat

Desire's clear

Tastes so sweet

Redirect my need

And my flame

Find levelheadedness again

Take this rapture

And energy

Redirect power back

Toward me

Extinguish Jealousy Spell

Ingredients
- Ace of Wands
- Temperance
- Red candle (lit)

Method, Visualization, and Meditation

Jealousy is a helpful emotion. It helps us identify what we want. Once jealousy or envy has served its purpose, it can make us feel terrible, especially if it lingers or affects our feelings toward others. This spell extinguishes feelings of envy.

The Ace of Wands represents the spark of desire, want, and need. The Temperance card helps us hone our desire. It brings our attention away from others and redirects it toward us. We take personal responsibility and perform the steps to make our dreams come true.

Place the Ace of Wands. Visualize what you want. Look within the fire of passion. Why do you want it so desperately? What would it mean to have this for yourself? What do you have to change in order to obtain this for yourself? How will it affect your life? Why will it make you happy?

Place Temperance. Enter the card. You work to extinguish the jealousy as you fuse the energy between the cups, moving it back and forth. The mountains behind you hold exactly what you desire. You can have them without negative thoughts toward anyone else.

Focus on the lit red candle.

Prepare to blow out the candle. When you blow out the candle, you extinguish any remaining jealousy. Blow.

Jealousy disappears with the tendrils of smoke from the wick.

Whisper the Wind Weather Spell

Ingredients
- Card representing your desire
- 7 dried or fresh flower petals
- Pen

Method, Visualization, and Meditation

The earth's winds are literally her breath. Hang chimes at the four corners of your home to connect with the element of air. Whisper or chant to the wind whenever you want to spread your desire.

Choose the card that reflects your desire. Check weather conditions. Determine which way the wind is blowing.

Focus on the card you have chosen. Enter the card. Using every ounce of concentration and determination, see the outcome you desire as determined by the card. What does it feel like as you satisfy your desire? Does your body feel different? Has your lifestyle changed? What does a typical day feel like now that you have been granted your desire? Take your time and imagine all scenarios.

After you have satisfyingly seen, felt, and understood the implications of what you are asking for, select seven flower petals. Carefully, without breaking the flesh of the petal, inscribe your desire on each petal. You may write a single word or a symbol.

Hold the petals in both your right and left palm and venture outside. Turn to face and greet the wind. Face into the rushing air and feel it invigorating you, waking you up from deep within.

Send your mind's eye foraging like a salmon moving upstream. Can it discover the source of the wind? Where does it spring from? When ready, turn in the opposite direction. Place your arms above your head and state your desire seven times. After the seventh utterance, open your fingers and let the wind carry the petals.

Weather work is one of the most pleasurable aspects of spellcasting. Today is National Weatherperson's Day. Try your hand at wind, rain, or snow magic, and see what happens. Where do your natural gifts lie?

INCANTATION
Whistling wind
And blustery skies
Bring to me
My heart's great prize

Today is sacred to Aphrodite, Greek goddess of beauty, love, and pleasure. Honor her sacred day by intentionally embracing your feminine aspect.

Aphrodite's "Face the World" Spell

Ingredients

1. The High Priestess
2. The Empress
- 2 tablespoons cooled green tea
- 5 teaspoons sugar
- 1 teaspoon honey

Method, Visualization, and Meditation

Perform this spell to put on a good face for any occasion.

The High Priestess reflects the inner goddess aspect. The Empress expresses the outer goddess aspect. Together, these cards represent the unstoppable female.

Place the High Priestess and Empress next to one another. Consider how these two dynamic cards create a whole. How do the cards interplay between darkness and light? How is the High Priestess reserved while the Empress is expressed? What is your deepest connection to the High Priestess? What is your brightest connection to the Empress? How does the essence in inner and outer beauty interact? What does beauty mean to you? What does it mean to be female?

Enter the High Priestess card. Sit in her throne. Look through her eyes. How does it feel? What changes?

Enter the Empress card. Recline in her throne. Look through her eyes. How does it feel? What changes?

Mix the green tea, sugar, and honey by the light of a candle. Repeat the incantation as you stir. Apply to your clean face. Rub in soft, gentle circles. Wash away with fresh water.

Look in the mirror with the eyes of Aphrodite.

You are ready to face anything.

INCANTATION

Challenges, stress
Away, away
Put my best face
Forward today
I shine with beauty
Charm and light
Sighs of love
Within my sight

1	2

Six of Swords Connection Ritual

Ingredient
- Six of Swords

Method, Visualization, and Meditation

Enter the arcana of the Six of Swords.

Step out onto a wooden dock that floats upon evening water. You balance on the bobbing dock as the dark water laps gently against it. A boat moves past you as you face an expansive bay. A man uses a stick to propel the boat in its intended direction. He reminds you of the legendary Charon, the ferryman of Greek mythology who brought newly dead souls across the river Styx.

You are certain the figures in the boat are not specters, ghosts, or the newly departed. You see a mother, draped in a cloak, and her small child. All three figures are hunched slightly forward as if leaning into the wind.

Yet, the Greek metaphor stays with you as you contemplate the nature of the dividing line of a river, the threshold that all journeys hold. The water on one side of the boat ripples with the oar while the other side remains passive. The shadowy depths of water beneath the boat represent the deep bonds of tender emotion between mother and child.

There is an air of escape as they move across your field of vision, as if better times lie ahead. You are strangely certain these people will not return. Their destination on distant shores is their final one.

Six swords have been stuck inside the boat like lessons that one carries forever. You note that the figures must look through the swords to see ahead of them. Are the swords obscuring the truth? Are the swords the filter through which the figures interpret the world? Are the swords a prison or protection? Perhaps the swords were the answers and information needed in order to create a new life on the opposite shore.

The Six of Swords was called the Lord of Earned Success by the magicians of the Golden Dawn, who assigned it the time period of January 30–February 8.

INCANTATION

Card of movement
Forward go
Where we land
We do not know
We have each other
That's enough
Whether currents be
Soft or rough

Magician Card Connection Ritual

INCANTATION

Tarot magician
Numbered one
Fill the night
Midnight sun
Your power's great
Your acts defy
What is seen
Is it a lie?
It is a trick
Or is it true?
Tremendous power
Lies in you

Ingredient
- The Magician

Method, Visualization, and Meditation
Enter the arcana of the Magician.

A funny feeling races around your tummy. A man stands before you. He is a magician. Knowing this, you stand in anticipation, waiting to see what trick he will pull. You have seen it in theaters and on television. You know that all magic tricks are illusion, that the magician's role is to deceive and surprise the audience, yet there is something about this magician who pulls you closer, intrigues you.

"I'm not here to perform or pull a bunny out of a hat," he says to you.

Surprised at the gentle sound of his voice, you remain wordless.

"I am nothing more than a reflection of you. I manipulate the energies of the physical world. I am you making things happen. Do you see the four suits of tarot lying before me?"

You nod your head up and down, looking at the cup, wand, sword, and pentacle on his table.

"All you need to create your reality is seen here in the four suits of the tarot deck. It is not the cards that are magic. It is you."

The magician utters words sounding unlike any language you have ever heard. He raises a wand to the sky. His other hand points to the earth. Flowers burst forth and bloom from out of nowhere. White lilies and red roses, the alchemical opposite—red representing masculine and white implying feminine—bloom and grow. Their vines move like snakes and the blooms fill the room with a heady fragrance.

"You create every day, every moment, every second. The question is, do you do it consciously or unconsciously?"

Connect to the Elements Spell

Ingredients
- Ace of Wands (Fire)
- Ace of Cups (Water)
- Ace of Swords (Air)
- Ace of Pentacles (Earth)

Method, Visualization, and Meditation

How do you connect with a new friend? You give the gift of yourself. Genuine gifts of the heart forge conscious connections. You can do the same thing to connect with the elements.

Bring each element inside your home. This is done in a variety of ways. Feng shui uses candles for fire, plants for earth, chimes for air, and fountains for water. A traditional Wiccan alter uses incense for air, salt for earth, a bowl of water for water, and a candle for fire.

Place the Ace of Wands. Enter the card. Consider how fire is a hungry element. It likes to consume, devour, and grow bigger. What gift could you give to the element of fire? What might you throw into a fire pit? What gift does fire offer you in return?

Place the Ace of Cups. Water is a mutable and changeable element; it likes to transform. Place an ice cube in the sun and allow it to melt, boil water for tea, or freeze ice pops in a tray while you contemplate the Ace of Cups and water.

Place the Ace of Swords. Air is an invisible element, yet it holds everything. Sing a song to the wind, hang new chimes, or play beautiful music while contemplating the Ace of Swords.

Place the Ace of Pentacles. Earth is a nurturing element and likes to encourage growth within its loamy soil. Plant seeds, transplant a plant, begin to grow seedlings indoors if the ground outside is still frozen, or create an artful rock or gem pile while contemplating the Ace of Pentacles and the element of earth.

The US Weather Service was created on this day in 1870. It is a perfect day to contemplate your connection to the four basic elements that make up tarot and the world we live in.

INCANTATION

Wands of fire

Swords of air

See you or not

You are always there

Pentacles of earth

And cups of water

Here I am

Your faithful daughter

Seven of Swords Connection Ritual

The Seven of Swords was called the Lord of Unstable Effort by the magicians of the Golden Dawn, who assigned it the time period of February 9–18.

INCANTATION

Seven of swords
Remove, subtract
And take away
Cultivation card
Let unneeded stay
Disappear under
Veil of day
No one knows
What's in play

Ingredient
• Seven of Swords

Method, Visualization, and Meditation
Enter the arcana of the Seven of Swords.

Seven is a mystical number, a lucky number. There are seven planets, seven notes on the musical scale, seven days of the week, seven planets in our solar system besides Earth, seven deadly sins, seven seas, seven colors of the rainbow, seven continents, and seven wonders of the ancient world.

You are walking in a familiar place. You look up from your footpath to see a lemon-yellow striped tent with flags flapping in the wind. The door is draped open to reveal dimness inside, as if to invite anyone in. You can't tell if the encampment belongs to the circus, soldiers, or gypsies. One thing is certain: tents are mobile, and this camp is on the move. It wasn't here yesterday and you are certain it will be gone by morning's light.

You see a figure dressed in colorful clothing. He is sure to be a magician or trickster as he carries the swords by their very blades yet bears no scars or bloody wounds. He appears to be getting away without anyone noticing him.

The murmur of voices and laughter graces your ears. It comes from distant dark figures gathered around a campfire that churns out puffs of billowy smoke. Their voices cause the gentleman with the swords to move faster in his evasive action. You watch as he gets smaller and smaller, swords in hand. He has left a few behind. You wonder why they were so important to him.

You recall that swords are the symbol of the mind. It strikes you that he has taken only what is important, only what will serve him in the future. He has discarded what was unneeded. You remind yourself to do the same in future scenarios and situations.

Love Your Body, Respect Yourself Spell

Ingredients
- The World
- Bath
- Fresh roses
- Your favorite music

Method, Visualization, and Meditation

It is said that when Ishtar approached the underworld, she was met by seven gates. At each gate she was to shed an article of clothing until she emerged into the underworld completely naked.

For this spell you will focus on the World card, dance, and enter a bath. Wear seven items of clothing that can be symbolically removed. The World card represents complete immersion in the moment and a moment of arrival. Roses are a symbol of love. Select your favorite music.

Prepare your bathroom with candles and flowers. Fill the bath, adding delicious scents, oils, and bubbles as you like. Pull the petals off a fresh rose and adorn your bathing waters with them.

Focus upon the World card. Look at the dancer for who she is: the gateway to all creation. The universe moves through her and is expressed by her. She is the eye of the universe. You are the eyes of the universe. You are the creative expression of all that ever was. You are nature incarnate. You are divine. You are an expression of the consciousness of the universe. Focus on the wreath as a gateway.

See how she dances and the universe revolves around her. Put your music on and move only when you are moved to do so, imagining the green wreath gate before you. Remove an item of clothing and dance through the gate. Feel love toward yourself at each gate. Continue to move until you have removed seven items of clothing and passed through seven gates. Enter the bath and luxuriate. Repeat the incantation as you towel off.

Invoke your inner goddess. Oscar Wilde's play Salome *premiered in Paris on this day in 1896. The Babylonian fertility goddess Ishtar is thought to have originated the Dance of the Seven Veils, which is the centerpiece of the play.*

INCANTATION

Source of creation

Light of life

I am divine

I discard strife

I'm here alive

In sacred space

A pure expression

Form of grace

Today is the ancient calendar date of Imbolc, the Celtic Fire Festival. Fire is the source of the Queen of Wands, a woman whose passion has no bounds.

INCANTATION

Queen of Wands
Goddess of fire
Woman who fans
Flames of desire
Magnetic lady
Attraction's gaze
Set a million
Hearts ablaze

Queen of Wands Connection Ritual

Ingredient
- Queen of Wands

Method, Visualization, and Meditation
Enter the arcana of the Queen of Wands.

The infernal heat of the desert greets your skin. Rocks and mountains spring around you from the sun-baked earth. The air is dry and hot. The scent of sagebrush and cedar fills your senses. Your muscles loosen, and you feel yourself beginning to relax.

The Queen of Wands sits in a throne before you. You walk up to her in awe. She is completely golden, the color of the sun. Her skin shimmers as if made of glitter that refracts the sunlight. Her eyes are of flame, her crimson hair wavy. Her throne is engraved with scorched red lions and sunflowers. The armrests of her throne lay on the backs of carved lions. A symbol of wicked magic, a loyal black feline stands at her feet, purring in protection.

The queen holds a wand that sprouts vegetation in one hand. The buds represent the activity and life that have sprung as a result of her passion. A sunflower rests in her other hand. The sunflower is a symbol of her great charisma and talent. She hands the flower to you as a gift. It has been said that men and women have traveled the world over to gain her audience and favor. Her feet are flat on the ground, her legs spread open. She embraces and purifies all who meet and greet her in this landscape of heat, flame, and smoke.

The Queen of Wand's fire carries the explosive power of creativity; her fire is the flame turning glass to liquid for the artisan, the fire that ignites the alchemy of food for the chef, the warm air that nurtures cold skin in winter, the heat that cleanses body and soul. She is the creative fire burning inside us.

Fertility Spell

Ingredients
1. The Lovers
2. Ace of Wands
3. The Empress
4. The Sun
- Your bedroom

```
        ┌───┐
        │ 3 │
        └───┘
┌───┐       ┌───┐
│ 1 │       │ 4 │
└───┘       └───┘
        ┌───┐
        │ 2 │
        └───┘
```

Today is Lupercalia, the most ancient of Roman fertility festivals and purification rituals. The festival is thought by some to be the root of our modern Valentine's Day.

Method, Visualization, and Meditation

No magic or lovemaking is quite as distinct as baby-making sex. Invoke intense joy and pleasure in the process with this spell, which may also be performed before a fertility treatment.

Place the Lovers card. Step into the female's position. If you have a partner, imagine them standing across from you. Feel the power of reproductivity inside you. Look up to see the hovering angel. The doorway to the other side opens through her. Your energetic channels open. Feel receptivity through your body. All your defenses fall away.

Place the Ace of Wands. Behold the wand of manifestation, the leaves sprouting and generating life before your eyes. The wand reverberates with power. It is a source of pleasure and holds the seed of life.

Place the Empress card. The flowing waters behind her give life. She offers life to the soft field of wheat she sits upon. Ask her for your blessing. She now holds the power of the wand in her hands. The red fabric beneath her represents life-giving menstrual flow. The waterfall falling behind her is the life-sustaining water inside you. Feel her pregnant belly. Feel yourself full of a child. Picture your belly expanding.

Place the Sun card. The Sun ensures a healthy pregnancy and a beautiful child. Hear the laughter of the child on the horse. Feel the warmth generated from the sun. From this moment forth, when you feel and see sunlight you are reminded of your good health and healthy pregnancy. Place these same cards at the four corners of your bedroom or tuck beneath the four corners of your mattress to bless your bed.

INCANTATION

Tiny fingers
Little toes
Silky hair
And baby nose
Your soul fills me
With such pleasure
You will be my
Little treasure

Send Love to a Crush Spell

This spell is an easy way to let someone know that you like them without saying or risking anything in daylight. Your thoughts are pure energy and contain power. Send your intention toward the object you are crushing on and request they make the next move.

INCANTATION

Eight of Wands
And speed of flame
Future lover
Hear my name
Passion is sound
And right and true
It reaches out
And touches you
My heart is sweet
This I'll prove
Now's your turn
Make your move

Ingredients
1. Card representing you and your feelings
2. Card representing your crush
3. Eight of Wands

Method, Visualization, and Meditation

Place the card representing you before you. Gaze at the card. Ponder the reasons you chose it. How do you feel in their eyes? Bask in the delicious feelings your crush provokes in you—the excitement, the coziness, the attraction, the nervousness. Take a moment to thank this person for how they make you feel. Thank them in advance for what is to come.

Place the card representing your crush. See them, smell them. Imagine their eyes, their lips, their hands.

Take all of the energy they provoke in you and turn it into an energetic ball that you hold in your hands. Hold the ball in front of your chest. Let the energy revolve, pulse, and reverberate. Take all the yummy feelings and place them into the ball.

Place the Eight of Wands. Like a meteor shower of energy, throw your energy ball to them. Imagine all your energy pouring into them.

1	3	2

Make the Right Decision Spell

Ingredients
1. The Hanged Man
2. Two of Pentacles

Method, Visualization, and Meditation

If you are having a tough time between two choices, cast this spell for guidance. It will aid in your resolution. Be sure to perform this when you have at least twenty-four hours to spare before making your final decision.

The Hanged Man reflects being stuck in limbo and indecision. The Two of Pentacles represents the active balancing of two options.

Place the Hanged Man before you. He echoes the crossroads, the place where paths diverse and lives change. While the Hanged Man exists in stasis and valuable information is gleaned here, it is important not to linger here too long. Not making a choice is still making a choice. Pick yourself up from the wait, untie your ankles, and free yourself from the Hanged Man's post.

Place the Two of Pentacles. Enter the card and become the performer. You have two disks in your hands. See your two choices clearly. Literally hold them in your hands. Toss them up and down—perhaps juggle one. One of them weighs more than the other. It falls on the floor. Which disk is it? Which choice have you made?

Sit on your decision for twenty-four hours before making it official.

1

2

Galileo Galilei, astronomer, thinker, and genius, was born on this day. Inspired by the brilliance of the father of modern astronomy, this spell was crafted for when you are facing a difficult resolution.

INCANTATION

Decisions, decisions
Choices all
Big picture—no difference
I will not fall
I'm safe, protected
My life is free
Make the choice
That best suits me

Pamela Colman Smith, illustrator of the Rider-Waite-Smith tarot deck, was born on this day in 1878. No matter what deck you favor, this ritual will bind you to your cards.

INCANTATION

Light of night, shadows fall

Give me power, show me all

Energize this deck

Let wisdom flow

I release all false ego

With love and light

And harm to none

This deck and I have

Become one.

Lunar Ritual to Connect with Your Tarot Deck

Ingredients
- Moonlit night
- Yourself
- Tarot deck

Method, Visualization, and Meditation

This exercise connects you and your deck on subtle subconscious levels. It imbues your deck with the mystery and magic of the moonlight, the night, and you. It will also bring powerful lunar insights to your tarot work.

Perform this ritual outside and under the light of the moon (full, if possible). Bring your tarot deck outside and let the moonlight wash over you. Focus on the light of the moon. Feel subtle power and eternal glow. Contemplate all who have come before to look at the moon. The eyes of da Vinci once gazed at this moon from the blooming gardens of Florence. Pamela Colman Smith looked at the moon as a child on the island of Jamaica. Here you stand, in their footsteps.

Exchange your energy with the moon. It should begin to feel a bit like a push and pull. Send an energetic wave toward the moon. Let the moon's energy fall into you. As the energy moves back and forth, hold your deck in your hands. Now let the energy flow through this third point: your cards. Feel the energy flow from yourself to the moon and down into your deck and back to yourself in a circuitous flow. It is a circle of flowing energy.

Leave the deck on the windowsill to charge in the moonlight as you sleep.

Invoke Kindness Spell

Ingredients
1. Ace of Cups
2. Two of Cups
3. Three of Cups
4. Six of Cups
- A kind act

1

2

4   3

Method, Visualization, and Meditation

Choose one act you will perform today invoking generosity, consideration, or friendliness. This shall seal the spell.

The Ace of Cups represents emotional flow. The Two of Cups is generosity of spirit. The Three of Cups represents heartfelt celebration. The Six of Cups reflects heartfelt gifts.

Place all four cards before you. Focus on the Ace of Cups. Open your heart chakra, find a moment or space of peace and kindness, and let it flow out of you like tendrils of energetic love. Feel it move outward, rejuvenating itself so more can flow out; it never stops. See the water moving like a chocolate or champagne fountain. The bubbling water fills the two cups below.

The Two of Cups reflects how acts of kindness draw us toward people, make them feel special, seen, validated, and counted. It feels amazing to let another person know that they are special. See yourself performing an act of kindness.

The waters from these two cups flow out and up into the Three and Six of Cups. Focus on each card. See the results of your kindness and care. It has multiplied.

The Three of Cups shows people you don't know benefiting from the butterfly effect. The Six of Cups shows gifts of the heart coming back to you. When you are finished, repeat the incantation, then perform your act of kindness.

Today is Random Act of Kindness Day. Sweet and considerate acts are committed randomly. Acts of kindness are like bandages for the soul. Perform them whenever you want to lift spirits and improve and enrich universal energy.

INCANTATION

I give of myself
Costs not a thing
Send love to all
With peace I bring
The world expands
Like the love of my heart
As passion for others
Becomes my art

Page of Swords Connection Ritual

Gertrude Moakley was born on this day in 1905. Ms. Moakley was the NYC librarian who linked the tarot majors to early Italian medieval processions. She was quick and clever, just like the Page of Swords, the detective of the deck.

INCANTATION

Page of Swords
Clever and bright
Travels like wind
With sword of might
Her mind moves fast
It soars and speeds
And genius ideas
She spreads like seeds

Ingredient
• Page of Swords

Method, Visualization, and Meditation
Enter the arcana of the Page of Swords.

The air is different inside this card. You stand in the highlands and feel the clean and thin atmosphere swirling around your body. You feel lighter, as if any problem, stress, or issue has been removed from your mind.

You spy a figure. It is the Page of Swords. Her hair, often tied back to conceal her feminine nature, flies free as she stands alone at the mountaintop. She is deft, and her soft leather boots cross the ground in silence. Spruce trees bend to the wind's will behind her.

Her element is air. As an air creature she travels far and wide. She communicates with the birds who soar above her, representing her ideas and thoughts. Her youthful nature is like spring wind carrying pollen that ignites ideas around her.

She follows nothing but her sword and her instinct. She can throw her instincts ahead of her on the far reaches of the wind. She anticipates what is to come. Her sword is magic, like her instinct. It points and quivers at truths undetectable to others but that are perfectly clear to her.

Her greatest gift is in understanding that by controlling her mind, she controls her world.

Imprison her—she will escape. Pit her against an enemy—she will win. Every mystery is a puzzle she hasn't unraveled yet. When you search for meaning, she whispers the answer in your ear.

Listen for the Page of Swords.

Mystical Visionary Pisces Spell

Ingredients
1. The Moon
2. King of Cups

Method, Visualization, and Meditation

Are you seeking visionary information? Perform this spell when you need to dive deep and seek information that cannot be discovered on the Internet or within books.

Place the Moon card. Enter the warm pool pictured on the card. Look up through the water and see the moon. Emerge your head and feel the moon reflected in your eyes. Your eyes are the white orbs of the moon. Emerge so the water is up to your neck. A crawfish is in front of you, but it is crawling from the water and toward the mountains. Howls fill the canyon, expressing ancient knowledge—hidden knowledge. Return beneath the water. The moon still glows through the rippled water. Water fills your ears and replaces the yelping and howling of dogs. Look down. What lies in the murky caverns and between the waving sea grass? Swim, dive deep, explore, and enjoy breathing without effort. There is nothing to fear.

Place the King of Cups. Push yourself up and toward the surface. You are the fish on the back left hand of the card! You swim quickly over the top of the waters toward the throne. The information you are looking for has been inscribed on the back. What does it say?

Once you have the message, jump into the chair. Become the king. You now have the power to make your vision a reality. You contain all of his resources and power.

1   2

Today is the first day of Pisces, who is symbolized by the fish. The culmination of all signs who have come before, dreamy Pisces is ruled by Neptune and Jupiter and is fiercely intellectual. Pisces carry a mystical nature with the capacity to travel shamanistic and artistic landscapes.

INCANTATION

Mystical truth
Information sought
For what I search
Can't be bought
Absorb this knowledge
As my own
New possibility
Can be sown

Path of Forgiveness Spell

Forgiveness heals. Today in 1712 the last recorded witchcraft trial took place in England. The accused witch was sentenced to death, but Queen Anne interceded on her behalf and gave her the royal pardon.

INCANTATION

I forgive you
I forgive me
With these words
I am free
(repeat as many times
as necessary)

Ingredient
• Ace of Pentacles

Method, Visualization, and Meditation

How to find forgiveness? Forgiveness can be understood as a path. Have you ever wanted to forgive someone but couldn't? Forgiveness—especially for extreme situations—doesn't happen overnight, and depending on circumstances, it shouldn't. And forgiveness never excuses behavior or makes what happened acceptable.

Perform this spell when you feel ready to walk the path of forgiveness. True forgiveness will alter your life in surprising ways, set you free, and offer a slew of unexpected gifts.

Focus on the Ace of Pentacles. Consider the golden pentacle. The circle is the true nature of our life. Let the circle remind you that when you hold on to anger, resentment, and hatred, it comes back around to you. It may revisit in other forms but will remain nonetheless.

This pentacle is the first seed of forgiveness. The ground is open and fertile beneath the hand. Watch as the hand turns the seed and drops it in the waiting ground.

Now that you have planted the seed of forgiveness, with your mind's eye, walk out of the garden and through the gate. You have set foot on a new path: a path of forgiveness. To walk this path you must try as many different ways to cultivate forgiveness:

• Set forgiveness intentions in a variety of ways
• Repeat forgiveness affirmations even when
  you don't mean it
• Imagine the person you want to forgive as a small child
• Recall the interconnectivity of life

Open Sacral Chakra Energy

Ingredient
- The Lovers

Method, Visualization, and Meditation

The sacral chakra is the center of your creativity, passion, and pleasure. As it opens, it will give you a wider sense of connectedness and responsiveness to the world around you. Our deepest sense of sensuality, intimacy, and connection to others is felt here.

The sacral chakra is located in your lower abdomen about three inches below the navel and two inches in. It sits above the root chakra.

Sit on a chair with your feet flat on the floor or sit in yogi position, legs crossed on the floor. Place the Lovers card before you. Focus on your lower abdomen. Feel the energy there begin to warm and glow. Imagine it is colored orange. You might even begin to spin the chakra's energy. Continue to allow it to glow as you sit straight. Perhaps you hear the energy, smell it, or even taste it.

Focus on the Lovers card. Note the vulnerable posture of the people on the card. Relax and become as open as they are. See their connection with the Divine. They embrace a triangle of energy with the angel above. Let the orange glow move from your sacral chakra to the card and back.

Move the energy from you to the female and back. Move your energy from you to the male and back. Move it from you to the angel and back. How does this change the energy? Allow the energy to move through the triad until it feels quite warm.

Move the energy back inside your body. Feel the energy rise through your spine, filling your entire essence with love.

Erotic novelist and diarist Anaïs Nin was born on this day in 1903. The sacral chakra rules our sensuality and sexuality. You know that belly flipflop when you lock eyes with someone you are attracted to? That's the sacral chakra.

INCANTATION

Sacral center

Place of love

Fill me with ecstasy

That poets speak of

Bewitching pleasure

Passion play

Invoke intensity

Every day

Wrong Side of the Bed Spell

Sybil Leek, witch, astrologer, psychic, and leader of the Neopagan witchcraft and modern Wicca movement, was born today in 1917. If there's one thing a witch enjoys, it's the practicality of her art form. Perform this spell when you need a restart.

INCANTATION

Swords are sharp

Can ruin a day

But I am strong

Will have my way

Started dark

But turned around

Because my magic's not lost

It's found

Ingredients
- Nine of Swords
- Ace of Swords

Method, Visualization, and Meditation

Perform this spell to switch your mood when you've woken up on the wrong side of the bed. If you can't hop back into bed, simply perform a meditative version of this spell and see it unfolding in your mind.

Place the Nine of Swords on the side of bed you got out of. Place the Ace of Swords on the other side of your bed. Put your pajamas/nightgown back on. Jump into bed.

Look deeply into the Nine of Swords card. Think about what has gone wonky for you this morning. Feel your cranky mood. Let any negative, annoyed, and exhaustive emotion pass through you. Adopt the position of the woman on the card. Place your hands over your face. Begin to massage your forehead and work the tension out of your head.

Imagine a white light in the center of your forehead. It is clean, purifying, and the light fills your body, wiping away any residual negativity.

When ready, get out of bed. Put your feet squarely on the floor on the opposite or "right" side of the bed. Grab the Ace of Swords. This sword is the positivity you have chosen to embrace. Hold it in front of you and point it toward what you would like to embrace. See a vision of you doing something you want to do today. Know you will do it.

Get dressed in a new outfit, if possible, and walk into your day with a fresh perspective.

Masonic Stability Contemplation

Ingredients
1. Three of Pentacles
2. Eight of Pentacles

Method, Visualization, and Meditation

The metaphor of building for modern and esoteric masons has come to represent the construction of knowledge within oneself that leads to enlightenment. This contemplation opens the door for the personal consideration of the metaphor of structures and building within oneself.

The Three of Pentacles and the Eight of Pentacles are heavily illustrated with masonic imagery. Place these two cards together. Enter them in quiet contemplation.

Focus on the Three of Pentacles. You are the builder. You hold a tool. What is the life you are building? What tools do you use to gain knowledge? Tarot? Books? Experience? You stand on a bench, symbolic of an alter. What lifts you up? What brings you to a higher perspective? How can you sustain support? Note the two additional consulting figures on the card. How well do you work with others?

Focus on the Eight of Pentacles. The Three of Pentacles is a card of collaboration, while the Eight of Pentacles works alone. Do you prefer to work with others? Are you more solitary in nature? What do you enjoy doing or making? What is your favorite way to spend focused energy?

If your life was reflected as a building, a structure, built by the hands of men, what sort of building would it look like? A Gothic mansion, a skyscraper, a treehouse? What do you need to know right now? What additions would you like to add?

| 1 | 2 |

Sir Arthur Conan Doyle, author of the beloved Sherlock Homes series, received his second Masonic degree on this date in 1887. Freemasonry began as a union of sorts for stone workers in feudal Europe. It became one of the biggest global fraternal organizations, with members from every walk of life.

INCANTATION

Building blocks
Stacked so high
Should I remove some
Should I try?
What have I built?
Where do I live?
What is done and over?
What needs to give?
What's cemented?
What demolished?
What in my life should
Be more polished?

Eight of Cups Connection Ritual

Ingredient
- Eight of Cups

Method, Visualization, and Meditation

Enter the arcana of the Eight of Cups.

The quiet inlet of an ocean surrounds you, and the sea air is salty. A lone moon shines in the sky, yet a shadow moves across its face. The waves' lapping ceases; the water becomes still. The rustling of sea moss and sage bushes pauses with the shadow. The light is supernatural. The sky darkens in a matter of moments.

Is your mind playing tricks? At first you see a shadow. You quickly realize it is a figure who moves past a small wall of cups. This traveler moves forth, onward and up the mountain. Where did he come from? It looks as if a cup from the wall is missing. Was he the ninth cup? Did he shapeshift from a goblet into a human? Did he appear from the water itself? Perhaps he was always there and you just didn't notice him.

His feet are covered with soft red boots that match his cloak. He leans on his walking stick that helps him ascend to new heights. It is the beginning of an adventure, a journey, or a trip. Watch him walk away and grow smaller. When you are alone, look into the cups stacked upon one another.

What lies inside the cups?

What has he left behind?

INCANTATION

Eight of Cups
The quiet flight
Begin again
Start tonight
Leave behind
What is not needed
Thoughts and wisdom
Deeply heeded
I'll travel quick
And alone
Who knows where these
Red boots might roam

Ace the Exam Spell

Ingredients
- King of Swords
- Rosemary

Method, Visualization, and Meditation

Japanese culture embraces the idea that words each contain a spirit or soul. This imbues language with a mystical power. It informs all Japanese mythology and also reminds us of the power of the spoken word.

The King of Swords is the intellectual giant of the tarot deck, with the power to ace any test. Rosemary, for remembrance, can be used to jog the memory.

Place the King of Swords. Enter the card. Imagine yourself taking the test as the King of Swords. Watch how quickly you correctly answer each question. See yourself writing with brilliance. Your mind moves as quickly and clearly as the wind he commands. All information you need is at your fingertips and in your mind's eye. See yourself receiving your grade. It is high, and you are pleased. How does it feel?

Keep the King of Swords out at all times while studying. Sleep with a sprig of rosemary under your pillow the night before the test. If possible, place a sprig behind your ear during the test.

The Plum Festival is celebrated in Kyoto today at a Shinto shrine. The festival is dedicated to the scholarly deity Michizane, patron saint of students.

INCANTATION

King of Swords
King of the hill
Your powers of perception
Within me fill
I ace the test
Get the answers right
And I sleep like a baby
Through the night

Today in 1930 New York City installed its first set of traffic lights. Car charms, used to promote safety, can be crafted and stowed away in glove compartments or hung under mirrors. This spell makes an oil to be dabbed on the steering wheel.

INCANTATION

Safety first
Safety now
Drive with pleasure
I know how
Drivers, animals, tickets
Away I steer
My path is open
Roads stay clear

Car Safety Oil

Ingredients
1. The Chariot
2. Ace of Swords
- Protection oil:
    1 ounce carrier oil (olive, almond, or sweet almond)
    3 drops lavender essential oil
    3 drops sage essential oil
    Bunch of mint
    White ribbon

Method, Visualization, and Meditation

The Chariot represents your vehicle. The Ace of Swords offers the protection of the element of air. The carrier oil is what you will place your herbal essences into. Sage and lavender are for protection. Mint is used for luck and white ribbon for added protection.

Collect all the ingredients and place on the table. Place the Chariot and the Ace of Swords next to each other. Bring your mind's eye into the Chariot.

See yourself in the driver's seat of your car, in full control of your vehicle. See yourself as the responsible, level-headed driver that you are. Look at the Ace. Picture the sword extending from the hood of your car, splicing the air and clearing your way. Imagine a protective white bubble extending around the entirety of your vehicle.

Add essential oils to carrier oil while repeating the incantation. Gather the mint and tie with white ribbon. Hang or place mint bundle in car. Dab oil on steering wheel and the four corners of your car.

1	2

Safe Crossings Travel Spell

Ingredients
  1. Six of Swords
  2. Knight of Swords
  3. Knight of Cups
  4. The Star

Method, Visualization, and Meditation

Journeys are marvelous metaphors. We cross a distance and come to a new place within ourselves.

The Six of Swords marks an important, evocative passage. The Knight of Swords protects your blind spots. The Knight of Cups emotionally clears your way. The Star shines optimism and clarity over you.

Place the Six of Swords before you. Imagine the trip ahead of you. Set your intention. What does this venture mean for you? Along with the actual transportation of your body, what else does the journey signify? Say it out loud. As you place the cards upon the table, imagine their image also surrounding your physical body so they move with you on your journey.

Place the Knight of Swords behind you. This knight acts like eyes at the back of your head. You are safe. Place the Knight of Cups ahead of you. He clears a safe and gentle passage for you. Potential obstacles are removed. Roadblocks are cleared and swept away as a path is opened.

Place the Star above you. Let her liquid fill your body with optimism and hope. Your energy should remain open on this trip so that wonders and unimagined possibilities will unfold.

Today is the sacred day of St. Honorina of Normandy, the patron saint of boatmen. Whether you travel by foot, bicycle, car, train, plane, or ship, this spell ensures your safety. Set an intention at the start of your trip so the journey itself becomes part of the magic.

INCANTATION

Knights of valor
Six of Swords
I travel forward
Seek rewards
My spirit travels
Fast as speed
Matching powers
Of knightly steed

```
        ┌─────┐
        │  4  │
        └─────┘


┌─────┐   ┌─────┐   ┌─────┐
│  2  │   │  1  │   │  3  │
└─────┘   └─────┘   └─────┘
```

Moina Mathers—occultist, clairvoyant, and the first female initiated into the Golden Dawn—was born on this day in 1865.

INCANTATION

Psychic vision
Come to me
I'm ready now
To truly see
With work with prudence
And with pride
So I'll be
A helpful guide

Clairvoyance Exercise

Ingredients
1. Queen of Cups
2. Page of Cups
3. Seven of Cups

Method, Visualization, and Meditation

Clairvoyance—derived from two French words meaning "clear vision" and denoting psychic ability—appears in different ways. The information and facility varies from one person to the next. Some people see visions. Others are struck with knowing. Do not predetermine how clairvoyance might happen for you.

The Queen of Cups is the most psychic queen in the deck. Her empathy and emotion are as deep as the ocean. The Page of Cups represents a child's wide and available psychic ability. The Seven of Cups represents visions floating in the air.

Place the queen before you. Reflect on all of the times in your adult life that you have had advance knowledge something was going to happen or been invisibly connected to a person or future event. When have you known something that you wouldn't have normally known? Do you know who is calling or texting before you get the call or text? Have you sensed an accident before it happened?

Place the Page of Cups. What did the world look like to you when you were a child? How was your perception of the world different? Can you remember a time before things had labels and names? Would you look at things without knowing what they were? Can you recall the senses and perspective of being a small person?

Place the Seven of Cups before you. Sit back, feet grounded on the floor. Look at each floating cup. See the ways psychic information may come to you: visions, sounds, knowledge, divination, voices, etc. Ask that information be given to you on your clearest psychic channel.

Leap Day Soul Realignment Spell

Ingredients
1. The Star
2. High Priestess
3. Temperance

Today is Leap Day. Leap years are essential to keep our modern Gregorian calendar (with 365 days) in alignment with the earth's revolutions around the sun. A leap day is added once every four years to save the calendar from moving out of whack.

Method, Visualization and Meditation

Physical and emotional alignment means that you are stacked up correctly and acting from a place of personal truth. Alignment means that you are plugged in and connected with your highest spiritual self and darkest shadow unconscious self. These places are akin to the shaman's three worlds. The high and low selves meet in the middle and play out in the daily goings-on of your life. When they are out of whack, you'll find yourself behaving in inauthentic or uncomfortable ways.

Just as leap year brings alignment to the calendar, cast this spell at any time to bring alignment to yourself.

Place the Star card. Focus on how she draws energy from above. Soaking in the starlight from the distant corners of the universe, she drinks in every bit of stellar energy. Imagine this card and all it contains and bring it to your crown chakra, located at the head. Feel all the parts of your skull—smooth front, squishy center, and hard back—all allowing Star energy to fill you.

Place the High Priestess card. Focus on the priestess's warmth, fluid and wet, undulating like water. She draws energy from unseen depths. Imagine this card and all it contains funneling into your root chakra, located at the base of your spine. Feel the front of your groin, the center above your sacrum, and the lower back.

Place the Temperance card. Focus on how she moves energy from her cup back and forth. The energy is colorful, alive, carrying a ringing sound as it moves. Imagine the liquid is from the high-level energy of the star and the deep-level energy of the High Priestess. Bring this image and the mixing and mutable energy to your heart chakra. Move the energy through your entire body from the tips of your toes to the top of your head.

INCANTATION
Time to check
Time to tune
Feeling better
Very soon
To thine self
Always be true
And what's not mine
I bid adieu

67

Stop Procrastinating Spell

Ingredients
1. Eight of Wands reversed
2. The Emperor reversed
3. Card representing emotional block
4. Card representing emotional freedom
- Paper and pen
- Lighter and fireproof bowl

Method, Visualization, and Meditation

This spell removes your mental block and eliminates what has impeded forward progress. Follow immediately with an action toward your intended goal.

Identify the reason for your procrastination. Express it in a single word. Write it on a piece of paper. Select a tarot card representing your emotional block.

Identify the end result of your follow-through. What would happen if you took action? What would change? How would you feel? Express this result in a single word. Write it down on a piece of paper. Select a tarot card representing your emotional freedom.

Place the reversed Eight of Wands and recall your past failed attempts to get started. Lay down the reversed Emperor and recall how you felt powerless.

Lay the emotional block card. Gaze at the card and pull apart the image in your mind. Like a CGI movie effect, watch the elements of the card dissipate. Take your emotional block word and light it on fire. Say goodbye and watch it incinerate.

Turn the Eight of Wands upright. Imagine all the energy and speed of this card at your back, aiding you and moving you forward. Turn the Emperor upright. Feel his power running through your veins. Place the emotional freedom card over the emotional block card. Let the symbolism of your chosen card wash over you. Embrace the results of your achieved goal. Embrace your power.

Author Truman Capote's final manuscript was due on this day in 1968. He procrastinated and ultimately died without ever finishing the book or fulfilling his contract.

INCANTATION

Growth is natural
Flowers bloom
Seek the sun
Brighten a room
Like a flower
My efforts unveil
Success upon
The highest scale
Extraordinary life
I do finesse
Move forward now
make progress

Lovers Card Connection Ritual

Ingredient
- The Lovers

Method, Visualization, and Meditation
Enter the arcana of the Lovers.

Musk, woodsy smoke, and the scent of plump scarlet apples take you by surprise. The air is heady and thick. A sumptuous garden encloses a naked man and woman. The scene is so private, you are tempted to turn away, to give them seclusion. You stay, knowing that to know this card you must experience it.

The Tree of Knowledge stands with a fecund snake wrapping itself around the trunk. The seductive reptile waits behind the ear of the woman, representing both choice and regenerative skin-shedding powers. The man's tree is raging with the fires of desire. His infernal passion informs his every move, clouds his vision, consumes his body. Every inch of his skin craves the woman's embrace, her scent, her warmth.

He looks at his companion with hungry eyes. The soft, fertile woman raises her gaze upward to the heavens. She gazes softly at the winged angel who blesses their private space.

The triad of figures represents the triad of manifestation, which is the ultimate creativity. This trio is found under many names: Mother, Maiden, Crone; Father, Son, Holy Ghost; Consciousness, Superconscious, Subconscious; Mind, Body, Spirit; Thought, Word, Action.

The angel bears the solar power of expansion and growth. The couple's sex act, desire, and choice keeps humanity alive. This arcana reflects all songs, poetry, and art.

Love. Romantic and intellectual love. This predates your mind's knowing. The instinct of arousal activated the body long before reaching the mind. It is the somersault of your belly, the flush of excitement, and the tendrils of electricity that create all. Witness the root of desire, the seeds of love, and the choice of ultimate creativity.

England's first ballet, The Loves of Mars and Venus, *was performed today in 1717. Romantic love and all its infinite beauty, devastating and life-giving power, sexuality, sensuality, and emotion is found inside the Lovers card.*

INCANTATION
Garden of Eden
Love and light
Linger among your
Sweet grass tonight
This card runs deep
Its powers strong
Choose wisely
Fear no harm
To myself and love
I must be true
And embrace that which
Calls me to you

Financial Manifestation Spell

The United States Mint was created today in 1791. It produces coins and change for general circulation. Coins are like the aces of tarot. They represent the seeds of financial freedom.

INCANTATION

Money trickles

Down the tree

Coming faster

Destination's me

Have what I need

There's more to spare

With friends and family

I will share

Ingredients
- Ten of Pentacles
- 10 dimes
- Peppermint tea
- Green candle

Method, Visualization, and Meditation

The Ten of Pentacles represents financial abundance and reveals the diagram of the Tree of Life in the pentacle formation. Place one dime on each sephiroth (sphere). Refreshing peppermint tea generates money magic.

Light the green candle. Begin with the top pentacle and work your way down, placing a dime on each sephiroth.

1. Crown: "This coin represents abundance I already possess."
2. Wisdom: "This coin represents acquired financial knowledge."
3. Understanding: "This coin is the utilization and culmination of financial knowledge."
4. Mercy: "This coin is the compassion with which I donate my money."
5. Severity: "This coin is the limit I place upon my financial universe."
6. Beauty: "This is the joy I experience attracting money."
7. Victory: "This coin is assured success with money."
8. Splendor: "This coin is the incandescence with which I radiate."
9. Foundation: "This coin is the manifestation of funds in the material world and the basis on which my spiritual and material wealth lives."
10. Kingdom: "This coin is the life in which I manifest riches."

Drink your tea and visualize yourself enjoying all aspects of financial freedom.

Envy Banishing Powder Spell

Ingredients
- Black candle
- Eight of Wands
- Banishing powder:
    Black pepper
    Cayenne pepper
    Cinnamon
    Sea salt

Method, Visualization, and Meditation

Desire's deviant little sister Envy reflects our wants and needs. Once we know what we want, we can set out to obtain it. Residual jealousy can be poisonous and doesn't feel good. To rid yourself of nagging envy, perform this spell.

A black candle absorbs all emotions. The Eight of Wands reflects a quick blast of energy. Banishing powder is used to rid yourself of anything you don't want in your life. It may be blown to the air, sprinkled, or added to a carrier oil to create banishing oil. Pepper and cinnamon reflect the fiery nature of the Eight of Wands and incinerate unwanted feelings.

Light the black candle. Place the Eight of Wands. Focus on its intense, rapid energy, gathering it inside your belly. The energy of the Eight of Wands is reflected in the fiery nature of pepper and cinnamon. Grind together peppers, cinnamon, and salt to create a fine powder. Sprinkle the powder upon the Eight of Wands card and repeat the incantation.

Go to your front door and check the wind, as you do *not* want powder blowing back in your face. Blow the powder off the card and into the air, dissipating all jealousy.

Cinderella was released today in 1950. The little cinder girl suffers at the hands of her jealous stepmother and stepsisters but triumphs with true love by the story's end. The bright flames of jealousy are powerful indicators of what we want for ourselves.

INCANTATION

Jealousy, Envy, let me be
Your energy flies fast from me
Find happiness myself
Depend on me
You were a tool
Of truth, now I see
Create my own reality
Clean and clear
True manifestation
Is mine this year

On this day in 1956 the Supreme Court upheld the ban on segregation in public schools, colleges, and universities. This highest of US courts is a living reflection of the Justice card.

INCANTATION

Justice, root of life and law

Look and feel in total awe

Actions count

Actions great

I'll never shrink

Or dissipate

Be earnest in all that I do

Stand right and tall

In front of you

Justice Card Connection Ritual

Ingredient
- Justice

Method, Visualization, and Meditation

Enter the arcana of Justice.

Enter familiar territory. You have been here before. Granite temples and courtrooms, pillars and statues surround you. Humanity conducts its formal justice proceedings here. It is a place of freedom and chains, guards and prisoners, right and wrong.

Attorneys battle, matching wits, honing arguments, and debating one another. Sentences are served on the cigar-stained breath of judges. Anxious plaintiffs sit, their sweaty hands knotted in nervous laps as their future weighs in the balance. Jurors retire to private quarters reeking of stale coffee and laminate chairs to reach their final decisions.

Limestone steps stretch out before you. You climb upward. The physical forms of Temperance, Fortitude, and Prudence are carved from white marble and form a semicircle around a large pink marble statue of a woman with scales and a sword: Justice.

Her direct gaze penetrates your eyes and pierces your soul. You can hide nothing from her, nor do you wish to. She knows you. She sees you from the inside out and knows everything about you. Her eyes have always watched. Her ears have always listened. She is the truth you cannot escape.

She oversaw every decision and calculation you have made. She sees your efforts, your failures, your indifference. She sees where you have been consistent and where you have faltered. Her balancing scales represent your freedom to choose.

This is the place where things become real. It is the arcana of consequence.

The white slipper pokes out from beneath her robe, symbolizing the chance to begin again. Her sword points to divine power above. Meet yourself, your morality and ethics, and begin anew.

Creative Boost Spell

Ingredients
1. Ace of Wands
2. King of Cups
• Camera or sketchbook

The sculptor, painter, and poet Michelangelo was born on this day in 1475. Call upon Michelangelo's energy when you need to get your creative juices flowing.

Method, Visualization, and Meditation

The Ace of Wands represents a surge of creative energy. The King of Cups is the artistic master.

Bring a camera or sketchbook outside. Look for spring-green shoots poking through the gray, matted grass. Search for any sign of new growth. Snap a photo to place on your phone or computer as its screen saver. Visual artists may want to sketch the image. This image is your creative boost image.

Place the Ace of Wands before you. This card represents a bolt of energy. Feel the heat, the creative fire. It is profound, deep, and will warm you from inside your bones. Let the energy of the Ace of Wands fill your spine, growing from the root to the top of your head.

Place the King of Cups above the ace. The energy shoots up your spine and into the king. See yourself on his throne. You are engaged in your creative pursuit as free, wild, and creative as the waves crashing against his throne. You are off and running. Begin your project now.

INCANTATION

Winds of change
And waves of art
Enthusiasm
Fills my heart
Movement, action
A strong kickstart
Fills my soul
Feeds my needs
Brilliance fuels
My future deeds

2

1

Nine of Cups Connection Ritual

The Nine of Cups was called the Lord of Material Happiness by the magicians of the Golden Dawn, who assigned it the time period of March 1–10.

Ingredient
- Nine of Cups

Method, Visualization, and Meditation

Enter the arcana of the Nine of Cups.

Soft white linens drape your body as you wander the aisles of a Turkish bazaar. Turmeric, cardamom, and cinnamon scent the dry desert air, and exotic spices spill from wooden barrels around you. Silk rugs with intricate designs of royal blue and scarlet pile as high as your eye can see, forming plush walls around you. Roasted rotating meats glisten and smoke over glowing coals. Purple figs, rosy pomegranates, juicy plums, and taut yellow and green grapes overflow from fruit stalls.

A single stall seems set apart from the others. The bustle of humanity, snorting camels, and bleating goats fades behind you as you move closer. A gentleman sits inside as if he's been awaiting your arrival. His eyes dance like flames and glimmer with merriment.

You draw closer as if under enchantment. The world behind you slips away. A great realization dawns upon you. You see with stunning clarity that what you focus on defines who you are. He nods slowly, letting you know you are correct in your assumption. He also tells you, without speaking, that what you focus on is what you manifest.

"I am a genie with the power to grant you any wish. But you are a witch with the power and foresight to weave your own destiny. I will travel with you always. I will remind you of one thing: you can always have what you want. Your wish is granted."

Nine cups—the number of fulfillment—dance behind him on a blue cloth. "Be careful what you wish for..." he whispers without whispering.

All wishes have unexpected consequences, both dark and light. These are what lie beneath his blue cloth and can be seen only after the wish has been made.

Honor Personal Magic Spell

Ingredients
1. The High Priestess
2. The Empress
3. The World

Method, Visualization, and Meditation

International Woman's Day is observed on this day around the world. Perform this spell to get in touch with your unique feminine powers. It doesn't matter if you are male or female, as aspects of both genders reside within our consciousness.

The High Priestess echoes all inner truth that has been forgotten and the knowledge you will retrieve in this lifetime. The Empress represents utter creativity and manifestation on the physical plane. The World card represents the state of enlightenment, living in the moment and merging with universal consciousness.

Place the three cards out together. Focus on how you embody the essence of each card. What have these cards taught you about yourself and where have you been able to go with them?

Who is your High Priestess self?

What are you bringing forth?

What is the essence of the Empress's creativity as she relates to you?

How do you create in the physical world?

What does it mean to embody the World card?

How is the World card a gateway?

How are you a gateway?

Ancient Aztecs worshipped Tlazolteotl, the female spirit of magic, love, sex, and desire and matron of midwives and healers. Women carry within them innate magic, as they are built for mystery and depth and are the gateways and guardians of life.

INCANTATION

Call upon you

Trio of power

Embrace your energy

In this hour

Personal magic

By any other name

Looks and feels

Quite the same

Refine intention

Effort and thought

Magic is cultivated

Not bought

1

2

3

Today in 1842 gold was discovered in California. Alchemy is the process of converting base metals into gold. It is a metaphor for the transformation of the spirit.

INCANTATION

Temperance card
Merge and mix
Qualities change
Consequences stick
Like a snake
I shed old skin
So I'll enjoy
The life I'm in

Alchemy Spell for Self-Transformation

Ingredients
1. Card representing how you feel
2. Card representing how you'd like to feel
3. Temperance
- Toast
- Honey bear

Method, Visualization, and Meditation

In springtime we watch the winter release its icy grip. We enjoy a front row seat to the spirit of transformation and regeneration. Do you know what you'd like to transform into? Perform this spell to usher in a personal metamorphosis.

Chose a card representing how you feel. Choose a card reflecting how you'd like to feel. The Temperance card represents the alchemical process of fusion and change.

This spell brings transformative properties to the forefront of consciousness. We then take the lead in how we transform from one day to the next. Add visual aids to your transformation spell.

Place card 1 before you. Contemplate how you represent the image and the archetype. Focus on all aspects, light and dark, positive and negative. Place card 2. Focus on the qualities you seek to embrace. Know this is entirely possible. What aspects of the card do you desire? Why is it helpful for you and those around you to embrace this archetype? What happens as a result?

Place Temperance between your two cards. She is the alchemical fusion card. Focus on the physical things you are actively doing to transform yourself. The golden crown glittering above the hill is your spiritual gold.

Prepare a slice of hot, crispy toast. Using golden honey, write a word that encapsulates your transformation. Utter the incantation. Consume your honey toast and consider this spell closed.

| 1 | 3 | 2 |

Attract Best Possible Relationship Spell

Ingredients
- Rose water
1. Two of Cups
2. The Lovers
3. The Star

Method, Visualization, and Meditation

The Two of Cups represents the recognition of a soul mate. The Lovers card reflects the commitment to give yourself to another. The Star card channels divine inspiration.

It takes twenty-four hours to prepare rose water. Use this time period to meditate and journal about the ways you envision, give, and receive love. To prepare the rose water, pick or select one cup of red rose petals. Place petals in a heatproof bowl and pour hot distilled water over them, steeping for thirty minutes. Strain the leaves out and pour the liquid into a glass jar. Set on a sunny windowsill for twenty-four hours.

To perform this spell, wash your hands in the rose water before handling your cards.

Place the Two of Cups. Feel the arrival of a heartfelt match. Feel simpatico and recognition of oneself in another.

Place the Lovers card. Feel the electric jolt of attraction, the sensual, physical sensation letting us know we are alive, here to love and create. Feel the fire and flames of desire radiating out of this card and explore its implicit sensuality.

Place the Star card. You are vulnerable, free and open to channel this greater higher passion and love that is so right for you, so full of what and who you are. Stars twinkle above you. One star contains the energy manifesting your best possible relationship. Let that starlight wash over you. Pour water from the jugs at your feet to let the emotion move through your body. You have begun true manifestation of this into your life.

1   2   3

Looking for passionate, healthy, and sublime love? The Hindu festival for Lord Shiva, the supreme matchmaking god, takes place today.

• • • • •

INCANTATION

Two of cups
Bring love close
Unfold before me
Like a rose
Lovers card
It's meant to last
Lonesome days
Left in the past
Star card refresh
Fill and inspire
My heart it catches
Passion's fire

Today is Johnny Appleseed day. Johnny Appleseed was famous for spreading apple seeds to American settlers. Botanically, apples are related to the rose, linking this fruit to love.

INCANTATION

Lover, hear my call to you
Come to me in joy you do
Love me long and
Hard and sweet
Our souls intertwined
Together meet
Outside of space and
Time and flight
Come to me under
The veil of night

I Want You in My Bed Sweet Apple Spell

Ingredients
- The Lovers
- 7 apple seeds
- Orris root
- Bag

Method, Visualization, and Meditation

Apples carry a long mystical tradition in ancient culture, associated with such goddesses as Hera, Aphrodite, and Freya. However, Christianity rebranded the apple as "forbidden fruit," so the apple became a symbol of temptation, sin, and witchcraft. Harvested in fall, it joins pumpkins as having a sacred association with Halloween.

An apple's sweet flesh circles the dark seeds that lie within and contain trace quantities of arsenic—a reminder of the inherent danger inside all beautiful things.

The Lovers card represents wanton sexuality and sensuality. Apple seeds are laced with attraction magic. Orris root powder is known as love-drawing powder in voodoo and hoodoo. It may be obtained online or in a magic store.

Place the Lovers card before you, and enter it with your mind's eye. Imagine the object of your desire being drawn to you and your bed. Place seven apple seeds in a bag with the orris root while chanting the incantation. Keep your bag in a secret place or on your person in a place where no one else will see it.

Bountiful Garden Spell

Ingredients
- Pen and paper
1. The Sun
2. Knight of Pentacles
3. Nine of Pentacles
- 1 seed (any variety or from a fruit)

	1	
2		3

Today is National Flower Day in the United States. It's a perfect day to plan a magical bed of creation and manifestation.

Method, Visualization, and Meditation

Some gardens are organized by the elemental association of the plants. A witch's herb garden planted near the home makes for easy pickings when crafting spells and recipes. Moon gardens scent nighttime air with flowers that bloom nocturnally and represent our subconscious. A simple vegetable patch can be a place of powerful manifestation and certainly of good health.

Sketch this year's garden plan with the help of three tarot cards. Seal the spell by planting a single seed. The seed is symbolic and need not actually grow in your garden.

The Sun card reflects solar, expansive energy. The Knight of Pentacles considers the act of creation. The Nine of Pentacles reflects the joy and contentment of your garden.

Place the Sun card before you. Consider the sun's pervasive power on earth. All physical things—animal, vegetable, and mineral—require the light of the sun. Channel the sun's expansive energy, the power generator of your garden.

Place the Knight of Pentacles. Embody him. Hold the seeds of your garden in hand. What does this year's garden represent? What requires growth and expansion? What shall you cultivate?

Place the Nine of Pentacles. See your garden blooming at the height of summer. See yourself surrounded by the bounty that you have created.

Begin to sketch your garden, planning what seeds will go where. Arrange the flowers, vegetables, and herbs.

Place the Nine of Pentacles atop the paper and repeat the incantation. Plant your seed, even if it means slipping it into some snow or under a rock.

· · · · ·

INCANTATION

Light of sun
And water of rain
Help my garden
Bloom again
The seeds I plant
Mean something more
Undeniable delights
Are in store

Uranus Technology Spell

The planet Uranus was discovered and identified on this day in 1781. Uranus represents sudden change, revolution, originality, and new technology.

Ingredients

1. The Fool
2. The Wheel of Fortune
3. The Magician
- Your computer, iPhone, or other technology

Method, Visualization, and Meditation

This spell counteracts Mercury retrograde and assures smooth technical workings among all your electronic and computerized equipment. Cast this spell in the evening, when you are finished using all devices. The cards and devices will lay out all night.

The Fool card represents the originality aspected by the planet Uranus. The Wheel of Fortune gets energy moving in the direction you desire. The Magician card directs this energy.

Place the Fool card before you. He is ruled by Uranus and wanders happily. Place the Wheel of Fortune and feel the whirring of the wheel. Freshly greased and oiled, working to perfection and in your favor, it brings the carefree energy of the Fool to the Magician underneath. Place the Magician, who takes Uranus energy, refines it through his magic, and casts it down to your technical devices.

Leave the cards and electronic device out overnight.

INCANTATION

Technology moves
At lightning speed
Devices meet
My every need
Working smoothly
And with finesse
Using tarot
These objects I bless

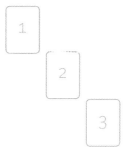

Entice a New Lover Spell

Ingredients
- Apple
- Honey
- Cinnamon
- Cayenne pepper
1. Card representing the best of you
2. Card representing your new lover
3. The Lovers

Method, Visualization, and Meditation

Apples are sacred to love. Honey extends wicked attraction magic. Cinnamon and cayenne are sexy and stimulating.

Place card 1 before you. Gaze at it. Consider why you chose it to represent yourself. Feel yourself brimming with those qualities. Place card 2, representing your soon-to-be lover. Gaze at the card. Think of this person. Imagine their scent, their gestures, the way they look at you. Place the Lovers. Feel the magnetic pull between you getting stronger. Imagine your lover coming to you, again and again.

Slice your apple in half horizontally. Write the name of your lover with honey on one half. Sprinkle their name with cinnamon while imagining your sweetness washing over them. Sprinkle with cayenne pepper and imagine their skin on your skin, the friction and the heat.

Recite the incantation below and eat the apple. As you eat, picture the two of you together.

Place the other half of the apple in your freezer. If you need to reverse the spell in the future, remove the half from the freezer, write their name in honey, and bury the apple as deeply as you can in the dirt.

White Day is celebrated today in Japan and Korea as men offer gifts of love to the women they adore.

INCANTATION
Apple of Eve, honey of bee
My lover, my crush
Come to me
Pepper that burns
And fire of spice
Lover, discover
My touch so nice
Come to me
Come quick, come now
Find your way
I'll show you how

[1]   [3]   [2]

Banish Nightmares Spell

Today is the Ides of March, the anniversary of the assassination of Julius Caesar in 44 BCE. The Ides of March has also come to express the dreary March weather: unexpected wet, heavy snows, drenching rains, and icy winds can feel like a nightmare.

INCANTATION

Fears and tears

Are gone from me

Restless night

You let me be

Gone away

Away with you

I sleep in waves

Of velvet blue

Ingredients
- The Devil
- The Lovers
- Eucalyptus leaves
- ½ pomegranate
- Chamomile tea

Method, Visualization, and Meditation

This spell will help you find restorative, uninterrupted slumber and sweeter dreams.

The Devil card represents fear, while the Lovers card represents love. The two cards are flip sides of the same coin. Eucalyptus leaves are said to repel evil spirits and ward off sickness. Pomegranates are evocative of deep slumber, as Persephone ate them and returned to the underworld. Chamomile is famous for its soothing qualities.

Eat half a pomegranate's worth of seeds for your evening's dessert. Before going to bed, fix yourself a cup of chamomile tea. Light a candle. Sipping the tea, place the Devil card before you. Enter the card in your mind's eye. Bring the core emotion of the nightmares into the card with you. Stand before the giant, seething Devil. He is like the great and powerful Oz, all artifice and nothing real.

Imagine the qualities of your nightmare as a symbol, something you can hold in your hand. It may be a dark ball of fuzzy energy, a present wrapped with shiny black wrapping paper, the bloody head of a corpse. Allow your imagination to express it.

Hold your fear in your hand. Walk up and place it before the Devil. Leave the fear with him. Walk backwards while chanting the incantation.

Place the Lovers card over the Devil card. The Devil has been transformed to light and sun and peace. Meditate on the beauty and bounty of this card as you finish your tea.

Scatter the eucalyptus leaves beneath your mattress. Devour a few pages of a favorite childhood book before turning off the light and falling into a deep sleep.

Spell to Unleash Magic in Your Day

Ingredients
- Coffee or mint tea
- Piece of dark chocolate
- Randomly selected card (don't look)
- Nine of Cups

Method, Visualization, and Meditation

Chocolate is an aphrodisiac and affects the pleasure centers of the brain just like really good sex. Coffee beans were first roasted and brewed in Sufi monasteries in the fifteenth century. The energetic properties of coffee are highly valued today. You can use the spirit of coffee to energize anything you like—in this case, as an activation of magic. A randomly pulled card reflects surprise magic. The Nine of Cups grants enchantment.

Devour a small piece of chocolate, knowing all the while that unexpected pleasures are headed your way. What will it be?

Sip your morning coffee (mint tea contains activation energy for tea drinkers). Feel the essence of the bean or herb whipping up the energy around you and filling your body.

Select a random card from your deck. Do not flip it over. Place the Nine of Cups over your randomly selected card. The genie on this card has already granted your wish. An essence of your unseen card is headed your way today. Finish your coffee and put the card out of your mind. Magic and the threads of the universe work best when left to their own devices and unattended.

At the end of your day, return and flip the card underneath the Nine of Cups. How did this card relate to the unexpected magic of your day?

Alice Hoffman, the prolific author of dozens of novels including Practical Magic *and* The Dovekeepers, *was born on this day. This spell provides you with an unexpected enchanted boost and is an excellent start to any day.*

• • • • • •

INCANTATION

Conjure magic
For my day
Marvelous delights
Head my way

St. Patrick Money Spell

Today is St. Patrick's Day. Keep the luck of the Irish with you all day long. This spell comes from the emerald gem of the western world. It has been adapted from Celtic Magic *by D. J. Conway.*

Ingredients
- Ace of Pentacles
- Bowl
- Water
- Silver coin
- Moonlit night

Method, Visualization, and Meditation

The Ace of Pentacles represents a windfall of finance. Silver is aspected by the moon and is the root of wealth.

Focus on the Ace of Pentacles. A hand offering a coin extends from a cloud. Imagine money coming at you from all directions. Think of what you could do with such money, how it would be spent and invested.

With the ace in view, fill a bowl with water halfway. Place a silver coin at the bottom. Place the bowl so the reflection of the moon plays across the water's surface.

Sweep your fingers across the surface of the water, symbolically gathering the moon's silver.

Repeat the incantation three times.

Pour the water into the earth when you are finished, and keep the coin.

Slip the Ace of Pentacles under your pillow before falling asleep.

INCANTATION

Lovely lady
Of the moon
Bring to me
Your wealth soon
Fill my hands
With silver and gold
All you give
My purse can hold

Send Healing Energy Spell

Ingredients
1. Card representing your healing energy
2. Eight of Wands
3. Card representing person receiving energy

Method, Visualization, and Meditation

This spell sends emotional or physical healing energy to a person in need, like long-distance healing.

Choose a card appropriate to the energy you wish to send. The Sun, Two of Cups, and Ace of Cups are excellent healing cards.

Lay the card of healing energy before you.

Gaze at the card and bring your mind's eye inside the card, aligning it with the energies and healing properties. Take all of these feelings and imagine molding them into an energetic ball.

Place the Eight of Wands on the table. Imagine you are taking all of these good and yummy feelings and sending them to the person in need of healing.

Place the card representing the receiver on the table. See all of your delicious white healing energy pouring into them.

1

2

3

Edgar Cayce celebrated his birthday today. Cayce found great fame in his prophetic abilities but was disheartened when his psychic fame overshadowed his work as a healer.

INCANTATION

Soft and warm

Right and true

I send healing thoughts

And energy to you

Stop discomfort

Stop the pain

Peace and love

Is what you gain

INCANTATION

Dark and negative
You are gone
Replace with light
The break of dawn
Your energy departs
Rest in dirt
No longer the power
To wound and hurt

Banish Negativity Spell

Ingredients
- The Star
- Flat rock
- Rusty nail
- Hammer

Method, Visualization, and Meditation

Negativity can plague a person or a home like the common cold. It's always out there lurking, like a dark shadow waiting for an unsuspecting person to give it the attention it wants and craves. The trick is not to be the person who fuels its energy. Casting this spell, you will be sure that when negativity is tossed your way, you can simply step aside. You can dodge it like a ball while remaining inside creativity, productivity, and peace.

The Star card is entirely open and positive. The negativity you banish is replaced with the inspiration of the Star card.

Visualize the negativity as you hammer the nail to the rock. You will want to score the face of the flat stone three times with the nail and hammer. When you are finished, bury the rock in the earth.

Place the Star card before you. Enter the consciousness of the card. Light. Expansive. Open. Allow the glow of starlight to form a protective white barrier around you. When you feel negativity coming toward you in the future, simply put up this shield and it will glide past.

Place the nail in a bag with a handful of dirt. Reserve this nail for future use when you need to banish negativity.

Ten of Cups Connection Ritual

Ingredient
- Ten of Cups

Method, Visualization, and Meditation
Enter the arcana of the Ten of Cups.

Stage curtains part as you enter the card and observe the ending of a play. The audience leaps to their feet. Hundreds of hands clap in approval as tears stream down wet cheeks and laughter escapes smiling lips.

A man and woman join together onstage and reach outwards as if they have created the glorious rainbow of cups above them. Two children, a boy and a girl, dance in circles upon the wooden stage, giggling in delight.

The carefully painted background depicts a bucolic scene: the sweet farm of this happy family. Moving your attention to the stage wings, a shadowy figure catches your eye. A female holds a paintbrush and looks at you as the curtain drops. The audience disperses and the actors retire to their dressing rooms.

You remain in the theater as the shadowy figure approaches you. You recognize her as Pamela Colman Smith. You remember Pamela worked for the Lyceum Theatre as a designer. A smile is set on her generous lips as she moves closer to you.

"This is a beautiful set, Ms. Smith," you say, complimenting her.

Wise, almond-shaped eyes settle upon you.

"Why is it beautiful? What did you see?" she asks.

"The happily-ever-after ending," you reply.

"Is there really such a thing?" she asks and disappears into the shadows.

The Ten of Cups was called the Lord of Perfected Success by the magicians of the Golden Dawn, who assigned it the time period of March 11–20.

INCANTATION
Happily ever after
The end
Hearts are healed
Wounds on the mend
Story's over, time to go
Emotions wavered to and fro
Drama's done
The battle's won
And just like that
Next story's begun

Today is the first day of Aries, the initiator, the ram, the one who gets things rolling. Aries is ruled by Mars and is represented by the horns of a ram.

INCANTATION

Action, forward

March and move

Forge ahead

The road is smooth

Action of Aries Spell

Ingredients
- Scarlet candle

1. The Emperor
2. The Chariot

Method, Visualization, and Meditation

Red candles reflect action energy. The Emperor gets things done. The Chariot card sets a course.

Light your candle while stating your intention.

Place the Emperor before you. The Emperor is ensconced in armor underneath his ruby robes. Ram horns, echoing Aries, decorate the four corners of his throne. The rhythmic drumbeat of his armies beats like a heartbeat in the distance. He controls these legions who will not stop until they reach their goal. Go to the Emperor's face. It has seen a thousand battles and an equal number of sunsets. He is strong but human underneath it all. He is willing to listen to your request.

Tell him what you want to take action on.

He looks at you earnestly, then raises his arm. It shall be done.

He turns to present you with a gift. It is a chariot.

Place the Chariot card before you. Step inside the cart. It rocks and roars. The Emperor's legions stand behind it. Visualize exactly what you must do and how you will take action.

Where would you like to go?

What road are you on?

Where are your current actions leading you?

What wonders unfold as you take action?

Pick up the reins and go!

Ritual to Align with Spring

Ingredients
- Ace of Wands
- Favorite spring items and symbols

Method, Visualization, and Meditation

Working with seasonal energy is like working within the moon's phases. The energy surrounds us; we need only be open to it in order to access its gifts. Energetic qualities of spring include birth, youth, freshness, newness, awakening, and expansion. Spring aligns with waxing moon energy.

Gather seasonal energy like a weaver pulling silken strands for her loom. Warm breezes, quivering green grass, drenching rain storms, and tender young buds support you and your magical intent. It is free, easy, and available.

Gather your favorite seasonal objects around the Ace of Wands. Enter the card.

See the flash of heat. It signals the beginning of manifestation. Torrid fire radiates from the wand. It is a primal heat, the very source of fire, the sun itself. The electric energy moves past your skin, warms your muscles and sinewy tendons, warms the blood circulating through your veins. The marrow inside your bones is heated, thawed, and rejuvenated. It extends back out and through all the molecules making up the rest of your body. The warmth of spring reverberates. This is the magic of life, of energy; like a purring engine, you glow with cardinal power.

This heart of spring, the essence of the sun, is the driving force of life. With this electricity you have the ability to grow anything you like.

How will you use this wand?

What do you want to grow this season?

What begs for expansion and energy?

What will be born?

The spring equinox falls on the modern calendar near March 20. The word equinox is derived from the root "equal." There are an equal number of daylight and nighttime hours. Spells cast for balance are especially powerful during the spring and fall equinoxes, when day and night call a tie.

• • • • •

INCANTATION

Awake, awake

Spring has sprung

Much magic waits

To be done

The ground is warm

The summer's near

Focus on things

That I hold dear

My garden's fertile

Full and rich

And I'm a clever

Seasonal witch

*The Two of Wands
was called the Lord of
Dominion by the magicians
of the Golden Dawn,
who assigned it the time
period of March 21–30.*

Two of Wands Connection Ritual

Ingredient
• Two of Wands

Method, Visualization, and Meditation
Enter the arcana of the Two of Wands.

You have entered the space of division. One has become two. In this space of duality, the wand has become aware of itself. Context is provided by means of a second. Opposition is born. Oppositional tension creates a new energy.

You view a sparkling vista from high atop castle ramparts. The air is fresh, full of the sea, and gulls squawk as they fly overhead looking for breakfast. A town is visible below. A shoreline meets red mountains who fall into the cool waters of the Mediterranean. A gentleman stands before you. His rich velvet robes convey wealth and stature. You recall how the suit of wands often relates to career and realize he is involved in business and commerce.

He stands with a globe in hand, utterly absorbed in it. A series of actions has been in motion. What began in his mind has been implemented. His passionate idea has become a reality and begins to take on a life of its own. The wheels are in motion. Like the Wizard of Oz's wicked witch who watches Dorothy through her crystal ball, this man watches to see what will happen.

Two red wands flank his sides, one anchored to the castle, the other in his hand. These wands represent the context he has created as he set his idea and plan forth. Doing so, he has created a new duality, and the wands are the physical proof. They represent the reality of his vision. The businessman stands between the two wands like the center pillar of the Tree of Life, echoing the High Priestess, Justice, and Hierophant cards. He represents each of us residing within the integration of two opposites.

Judgement Card Connection Ritual

Ingredient
• Judgement

Today is sacred to archangel Gabriel, who appears on the Judgement card.

Method, Visualization, and Meditation
Enter the arcana of Judgement.

A pontoon supports you upon the peaceful waters of a glacial lake. Though you are alone, expectation hangs in the crisp air as if something is about to happen.

Distant rumbling, like rolling thunder, breaks the silence. Like an approaching freight train it draws close to you, becoming louder.

Bruised purple and blue clouds billow in turmoil over you. They are skyscraper high on one another, swirling like soup. A blond figure emerges through the top of the clouds. He is a creature born of air, fire, and energy. His form pulsates, creating the visage of a human figure, but you know there is nothing human about this airborne entity. His eyes are wide and look past you to the four corners of the earth.

Scarlet wings unfold behind him as he raises a golden horn to his lips. An ear-splitting sound so loud it becomes silence, then noise again, startles every creature on earth awake. The waters of the peaceful lake roll, churn, and splash, echoing the clouds above as granite coffins break the water's surface. They bobble up and down like plastic toys in a child's bath. Each splash reveals a new coffin. The creature continues to blow his golden horn. Amidst the mayhem, the coffin lids spring open. Out of boxed darkness, soft, naked bodies rise. Dead eyes pop open, renewed. Men, women, and children, with arms of surrender and exultations of ecstasy, embrace the angelic creature above.

This is revelation, rebirth, and transformation. There is no going back. The transformation is nearly complete.

> There is no going back.
> Nor do you wish to.
> You move into what is.

INCANTATION
Judgement card
The end of days
I've evolved my life
Changed my ways
Altered my very
State of mind
The World card is
Not far behind

According to legend, Venice was founded on this day at noon. Cast the Venetian Shadows and Mist Spell when you need to sink back invisibly and observe without drawing attention to yourself.

INCANTATION

Darkness cover

Me from light

Gain what I need

Power of sight

I watch, I listen

Observe all

Gloom and mist

Does inthrall

I'll slip and slide

No one will see

The shadow that

Is cast by me

Venetian Shadows and Mist Hot Chocolate Spell

Ingredients
- The Moon
- 2 tablespoons sugar
- 2 tablespoons unsweetened cocoa
- ½ teaspoon arrowroot powder
- Scant pinch of salt
- 1 cup milk
- Dash of vanilla extract

Method, Visualization, and Meditation

Sometimes we like to be front and center. Other times sinking into the background and simply observing will help us uncover great truths that deserve our attention.

Venetians are famous for their thick hot chocolate. The Moon card helps us discover secrets illuminated only by a lunar glow. Powdered arrowroot, a thickening agent, aids in spying unseen opportunities and increases luck. The pleasure of chocolate can be used as mindful experience.

Place the Moon card. Gaze past the double dogs, beyond the crawfish, and into the darkened windows of the double towers. Sit inside the tower on the right. Cast your eyes upon the shadowy recesses of the valleys below. Feel yourself melting into the darkness of the tower. Blend in like a chameleon to the dimness around you.

At this moment you are invisible. Carry this sense of invisibility as you venture out into the world, using it to cloak you as you wish.

Prepare your hot chocolate mindfully. Mix sugar, cocoa, arrowroot, and salt in the bottom of a cup. Place your milk over a low flame and heat until not quite boiling. Pour into the powdered mixture and blend. Sink into the darkness of the cup. Drink and enjoy your view from the shadows.

Ace of Swords Connection Ritual

Ingredient
- Ace of Swords

Method, Visualization, and Meditation
Enter the arcana of the Ace of Swords.

You stand on the side of a cliff overlooking a deep valley. You are safely ensconced in climbing gear. The altitude is high, the air crisp and clean. You gaze back to the valley where you began. Down below, the air was warm and calm. Spiders cast silken strands, allowing themselves to be pulled up and away, as gently as a thought. Down in the valley the birds soared above you while butterflies erratically bounced to and fro.

The arctic gulf stream blasts you in the face. You watch a distant airplane inch across the sky, leaving a thin white trail in its wake. Clouds move like mountains, nebulous formations changing with the wind. The air changed the higher you went. Thoughts move freely, quickly at higher altitudes. You realize this is the place in your mind where you seek clarity. This is the source of originality and higher thoughts.

A distant howling, like a coyote or wolf pack, grows louder in the distance. You wonder what it might be. The swaying valley trees warn you it is the wind. A rushing sound like roaring water fills your ears, moving past you and onto the mountain peaks.

This is the essence of air, the soft bubble surrounding the earth, protecting us from the black emptiness of space. A hand appears before you, grasping a gleaming silver sword. You realize if you remove the "s" from "sword" it becomes "word." Words heal, encourage, protect, hurt, damage, and destroy, just like a sword. You now understand why the sword is the symbol for our thoughts.

This sword is yours.

Spring winds are blowing wild and free. It is time to connect to the Ace of Swords.

INCANTATION

Gleaming sword
Powers speech
Calculations, meditation
And where I reach
Acting swift, decisive
Super fast
Good decisions
Are made to last

INCANTATION

Flight

Passports

Excitement

Wow!

Plan a trip

Do it now!

Manifest a Trip Spell

Ingredients
1. Page of Wands
2. Six of Swords
3. The Sun

Method, Visualization, and Meditation

The Page of Wands is the intrepid traveler of the deck. The Six of Swords reflects a journey. The Sun card represents the exuberance and personal expansion that traveling provides.

Place the Page of Wands. Join her in the desert landscape. Let your bare toes dig into the grainy, hot sand beneath your feet. Feel the sun in your hair. See pyramids rising in the distance.

The Page of Wands contains the power of travel in her wand. See the place you wish to visit. It appears before you like a mirage on the desert sands. What does it look like? What does it smell like? What lodgings are you staying in? What does the food taste like?

Once you have the destination alive in your mind's eye, the page gives you her wand. It reverberates and shivers in your hand. You point it toward your destination. Your intention brings you there.

Place the Six of Swords. See your departure. Who travels with you? Do you travel by train, plane, car, or bus? Feel yourself inside your transportation—the slow rocking of the train, the plane lifting from the earth, or the nighttime highway lights zipping past you. Reach into your pocket. Find a roll of cash. You have the resources you need.

Place the Sun card. An jolt of energy moves through you as you arrive at your destination. Sunflowers wiggle, mirroring your excitement. The open arms of a child welcome you, embracing you in the excitement of a new adventure. Scratch the white horse and turn to look at the potential you have unlocked. Walk out of the hotel and down the street to your destination.

1   2   3

Permission to Explore My Creativity Spell

Ingredients
1. The Star
2. Ace of Wands
3. Ace of Pentacles

Method, Visualization, and Meditation

Have you been challenged in expressing personal creativity? To be alive utilizes an incredible amount of creativity. In past generations we made our own clothes, built our own homes, grew and cultivated our own food, hunted and prepared our meals, even provided our own entertainment. These things are done for us in modern times. We specialize in our jobs or careers. Creativity is lumped into "the arts" and described as something "artists" do.

Giving ourselves permission to be creative is important. It opens up the gateway to freedom, expression, and, yes, magic.

Place the Star before you. She is the muse. She is the artist's channel. Inspiration comes from above and below. She blesses your creativity. Open your energy from the top of your head and the bottom of your feet. Allow yourself to become the vehicle for your chosen art/work.

Place the Ace of Wands. The Star's energy lights the wand's flame. The wand glows and grows bigger. The more attention you shed on your project, the greater your passion grows. It warms and feeds you. The process of making becomes an end to itself.

Place the Ace of Pentacles. A pentacle appears in the material world. See the finished work. It is there. You simply bring it into being.

1

2

3

The painter Raphael was born on this day in 1483. Raphael, da Vinci, and Michelangelo are the holy trio of Renaissance masters. Cast this spell to grant yourself the permission and right needed to access materials, inspiration, and space to engage personal creativity.

INCANTATION

Gather items
That I need
Of negative words
I take no heed
Creative project
From my heart
I give permission
And will start
Follow through
Until it's done
Having ridiculous
Crazy fun

Knight of Cups Connection Ritual

INCANTATION

Knight of Cups
Lover of emotion
Handsome and deep
As the ocean
Bear a message
Words for me
Once revealed
I can see

Ingredient
• Knight of Cups

Method, Visualization, and Meditation
Enter the arcana of the Knight of Cups.

Lavender and rose shrubs nestle into cliff walls, sage bushes and cedar groves mingle with saltwater air. A man and horse appear like a desert mirage. He is dressed in armor that glints in the overhead sun. The armor looks silver and slippery, like a sardine who has leapt from his waterlogged pack and appeared before you in human form. The figure glistens like the sea and smells of ocean. Gazing into his eyes, you see eternal waves crashing there. His eyes carry the depths of the sea and forty shades of blue. His body is sheer Caribbean blue liquid.

Red fish adorn his tunic, which rests over fine sheathed metal pounded out to protect this sensitive knight. He is not meant for battle or war. He would sooner write a sonnet under a tree than kill a foreign enemy or sing a gentle song than yell the cry of war. He is the protector of the human heart and cultivator of emotion. He is a knight of communication and feeling. The knight contains the uncanny ability to see right through you and to understand and know what you want and need. If he were to turn on his powers of seduction, you know you would be powerless to resist him.

He descends from his horse and walks to you. Bending down, close to your face, he traces his finger across your cheek and whispers a message into your ear. It sends a ripple of shivers down your spine.

As quickly as he appeared, he vanishes. The son of the sea is the ultimate shapeshifter. He dissolves like mist caressing the pounding waves.

You stand alone with your message.

What did he say?

Ensure Good Health Kale Charm

Ingredients

- The Sun
- A diced apple
- Shredded coconut
- Dried cranberries
- Kale that has been chopped fine
- Your favorite salad dressing

Method, Visualization, and Meditation

Something as simple as the preparation of lunch can be turned into a spell or charm if done with focused intention. The Sun card invokes wellness. Apples, kale, and cranberries are all associated with good health. Coconut is a sacred moon food.

Place shredded coconut on a baking sheet and bake in a 350-degree oven for eight minutes. While the coconut toasts, turn to your cards.

Focus on the Sun card. Feel the sun shining light into your heart center. When you feel the solar light strong and warm inside your chest, express it outwards. Expand the warmth. Allow it to grow larger. Feel the heat across your entire chest, down your arms, up your neck and into your head and right down each leg to the tip of your feet. Circulate the warmth. Feel the health glowing inside you.

When the coconut cools, toss all the ingredients together with your favorite dressing while saying the incantation.

Today is the Roman festival of Salus, goddess of health, preservation, and good fortune. As seasons change, this charm invokes an aura of good health from the inside.

· · · · ·

INCANTATION

Greens of health
Card of wealth
The body glows
My mind knows
I'm healthy, healthy, healthy

Today marks the Roman festival of Luna, who is the divine embodiment of the moon. Use this energy to connect to the moon's evocative, mysterious, and intuitive qualities.

Moon Card Connection Ritual

Ingredient
- The Moon

Method, Visualization, and Meditation

If possible, perform this ritual on or near the night of the full or new moon.

Enter the arcana of the Moon.

All would be dark in this landscape were it not for the light of the moon. You stand safe and dry next to a pool of water. A crawfish scurries out of unconscious depths. This water hides desires, needs, and wants that dare not cross whispering lips. What would people think if they knew what your water conceals?

Allow what is hidden below the pool to venture forth so you alone can see them. A blanket of darkness conceals what the moon reveals.

Nothing is what it seems when it stands between the two beasts of instinct and the two towers. Moonlight blurs the lines between unknown and known. Each new desire rising to meet your skin and break from your water is frightening. It has not been acknowledged before. Yet, under lunar light, you can softly examine what wants to break through and cross the threshold of reality into your world.

Your guides wait patiently in the shadows. The path of the shaman extends before you. It begs you to take the first step.

Embrace the milky ivory rays of the moon.

The alchemical process is reversed and our souls are laid bare as the lunar sphere reflects the golden light of the sun from its bone-white surface, shedding the uncanny light of truth that no one can turn away from.

Do not fear. Embrace the unknown.

INCANTATION

Between right and wrong
Lies the gray
Between the poet's lines
Lies her truth
Between wake and sleep
Lies dreams
Between life and death
Lies the other world
Between day and night
Lies twilight.
I cultivate my shadows

Fool Card Connection Ritual

Ingredient
- The Fool

Method, Visualization, and Meditation

Enter the arcana of the Fool. He is the true mascot of tarot. Stand on the threshold.

Everyone ignores the madman dancing on the edges of reality. Are you mad to enter the tarot? You cannot turn away; you follow his maniacal laughter and stand atop a mountain peak. The Fool prances before you. The sun casts blinding white light of potential upon your upturned face. The Fool carries a white rose, symbolic of innocence. Only the innocent would follow his example. Only those who are pure of heart can follow his course. Can you forget all you know? Would you risk it? The Fool risks everything because he has nothing. With nothing to lose, you have everything to gain.

Leave your preconceived notions at the door. Shed your clothing. Rules? Throw them out the window. The Fool knows neither up nor down. The Fool is ridiculous. The Fool is an opening. Can you hear his maniacal laughter?

The sacred symbol of all life, the circle, the zero, hangs above his head. *No thing.* The circle is the shape of the solar system, our planet, your z, a clock, an egg, the shape of the molecules building your body. To enter the O is to enter the physical world. O is manifestation of physical reality. O is us as far as we can explain and experience ourselves. O is the beginning of the tarot. It is also the end. The Fool is ascended master and novice. Enter the mystery.

Begin your adventure.

Start.

Now.

Today is April Fool's Day. Spring bursts forth in unexpected ways, as does the trickster pictured on this card. It is the perfect day to connect with the archetypal energy of the Fool's folly.

INCANTATION

Doorway, threshold
Ground I stand
What is this foreign
Mystic land
Answers sought
Questions known
Through this territory
I shall roam
Trod this path
Like souls before
Search until
I find my door

Raise the Wind and Your Energy Spell

Over sixty tornados broke out in the United States on this day in 2006.

INCANTATION
Queen of Swords
Goddess of Air
Your magic flows
Like wind in my hair
The change is quick
True and fast
The results we bring
Are meant to last

Ingredients
- Queen of Swords
- Dried flower petals or milkweed or dandelion fluff

Method, Visualization, and Meditation

It once was a commonly held belief that witches could control the wind. It was also said that a woman during childbirth and shortly thereafter had the power to raise the wind. Try your own hand at raising the wind with this spell. At the very least, you'll blow fresh air into your life and change your luck.

Place the Queen of Swords. This queen is direct, pointed, and precise. Venture toward her throne; feel the wind and billowing clouds surrounding her. The air is clean and crisp. Your thoughts are already beginning to sharpen. Her profile looks as if it has been carved from porcelain. She hears the scuffle of your footsteps and turns to look at you.

Bid her hello and tell her how you would like to change and adjust your energy. When you are certain she has heard you, carefully enclose the petals or the fluff from milkweed or dandelions in each of your fists. Walk to the largest open space you can find.

Stand with your arms spread apart and gaze at the sky. Place an image of the Queen of Swords across the entire expanse of the sky from the horizon upward. She should appear as enormous as the entire sky. When she is crystal clear in your vision, repeat your request.

The moment you feel a breeze, open your hands to release your petals/fluff to the wind.

Pentacle Pomander for Financial Wealth Spell

Ingredients
- King of Pentacles
- Orange
- Cloves

Method, Visualization, and Meditation

The King of Pentacles is the wealthiest and most financially secure card in the tarot deck. Pomanders were first created in the Middle Ages for protection and sweet scents. Even Nostradamus wrote pomander recipes. You will craft a pomander out of the orange and cloves. Oranges are associated with the power of the sun, and cloves are known for their money attraction.

Gaze at the King of Pentacles. Step inside the card so you are standing before him on equal ground. His rooftop garden is lush. Greenery and bursting flowers surround him. Creeping ivy represents the stratification of his ever-growing wealth. The surrounding castle is his. All that is available to him is also available to you. Around you wealth grows like spreading ivy. Feel it sprouting from your feet and ankles and up the back of your chair and the wall behind you. Ivy will grow, untethered, like the King of Pentacles' riches. Spin the web of your own wealth, which multiplies.

Note the pentacle the king holds. Now you can create your own.

Bring the orange before you. Focus on the circular nature of the orange. Like the sun, it holds the energy of growth and expansion. Decorate the orange with cloves (use a sharp point to make room for the clove rather than the clove itself), making the shape of the pentacle or the money sign.

Place your pomander somewhere warm. Each time you catch its scent, smell the money you are drawing.

The first casino opened on the Las Vegas Strip today in 1941. Why gamble when you can make your own financial luck with a Pentacle Pomander?

INCANTATION

Solar rays

Soak into me

Money growing

Wild and free

King of finance

Inspire me

You show me how

I follow you

Wild wealth

I now pursue

Three of Wands Connection Ritual

The Three of Wands was called the Lord of Established Strength by the magicians of the Golden Dawn, who assigned it the time period of March 31–April 10.

INCANTATION

Three of Wands
Creativity unbound
Set forth your ships
Send them round
They will return
Someday, somehow
Make your plans
Plan well now

Ingredient
• Three of Wands

Method, Visualization, and Meditation

Enter the arcana of the Three of Wands.

A new possibility has been born from two. Threes are the sacred triad of manifestation. A third option has emerged. This is the birth of creativity from the tiniest grain of sand to the furthest galaxy in the known universe.

The brilliant lemon yellow light of morning fills a bay. A merchant waterway bustling with boat traffic spreads before you. Great ships with decks of a hundred men sail over churning waters. Pungent rosemary bushes dot the rocks along the seashore.

A figure stands before you. He is dressed in colorful clothing and a cherry-red cloak.

Wet and shiny sea moss creeps across the rocks he stands upon. Two wands, sprouting leaves, align next to him. They protrude from the sea cliff. His hand reaches out and grabs for a third wand. His stance opens toward the water, toward the sailing ships.

He has put a plan into action; wheels are in motion, the stage has been set. The wheels of fate have turned by his very own hand.

The Three of Wands is the creativity of fire, the coming together of passion, ideas, and potentials.

The figure causes you to reflect on the nature of what you have created in your life. What have your passionate desires created in your life? What have you set into motion? What has been born through you?

Peaceful Homecoming Spell

Ingredients
1. Eight of Cups
2. Ten of Pentacles
• Favorite grounding stone or rock

Method, Visualization, and Meditation

Returns can be joyous, heartfelt, and unexpectedly poignant. Usually they come with a combination of emotions. Sometimes we return home wearing our accomplishments like badges upon our sleeves. Other times we return home to care for a loved one or clean up someone's mess. Sometimes we return to find ourselves.

This spell promotes a centered grounding. No matter your homecoming's reason, you will remain peaceful and centered inside of it.

Place the Eight of Cups. Enter the card. Feel the warm, red cloak upon you. Embark on the upward climb. See the return journey. The cups behind you are the lessons you've learned and the experiences you have had while away. The eight cups represent your current identity, the physical ways in which you now define yourself. You know, as you walk, that to return home means coming back into the world of preconceived notions about who you are. You define you. Others do not.

Place the Ten of Pentacles. This card represents the rich tapestry you are walking into: the heady combination of people, place, and memory. Move through the card for a moment, past the wise grandfather. Feel the soft canine fur against your knees. Wink at the child who hides and moves to the banner in the back. Upon it you will find the scales of balance. This scale is your center, your saving grace. Though the wheels of emotion and the affects of others are felt, with this scale in hand you will find your inner balance. Nothing will throw you. You are a rock.

Feel your stone in hand with its grounding and centering energy. Keep this with you at all times on your trip, touching it when and where you need to center yourself.

The Mayflower set sail from Plymouth on this day in 1621 on its journey back to England. This spell is useful for class reunions or visits to a former home after being away for a long time.

INCANTATION
Home sweet home
I'm coming back
Full of heart
I feel no lack
What is old
Becomes new again
This time I say
Where and when
No matter what
I find peace
Conflicting feelings
Come to cease

INCANTATION

Queen of Cups
And god Apollo
Fill me up
When I am hollow
Let the words I speak be clear
Be the words we need to hear
Let me give them
What they need
Provide wisdom
They can heed

Powers of Prophecy Tarot Reading Ritual

Ingredients
• Candle reserved for tarot reading only
• Queen of Cups

Method, Visualization, and Meditation

The Queen of Cups carries an empathy as deep as the ocean, and as such she is the glorious tarot reader of the deck. She is psychic, able to see visions in sea foam, scry across placid waters, and navigate storms.

Place the Queen of Cups, the most empathic card of the deck, beneath your lit candle. Look at the light of the candle. As a tarot reader, you become the shining light for your querent. The light you shed is found in the words you say, the compassion you offer, and the counsel you give. How do you act as the shining beacon for those who sit across the cards from you? As a reader, it is not the time to spout your opinions and projections onto your client or friend.

Focus on the candle and feel yourself becoming hollow. Feel all preconceived notions falling away from you. Become the vehicle through which truth and kindness flow. Let your light reflect the querent in the best possible way. Remind them of how special they are. Become the witness to their truth. Become the candle.

Allow the invisible rising heat of the candle to let your spirit open to the wisdom above so that the best possible words are spoken.

Empress Connection Ritual

Ingredient
• The Empress

Method, Visualization, and Meditation

Enter the arcana of the Empress. You are walking through a field of gold. You run your fingers across soft tips of wheat. The wind blows like waves in the field, and the sweet smell of hay and poppies makes you dizzy. White dandelion fluff flies past you like Victorian fairy kingdoms in flight. It is late afternoon, and the sun casts a rich orange glow across the meadow.

Do your eyes deceive you or do you see a woman? You feel confused. Refracted light pings back and forth in a million fractals. The excitable quality of summer hums, confusing everything in a golden haze. The closer you get, you see it is, indeed, a lady.

She reclines on a chaise lounge that is covered in velvet pillows. Her belly grows round with new life warm and safe inside of her, ensconced within watery darkness. The signs of Venus are engraved inside a heart beneath her. She is adorned with a crown of twelve stars, each shining for a sign on the zodiac. She carries the secrets of the heavens, yet this woman is made entirely of earth.

Her neck is strewn with a pearl necklace, and she bears a glowing scepter. Her gown is covered in pomegranates, and her ruby slippers caress the ground beneath her. A waterfall flows behind her, its waters churning a sparkling rainbow mist.

"Come to me, my darling," she bids you. You walk forward and sit before her. Her voice purrs, throaty and full. She strokes the top of your head in a motherly fashion.

"Child, I know how I must appear to you, but do not be confused. I am merely a reflection of you."

"Of me?" You shrink back, shocked.

"Yes," she answers knowingly. "I am the epitome of your creative self."

The self-declared Empress Matilda prepared to become the first female ruler in England on this day in 1141, though she never quite managed to take the throne.

INCANTATION

Empress, goddess
Warmth and light
You are dazzling
In my sight
Your gifts of creation
Are love and birth
You spread joy
Exuberance and mirth

Japanese Buddhists celebrate Buddha's birth today in a festival called Hana Matsuri, or the flower festival. Serve this empress tea to become irresistible and have your way with anyone who drinks it.

INCANTATION

Cherries red
Passion bright
My wish is granted
By evening's light
I serve this for
The things I crave
And to their hearts
I do enslave

Irresistibility Empress Tea Spell

Ingredients
- The Empress
- 8 cherry tea bags
- 1 cup water
- 1 cup sugar
- 1 lime

Method, Visualization, and Meditation

Baby Buddha statues are erected in temples during Hana Matsuri. These baby Buddhas stand like the tarot Magician: their right hands point to heaven and their left hands point toward the earth. Sweet tea is purchased by the faithful, who pour the tea over the baby Buddhas. This occurs just as the cherry blossoms bloom.

You can pay homage to this festival by preparing a brew to become irresistible. Cherry fruit has a long history of attraction magic—who can resist sweet cherries?—and cherry juice can be used as a substitute for blood in spells and recipes. The Empress card is used because she has her way with all who cross her path.

Focus on the Empress card with your mind's eye. There is nothing she cannot create, manifest, or influence. She represents the ultimate in female desire and creation.

What do you desire from your guest or guests? See them bending to your desire. Slip into her dress, feel the light weight of her crown. Embody the Empress as you whip up this tea.

Dangle eight cherry tea bags near your lips and whisper your desire into them before steeping them in a pitcher of cold water. Place in the sun to catch its rays and infuse the tea. Dissolve sugar in water over a low flame until the sugar has dissolved. When the tea water has turned the ruby color of passion, remove the bags, add the sugar water and the juice of one lime.

As you stir everything, repeat the incantation.

Activate Crown Chakra Energy

Ingredient
• The World

Method, Visualization, and Meditation

The crown chakra is the spot where all the chakras of your body integrate. It represents spiritual connectiveness, consciousness, and enlightenment. It is the soul level of self-knowledge, often depicted in saints as the golden halo glowing around the head. This is seen in the arcana of the Hanged Man.

The crown chakra is located at the top of your head, in the very place the circle of a royal crown sits. Sit on a chair with your feet flat on the floor or sit in yogi position, legs crossed on the floor. Place the World card before you. Focus on the top of your head. Feel the energy there begin to warm and glow. Imagine it is colored violet or pure white. You might even begin to spin the chakra's energy. Sit straight. Perhaps you hear the energy, smell it, or even taste it.

Focus on the World card. See each and every element of the card dancing, moving in tune with the flow of the universe. Feel the connection of divine love, and let the violet or white energy move from yourself to the card and back again. Toss the energy back and forth between you and the card. Each time the energy returns to you, your sense of the present becomes more ingrained. You engage with the fluidity of life.

Feel the ball of energy move through your spine, filling your entire essence with love.

Henry the Fifth was crowned King of England on this day in 1413. Royal crowns rest on the top of the head and denote the connection between royalty and divine right.

INCANTATION

Divine connection
Love and light
Bring conscious awareness
To me tonight
An open channel
Crystal clear
Angels and guides
Are always near

Tree Journey with the Four of Cups

The first Arbor Day was celebrated on this day in 1872.

Ingredients
- Four of Cups
- Your favorite tree

Method, Visualization, and Meditation

In almost any tarot deck the Four of Cups card reflects a figure sitting beneath a tree. The traditional meaning of this card describes unseen opportunities. The entire universe is your personal unseen opportunity. Infinite realities are awaiting your discovery. True magic exists in what you place your attention on.

Trees are the lungs of the planet and are representative of the human journey. Did you know trees can serve as thresholds to other realities? For this journey, you will embrace the gateway quality of a tree.

If you have a favorite tree, take your card to the actual tree. If you don't have a relationship with any particular tree, take a walk until a tree catches your eye. If you do not have access to trees, simply use the Four of Cups.

Focus on the Four of Cups as you sit beneath the tree or move inside the card if you are only using the card. Feel the soft grass beneath your crossed legs. Note how the towering tree's leaves dapple you in sunlight. Spend twenty minutes observing the tree. Look at the bark. What does it look like? What does it remind you of? Examine its leaves. See if you can follow its root system under the earth.

Sit beneath the tree, back to its trunk. Align yourself with the tree's energy. As you do, allow yourself to drift off to the state between wakefulness and sleep. What happens? What do you notice? Hear? See?

Record your findings in your grimoire or journal with the Four of Cups in sight.

INCANTATION

Leaves and bark
Sun and sky
Through your branches
I will fly
Travel up
Travel deep
Enter you
In twilight sleep
Move inside
Move between
Enter realities
Quite unseen

Ace of Wands Cloud Divination

Ingredients
- Ace of Wands
- Sky clouds

Method, Visualization, and Meditation

Nephomancy is the fancy name for cloud divination. It is one of the oldest forms of oracles. Ancient people sought favorable weather conditions for crops. They looked skyward for sustenance. Historically, cross-cultural gods manifest themselves through clouds. The World card and the Wheel of Fortune appear as if in the sky amongst the clouds. Each ace in tarot is expressed as a gift coming forth from a mysterious cloud.

The mutable nature of clouds provides an excellent canvas for the subconscious. Choose an optimal day for cloud observation, but before observing the clouds, place the Ace of Wands. Wands represent the energy you will want to tune in to before performing nephomancy.

Focus on the Ace of Wands. See the hand emerging from a burst of clouds. Let this sudden burst remind you that answers are always at your fingertips. The spirit of fire running through you is tenacious. Your subconscious will pick up on messages if you direct it to do so. Feel the energy of wands moving through you and warming your body like the heat from a campfire.

The castle in the distance of the card holds the treasure you will receive by listening to the messages sent from your subconscious to your conscious. Repeat the incantation as you look upward.

Today in 1903 marks the death of Italian mystic and saint Gemma Galgani. Gemma purportedly produced the stigmata, communicated with guardian angels, was often found in states of ecstasy, and had powers of levitation in which she rose to embrace crucifixes.

INCANTATION

Ace of Wands
Clouds of sky
Bring me messages
While rushing by
Crystalline, wet
Water and white
Shed information
In billowing light

Interview with a Vampire, *Anne Rice's infamous vampire tale, was published on this day in 1976. While vampire wounds heal immediately, mortals can use the vampire metaphor when we need to find rejuvenated love for another person.*

INCANTATION

Love of mine
You're worth the fight
Peace and openness
With you tonight
Past is gone
It slips away
Together find
New ways to play

Vampire Regeneration Love Spell

Ingredients
1. The Moon
2. The Lovers
3. Ace of Cups

Method, Visualization, and Meditation

The Moon card is indicative of the nightwalker. It carries the only sunlight a vampire can tolerate. The Lovers card represents your relationship. The Ace of Cups represents the cup of immortality and the liquid a vampire thrives on to survive.

Place the Moon card. You are inside the pool of water, looking at the landscape of the card. The shellfish rises before you. It begins its arduous journey toward the mountain. Wolves howl, and the moonlight sheds itself and everything in mysterious light. Quiet supernatural power emerges from you. Smell the air. Hear the howling. Feel the potency coursing through your veins. This power is eternal, like the vampire. It is the power of love.

Place the Lovers card. It rests in stark opposition to the Moon. The sun is hot on your head. You and your lover stand in the card. A snake hisses behind you. Fire snaps and crackles behind your lover. You are naked and vulnerable. The act of love is dangerous. You are unafraid. You proceed.

Place the Ace of Cups. Everlasting water and immortality fall on the cards beneath. The Lovers card is refreshed and reinvigorated, the couple saved from the unrelenting sun. The powers of the Moon, the mystery of the subconscious, cycle through the Lovers card. All cards connect, circling, regenerating. See the face of your lover. See them naked, open, and available to you. Let all preconceived notions fall away. Past arguments dissipate and lose their importance. It is just the two of you, open, free, and filled with the waters of regenerated love.

3

1

2

Wash Away Past Pain Spell

Ingredients
1. Three of Swords
2. The Star
3. Ace of Cups
4. The High Priestess
- Swimming pool or shower

Method, Visualization, and Meditation

Water is a baptismal and cleansing agent. If you don't have access to a pool, a shower will work.

Place the Three of Swords before you and take an honest look at the pain you have endured. The piercing of the swords have served their purpose. Their lesson was taught. You have been marked. Look at them honestly, piercing the soft tissue of your heart. Recognize them for what they are. You will not allow this pain to become a habit upon which further truths are made. It is time to extract them. You will pull each sword out of the heart with the help of another card.

Place the Star card. Pull the first sword out. In its place feel her cool waters of refreshment and inspiration filling the sword space. This heals the wound. Say the incantation.

Place the Ace of Cups. Pull out the second sword. Feel the waters of renewal and peace fill the space left from the blade. Repeat the incantation.

Place the High Priestess card. Pull the third and final sword out. Her dress turns into currents of moon water that fill the open gap left by the sword. Repeat the incantation.

Dive into a swimming pool or take a shower. As you do, feel the effects of your operation and all attachment to pain wash away. Embrace renewal on all levels.

The Songkran Festival begins today, marking Buddhist New Year in Thailand, Burma, Cambodia, and Laos. Temples are visited and water is poured over the hands of monks and Buddha images. Water is symbolically splashed to wash away the old year.

INCANTATION
Though the mark
Will remain
I no longer
Endure pain

Today is Black Day in South Korea, an unofficial holiday focusing on singles. Matchmaking and speed dating events are held in order to get couples together.

INCANTATION

Mint of fire

Sparks desire

Laughter and fun

Take us higher

Magical night

Magnetic attraction

Brings us each

Much satisfaction

Hot Date Spell

Ingredients
- Red candle
- Favorite moisturizer
- Cinnamon mint
1. The Lovers
2. Queen of Wands
3. King of Wands

Method, Visualization, and Meditation

Cast this spell for a hot night out on the town when you want to feel alive, sensual, and sexy. This is not a spell for long-term romance. This is a spell for the delicious feeling of being a sexual creature and enjoying yourself. However, the casting of this spell will not prevent true love from blooming.

A red candle sparks attraction. The Lovers card represents desire. The Queen of Wands is the sexpot of the deck. The King of Wands is the ultimate passionate lover.

Light the candle. Place the Lovers card before you. Smell the musk of the lover's skin. Feel the magnetic attraction between them and feel the same desire rising within you. Let it fill your body from your feet on up. Feel your body and skin glowing red with desire and arousal.

Place the king and the queen cards on opposite sides of the Lovers. Feel them coming together with a magnetizing energy through the Lovers. Send out tendrils of attraction to your date.

As you prepare for your date, apply moisturizer over every inch of your skin. As you apply, imagine your date's lips on every inch of your skin. Before meeting your date, place a spicy cinnamon mint in your mouth and utter the incantation three times.

| 2 | 1 | 3 |

Da Vinci Follow Your Passion Spell

Ingredient
- The Sun

Method, Visualization, and Meditation

You needn't be a painter to realize your passion. You can be a passionate stamp collector, dog walker, or number cruncher. It matters little what form your passion takes. Embrace an attitude of allowance and acceptance of who you truly are.

The Sun card gives power to you.

Place the Sun card before you and feel yourself as the naked child standing there. Solar power generates all life on earth. It has even stirred the molecules of your body. Feel it. Feel the power you have coursing through your veins. Feel the things you are passionate about. This passion, this truth, is stronger than the blocks that stand in your way. See road blocks being erased. They have been placed by your mind and may now be removed.

Your passion is the roadmap you can follow that will always lead you where you need to be. The sunlight illuminates this path for you. The horse will take you wherever you need to go. Grant yourself permission to follow your heart.

Artist Leonardo da Vinci was born today in 1542. He is the iconic archetype of an artist, a person who follows their passion and creates great works of art. This spell gives you permission to blaze a trail of passion.

INCANTATION
Sun of light
Sun of fire
From this moment
Feed my desire
Walk passion's path
Follow through
Swap fear for integrity
This I do

The Four of Wands was called the Lord of Perfected Work by the magicians of the Golden Dawn, who assigned it the time period of April 11–20.

INCANTATION
Four of Wands
Passion stable
Use enthusiasm
You are able
Create a life
Of joy and fun
Be an example
For everyone

Four of Wands Connection Ritual

Ingredient
• Four of Wands

Method, Visualization, and Meditation
Enter the arcana of the Four of Wands.

Fours represent stability. The arcana of three bursts forth creatively and has evolved to the next stage. A fourth appears; stability is reached. A square. A home. A haven. The structure is complete. Four seasons. Four directions. Four elements. Four suits of tarot. Reality in the physical world has been achieved.

A classic European fairy-tale scene appears before you. It is complete with a turreted castle and revelers dressed in long, flowy gowns. You discover the symbol of wands and see they are being used for a party. Four wands are draped for celebration. Cheerful garlands are suspended between the wands, which are tied with charming ribbons. Flowers, grapes, and citrus drape from curly ivy and lush greens.

This marks the celebration of the harvest. Noting the suit of wands, you recall how wands represent passion, fire, and energy. You realize the party is held to honor what has manifested as a result of clear intention.

The four wands are a gateway and a structure. You move to stand inside of them. You feel the grounding nature of intention made real. It surrounds you from every side. Can you feel the support? What happens when the stability of passion blossoms in your life? What happens when you support what you love?

A maiden moves toward you. She leans in. You smell lemon and jasmine in her hair. Her sweet breath whispers a secret into your ear. This message is meant for you and you alone. What does she say?

Bring this message back with you.

Grow My Money Spell

Ingredients
- Mint root
- Box
- Penny, nickel, dime, quarter
- Page of Pentacles
- Seven of Pentacles

Method, Visualization, and Meditation

Mint root will make your money grow. The box represents structure and protection. The coins represent small denominations of money that grows in value. The Page of Pentacles represents a person about to plant a seed. The Seven of Pentacles reflects the harvest of that seed.

Place the root inside a box. Place the Page of Pentacles before you. See the rich, upturned earth. The sweet smell of poppies and hollyhocks flowers the air. Hold the penny before you the same way the page gazes at her pentacle. It represents the beginning of manifestation. Whisper the incantation and place in the box.

Hold the nickel. Your money grows five times. Repeat the incantation. Place in the box. Hold the dime. Your money grows ten times. Repeat the incantation. Place in the box. Hold the quarter. Your money grows twenty-five times. Repeat the incantation. Place in the box, then close the box.

Place the Seven of Pentacles next to the page. The single pentacle has divided and multiplied, just like your finances. It is the singular nature of growth. All things innately seek growth and expansion. Imagine the money in your account growing; see it multiplying.

Choose one way you can help another person with your money. It can be an act as big or as small as you like. A surprise gift for someone you love or a donation to the charity of your choice. Perform that action to seal your spell.

Spring is underway. Bulbs quiver and grow, hibernating animals awake, and the sun grows warmer with each passing day. The earth is awakening and so is your bank account with this money-growing spell.

INCANTATION

Pentacle, seed
Coin and bill
Multiplication
Is my will
My money grows
It builds up high
It is an endless
Continuous supply

April • 18

Beauty and the Beast *opened on Broadway on this day in 1994. The story meditates on the nature of inner and outer beauty. Is beauty skin deep or does it lie in embracing the ultimate truth of who you are on the inside?*

INCANTATION

Beauty and grace
Allure and bloom
Provide peace
Inside this room
Allow myself
To shine and see
Exactly who
I'm meant to be

Inner Beauty Salt Bath Spell

Ingredients
- Candles
- 1 cup Epsom salt
- A bath
- Your favorite ambient music
- The High Priestess

Method, Visualization, and Meditation

A person in touch with themselves who acts out of personal authenticity reflects a universal principle of growth. Nothing is more rapturous or beguiling than an individual who knows who they are.

The electricity occurring inside a person operating from their inner truth is felt by all who connect with them. It can't be applied with makeup or bought in a store. It cannot be found in any person, place, or thing other than you.

Invoke inner beauty here and now.

At night, preferably by the light of the moon, safely fill your bathroom with as many lit candles as you can find. Fill your tub and add one cup of salt to the water. Play your favorite ambient and transporting music.

Place your High Priestess card as the waters rise. Enter the milky moonlight of the card. Stand before her. She is you. You are her. She is your reflection in the mirror, existing to remind you of who you are, of what you have forgotten, and of what you are to recover. Make a solemn promise to be true to her. The secrets behind her veil were once known and available to you. It is your journey in this lifetime to recover them. She will give you a glimpse. Are you ready? Allow her to pull back the veil. What do you see?

Remove your clothes and enter the sacred waters of your bath. Sink as far into the depths as you can, and close your eyes. Contemplate what you saw. Spend the rest of your tub time basking in the beauty that is you.

Primrose Hidden Treasure of the Soul Spell

Ingredients
- Seven of Cups
- Primrose seedlings

Method, Visualization, and Meditation

Our days lay like a deck of cards, unturned, unknown, until the moment greets us. Life remains an intrigue, surprises are numerous, and life can be lived as a revealed joy. Tarot steers you in desirable directions but will not reveal the deepest joys. Hidden treasure must be cultivated and experienced yourself.

The Seven of Cups reflects potentials, surprises, and unseen choices suddenly revealing themselves to you. Primrose seedlings will unlock hidden potentials.

Gather all of your transplanting materials. Place the Seven of Cups before you. Enter the card. Consider the mysterious cups floating before you in the air. Each cup represents a hidden treasure that has yet to spring from your soul. Reflect for a moment on the quality of surprise in your life. Think of the last thing you acquired a new taste for. What was the last reversal of opinion you experienced? When did you discover something paying off in ways you couldn't have imagined at the time? Consider what you have unexpectedly accomplished.

Move around your home or garden and transplant each tender primrose. Knowing that as you do, you are planting hidden treasures to be revealed when the time is right.

Primrose Day is celebrated today in Britain. Primroses, sacred to Venus, are known to reveal truth. Germanic culture calls them "cowslip" and describes how they will open locks to reveal hidden treasure. Transplant primrose around your home and reveal hidden treasure existing inside of you.

INCANTATION
Seven of Cups
The magic of rose
Enchantment and treasure
Around me grows
Wild sorcery I weave
Around this home
Embrace a happiness
I have always known

Today is the first day of the sign of Taurus, who is ruled by Venus. Taurus is renowned as the best kisser of the zodiac. Ancient Mesopotamians created Taurus before all other signs.

INCANTATION

Sensual pleasure

Fill me up

Life is elixir

Drink my cup

With attention and cultivation

I soon see

All life's pleasures

Revealed to me

Sensual Pleasure of Taurus Spell

Ingredient
- The Hierophant

Method, Visualization, and Meditation

Your senses are the gateway to the invisible and a direct route to pleasure. You have the ability to fill yourself with pleasure at this very moment, no matter your circumstance. You can also turn this into a sex spell and perform with your lover and a little imagination.

The Hierophant resides over formal spiritual matters.

Place the Hierophant before you. Enter the card. Step up to his feet and listen to his words.

"Senses are the gateway to the spiritual. This is why incense, flowers, candles, music, performance, and beautiful clothing are so often utilized in cross-cultural religious ritual. Let's embrace your senses right now to increase pleasure, compare and contrast. This hones your power of observation.

"Create your own compare and contrast experiment. Set aside one hour. Find the items I have described or similar items. Compare and contrast them. But you must take your time doing so. When you see, really see. When you smell, really smell. Move inside the source of the sight, smell, taste, feeling, and sound. Move through to experience the other side of it as well.

"Repeat the incantation with each sense. When you are finished, walk out of my cathedral. Exit the card. Move back to your life."

- See: farthest thing you can see vs. closest thing
- Smell: ripe fruit vs. ground coffee beans
- Taste: dark chocolate and goat cheese
- Feel: favorite sweater vs. the skin of your forearm
- Listen: Mozart's Requiem in D minor vs. Nirvana's "Smells like Teen Spirit"

Continue to compare and contrast on your own.

Chariot Card Connection Ritual

Ingredient
- The Chariot

Method, Visualization, and Meditation

Enter the arcana of the Chariot.

A radiant golden figure stands before you. His creamy skin is youthful and plump, while his hair is speckled with flecks of sunlight. Light radiates from within him as if a fire were lit and flickering inside. He stands motionless, awaiting your instruction. The crown on his head bears the northern star, plucked from the galaxy like a grape; it will guide you on your journey. His metallic armor reflects silver lunar powers that combine with the yellow generation of solar energy. The veil upon his canopy has been fashioned from the Empress's clothing, as he carries her essence with him. His two sphinxes—one black as night, the other white as bone—mark the choices we make.

The Chariot pulls Earth in its circular pattern around the sun. The Chariot pulls your own body through its linear experience of time. We would experience all things at once were it not for the presence of the charioteer. The charioteer brings us toward the destiny we weave for ourself through personal choice and action. We act as charioteer when we get behind the wheel of our vehicle, literally and figuratively. The Chariot makes dreams a reality.

To greet him, you leave what is known and comfortable and move into the wild providence of nature.

Point him in any direction you choose. Let him guide you or take up the reins. He will let you embody him if you choose. Though your feet may never touch the ground, an airplane lift you to the clouds, the wheels of a car spin under your feet, or your passport get stamped, you journey still.

Every day, every hour, every minute of your life is a journey.

Today is Rome's birthday. Roman charioteers entered arenas such as the Circus Maximus and raced to honor the gods and achieve love, adoration, and glory.

• • • • • •

INCANTATION

Chariot card

Of travels speak

What experience

Do I seek?

My intention always

Sets the course

Take the reins

Control my horse

Hone desire

Fashion will

As I move

My center's still

The United States celebrates Earth Day today.

World Card Connection Ritual

Ingredient
- The World

Method, Visualization, and Meditation
Enter the arcana of the World.

To enter the World card is to enter the luminous state: true enlightenment and the remarkable present. The possibility of the World is always there. We are free to enter and inhabit at any moment.

You discover yourself sitting in a yogi position. The legs of your lithe body are crossed, your spine is straight, and you sit atop a green, grassy hill. This is a space of meditation. You've been coming regularly for days now. This is the peace amidst the chaos of your day. As always, you finish your practice with a deep final breath. Breathe in sweet air, inhaling into your lungs, and exhale through your mouth.

Empty blue sky stretches before you. A goddess-like naked woman dances before your field of vision. Nothing but a long scarf conceals her body. She looks to the side in an expression of ecstasy. She balances two white wands in her hands. She is circled by a bright green wreath, the magical threshold to her world. It is clasped by red ribbons on the top and bottom. Swirling clouds have broken out at her four corners, and creatures appear there in the shape of man, beast, and bird.

The figures move and bounce. You feel yourself growing lighter as she lifts you off the ground and you become weightless. Your body mirrors hers as she rises higher into the sky with you. She floats in the ecstasy that is complete immersion in the nature of life. Time ceases. You are released from your body. You no longer sense any physical boundary between yourself and what lies beyond the exterior of your physical body. You have become one with the energy of magic. You have merged with the essence of the universe.

You are nirvana. You are. You.

INCANTATION
World card
Earthly goal
Peaceful goddess
Eyes rimmed with kohl
Together dance
Together fly
Entwined alight
Through the sky

Charmed Grimoire Spell

Ingredients
- Sketchbook, journal, or grimoire

1. Ace of Cups (east)
2. Ace of Wands (south)
3. Ace of Pentacles (west)
4. Ace of Swords (north)

Method, Visualization, and Meditation

Place the book before you and repeat the following in the exact order listed.

Place the Ace of Cups and say:

> Ace of Cups, your waters run true
> Wash over my book, your powers imbue.

Place the Ace of Wands and say:

> Ace of Wands, passion's spark
> Fire's light illuminated the dark.

Place the Ace of Pentacles and say:

> Ace of Pentacles, the words I write
> Magic inside these pages take flight.

Place the Ace of Swords and say:

> Blades of intellect and steel
> Express the way I always feel

To the whole book, say:

> With love and light and time to rest
> I do declare this book be blessed.

World Book Day is celebrated today. Mark the day by creating a first edition of your very own. A grimoire is a place for spells and sketches, dreams and ideas, poetry and secrets.

FYI

The first World Book Day was celebrated April 23, 1995. This date was decided on in part because it was also Shakespeare's death and birth anniversary.

	4	
3	book	1
	2	

Give It Up Spell

Today marks the traditional 1182 BCE date of the fall of Troy. Do you, like the Trojans, need to give it up? When an issue continues to plague us, this spell will help us let it go. Rest assured something new and wonderful will fill its place.

Ingredients
1. Eight of Swords
2. Nine of Pentacles
- Bowl of dried rose or loose flower petals

Method, Visualization, and Meditation

Make dried rose petals from the flower petals of your bouquets to extend the usage of the rose. Dried petals can be used for pot-pourri, homemade oils, and rose water, sprinkled on tables or beds for decorations, and are always welcome additions to spellwork.

The Eight of Swords represents being held hostage. The Nine of Pentacles reflects glorious, self-empowered freedom.

Place the Eight of Swords before you. Enter the card. Come to terms with the headspace you are in. How does your situation hold you in its grip? What must you break free from? Contemplate the ways in which you are held hostage by this idea or situation. You crave freedom. You need to unravel it. You will do so now.

Mix the bowl of dried flower petals with your hands while reciting the incantation. Let the sweet scent enliven you. Repeat the incantation until you feel you have been released from the bonds of old behavior.

When you believe the words you are saying, release a palmful of flowers to the wind.

Place the Nine of Pentacles before you. Bring your mind's eye into the card and see yourself standing tall, proud, and independent in the garden of manifestation. Look at the garden. Allow a new reality to unfold before you.

INCANTATION

It's over

It's finished

This I know

Bonds release me

Let me go

bowl

1	2

King of Cups Connection Ritual

Ingredient
- King of Cups

Method, Visualization, and Meditation
Enter the arcana of the King of Cups.

Soar across silky, blue-green waters like a bird to locate the King of the Sea. He floats on ocean waves in his throne. Beneath him minnows dart back and forth. The dark shadows of a sperm whale and her calf pass silently beneath him. To the passing ship he appears in the mist, perhaps as a pirate or a sea ghost. Sirens sing to him in the briny wind.

His eyes are blue marble. His skin is oxygen and water. His voice rushes over you like crashing surf, soothing you, repeating in rhythmic cadence the words you need to hear again and again. His crown is made of compact shell, his jewels of volcanic rock.

Dolphins, mermaids, and manatees leap around him, his willing playthings. He forms rogue waves that will destroy a coastline or tickle your toes with sea foam. His emotions are wide and deep. The ocean contains his breadth of feeling. He dreams as far and wide as the ocean is deep. He carries these dreams to completion.

His slippers are rainbow scales of tropical fish. His breath is the fog that creeps across the ocean in the early dawn. Like the ocean, he will wipe your slate clean, cleanse you, and erase all stress, all fear, so you are set back into place.

The King of Cups, as a creature of the ocean, is a shapeshifter, taking on any form needed to complete his task. You hold all of these abilities inside yourself. You are a creature of water: a singular, unique point of energy on the event horizon of your life.

A feast honoring Saint Mark, patron saint of Venice, is held today. The King of Cups is the watery and aquatic King Neptune, ruler of emotions, who, like the city of Venice, sits atop the high seas.

INCANTATION
King of Cups
Where sea meets sky
His ocean's deep
His waves grow high
He dreams the mist
Of fish and foams
Imagination's landscape
Freely roams

INCANTATION

Work of love

Work of me

Toil and sweat

No complacency

I worked you hard

I worked you well

Now use my magic

For this spell

We finish quick

With joy and fun

I do declare

My project done!

Finish a Project Spell

Ingredients

1. Eight of Wands
2. Ten of Wands
3. Ten of Swords
4. Ten of Cups
5. Ten of Pentacles
6. The World

Method, Visualization, and Meditation

The start of a project is often more interesting than the finish. Some creative projects are like childbirth, exciting and full of surprises in the beginning. As the project ends, though, it's filled with temporary contractions, sharp pains, even terror. This leads to unfinished projects and potentials who hang in midair, half-way done. Give yourself the gift of working through the pain and delivering a completed project.

Lay the Eight of Wands. Feel the energy of passion taking you to where you need to be.

Place the Ten of Wands. Put the final bits into place. You have already done so much. He will help you over the finish line. Your original spark has manifested into a finished project.

Lay the Ten of Swords. It is the end of the drama; the show is done. You have nailed down what needed to be said and done.

Place the Ten of Cups. Feel the celebration on the card. Feel the exuberance and joy of accomplishment. Feel your happiness once the project is complete.

Lay the Ten of Pentacles. Marvel at the manifestation within the card. It is your nature to be creative.

Place the World card. See your project in its perfect state. You are the creator. Feel the pride coursing through your veins. Feel unexpected delights coming your way.

You did it. It is already done. Just add those finishing touches, and you are there.

2		3
	6	
1	4	5

Five of Pentacles Connection Ritual

Ingredient
- Five of Pentacles

Method, Visualization, and Meditation
Enter the arcana of the Five of Pentacles.

Fives imply challenge. Fives are the halfway point, the turning point, the space where a new chapter begins. What has manifested up until this point begins to build on itself. This required challenge provides perspective for the ultimate outcome in the finality of the ten. Inside every challenge lies a gift. Can you discover it?

Wicked winter howls through white, snow-covered alleyways. The silence of city streets is broken only by the wind's whistle. Residents avoiding the bitterness are tucked away in their homes, sitting before crackling fireplaces and warm tables laden with hearty soups and stews.

Two souls, looking lost, wander amidst the fray. One hobbles on crutches, a bell at his neck. A bandage covers his head. The figure leading the march gathers her scarf close to her chin. They appear as penniless beggars even though their clothing is richly textured and colored. Their feet are wrapped in paltry fabric, toes exposed to the bitter, numbing air as they trod through the snow.

The wall of a church looms next to them, laden with heavy stone. A stained glass window radiates the richness of heat, shelter, and sustenance. The lit glass reflects five pentacles as seen at the top of the Tree of Life. Where is the couple walking? Why do they not see salvation before their eyes? Will they pass by safety and comfort? Are they looking to find the entrance?

How does the manifestation of money, objects, or people in the physical world become problematic? How do these problems serve as lessons?

The wind continues to howl, and the couple moves on.

The Five of Pentacles was called the Lord of Material Trouble by the magicians of the Golden Dawn, who assigned it the time period of April 21–30.

INCANTATION
The ups and downs
Of relationships go
Insights most people
Don't even know
Through times of tough
And times of sweet
How does your soul
Rise to meet
The challenge of
The pentacle suit
Your inner strength
Is outer fruit

*George Balanchine's
"Orpheus" premiered today
at Lincoln Center in 1948.
Orpheus is the Greek god
of music. His singing and
playing was so beautiful
that animals, reptiles, and
birds were seduced by him.*

INCANTATION

Felines teach us

To be ready

Buzzing bees

Are slow and steady

Spiders teach us

How to weave

Geese show us when

It's time to leave

Bats enhance

Nocturnal visions

Owls guide us

To wise decisions

Totem Animal Discovery

Ingredients
1. The Star
2. Nine of Pentacles

Method, Visualization, and Meditation

Discovering your totem animal is an enjoyable, often surprising process. You may find your animal changes seasonally, even yearly, as you evolve. You may have one special animal for a lifetime. Your spirit animals could be the ones appearing in your yard or at your window on a daily basis. This meditation into the tarot will help you move closer to animal essence.

Place the Star card. A landscape of tender grass and fields of hay caresses your senses. The night sky brims with subtle energy. A sweet song escapes a bird who perches on a branch behind the female. The woman in the card puts down her watering jugs. She wants to have a conversation with you. Ask her questions about yourself. She will answer each question:

- What animal have I always been attracted to?
- What animal am I terrified of?
- What animal have I dreamed of?
- If I could shapeshift into an animal, what would I become?
- Did I have profound animal experiences as a child?

Listen to her answers carefully.

Place the Nine of Pentacles. Enter the card. Hear the same birdsong around you. An airplane engine hums overhead. Green vine leaves bow in the breeze. There is a gated area just to your left. Lift the rusty latch, enter, and find yourself inside a secret garden. An ancient stone fountain stands in the center. You enter to look inside the deep waters of the fountain, seeing your reflection in the placid water. You hear something behind you. It is your spirit animal.

Turn around to discover who and what it is.

| 1 | 2 |

Happy Marriage Spell

Ingredients
- Rosemary plant
1. Two of Cups
2. Four of Wands
3. The Lovers

plant

| 1 | 2 | 3 |

Kate Middleton and Prince William were married on this day in 2011.

Method, Visualization, and Meditation

Rosemary sprigs were often worn in bridal crowns. The Two of Cups reflects the emotional union of two people. The Four of Wands represents a home filled with love, laughter, and passion. The Lovers card shows the spiritual and physical union of opposites.

Place the rosemary plant before you. Inhale. Note how rugged and strong its branches are. Consider the history embedded in its scent.

Place the Two of Cups. See the couple standing gazing into each other's eyes. They are separate, unique individuals, yet their unique aspects complement one another. Her beauty reflects his handsomeness and humor. He admires her strength and beauty. He reaches for her. She accepts his hand. Both raise their cups and sip from the healing liquid of love. See yourself in this card.

Place the Four of Wands. Laughter floats up to the sky like tendrils of incense. A crowd gathers to celebrate the happy occasion. The four corners of the home, aligning with the four suits of tarot, are in balance. This creates structure and stability for the life to be lived inside these walls. The passions and pursuits of the bride and groom are reflected in the decorations. Baby leaves sprout from the wands, a sign of growth and expansion due to this union.

Place the Lovers card. The couple stands naked before each other. Their bodies join in the mystical experience of lovemaking. The scent of musk, sex, and sweetness fills the card. Emotion in motion. Love mingles with toe-curling desire. Nightly they worship each other on the altar of creation magic.

Plant or place the rosemary outside or close to the door of your or the newlywed's home.

INCANTATION
Union of two
Life of love
Aspects from
Divinity above
A life together
Is work and play
Consider the other
Every day

127

Charm to Gain Your Heart's Desire

Cast this nature charm to gain your heart's desire. As the moon rises tonight, it marks the beginning of Beltane, the Gaelic May Day festival. Bonfires are lit, homes are decorated with flowers, and magic runs rampant through the evening air.

INCANTATION

Flesh of darkness

Born of death

Give my will

Thy life and breath

Wither dry

And shrink to dust

My hearth shall feed

Upon thy crust

Ingredients

- Nine of Cups
- A large wild mushroom
- Red cloth bag
- Needle and thread

Method, Visualization, and Meditation

This spell is adapted from a personal favorite, Valerie Worth's *Crone's Book of Charms & Spells.* The Nine of Cups is incorporated to ensure you gain your heart's desire.

Place the Nine of Cups. The genie inside is ready and willing to grant you your wish.

In wet weather, walk across the fields until you find a large white mushroom. Capture the largest you can find. Bring it home with you. That evening, by candlelight, take out your Nine of Cups again so the genie sees the work you are doing. Take a large needle and inscribe your heart's desire on the mushroom's upper skin. Breathe upon your words and utter the incantation. Lock your mushroom away for the rest of the night.

In the morning, cut the mushroom into a multitude of tiny pieces. Set them in an oven until they are quite dry. Sew the pieces into a red cloth and carry with you, as close to your heart as possible, until you have your desired effect.

When your heart's desire is granted, go back to where you found the mushroom and bury the bag.

May Day Grounding Spell

Ingredients
- Temperance
- One raw onion
- Olive oil
- Water
- Fresh feta cheese
- Salt, pepper, and thyme

Method, Visualization, and Meditation

Onions belong to the allium family of garlic, chives, scallions, scapes, and leeks. Onions are used for spiritual resilience. Feta cheese relates to lunar energy. Thyme is used for courage. Onions relate also to the Temperance card's flowering yellow pond irises, which also bloom from bulbs. Temperance represents balance, synergy, and alchemy.

You will bake an onion stuffed with cheese, which combines grounding (onion) and feminine lunar connection (cheese).

Place the Temperance card. She is the synergy between the two cups. Yellow flowers bloom. Follow their green stalks down, past the buzzing bees, spider webs, and scampering ants. Find the circular bulb at its base. Like a lotus flower, the pond iris is rooted in the murky, muddy darkness. Allow yourself to feel the rooted-ness. In your mind's eye reach for the bulb and retrieve it.

Set the oven to 350 degrees. Prepare the onion. Slice the bottom of the onion so it will sit upright in the pan. Slice off the top and discard. Scoop out a tablespoon of center onion flesh but do not pull it out yet. Place in pan. Splash with olive oil. Sprinkle salt, pepper, and thyme over the onion to taste. Add a touch of water to the pan bottom. Cover pan in foil and pop in oven.

Mix feta with thyme and set aside.

Cook for 45 minutes. Remove from oven, remove scooped flesh, and fill with cheese mixture. Return to oven and bake for another 15 minutes.

Eat the onion while pondering earth connection and the value of being grounded during spiritual work.

Today is May Day. As nature flourishes and spring energy abounds, this grounding spell will help you keep rooted as expansion blooms. Repeat as needed.

INCANTATION

Root of growth
Onion's layer
Over this dish
I cast a prayer
Keep me grounded
Centered and still
As I cast and
Invoke my will

129

The Queen of Swords has earned herself quite the reputation, much like another famous monarch. Anne Boleyn was arrested on this day in 1536 and charged with adultery, treason, incest, and witchcraft.

INCANTATION

Queen of Swords

Goddess of thought

Select my ideas

Self-sabotage naught

Be articulate

Swift and fast

Indisputable change

Built to last

Queen of Swords Connection Ritual

Ingredient
- Queen of Swords

Method, Visualization, and Meditation

Enter the arcana of the Queen of Swords.

Stand amidst the mountaintop of the kingdom of swords. Birds swoop in the sky, airborne and free. A burst of churning, growing cumulus clouds looms in the distance. These are billowy, white reminders of what lies between spirit and nature. A storm is not far off.

A female sits in a royal throne. The lines of her face are so sharp and precise, it looks as if she could cut glass with her profile. She has summoned these clouds and you to her side.

She wears the image of clouds on her cloak. Like the tension of a string pulled tight, the barometer drops, and a change is felt in the air. The queen, aware of the mutable nature of the air, sits straighter in her throne. It is adorned with butterflies and moths, ancient symbols of psychic self-renewal and immortality. Like the butterflies who adorn her golden crown, this queen will usher the transformation of your soul.

A small stream connects this queen to the High Priestess. The water flows under a tree in the distance. The High Priestess ushered silence, but this queen speaks her mind and her truth at all times. The waxing and waning moon is carved into her throne, connecting her to the changing nature of her highest self.

Her hand reaches forward, and she speaks. "Are you ready to take control of your thoughts? Are you ready to speak your truth? Can you use your power of language and articulation for the highest possible good?"

Four Directions Spell

Ingredients

1. Ace of Pentacles (north)
2. Ace of Wands (south)
3. Ace of Swords (east)
4. Ace of Cups (west)

```
        ┌─────┐
        │  1  │
        └─────┘
┌─────┐         ┌─────┐
│  4  │  you    │  3  │
└─────┘         └─────┘
        ┌─────┐
        │  2  │
        └─────┘
```

It is planting season. Embark on a spell that requests what you need from the universe. Let the universe's infinite wisdom decide what you require. Allow the mystery of the unexpected to delight and inspire you.

Method, Visualization, and Meditation

Aces are the most highly concentrated form of suit energy. Like seeds, spread the aces around you in the four directions.

Sit cross-legged on the floor, facing north. Place the Ace of Pentacles before you. The flutter of hummingbirds fills the breeze, which plays softly on your skin. Smell the jasmine and abundant honeysuckle. An ivy-covered gate of golden opportunity is ahead of you. Swirling clouds loom and a hand emerges with a physical gift for you.

Place the Ace of Wands to the south. Feel toe-curling warmth emanating. The landscape is hot and lush. A cloud appears before you. A blinding spark, white at first then glowing red, extends. Incendiary passion alights inside you.

Place the Ace of Swords in the east. Overlook a tall mountain range and feel wind, cool and exhilarating, hit you from every direction. Your hair flies in the air. Oxygen fills your nose and mouth. Swirling gray clouds appear before you. A hand emerges with a massive silver implement in its grip. A genius idea forms in your mind.

Place the Ace of Cups in the west. You are floating above water filled with lotus lilies, smelling sweet and salty sea air. Frogs and fish dart beneath the surface of the water. The waves lick your toes and seagulls call out. A billowing cloud appears. A golden cup is presented to you. It is full of water, gushing like a fountain. White doves appear bearing wafers. The wafers dissolve in the water. The emotional essence of purity cleanses you, leaving your emotions refreshed and expressed. Your emotional state is open and balanced, free and flowing—nothing repressed, everything expressed, all blocks removed.

INCANTATION

Aces of power
Elements of life
Bring needed things
Remove all strife
I send intention
Hear my call
Manifest what I need
Surprises and all

131

Today is National Bird Day. Utilize the power of bird energy to craft a financial spell for long-term security.

INCANTATION
Financial nest
Savings and security
Money protect
And grant opportunity

Financial Nest Egg Spell

Ingredients
- Nine of Pentacles
- Pen and paper
- A plastic pull-apart Easter egg
- Nest

Method, Visualization, and Meditation

This spell calls for an old bird's nest. Nests are carefully built and provide long-term protection for growing and nurturing. The hunt for a bird's nest may become part of the fabric of the spell. A nest should only be taken if you are absolutely sure it is not in use. Leave an offering of birdseed or granola as thanks. Alternatively, you can craft a nest using mud and dried twigs.

Cast this spell in conjunction with a long-term savings plan or investment plan or right before you make a deposit. The Nine of Pentacles represents a woman who enjoys complete financial security.

Place the Nine of Pentacles. Enter the card. Focus on the card and see yourself as a confident person with no financial pressure. Enjoy sumptuous clothing and the garden of bounty. Everything you could want or need is before you. A laptop computer sits on a stone table in the corner. Look at the screen. You see your bank account statement. You have planned properly; the money has built upon itself, and you no longer need to work or concern yourself with the generation of money. What does the account balance say?

At your regular table, write as many positive reasons for long-term investment on a slip of paper that you can think of. Place paper inside plastic egg.

Place the egg inside the nest. Secure in the basement portion of your home.

Mexican Love Truffles

Ingredients

- Ace of Wands
- 8 ounces semi-sweet organic chocolate, chopped
- ½ cup heavy cream
- 1 teaspoon vanilla extract
- 1 teaspoon cinnamon
- ¼ teaspoon fresh cayenne pepper
- ¼ teaspoon sea salt
- Cocoa powder

Method, Visualization, and Meditation

Sprinkle spice and incantations of love over truffles to bring passion to your bedside. Prepare and feed or gift these delicacies to the person you desire intimacy with.

Chocolate is an aphrodisiac known the world over. The Ace of Wands is the spark of desire. Cayenne pepper inspires passion. Cinnamon enhances the libido and attracts love. Vanilla is used for sex magic. The cacao tree was revered by the Aztecs, who mixed cacao seeds into their ceremonial beverages.

Gather your ingredients upon the kitchen counter. Place the Ace of Wands. Enter the card. Stoke the passion of the wand by making the flame grow bigger.

Place chopped chocolate in a heatproof bowl. Heat heavy cream on your stovetop; right before it boils, take it off the heat, pour it over the chocolate, and mix until the chocolate is melted and smooth. Whisk in vanilla, cinnamon, cayenne, and salt.

Refrigerate until the mixture becomes thick. Scoop small tablespoon mounds onto a baking sheet lined with parchment paper and place back in the fridge to firm up for about half an hour. Form each mound into a ball. Roll in the cocoa powder while whispering the incantation. Truffles keep in the fridge for up to one month, but feed them continually to your lover to keep things spicy.

Ready to invoke powers of seduction? Cinco de Mayo is celebrated today, a Mexican holiday invoking pride and honoring a victorious battle. Make Mexican Love Truffles to conjure the heat of Mexico in your bedroom.

INCANTATION

Greedy lover
Like nectar to bee
Caress my body
Love on me
Bring me pleasure
To my bed come
Kiss me, lick me
I'm your plum

May • 6

Today is the Feast of Saint George, Bulgaria's patron saint of bravery. Invoke courage on any day with the Strength card.

INCANTATION
Strength of spirit
Strength of mind
Cultivating power
Can I find
Source of strength
Right and true
And will it lead me
Right to you?

Strength Card Connection Ritual

Ingredient
• Strength

Method, Visualization, and Meditation
Enter the arcana of Strength.

You stand inside a green pastoral European landscape. A female figure adorned in white charmeuse stands before you. The air of familiarity, of déjà vu, sweeps over your body. A strange symbol glows above her head as if tiny molecules of energy have conjoined above her crown chakra. You realize it is the same symbol the Magician carries above his head: it is the lemniscate, representing infinity. It is in the shape of the sideways eight, which is also the number of the arcana of Strength. The lemniscate mimics the female curvature of a reclining woman.

Her gown is held at the waist by a belt of honeysuckle flowers and berries. It matches her flowery crown. She bends in a gentle curve over a tawny lion. The beast submits to the will of his mistress. His tail hides beneath his belly, winding through his legs. His body shudders under his orange fur as the woman gently opens the beast's mouth. His silky red tongue flicks out to catch a lick of salt from her delicate wrist. The thick hair of his mane curls thickly down his neck, and his sharp nails claw the green grass beneath his feet.

Her left hand firmly holds his snout while her right palm opens his jaw. The female opens and closes the jaws of this great beast with ease. Great power lies inside his mouth. These jaws possess the ability to rip another animal limb from limb. In a way, it is like the power we all share: the ability to empower or destroy with our actions.

Marie Laveau Lawsuit Spell

Ingredients
1. Justice
2. The Wheel of Fortune
3. Temperance

Method, Visualization, and Meditation
See your desired lawsuit outcome with crystal clarity in your mind's eye.

The Justice card rules over all court proceedings. The Wheel of Fortune can be persuaded to turn in your favor. The Temperance card depicts the archangel Michael, who is the defender of all humankind.

Place Justice before you. Stand before the pillar of right and wrong. This figure is not blindfolded. It will not turn its cheek on you. The consequences that emerge are the result of the efforts you put forth.

Place the Wheel of Fortune card below the Justice card. See Justice revolving the wheel. It spins faster and faster. In doing so, it aligns with your personal energy.

With the wheel still spinning, place Temperance beneath the wheel. Using the energy of the spinning wheel, the cups pour back and forth. This is the tension of Temperance. This angel will come to your defense. He will be sure things work in your favor. See yourself walking out of the courtroom satisfied with the outcome, your heart's desire met.

Slip the Temperance card into your bag. Bring Temperance with you to all lawyer meetings and court appointments. Repeat this spell as often as needed until a verdict is reached.

1

2

3

New Orleans was founded on this day in 1718. The town would become synonymous with Voodoo queen Marie Laveau. Miss Laveau, who practiced magic in all areas, was especially known for her spells regarding legal issues.

INCANTATION
Justice card, you see the truth
I am walking, living proof
My conscience clear
My hands washed clean
In my favor
Decisions lean
The outcome is true
Just and fair
Lessons learned
I'm free of care

White Lotus Meditation

White Lotus Day is celebrated today by Theosophists. It marks the death of their enigmatic founder, Madame Blavatsky. The flowering lotus is a common symbol in cross-cultural mythology; engage in this meditation to discover why.

INCANTATION

Lotus life
You are for me
Opening petals
Set me free
My life reflects
Upon the water
Blessed I am
Fortune's daughter

Ingredient
• Ace of Cups

Method, Visualization, and Meditation

Lotus flowers contain spectacular genetic coding that enables them to live an unusually long lifetime. Thousand-year-old lotus seeds were discovered in a Chinese river bed and germinated. In Egyptian myth, the lotus emerges from the primordial ocean as a representation of the manifestation of spirit and reveals the sun god Ra. What could the lotus represent to you? Why did Pamela Colman Smith choose to place them on the Ace of Cups?

The lotus flower opens in the morning. In what way do you open in the morning? The lotus closes in the evening. How do you wind down in the evening?

Note the lotus is the perfect symbol of a cup. Lotus petals open and close to maintain the temperatures inside the flower chamber. Bees enjoy hiding in this warmth. What would it feel like to hide in a lotus flower?

The lotus flower is considered sacred by many cultures. Preferring the still waters of lakes and ponds, it sprouts from the mud, shoots through the water, and flowers at the top.

Place the Ace of Cups before you.

Sit on the floor, legs crossed in yogi position, with a straight spine. Feel yourself grounding into the floor while your head floats in the air. Imagine yourself secure in a bed of mud. Feel waters surrounding your torso. Grow your spine straight and tall. When ready, open your arms to the sky, emulating the flower petals of a lotus. Feel the sun against your outstretched arms.

When you bring your arms down, sit inside the space of a closed lotus flower. What does it feel like? What does it smell like? How does it inspire you? What animals and insects surround you?

Six of Pentacles Connection Ritual

Ingredient
• Six of Pentacles

Method, Visualization, and Meditation
Enter the arcana of the Six of Pentacles.

Six implies advancement. The challenge of the five has been met. Small victories support forward momentum. Hierarchy is achieved.

Bringing your awareness into the card, you find yourself miniaturized like Alice in Wonderland inside a child's play box. It seems you have entered the midpoint of a play already in progress, yet these actors continue. They break neither their fourth wall nor their concentration.

You note that, as in the other "six" cards you have seen, one figure stands above the others. It denotes hierarchy and reflects a goal that has been achieved.

A man stands over two others. He wears the ruby red colors of a merchant costume. He doles out coins to beggars while making a big show of his generosity. He holds a scale in one hand, as if to measure out the precise amount of what is due. The hand dropping coins offers the same blessing sign as the Hierophant. The Hierophant offers spiritual blessings while this merchant offers financial blessings.

The two figures beneath him dress in beggars' clothing. One has a bandage wrapped around his head. The scene is so theatrical in nature, you wouldn't be surprised if the beggars were to stand, toss their cloaks, and surprise the merchant with a wealth that outshines his own, yet they continue to play along.

Six pentacles hang in the air, framing the picture. A merchant speaks: "It is a little-known secret that the key to wealth is in sharing your good fortune with others. Why, might you ask? The ancient law of magic. What you put out comes back threefold. This secret has been known for ages, yet only a few apply it. Try it for yourself and see."

The Six of Pentacles was called the Lord of Material Success by the magicians of the Golden Dawn, who assigned it the time period of May 1–10.

• • • • • •

INCANTATION
Six of Pentacles
Generosity, gifts
Give of myself
My spirit lifts
Heart center of
The Tree of Life
Is Six
Benevolence and bounty
No silly tricks

Han Dynasty astronomers observed one of the earliest recorded sunspots today in 28 BCE. Connect with solar power to embrace the energizing essence of all manifestation magic.

INCANTATION

Golden sun

Your energy heals

You keep me going

Through fortune's wheels

Life's up and down

Like change of season

You bring to light health

And love and reason

Sun Card Connection Ritual

Ingredient
• The Sun

Method, Visualization, and Meditation

Enter the arcana of the Sun.

Smiling before you even realize you are doing so, you stretch your arms above you to expand your body and take in the delicious heat of the sun glowing before you. You are drenched in yellow light and feel it healing you from toes to fingertips. The breeze smells of coconut and sweet mango. You detect the faint sound of breaking waves in the distance.

The Empress's child rides toward you on a white horse. Childlike giggles and laughter alight on the soft air.

Golden-tipped sunflowers dance from the top of a wall. The child wears a garland of mini sunflowers. He carries a radiant red flame-shaped flag. It looks as if he swiped it from under the Empress and now waves it at the world. This is the essence of creativity on display. It is not just individual creativity but the mad expansion of simultaneous growth occurring in every sector of the planet.

The grass beneath your feet is warm and soft. The child's horse bends to nibble the sweet blades. The horse's color is a brilliant, shining white and represents the unfulfilled potential resting inside this little human. His future is yet to unfold.

The trees are green and lush, flowers are blooming, and animals are frolicking. It is the height of summer. The natural world has hit its peak. It is as if the entire earth has unfolded to let the sun see what it can do. And the sun is generated through every material thing.

What can you do? What blooms inside you?

Banish a Ghost Spell

Ingredients
- Six of Swords
- White candle
- Black beans
- Four of Wands

Method, Visualization, and Meditation

The Six of Swords echoes the journey of the departed souls who cross over to the afterworld. The Four of Wands reflects a happy and secure home that is free of any plaguing otherworldly pests.

You will embody the ferryman on the Six of Swords.

Twilight is the threshold hour. Doors open in growing shadows. Possibility emerges by the light of the stars.

As darkness falls, focus on the Six of Swords. Feel the quietness and stillness of the place that is a gateway between worlds. Enter the card. Become the ferryman. You are making this boat ready for your ghost.

Light a white candle and begin walking backwards through your home, reciting the incantation. *Domun* is Latin for "go home."

When you reach the topmost point in your home, extinguish the candle.

Bury black beans in the four corners outside your home, beginning in the east and working clockwise.

After you have buried the beans, finish circling your home counterclockwise while throwing beans over your left shoulder.

Return inside.

Meditate over the Four of Wands, feeling peace and safety.

Lemuria, the ghost-banishing feast of ancient Rome, started today. To rid the home of ghosts, Ovid describes rites that include waking up at the stroke of midnight, reciting incantations, and walking barefoot around the home while throwing black beans behind you.

INCANTATION
Spirit, soul
Ghost or sprite
With love and light
Depart tonight
Domun
Domun
Domun

Mother's Day was first celebrated on this day in 1907. Being a mom is tough, important, and worthwhile. This meditation examines your own mothering gifts and challenges. It cultivates love, support, compassion, and boundaries.

- - - - -

INCANTATION

A passion-packed
word: mother
First figure we that
We see as other
Nurture, grow
Embrace and live
Forgiveness and love
To you I give

Mother's Day Meditation

Ingredients
1. Two of Cups
2. Four of Wands
3. Six of Cups
4. The World
5. The Empress

Method, Visualization, and Meditation

Ponder the relationship you have with your mother. How do you strive to be like her? How do you strive to be different?

Place the Two of Cups. Recall meeting your child or children for the very first time. What did it feel like to look in their eyes? How has the experience of love changed since that day? How has it grown stronger? Has your capacity for love surprised you?

Place the Four of Wands. Note the four wands supporting the garland. How do you support your children? How do you support their goals? How have you created a stable structure for them? How do they count on you?

Place the Six of Cups. How do you give of yourself to your children? How does it feel to look at your children through the eyes of compassion? What does it mean to have compassion? Can you see what you look like through their eyes?

Place the World card. How do you set boundaries for your children? Where is their safe space from which to explore the world? How do your children embody the World card?

Place the Empress in the center of the mandala. See how she touches all four cards. You embody all four sectors of these archetypes. The Empress is the mother archetype, but remember: you are not an archetype; you are human. And no human is perfect. Know you are excelling at the toughest job on the planet with grace and elegance.

Stop Obsessing Over Someone Spell

Ingredients
- Pen and paper or computer
1. Nine of Swords
2. Ace of Swords reversed
3. Queen of Swords

Method, Visualization, and Meditation

Anyone can be susceptible to an obsession. Compulsive thoughts seem to take control and possess the mind. Cast this spell to move on with your life.

Write a letter to the person you are obsessing over. You WILL NOT SEND this letter. Write down all of the thoughts that roam through your head. Write down what they represent to you. Write down how they make you feel. You can even write this out as a series of lists. It doesn't need to make sense. You will not show this to anyone. It is imperative you get all your feelings on paper.

Once you have written everything down (and take as long as you need), examine it. Do you note any patterns? Has the process offered any revelations about the nature of your obsession? Put the letter aside.

Place the Nine of Swords. Become the figure in bed. Look at the pain and turmoil you are suffering. Leave the card. Imagine yourself in the future, when your obsession means nothing to you. Cultivate that feeling by severing the psychic ties through tarot.

Place the reversed Ace of Swords above the nine. Slowly bring the card down with your finger. As you do, imagine it cutting off each of the nine swords, or psychic ties. Those swords stand for cords on connection. You are severing each one.

Place the Queen of Swords before you. She is strong and in command. She faces the future with her hand outstretched, ready to greet a new day. She represents your new state of mind.

Lemuria, the feast of exorcising ghosts in ancient Rome, continues on this day. Are you caught up in an unhealthy obsession? Have you passed the point of what would be considered "normal" thinking about another?

INCANTATION

Nine of Swords
I've broken free
No more obsessive
Attraction for me
What's done is done
It's buried, passed
I am free
Free at last

The Seven of Pentacles was called the Lord of Success Unfulfilled by the magicians of the Golden Dawn, who assigned it the time period of May 11–20.

• • • • •

INCANTATION
Seven of Pentacles
Garden's growth
Tend my seeds
And utter this oath
There's magic in
The deeds I do
I make my mark
With all things true

Seven of Pentacles Connection Ritual

Ingredient
• Seven of Pentacles

Method, Visualization, and Meditation
Enter the arcana of the Seven of Pentacles.

Seven is a mystical number. Seven is a lucky number. There are seven notes on the musical scale, seven days of the week, seven planets in our solar system besides Earth, seven deadly sins, seven seas, seven colors of the rainbow, seven continents, and seven wonders of the ancient world.

It is overcast. It's one of those days where the sky looks like a gray sheet of construction paper from sunup till sundown. The humid air carries the smell of sweet grass and vegetation. A gardener stands before you, leaning on a farming tool she was using to dislodge weeds from the rich soil. Her gaze is drawn to a pile of magical pentacles. The pentacles are bursting with life, ripened like fat juicy peaches and weighing down their branches.

Heart-shaped leaves offer shade to the deep innards of the plant. Slender corkscrew tendrils slither along the ground. They extend up and around the figure as if reaching for her life force.

The worker's face is solemn. Is she dreaming of a far-off enchanted place? Is she being drawn into the world of the plant? Either way, the number seven lets you know it has been a lucky harvest.

There is still more to come.

But what shall grow is completely unexpected.

The pattern has changed.

Mercury Retrograde Protection Bag

Ingredients
- The World
- 10 dimes
- Feather (preferably found outside)
- Loose sandalwood incense

Ancient Romans believed today was Mercury's birthday. Mercury was Zeus's messenger, and he traveled at the speed of light.

Method, Visualization, and Meditation

Mercury retrograde is an astrological term used for when the planet Mercury creates an optical illusion to earth gazers. It passes Earth and appears to slow down, stop, and begin moving backwards. Even though the planet isn't actually stopping and moving backwards, Mercury retrograde is known as a time period where well-laid plans, contracts, and technology go haywire. It is impractical to stop your life, cancel trips, stop legal proceedings, etc., when a retrograde occurs. If the retrograde bothers you, craft this protection bag and let the effects of retrograde roll right off your back.

The World card represents all aspects of your life operating with ease. Dimes and their silver tint are sacred to Mercury. Each dime has an edge with 118 ridges. This number reduces to the number one and represents the continuation of a cycle. Feathers connect to the element of air and speed.

Place the World card before you. Focus on the revolution of the items on the card around the world dancer as if you are observing the solar system itself. Everything is moving in perfect time. Everything is where it needs to be. When you are centered, when the world dancer is centered, nothing will throw you off balance. Remember, you are your center. Nothing shall throw you or your life off balance.

Divide the incense in half. Light one half, placing the other half in the bag. Take each dime and move it in a circle over the World card, pass it through the lit incense smoke, and place in the bag. Take the feather, your gift from the sky, and make a circle over the World card, pass through the incense smoke, and place in the bag. Secure bag and chant the incantation three times.

· · · · ·

INCANTATION
Mercury retrograde
Let me be
Your influences stay
Far away from me

The first Academy Awards was held on this day in 1929. Harness the spectacular power of seduction and the sparkling essence of Hollywood glamour to cast an enchantment upon your chosen jewels, gems, silvers, golds, and beads.

INCANTATION

Glinting gems
Refracted light
Be my aid
Shimmer tonight
Radiance is mine
I shine and delight
Enchantment I weave
On this night
With love and with light
And with harm to none
I do declare this
Enchantment is done

Glamour Jewelry Spell

Ingredients
- The Empress
- Gold candle
- Jewelry

Method, Visualization, and Meditation

The word *glamour* is often used in the context of fairy power. It is also used interchangeably in vampire lore where a vampire glamours his prey into yielding to his dark will.

You can glamour a piece of jewelry for any occasion. It gives you a boost of sparkle and seduction to all who cross your path. It is a simple and easy process. As always, use your powers wisely and kindly, and for the greatest good.

Earrings will catch someone's eye. Choker necklaces mark the throat chakra when you wish to seduce or charm with words. Dangling pendents over the chest invite someone to your heart. Charm bracelets mark the place where need meets desire.

Take a bath or shower on the evening in question. Light a small candle. Place the Empress card before you. The Empress is warm, pliable, and alive. She sits in a field of yellow wheat where sustenance abounds, rivers flow, and magical, creative energy circulates. Cool glades stand behind her; a warm field spreads before her. She represents all that is alluring and desirable. She is the source of warmth who cannot be ignored. Channel her power as you look at the card. Feel her rich desire coursing through your body. Feel her in your veins. The desire pools into your belly. Bring it up and reflect it out of your eyes.

Place your jewelry upon the card.

See the sparkling stars in her crown—the energy of the universe, the light of the stars—imbue your jewelry.

Adorn yourself with your shimmering objects. Enjoy as the evening unfolds.

Powered-Up Pendulum Charm

Ingredients
- Your chosen pendulum
- The High Priestess
- Incense of choice

Method, Visualization, and Meditation

You can purchase a pendulum, slip a ring over a necklace, or use a crystal on a string. Root workers use a root for a pendulum, setting a special place on their altar to honor it as a sacred tool, just like the tarot.

Using a pendulum over a spirit board is an excellent way to dowse your unconscious. The pendulum becomes an extension of oneself, a tool to discover personal truth. When we can't discern the truth for ourselves, a pendulum will help us do it. Let the pendulum speak and articulate when we can't for ourselves.

Choose your pendulum. Hold it in the warmth of your hands, examine it, and mentally make friends with it. Welcome it into your life.

Place the High Priestess card before you. Focus on the quiet truth the High Priestess bears. She is silent yet knowing, just like your pendulum, and she will answer your questions. Focus on her lunar energy. Her milky-white moon glow envelops your body. Hold the pendulum over the card and allow the glow to move from you to the pendulum and to the High Priestess in a circular fashion. Remove yourself. Watch the energy exchange between the pendulum and the card.

Pass your pendulum through incense smoke while whispering the incantation.

The Pit and the Pendulum by Edgar Allen Poe was published on this day in 1845. Pendulums can be used over a spread of cards, over Ouija or spirit boards, and even swung over a pregnant woman's belly to determine the baby's gender.

INCANTATION

Pendulum swings
Over airs of fate
Your power
I do not debate
Speak the truth
And tell me so
This way I will
Always know
The path is right
And it is true
This charm binds
Myself to you

Queen of Pentacles Connection Ritual

*Eleanor of Aquitaine,
one of the most powerful and
wealthy women in the Middle
Ages, was wed on this day
in 1152. Wealth, abundance,
manifestation, and the glories
of the physical world all belong
to the Queen of Pentacles.*

Ingredient
• Queen of Pentacles

Method, Visualization, and Meditation
Enter the arcana of the Queen of Pentacles.

A trellis filled with red roses and climbing vines frames a beautiful woman as if she were a painting. She looks down adoringly at a magical disk on her lap. She is still, as if she were posing for a painter and offering the artist her generous, sloping profile. Wild violet and green moss reveal a bunny; his fast, warm breath and twitching nose remind you this is no snapshot but a living, breathing scene.

Her throne is carved with pears, goats, and cherubs. All manner of animal, vegetable, and mineral have declared allegiance to her. The red of her cloak denotes passion, while her yellow fabric informs you she is a woman to be counted on. Dusty mushrooms poke through the fertile earth, looming large to the ants who scurry past. A lazy river meanders in the distance against the base of cool blue mountains who reach toward a cheerful sky.

The scent of apples wafts from the fruit trees behind you. Immense gardens continue in every direction, organized, tended, and bursting with life. This woman is a natural healer who has harnessed the power of earth.

INCANTATION
Queen of Pentacles
Goddess of earth
Together, with love
We give birth
Soil, clay
Moss and loam
Through abundant gardens
We will roam

"Come, child. See what I have created? You have this power too. You can organize the physical world however you like. It is the nature of the world to grow and expand. You help it along. Doing so, you cultivate a life for yourself, for what you plant in a garden, you plant in your life. All answers are found there, amidst the soil and roots, between the stalks and leaves. You are the source."

Home Protection Spell

Ingredients
- Four potted geraniums
1. King of Swords
2. King of Wands
3. King of Cups
4. King of Pentacles

```
        [ 1 ]
[ 4 ]  home  [ 3 ]
        [ 2 ]
```

Method, Visualization, and Meditation

Geraniums are known to repel negative mojo. Place pots at the boundary of your home or simply sprinkle their petals at the four corners of the building or block.

A king's protection and favor has always been desirable for security. Place four potted geraniums before you.

Place the King of Swords before one geranium. This will be placed on the north side of your home. He commands the northern winds and deflects the thoughts of those who would cause harm. His shield is up.

Place the King of Wands at the second geranium. He commands the power of fire, so fierce and protective that no one will cross its boundary for fear of being devoured by the hungry flame. This king harnesses the sun's power for growth and expansion inside your four walls. His shield is up.

Place the King of Cups at the third geranium. He commands the water that churns and nourishes the imagination. This water would drown all enemies. He is placed at the space of potential, the place of possibility, so that nothing but inspiration seeps through your walls. His shield is up.

Place the King of Pentacles at the last geranium. He is the king of manifestation, the place where things manifest. He contains the power to provide stumbling blocks to all who would cause harm. He commands the space where the sun sets and casts its rosy glow upon your home. His shield is up.

Plant or place each geranium around your home, looking up at the sides of your house as you do so. In your mind's eye, project the image of each king's face across the side of your home. Repeat the incantation in each direction.

Queen Elizabeth ordered the arrest of Mary, Queen of Scots, in her house on this day in 1568. To protect your home and keep the good thriving inside, perform this spell of protection.

INCANTATION

Walls of wood
Foundations deep
Protect the place
Where I do sleep
This is my house
This is my home
Protect all the things
Within I own
Kings protect
What is most dear
Keep them safe
From year to year

INCANTATION

Speed of Hermes

Cups of fun

Let this journey

Be filled with sun

Move fast with comfort

And with speed

Like the knight

Upon his steed

Go with the flow

Surprises await

Greet delight through

The traveler's gate

Ease of Travel Spell

Ingredients
- Knight of Cups
- Feverfew
- Mugwort

Method, Visualization, and Meditation

In the old days travelers put themselves at high risk. Travel meant camping out, braving the elements, hungry animals, and roving bandits. Dirt roads led to unimaginable dangers. These days travel nightmares include rude fellow travelers, disrupted flight patterns, and unfriendly TSA agents. This spell ensures comfortable traveling for everything from short lines at passport and luggage checks to upgrade and smooth sailing.

The Knight of Cups bears the mark of Hermes, messenger of the gods and master of speed and communication, on his helmet and heels. He provides a speedy journey. The sweet, optimistic flowers of feverfew are used medicinally to treat headaches. Mugwort is a traveler's talisman.

Place the Knight of Cups before you. This knight stops for a moment to indulge in the joys of the cup. He does this even though he has speed and power. Let his action be a reminder as you travel: joy exists in the journey as well as the destination. Whisper the incantation over him.

Tuck the feverfew into your suitcases, folded clothes, wallet, and bag to protect you from travel headaches and snags along the way. Do as Roman foot soldiers did: tuck a sprig or sprinkle of mugwort into your shoes. Remember to bring along enough for your journey home.

Gemini Lighten Up Spell

Ingredients
- Popcorn (such as Jiffy Pop)
1. The Lovers
2. Queen of Cups reversed
3. Page of Cups reversed

Method, Visualization, and Meditation

Native Americans believed a spirit lived inside every kernel of popcorn. When the kernel heated up, the spirit grew angry and exploded the kernel. We now know a small drop of water exists inside every popcorn kernel. When the temperature is high enough, the tiny kernel explodes into fluffy, delicious popcorn.

This popcorn spell will lighten your spirits and provide a tasty snack in one shot.

The Lovers card represents the dual aspect of Gemini and two sides of a situation. The reversed Queen of Cups represents bottled emotions. The reversed Page of Cups reflects a resistance to fun and good feelings.

Place all the cards before you. Consider the Lovers card and the strength of Gemini, the most adaptable sign of the zodiac. Focus on the nature of the twins as seen by the lovers on the card. Look at the two court cards. Turn the Queen of Cups right-side up. Turn the Page of Cups right-side up.

You have released the blocks.

Move to your stove or popper. Make a batch of popcorn. With each pop, allow yourself to lighten up.

Today is the first day of the sign of Gemini, the Twins. Gemini is assigned the Lovers card and ruled by Mercury. Geminis are known for their adaptable and intellectual qualities. Cast this spell when you need to loosen up on any situation and find renewed enthusiasm.

INCANTATION

What goes down
Must come up
Release the darkness
From this cup
Lighten up this mood
Say I
Harness the spirit
Of Gemini

Today is the feast day of Italian hermit Romanus of Subiaco. The Hermit is the archetype of the wise man who removes himself from society and distraction so he can master his spiritual journey.

INCANTATION

Hermit's light

Can you see

The answer's right

In front of me

Do the right things

You've done before

The answer's right

Outside your door

Go on the journey

Take the leap

Enlightenment

You will reap

Hermit Card Connection Ritual

Ingredient
• The Hermit

Method, Visualization, and Meditation

Enter the arcana of the Hermit.

Snow crunches beneath the feet of the man who is about to summit this mountain. He walks with a solar yellow walking stick that glows in the starkness of his surroundings. Though you are high on a mountain peak, the winds are still and the evening quiet. The night sky expands behind him, and the moon is new, dark, and pregnant.

He looks at the valley below with tired yet twinkling eyes. He raises his lantern up before his face, and it begins to glow. A brilliant six-pointed star permeating with light casts warmth on the old man's face. His skin is etched with the mark of experience and the wisdom only maturity can bring. He bends his head forward as if in reverence and thanks for all he has seen, all he has done, and all he has experienced.

You look down at the valley below and can barely believe your eyes. Yellow lights, lanterns, and fires are lighting up like fireflies, one after another. The entire alpine valley is illuminated with twinkling lights stretching for as far as the eye can see. It seems this man has sent out a signal, and the valley responded in turn. For what we do and what we share—how we act—echoes its consequence and mark forever. It leaves a footprint and changes the very nature of the world.

His message remains a mystery to you. The man lowers his lantern, closes his eyes for a moment, turns, and retreats back down the mountain.

Mesmerizing Spell

Ingredients
1. Queen of Wands
2. The Hanged Man reversed
- Vanilla oil
- Coconut oil

Method, Visualization, and Meditation

The Queen of Wands reflects the magnetic power of attraction. The Hanged Man represents a person held captive by charm, wit, grace, and intelligence. Vanilla is used for sensuality. Coconut connects to magnetic lunar power.

Place the Queen of Wands next to the reversed Hanged Man. See how her magnetic gaze lights him up? He has a yellow halo around his skull. He is a slave to the queen and will do her bidding—whatever she desires; he is mesmerized by her. She uses the strength of passion to radiate her energy toward him. She is also aided by the magical powers of her feline companion, whose green eyes can stop anything in its tracks.

Walk close to the Queen of Wands. Embody her. What does it look like when you see the world through her eyes? How does it feel to sit in her skin? How does it feel to contain the power to attract others like a moth to a flame?

Get dressed for your day or evening but prepare yourself exactly like the Queen of Wands would prepare herself for an evening out. Bathe in the finest of oils; dress with reds, scarlets, and crimsons. Anoint yourself with vanilla oil, sacred to the great love goddesses. Moisturize your body with coconut oil, which the ancients used for their lanterns.

When you are ready to leave the house, go to the mirror and stare deeply into your own eyes. You are now the Queen of Wands. You are prepared to mesmerize the crowd or that special someone.

The word mesmerize *comes to us from Franz Anton Mesmer, proponent of animal magnetism energy work, who was born on this day in 1734.*

INCANTATION

Magnetic power
Draw to me
Hear my voice
Follow my plea
Can't resist
My strong allure
Your feelings strong
And oh so pure
You are putty
In my hand
Leap to try
And understand

1   2

Queen Victoria, for whom the Victorian age was named, would be celebrating her birthday. She was born on this day in 1819.

INCANTATION

Happy birthday
Happy birthday
Happy birthday to me
Life unfolds with joy and glee
Magic prevails
My wish comes true
My gorgeous birth year
Begins anew

Birthday Wish Spell

Ingredients
- Journal
- Tarot card representing your wish
- Candle colored to correspond to your wish
- Carving tool
- Glitter
- Oil

Method, Visualization, and Meditation

People blow out birthday candles without realizing they are performing an elementary form of candle magic. A person's life breath extinguishes the flame, and in doing so their desire is released for manifestation.

Take some time to journal and write about the year that has passed. Consider the year to come. Write specifically what your birthday wish is. Describe every detail. Why do you want it? How will it affect your life? When you are ready, select the card best representing your wish.

Focus on your card. Enter it with your mind's eye. Touch, smell, and examine the world inside the borders of the card. See yourself gaining your wish.

Anoint your candle with oil. Rub it upward, filling the wax with your energy and intention. Using your carving tool, carve the candle, inscribing your name, astrological sign, and desire. If there is room, make any marks or images that correspond to your wish. Your glitter will adhere to the oil; cover the candle with glitter, getting it into the crevices you have created.

When you are satisfied, light the candle. Doing so, you see your desire unleashed.

Meditate on the flame and focus on the candle as long as you like to align your energy with it.

Night Visions Oil

Ingredients
- The Star
- The Moon
- Mason jar
- Gardenia petals
- 1 cup coconut oil

Method, Visualization, and Meditation

Gardenias are known to be prophetic and beckon friendly spirits. The Star reflects inspiration from above. The Moon reveals unseen mysteries of the night.

Place the Star and the Moon card together as you prep for the oil.

Place the petals in the mason jar and cover with coconut oil. Gently warm the oil if it has solidified, so you can pour it over the petals.

Look at the combination of nightscapes between these two cards. They reflect the duality of night: the light and the dark, the rejuvenating and the murky.

Place the Star card against your oil jar. Under a dance of stars, all things are possible. Boundaries are erased as you move from one reality to another as easily as switching channels or opening webpages.

Place the Moon card against your oil jar. The Moon card beckons to your sleeping self as your subconscious fills the base of the card. Unknown desires creep to the surface. Creatures emerge from the shadows to grant your bidding.

Cover and let the mixture infuse in a warm place from one to six weeks, depending upon the intensity of the petals.

Anoint your third eye with the oil and contemplate the Star and Moon card before bed or prior to nighttime rituals and magical or creative work.

Gardenias are in season from May through July. You'll need to find them fresh to create Night Visions Oil. Dream oil may be added to an evening bath or dabbed on your feet before bed for rich and enigmatic dream experiences.

INCANTATION
Star and Moon
Hypnotic's delight
With Night Vision Oil
I glide into flight
Psychedelic dreams
Fancy of truth
Gardenias bring fun
And the joy of youth

Bram Stoker's infamous novel Dracula *was published on this day in 1897. A psychic vampire is someone who sucks energy from you and leaves you feeling depleted, tired, and worse off than when you first encountered them.*

Psychic Vampires Begone Energy Shield

Ingredients
1. The High Priestess
2. The Fool
3. Eight of Cups

Method, Visualization, and Meditation

You can banish vampire behavior and protect your valuable energy. Cast this energy shield and watch as the vampire slithers off in search of a more willing victim.

Psychic vampires can be tricky to deal with; sometimes you initially tried to help them, maybe they are a member of the family, or perhaps you work for one. What you resist tends to persist. Consider how your own energy contributes or reverse attracts their attention upon you. Once you cast this spell, put them far from your mind.

The High Priestess provides a shield of psychic protection. The Fool represents the person you are sending away. The Eight of Cups marks their departure.

Ground yourself, feet on the floor and spine straight. Place the High Priestess before you. A silver shield of power, the reflective moonlight protects her. Begin to build a bubble of protective energy around yourself. Be sure it engulfs your entire body. When it is strong and pulsing, feel it reflect any negative succubus energy that comes toward you by bouncing it back to the person who sent it.

Place the Fool card. Watch as he journeys. Imagine your vampire walking away from you, their attention turned to something else.

Place the Eight of Cups. Celebrate their final departure as their figure moves away from you, becoming smaller and smaller in the distance.

INCANTATION

The powers inside
Are mine alone
You cannot take them
Will not roam
You've robbed me before
But never again
I give myself only
If I say when

2	1	3

Page of Cups Connection Ritual

Ingredients
- Page of Cups

Method, Visualization, and Meditation

The Page of Cups is the most psychic figure of the tarot deck. She is a youth whose perceptive qualities are wide open. No preconceived notions hold her back or taint her visions.

Enter the arcana of the Page of Cups.

A smooth-faced girl stands upon a yellow stage, one hand on her hip, the other grasping a cup. A fish pokes its head out as if she's telling it a joke. Her posture is animated and stagey. Two hundred pairs of eyes belonging to the audience watch her every move. Behind her, the painted scrim depicts ocean waters that flow, watery symbols of the cup.

What the audience doesn't know is that this actress is the daughter of the ocean. As such, she carries prophetic visions and a sight that sees far and wide. As she opens herself up to creative inspiration for her role onstage, true psychic visions occur to her. She can tell you that the woman in the front row hides pound cakes in her pantry and devours them when no one sees. She sees Mrs. Poundcake's husband kissing the neighbor after sunset. She senses the deepest of secrets, even secrets she doesn't understand: ghosts, flashes of truth, glimpses of the past, visions of the future. It is hard for her to discern what is of the physical world and what is not; therefore, she lives with a foot inside each.

And she never breathes a word of the visions she sees. She allows them to wash over her without ever being swept away.

Marie Anne Lenormand, French fortuneteller and psychic, was born on this day in 1772.

INCANTATION

Page of Cups
And bubbling cup
Drink your visions
Drink it up
Past, present, future
They collide
Who knows what
People hide inside
Page of Cups
Daughter of the sea
She knows the depths
Inside of me

Fly Your Freak Flag Solar Eclipse Spell

Ingredients
1. The Hierophant
2. Eight of Cups
3. The Star

Method, Visualization, and Meditation

Solar eclipses have a long and torrid history of being associated with black magic, dark omens, and fear. It is not hard to understand why a shadow passing over the daytime sun would strike fear into the hearts of people.

Though science helps us to understand today's world in a better way, people still fear the unknown. Unique and creative people can often have a hard time fitting in, especially in small communities where everyone seems to be watching and judging. Perform this spell when you want to be seen as you truly are.

Place the Hierophant and the Star before you. The Hierophant represents all of the rules of society, traditions, and old ways. Note his heavy and concealing clothing. In comparison, the Star kneels in her naked skin, fully revealing who she is. A child of nature, she needs no cathedral, church, or building with which to trap the idea of god. There are no followers, no proselytizing; she has no interest in telling others what to do. She is content to be the channel of her true self.

You are moving away from "rules" and into the nature of who you are. Place the Eight of Cups to facilitate this journey. In doing so, move the cards so they are moving in an upward diagonal.

Note the eclipse on the eight. This is the genesis of a personal revolution of personal expression. Your back is turned on the old and outdated. From this moment on, you will be authentic to your true self in every way you can be.

Eight of Swords Connection Ritual

Ingredient
- Eight of Swords

Method, Visualization, and Meditation
Enter the arcana of the Eight of Swords.

The wetlands are damp, the bay is cloudy, and the water matches the dullness of the sky. From your bird's-eye viewpoint in the great tower, you look down upon the shoreline. A strange apparition meets your eyes. It appears a creature has been captured and bound, held within a silver prison. Seagulls circle and mists roll across the marsh. You try to bring your attention back to the words you are reading but you find your curiosity has gotten the best of you.

You exit the castle at once and make for the beach. You trudge through wet sand to approach the figure. It is a human female. She is bound and blindfolded in white tatters of fabric. A piercing prison of swords surrounds her. The mystifying part of this vision is how she bobs up and down, her slippers never touching the ground, as if held by invisible tethers.

Not knowing what else to do, you run to the first sword and dislodge it. You throw it flat to the ground. As the steel breaks free, you hear the figure gasp. You work quickly now, and with each freed sword, she comes closer to the ground. You free the last sword and watch in astonishment as her binds loosen, falling from her body and eyes. She looks gratefully at you.

She seems familiar.

Your doppelgänger stands before you.

The Eight of Swords was called the Lord of Shortened Force by the magicians of the Golden Dawn, who assigned it the time period of May 21–31.

INCANTATION
Eight of Swords
And binds of white
What has gripped
Me on this night
Am I a willing initiate
Or held a slave
Regardless, it's freedom
And new sight I crave

Leadership and Inspiration Spell

*On this day in 1431
Joan of Arc, at age 19,
was burned at the stake.
Her efforts to free France
from the grips of the English
throne have made her a
legendary figure. Confidence,
commitment, communication,
and delegation are all
marks of a good leader.*

INCANTATION

Joan of Arc
And Page of Swords
Fill me, gift me
I need the words
Pass the passion
Spread my light
Give me the strength
I need tonight

Ingredients
   1. Ace of Wands
   2. The Hermit
   3. Page of Swords

Method, Visualization, and Meditation

The Ace of Wands represents a spark of excitement. The Hermit card reflects knowledge. The Page of Swords represents Joan of Arc and contains the ability to guide others without compromising one's sense of self.

Lay the Ace of Wands and contemplate the reason you are being called upon to lead. What was your initial spark of enthusiasm and excitement? Does it still glow within you? Fire and this wand radiate outward. Feel how enigmatic you are when you are excited and passionate.

Place the Hermit card above the ace. Watch his lantern glow as the ace ignites the flame of knowledge. The Hermit is secure with what he has gained through study, seclusion, and reflection. He has come to the mountaintop to spread his word, and, indeed, the mountain he stands on spreads below the card's border to the fertile green valleys below. Do not doubt yourself for a moment. Your light shines.

Place the Page of Swords above the Hermit. Now is the time to become the fearless leader, sacrificing none of yourself. You do not need to become someone else to move crowds. Simply bring compassion and confidence out of yourself. The swords are the cards of communication. Like this knight who embodies Joan of Arc's spirit, you will forge new ground and become a passionate leader.

Wheel of Fortune Card Connection Ritual

Ingredients
- The Wheel of Fortune

Method, Visualization, and Meditation
Enter the arcana of the Wheel of Fortune.

Close your eyes and listen very carefully to the room around you. What do you hear? Are birds calling to each other from the branches extending past your window? Is the refrigerator humming as it cools the eggs, milk, and cheese? Are the honks of frustrated commuters reaching your ears? Does soft music drift from your computer? Underneath normal everyday sounds, if you listen, lies a whirring sound. It lies just beneath the normal sounds of your everyday life.

It is like the gentle whir of a playing card in the spokes of a child's bike, the subtle sound of circulating electrons around the nucleus of an atom, nothing more than the whisper of the wind. But, were you to pull away the fabric of reality like the drapes of a curtain, you would find the Wheel of Fortune spinning everywhere: under your sink, beneath the bed, inside the dishwasher, inside your own body.

The Wheel of Fortune reflects how we experience time. Slow it down by paying attention to what you are doing.

The Wheel of Fortune is the energy that revolves solar systems, controls the tides, and directs the wind. The Wheel of Fortune controls the seemingly uncontrollable events of your life. The four corners of the card represent the four suits, seasons, and directions. The word "taro" spins across the wheel.

The Wheel holds all future and past secrets. It may be that every experience is happening at once, simultaneously. Experience is only revealed as you inhabit it.

Big Ben, London's famous clock, went into operation today in 1859. Clocks spin like the Wheel of Fortune, reminding us of the nature of luck and good timing.

INCANTATION
Wheel of Fortune
Spinning time
I'll slow you down
And make you mine

159

Magnetic north was discovered on this day in 1831.

Lodestone Attraction Spell

Ingredients
- Lodestone
- Olive oil
- Pouch
- Handful of dirt
- Tarot deck

Method, Visualization, and Meditation

Lodestones are attraction stones made of magnetic iron ore and will act as a magnet to bring desired energy to you. Choose a lodestone from a shop or online retailer. Select a phallic-shaped stone for masculine energy or a round stone for feminine energy. Rub your lodestone with olive oil. Align your energy with the stone, welcoming it into your life, feeling its innate magnetic pull. Place the stone in a pouch and cover the pouch with dirt for three days. After the third day, your stone is charged and ready to go. Lodestones are said to have an intelligence all their own.

Place the lodestone over any tarot card whose energy you would like to attract into your life. Choose a court card to represent a specific romantic object, such as the Knight of Cups for a romantic and artsy guy in his twenties. A major arcana card can represent and experience you would like to attract: choose the Chariot for a new car, the Hermit to find inner peace, Death to facilitate change, etc.

Place your desired card before you and meditate into the card, imagining the scenario you desire. Place the lodestone over it for three days. Each morning recite the incantation:

INCANTATION

Magic card and stone of ore
I call upon you, I want more
Bring _____
To me this year
Universe, this I know you hear
What comes if right
And true and good
Receive the bounty
That I should

Evil Eye Protective Charm

Ingredients
- Nine of Wands
- Bright yellow lemon
- 9 iron nails
- Red thread

Method, Visualization, and Meditation

Sicilian folk magic is called Benedicaria, meaning "Way of Blessing," and is often practiced by devout Catholic women. The practice differs according to the individual but it does make extensive use of candles, olive oil, eggs, and herbs.

The Nine of Wands emulates protection energy. Lemons are used around the world for protective charms. Iron nails are said to repel evil. Red thread can be used to connect us to the other side.

Place the Nine of Wands. Enter the card. See the gentleman warrior step forward from the line of wands. Walk up to him and invite him to become your house genie. Request his protective eyes and ears protect your home. His battle wounds only serve to show where he has been and what he has been through.

He reaches into his belt and hands you a lemon. He says something as he hands it to you. What does he say? Bring this message back with you. Look and listen for other responses from him in the natural world around you.

Pierce your lemon with the iron nails. String with red thread. Hang by the front door to ward off the evil eye and any negative energy from entering the home. Every time you sweep the floors, finish by sweeping the last bit out the front door to ensure negativity stays at bay.

Sicilian occultist Count Alessandro di Cagliostro was born today in 1743. He sold secret Egyptian magical amulets while working for a Roman Catholic cardinal and is credited with creating Freemason rites. Aleister Crowley claimed he had lived as the Count in his former life.

. . . . .

INCANTATION
Buon giorno charm
Protect my home
From harm

Halt the Haters Spell

Today was the sacred feast day of Bellona, the Roman goddess of warfare.

Ingredients
- Six of Swords
- Black peppercorns
- Kosher salt
- Computer/laptop/phone

Method, Visualization, and Meditation

Haters, naysayers, and gossips only have the power you give to them. This spell does nothing to physically harm or move the haters; rather, it removes any effects they have upon you and your psyche or any ramifications their words or gossip might have.

The Six of Swords reflects negative people moving away from you. Peppercorns have been used in protective and defensive folk magic for years. Salt is used for protection.

Mix black peppercorns and salt together in a dish while uttering the incantation.

Place the Six of Swords before you. Enter the card. Stand on the dock and see a boat before you. The figures in the boat are the people who have caused you strife. The childlike figure represents their immaturity. Tell the boatman you are sending them away. They no longer have the power to wound you. Shake his hand. He agrees to ferry them to distant shores. Watch the boat leave the dock. Observe the figures get smaller and smaller. Their emotional impact disappears as their figures disappear into the horizon.

Sprinkle the salt-and-pepper mixture around the perimeter of your home, repeating your incantation.

At bedtime sprinkle a circle of salt and pepper around your computer and cell phone. Wipe it away in the morning, knowing you have been cleansed.

If anything negative should catch your eye, simply turn away. Focus on something wonderful.

INCANTATION

Jealous thoughts
And tongues of spite
You are banished
On this night.
Stop, turn, and
Go back, away
You'll be gone by
The light of day

Emperor Card Connection Ritual

Ingredient
- The Emperor

Method, Visualization, and Meditation

Enter the arcana of the Emperor.

You hold an invitation in the palm of your hand and watch as the messenger who brought it departs. The ancient parchment scroll has been read. Black ink, scratched in feathered calligraphy, requests your presence. You are to have an audience with the emperor.

You have traveled across the mountains and plateaus of his domain. You have stood at the dry riverbed and watched as the high priestess and the empress opened the floodgates, allowing their waters to rush through.

Saffron, myrrh, and cinnamon incense scent the air as you approach the emperor. You wonder at first if he isn't asleep with his eyes open. His face is set with a firm expression, like that of a British guard who is not allowed to break face.

You walk closer, respectful yet extremely curious. There is tension in his fingers as they grasp a metallic scepter. His crown is pure gold, encrusted with glittering gems. His royal cranberry colored cape covers embalming armor. You consider the battles this man has seen and waged.

Running your fingers across his throne, you finger the horned rams. They appear ornery and bullheaded. Leaning closer to his impassive face, your eyes trail his long beard. This is a man who has seen many winters pass, yet his lips contain the lush plumpness of youth.

"What do you want?" he softly asks.

"You sent for me," you respond, unafraid.

"You needed to be reminded," he says.

"Of what?" you ask.

"That I am always here for you," he states. "My strength is your strength. You are me. I am you. My kingdom is your kingdom."

Today, in 1039,
Henry the Third becomes
Holy Roman Emperor.

INCANTATION

Emperor card
Man of type A
What is your lesson
For me on this day?
You provide me
With structure
Solidity to life
Greatest warrior of all
You protect me from strife

Love Yourself Spell

INCANTATION

Priestess moon

And Empress sun

The web of magic's

Just begun

Heal the wounds

That once I placed

Across my body

I do replace

With light and love

And love and light

Love myself

With all my might

Ingredients
- The High Priestess
- The Empress
- Honey bear
- Bath

Method, Visualization, and Meditation

The High Priestess reflects our shadow, invisible self. The Empress reflects our physical, outer self. The gentle integration of this duality reflects who we are. When we listen and respect our instincts (Priestess) and love and revere the physical body we have been lent for this journey (Empress), we integrate with love toward ourselves. With love and respect firmly set inward, we can then shine it outward to the people, places, and things we care about.

Place the High Priestess. Enter the card. High above the ocean, brilliant torches alight her temple. Her eyes are trained upon you. She glows with the luminescence of the moon. You walk to her throne. Turn and sit in her place. Become the High Priestess. White and blue robes rest upon your skin as light and silky as your favorite nightgown. The triple goddess crown rests firmly upon your head. A scroll is on your lap bearing a language you cannot decipher. It is the book of your life.

Place the Empress card. Enter the card. The soft flesh of your bare feet tiptoes over wheat. The sun is warm on your head. The dazzling illumination of the Empress is revealed. Sit in her place to invoke her. The brilliance of the universe beams from the stars upon your crown. Your hair cascades softly around your face and neck. The power of all creation glows from your scepter. A luxurious gown flows around you. Sit back against silken velvet pillows. Your belly is pregnant with potential.

Remove your clothing. Your body is borrowed for this life's journey. One day it will pass back into nothingness. Love it while you live in it. Write loving statements all over your body with the honey bear, like *love*, *peace*, etc., then enter your bath.

Nine of Swords Connection Ritual

Ingredient
- Nine of Swords

Method, Visualization, and Meditation

Enter the arcana of the Nine of Swords.

Nines in tarot reflect the near close to a cycle. Nines are akin to standing at the front of a long line, knowing you are next to be called. Nines provide what is wanted: wishes are granted, actions have culminated. The experience of manifestation is at hand. In the best cases we sit on cloud nine.

The witching hour rings with twelve hollow gongs. A figure rises from her slumber. The blackness of night cloaks this figure despite the cheerful hand-stitched quilt covering her lower body. The signs and symbols of the zodiac have been lovingly embroidered upon the quilt, a reminder of the night sky, who unveils itself over her every evening. The wheel of the year spins as she enters her dreamtime, where linear time has no meaning and she travels with the speed of her thoughts.

Evening primrose and Casablanca lilies, who open their blooms only at night, fill the dim air with sweet fragrance, yet she does not smell them.

Her gruesome thoughts have taken a turn for the worse, and she buries her face in her sweaty hands. The pallet on which she rests is thin, and the wooden frame carries the relief. It is inscribed with the scene of a duel, perhaps echoing the troubled scene of her mind.

Nine swords are displayed above her. Have they formed a ladder? Can she scramble up the swords to safety or are they the beleaguered thoughts running like a freight train through her mind?

To rule one's mind is to rule your world. Should she straighten her back and drop her hands upon her knees, she would find the peace of the lotus and begin to take control.

The Nine of Swords was called the Lord of Despair and Cruelty by the magicians of the Golden Dawn, who assigned it the time period of June 1–10.

INCANTATION

Nine of Swords
Strife of mind
Change my thoughts
Peace I'll find

Today is sacred to Vespa, Roman goddess of the house and home, hearth and fire.

INCANTATION

House and home
You've been good
I've enjoyed
This neighborhood
The time has come
It's time to go
Watch my bank account
Inflate and grow

Sell a House Spell

Ingredients
- Ten of Pentacles
- Mint essential oil
- Distilled water
- Spray bottle
- Vanilla extract

Method, Visualization, and Meditation

The Ten of Pentacles will attract the highest bidder. Mint activates financial channels. Vanilla creates desire and provokes the love of others for your home.

Place the Ten of Pentacles. Enter the card. Focus on the energy connecting the grandfather figure to the young couple and the small child who hides in his mother's skirts and the family of dogs. Focus on the dazzling money decorating the card. Hear coins ringing and clinking onto each other like a winning Las Vegas slot machine.

Examine archway and threshold of this card. See your buyer walking through that arch. Your buyer brings you even more than your asking price. After a firm connection to the aspects of this card, take it with you through your home.

The direction of east marks manifestation. Begin at the lowest level, in the basement or lower floors. Cast a mental projection of this card on the east wall. Move though each room, casting the image of the Ten of Pentacles on each eastern wall.

Prepare a mixture of a few drops of mint essential oil with distilled water in a spray bottle. Spray in each room of the home before a potential buyer passes your threshold. Place two capfuls of vanilla extract in a heatproof container in a 300-degree oven for one hour to release its scent and tempt the buyer.

Release Sadness Beach Spell

Ingredients
- Queen of Cups
- Found black stone

Method, Visualization, and Meditation

Don't you feel rejuvenated and tired when you return home from a day at the beach? Cleansing powers are rampant in natural power spaces where elements collide: where sea meets shore, where mountain meets sky, at waterfalls, in hot deserts, inside frozen landscapes. If you are not located near a beach, find the closest spot where the elements converge to perform this spell.

The Queen of Cups is the glittering mermaid and sea siren of the tarot deck. Her empathy is so deep, her feelings so broad, she has the greatest capacity to experience every side of the emotional spectrum, from deep sadness to buoyant happiness.

Bring the Queen of Cups to the beach with you. Enter the card. Sit yourself down in her ocean throne. Look at the expanse of the ocean before you. It moves as far as the eye can see. Feel the eternity of the waves crashing. Sense the depths and brimming life in the waters before you. Embrace your feelings. Feel your sadness. Allow the crashing waves to pulverize the walls of emotion inside you, rubbing you raw. Let sound, wind, air, and mist wash over you.

Walk along the surf. Search for a shimmering black stone. When you find one, sit with it in the sand. Allow the rock to dry in your hand and warm in the sunlight. Make friends with the stone as you align your energies into it. It will absorb all your emotions.

Release all sadness or distress into the stone while whispering the incantation. Once it has been released, you can throw the stone back into the waves. If you choose to bring the stone home as a healing tool, bury it for three nights to cleanse its energy.

Today World Oceans Day is celebrated worldwide. Among its many attributes, the ocean has the ability to cleanse your aura and transform your soul. This spell erodes sadness and encourages you to find a valuable healing treasure.

INCANTATION

Queen of Cups
Heart of mine
Absorb my pain
So peace I'll find
Joy in my heart
Runs free
The gift of love
I give to me

Today in 1963 the film Cleopatra *premiered in New York City. A fearless leader, Cleopatra spoke multiple languages and embarked in legendary love affairs with Mark Antony and Julius Caesar. Her myth-making beauty was legendary.*

INCANTATION

Epic beauty

You are mine

Attract to me

Romance divine

Get Lucky Tonight Cleopatra Spell

Ingredients
1. Ace of Cups
2. Ace of Wands
- Avocado
- 1 tablespoon honey

Method, Visualization, and Meditation

Cast this spell when you are heading out for a night on the town and want to attract and inspire spicy love and lust all around you or toward a specific someone.

The Ace of Cups reflects the ultimate receptive power of the female. The cup springs forth while it waits to be filled. The Ace of Wands reflects the phallus of male desire. Avocados inspire love, lust, and beauty. They are sacred to fertility and inspire amour. Honey is sticky and sweet and can be used to attract your heart's desire.

Place the Ace of Cups before you. Place the Ace of Wands sideways so the phallic wand is pointing at her.

In your mind's eye look at the cup. It bubbles with the ancient Egyptian liquid of magnetism. Reach forward, grasp the cup, and drink heavily. You are now empowered with the liquid of Cleopatra. The Ace of Wands coming toward you is the very thing you desire. Draw it toward you like a moth to a flame.

Blend the flesh of the avocado together with the honey while chanting the incantation. Apply to your freshly cleaned face. Leave on for twenty minutes while you do something to invoke pleasure—watch a snippet of a favorite film, listen to your favorite music. Wash off with cool water and proceed to get ready for your evening.

Enjoy what you attract.

1	2

Peace in the Workplace Spell

The Equal Pay Act was passed today in 1963. It stated that men and women must be paid the same amount of money— equal pay for equal work.

Ingredients

- Ten of Cups
- Your favorite "made from scratch" cookie recipe

Method, Visualization, and Meditation

This kitchen magic spell should be cast when things seem out of control at work. This is a tasty and lovely gesture when you'd like everyone to settle down and return to a space of calmness.

The Ten of Cups represents happiness and gleeful feelings shared by a group of people.

Place the Ten of Cups. Enter the card. Feel your spirits raised by looking at the magnificent rainbow's endless colors refracted in the moisture. Can you hear the joyful music playing? Everyone smiles at each other, happy and playful. This happiness is what you shall provoke and project in your workplace.

Make your favorite cookie recipe from scratch. As you arrange your ingredients on the counter top, think of the people at work.

When you add the sugar, think about the sweetness shared between people.

With every egg you crack, a new, positive potential being is unleashed.

Add the baking powder or baking soda and see your coworkers rising to the top of the situation.

The butter reminds everyone of the richness of diverse per-sonalities.

Chips and sweet additions are the unexpected delights of knowing each other.

Shape the cookies with your fingers; as you do so, alter the real-ity of what you experience at work. Fold it into the shape you desire.

Repeat the incantation as each sheet bakes.

Serve at work with gratitude to your coworkers.

INCANTATION

Ten of Cups
And cookies bake
Joy and love
Are free to take
The happiness
Is spread around
Negativity is banished
To the ground

Stop Nasty Gossip Spell

Today is National Corn Cob Day in the United States. Corn is used for magic involving growth, transformation, or fertility goddesses. To stop gossip, you will construct a corn doll.

INCANTATION
Eight of Swords
Binds and ties
Spread no more rumors
No more lies

Ingredients
- Eight of Swords
- Sharpie marker
- Dried corn cob with husk
- Piece of string

Method, Visualization, and Meditation

This simple spell is created to stop the spread of rumors. It is of utmost important to focus on the binding quality and the effect of the *words* people are saying. You will *not* create a doll representing a specific person and wish them harm. Always remember that what you put out—in magic and in the actions of everyday life—returns to you threefold.

And at the end of the day know that the truth will always surface—and that people have short memories.

Place the Eight of Swords. Enter the card. See the harmful talk and gossip as being inside the figure who is bound. In this instance it will be held until its power loses potency.

Hold the corn cob husk. Pull back the leaves of the husk to reveal the corn underneath. You have exposed the truth.

Using the marker, write "null and void" across the kernels. When you are finished, pull the husk back up while repeating the incantation, then tie the husk tight with string. Place in your freezer for one week.

Outdoor Sigil Magic

Ingredients
- Pen and paper
- Tarot card expressing your desire
- Cornmeal
- Offering of choice

Method, Visualization, and Meditation

The word *sigil* is derived from the Latin word for "seal." Sigils have been employed for magical practices since antiquity.

Cornmeal echoes manifestation and is used in Central and South American magic. Outdoor sigils are still widely used in Haitian Voodoo. Use a pen and paper to articulate your desire and design your sigil. A chosen tarot card will reflect your desire. Choose an appropriate offering: for love, offer chocolate; for money, offer coins; for beauty, offer flowers; for travel, offer tickets.

Use your pen and paper to simply and specifically express your desire. Once you have written it down, cross out all vowels and repeating letters. Using the letters that are left, combine them into a glyph. Play around, making as many sketches as you like in order to find a design that appeals to you.

Once your design is set, select the tarot card that aligns to your intended desire. Meditate on it.

Sigils are best placed in threshold spaces like crossroads, graveyards, groves of trees, or at the foot of a tree. Re-create your sigil design outside on a non-windy day or evening. Using the cornmeal, centering and focusing on your intention, pinch the sigil design out. Create a small hole in the ground inside your sigil and place your offering.

Today is National Magic Day, a perfect day to perform a powerful enchantment. Sigils can be used to call upon a particular god, raise the dead from the underworld, act as a threshold to another world, or to simply manifest your explicit desire.

• • • • •

INCANTATION

Manifestation place of mine
Heart's desire intertwine
Come to pass and come to be
The very thing I want for me

W. B. Yeats was born on this day in 1865. Yeats, one of the twentieth century's most influential poets, was an active member of the Golden Dawn. Like the angel of Temperance, Yeats fused his occult fascination and spirituality with his work.

INCANTATION
Temperance card
Balance, mix
Anything I face
I can fix
Practice makes perfect
You show me how
Life's results
Are different now

Temperance Card Connection Ritual

Ingredient
• Temperance

Method, Visualization, and Meditation
Enter the arcana of Temperance.

You followed the croaking song of frogs and peepers through the fields. Past a line of pines, walking through the fresh dried pine floor, you come into a clearing. There is a pond before you, serene and still on a warm summer day. A clump of green reeds rustles as a startled bird alights from its nest. Water lilies dance back and forth in delight as the bird takes flight.

A white butterfly dances and dips over the placid pond surface. It reflects sunlight, taking shape as a misty vision. You rub your eyes to be sure you aren't dreaming. Hundreds of ruby feathers rustle as the angel extends immense wings. One of the angel's feet touches water but the other touches ground. You understand this posture is meant as a sign. Maintain duality above and below, in this world and the other, in the seen and unseen. The angel holds two cups and pours liquid from one cup to another. A rush like a waterfall roars in your ears from the angel's combinations. He teaches you with his actions to refine and reshape every thought, every action. His energy exchange reminds you of the power you have over your reality.

The angel's silk gown shimmers with an incandescence like the wings of dragonflies. His hair is golden like the sun, sparkling and glowing. A path leads from the root of the pond. You know you must take it.

The only way to take this road is to dive into the water and pass this great being.

You are certain some answer lies at the top of those distant peaks.

Taking a deep breath, you dive into the water...

Third Eye Diamond Spell

Ingredients

- Peppermint oil
- Frankincense incense
- Queen of Cups
- Diamond

Method, Visualization, and Meditation

Peppermint carries an awakening energy. Frankincense is a Jewish holy incense used in pre-biblical times and can be used to encourage psychic energy. The Queen of Cups is the most psychic queen of tarot. She is capable of deep visioning and insight.

You can make excellent use of a personal diamond with this spell. If you do not own a diamond, you may use a clear crystal quartz.

Place a dab of peppermint essential oil on your third eye. Light your incense. As smoke tendrils curl upward, allow your senses to be transported. Let your third eye open. As the smoke spreads to fill the room, so does your vision expand.

Place the Queen of Cups before you. Enter the card and feel the salt sea breeze rush against the baby hairs of your neck. Your feet stand on the wet sand and warm water laps at your toes. The ebb and flow of the great ocean behind you caresses your ankles. The ocean contains a power vast and deep. Its depths are hidden. Only your wildest dreams might begin to comprehend and understand the secrets that it holds.

The Queen of Cups sits holding a chalice. Inside she has scooped magical sea water. Take the cup from her. Its inlaid gold glitters in the sun. The cup is heavy in your hand.

Look inside the cup. What do you see?

Hold the vision clearly in your mind before giving it back to her. Thank her.

Place your diamond over your third eye. Meditate and fill the diamond with your refracted physic energy, and feel the white light inside you expand like a bright explosion of energy.

The Hastings Diamond, a large and uniquely brilliant gem, was presented to King George the Third on this day in 1786. Diamonds reflect the power of light itself. Their high frequency enhances personal creativity and psychic development.

INCANTATION

Queen of Cups
Diamond of depth
Empathy inside
Where once I wept
Help me to vision
Help me to see
Your knowledge is safe
And true with me

The Spiritualist Church was founded by the Lily Dale Assembly today in 1873. Spiritualists train mediums to receive messages from the other side and perform séances.

INCANTATION

[State their name]
Come speak with me
I'd like to see
What you can see
Your wisdom is needed
I want to talk to you
My magical cards
Offer me a clue

Necromantic Tarot Reading

Ingredients
- Wisteria branch
- Grave, burial spot, ashes, a photo, or personal item of the deceased
- Tarot deck

Method, Visualization, and Meditation

Do you ever find yourself talking out loud to someone who has passed? Using tarot, you will receive specific answers back from willing spirits. Tarot cards are an excellent way to communicate with the deceased.

It is said that trees planted over the grave of a loved one can be used as a communication device. Wisteria has been used to communicate with those who have passed.

No matter where you perform this reading, in a graveyard or in your bedroom, it is important to ground yourself and focus before beginning.

Place the wisteria and the personal item before you.

Address the deceased, using your tarot cards to answer back. Ask your questions out loud. Flip cards as your answer.

Talking with the dead can be a tricky business. Everyone is wired differently. Trust your instincts and your inner compass as you converse. Allow yourself to experiment in the beginning until you feel confidant with the process.

When you are finished, take a sea salt bath to cleanse and renew your energy.

Keep Enemies at Bay Spell

Ingredients
- Violet leaves
- Carrier oil (such as olive or canola)
- Justice
- White candle
- Carving tool

Method, Visualization, and Meditation

Violets are the plant of truth. If negativity is close or rumors are spreading, this simple spell should allow the truth to shine through. Justice doles out a fair outcome. White candles purify a situation.

Infuse violet leaves in carrier oil. Strain and cool. Carve a white candle with symbols representing positivity (pregnant belly, flowers, smiling face, etc.) and protection (a peace sign, heart shapes, sigil, etc.). Dress the candle with oil, then light it.

Place your Justice card before you. Enter the card. Expand the image of Justice. Allow her to loom above you five stories in the air, like a great Buddhist statue. Kneel at the steps before her. Bow your head for a moment.

The only justice you can wield is that of being true to yourself. Truth will unfold; the universe works in its own mysterious ways and in its own time. Truth will be revealed; karma reverberates. Know the work, the energy, you emulate will be returned to you. It is not for you to judge others.

What lies behind Justice's curtain? Synchronicity, mystery, invisible hands, and the laws of nature. Know you are protected by the unseen.

Remove the "enemy" from your vocabulary.

Allow the candle to shed the white light of protection around you wherever you step.

Today marks the last major engagement of the War of the Roses in 1487. It was the end of a thirty-year period of war over who would control the throne of England.

INCANTATION

Light of Truth

Balance of Scales

Wicked words

Shrieks and wails

Reject all drama

To the sender return

Protect myself

Leave them to churn

With love and light

And harm to none

I do declare

This spell is done

The Ten of Swords was called the Lord of Ruin by the magicians of the Golden Dawn, who assigned it the time period of June 11–20.

INCANTATION

Ten of Swords, story's
finished, done
Theres other battles to be won
Its over now, forget the past
Don't allow old
narratives to last
Write things fresh,
embrace today
Let old stories slip away.

Ten of Swords Connection Ritual

Ingredient
• Ten of Swords

Method, Visualization, and Meditation
Enter the arcana of the Ten of Swords.

Like icy fingers, a frigid wind pries under your clothes. You pull your coat closer as you observe a bay. Distant mountains rise up to caress the breaking dawn. A newborn sunrise warms their icy peaks and chases away the blackness of night. As the night rolls back willingly, the breaking light illuminates a dastardly scene.

A body lies before you. The pooling blood turns black as it soaks into the thirsty earth. The man's spine has been pierced with ten silver swords. From his sacrum to the soft flesh of his cheek, each chakra is pierced. His hand quivers. He makes a strange sign with his fingers.

"Cut!" yells a voice. A film crew leaps to life around you.

"Great work," yells the director.

"Did you get it on that take?" asks the actor, still lying on the ground.

"Yes, that's a wrap," assures the director.

"What's going on?" you ask.

"We are wrapping a movie," says the actor as assistants pull the fake swords from him.

"A movie?" you ask.

"Yes," he responds. "You see, the entire suit of swords reflects our thoughts, decisions, and calculations. Our thoughts move as quick as the air. Swords are the stories we create about our life, our experiences—our past, present, and future. They are the movie of our life that we see in our head."

"Latte?" asks an assistant, who offers a steaming cup of milk and bitter coffee.

"Yes," you answer. "Thank you."

You take a sip of the coffee. It is delicious. Every person has vanished. You have been left alone with the sunrise. The light caresses your face as you take another sip of the coffee and look at the new day before you.

Picnic Spell for Excellent Health

Ingredients
- Picnic blanket
- Four collected stones
- Healthy lunch
- Tarot deck

Method, Visualization, and Meditation

Ceremonial magic marks out the sacred space where magical operations are performed. The very same thing can be done with a picnic blanket and stones. Pack a lunch and bring it to your favorite outdoor spot on a sunny day. A grove of trees and a place close to running water add wonderful energy.

Collect four stones from the spot you have chosen. Cast your blanket across the ground. Place the first stone in the east and state aloud, "I call to the power of Cups." Place the second stone at the south edge of the blanket and state aloud, "I call to the power of Wands." Place a third stone on the western edge and state aloud, "I call to the power of Pentacles." Place the last stone to the north and state aloud, "I call to the power of Swords."

Shuffle and spread your deck on the center of the blanket. As you shuffle, ask for a card aiding you in achieving all of your health and wellness goals. This will be a card you focus on when engaging in health-related tasks such as shopping and health routines. When you are ready, select one random card. Meditate with it as long as you like to gain full wisdom from it. When you are finished, lie down upon the blanket with arms and legs spread open to contemplate your connection to nature.

Touch each stone and thank the suits for joining you. Enjoy your healthy lunch and finish up by journaling, reading, or performing any pleasant activity. Be aware of any message coming from the natural world, such as birds, animals, or cloud formations.

Today is International Picnic Day, a day to celebrate the pleasurable activity of feasting outdoors with friends and family.

INCANTATION

Grass so green
And trees so tall
Protect my body
Hear my call
Picnic spell
For wealth of health
Let me always be
Super stealth
Find the fastest path to well
By the casting of this spell

The first Father's Day celebration took place today in 1910.

Father's Day Spell

Ingredients
1. The Emperor
2. Page (pick one representing you)
3. Temperance
- Cinnamon chai tea

Method, Visualization, and Meditation

Forgiveness is the cornerstone of any relationship. Perform this spell to open the channels of communication and forgiveness between you and your father figure.

The Emperor reflects the Father archetype. Choose the page whose temperament most suits yours: Cups for your emotional, creative self; Wands for your passionate, fiery self; Swords for your analytical, intellectual side; Pentacles for your practical, productive side. Temperance reflects the balance of energies between you and your father. Chai tea activates warmth and compassion.

Place the Emperor before you. Enter the card. Smell the cinnamon and cardamom incense that burns at his throne. This warrior is capable of a love that can nurture or destroy in a single look. An orange landscape surrounds him. The peaks and valleys, the rivers that run underneath—this is the emotional landscape he created for you knowingly and unknowingly.

Place your page card next to him. This card embodies you. Enter the card. Consider all of the good and negative ways that he helped you to become this page.

Place the Temperance card between the two cards. Feel the energy that moves between the two of you. What color is it? Turn it the color white in order to cleanse it.

Discard Temperance and place your page card upon the Emperor, covering him up. Your father is not an emperor at all but a child, as we all are; infallible, imperfect, and finding our way with each passing day. Forgive him. Forgive the hurts he placed upon you and passed onto you.

Sip your tea and write a letter or journal if needed.

INCANTATION

Emperor, father
Man from who I came
I'm willing to let go
Of my anger
Are you game?
I open the way
Let go of fear
Forgiveness is granted
My conscious is clear

1   3   2

Ritual to Connect with Summer

Ingredients
- The Sun
- Favorite summer items and symbols

Method, Visualization, and Meditation

Working with seasonal energy is like working within the moon's phases. The energy surrounds around us; we need only to be open to it in order to access its gifts. The energetic qualities of summer include expression, vitality, harmony, contentedness, and celebration.

Gather seasonal energy like a weaver gathering silken strands. Sultry nights, plump stone fruits, wildflowers, fresh vegetables plucked from the garden, lazy days of swimming and frolicking, and tangerine pink sunsets support you and your magical intent.

Collect your favorite summer objects to place around the Sun card. You might select your fresh-picked flowers, suntan lotion, scattered flower petals, seashells, glitter, lemons. Place all items around the Sun card and then enter the card.

The warmth of this card is echoed in the warmth outside your window. What is the child looking at in the card? Turn your attention around so you can see the lush bounty blossoming behind you. Examine the stone wall; run your palms across it. This wall is the natural barrier of what you have known and experienced in your life. You see the sunflowers growing beyond it. This is the undiscovered, uncultivated possibility that exists for you. Walk to the flowers and hold them in your hand; stroke the inside of them with your finger. Acknowledge the wild magic of the unknown and unexpected that will burst forth in your life by keeping an open mind and heart.

This space is the result of your passion, work, and personal exuberance. Bask in the glory you have created. Explore into the card as far as you can go on your own.

The fire and water festival of Litha coincides with the summer solstice and is celebrated between June 20–24. Love and romance spells are well cast at this time of year. Summer aligns with full moon energy.

INCANTATION

Summer sun
Expansion bright
Warmth, growth
And filled with light
Blossom, bloom
All things grow
And in my heart
I always know
The seeds I plant
Will come to be
And fill my life
With joy and glee

Invoke Empathy for an Annoying Person Spell

Today is the first day of the astrological sign Cancer, the Crab, who is known to embrace all realms of human emotion. As such, Cancers act as natural empaths. Break your cycle of annoyance with this gentle spell, transforming annoyance into compassion.

INCANTATION

Compassion is what
I feel for you
I won't get angry
I'll make do
You are human, after all
No one's perfect
We all can fall
You affect me no more
And I open a brand-new door

Ingredients
- The Chariot
- Clear glass bowl of water
- Photo or sketch of person or their name on paper

Method, Visualization, and Meditation

This is a helpful spell when you are annoyed with someone who you can't avoid contact with. This includes coworkers, family members, etc.

Place the Chariot before you. Imagine what it means to travel the human psyche. Inside the chariot you can move from your highest high to your lowest low in a flash. Consider the speed with which our emotions color our actions. How often do we allow our emotional landscapes to motivate our actions?

From this moment forward, you will control your chariot by acting how you decide, not how you feel.

Place the photo, sketch, or name of the person before you and put the bowl of water over it. Looking through the water, feel their emotional state. Understand they are as emotional as you. They are only human. Accept that you have projected many of your own issues onto them.

Utter the incantation.

Sensitive Breakup Spell

Ingredients
1. Knight of Wands
2. Page of Pentacles
- Black beans

Method, Visualization, and Meditation

The Knight of Wands reflects the "breakee." The Page of Pentacles reflects your present reality. Black beans will banish.

Place the Knight of Wands before you. See the person in question moving away from you. They do so quietly, by their own accord and with no drama, yet the Knight of Wands is fiery and passionate. This person moving away from you searches for someone or something else to focus their attention on. Their attention is no longer on you.

Place the Page of Pentacles in front of you. Consider your new reality. You have taken what you needed from the relationship. The pentacle represents knowledge gained. By holding the seed and looking at the situation dead in the eye, you will not repeat any patterns or holdovers from the last relationship. You have learned your lessons. You will move on.

In your mind's eye picture your gentle breakup. Find kind words and eloquence. Slowly begin to move the cards apart from each other.

Picture your soon-to-be-ex partner standing in front of you. Take the beans and begin walking backwards. Toss the beans on your footsteps as you go. Take exactly twenty-one steps backwards, seven times three for luck, and repeat the incantation.

King Henry VIII separated from his first wife, Catherine of Aragon, on this day in 1527. Henry's beheaded wives wouldn't say he was the sensitive or judicious type. We all must face severing bonds sometimes. This spell fosters kindness in the deed.

INCANTATION

I release you
[Repeat with each step]

1	2

1	←	2

Tonight is St. John's Eve, celebrated with purifying bonfires. Herbs collected on this night are thought to contain the height of their botanical richness.

INCANTATION

Inherited patterns

Slice you away

Banish from my life

Today

You've hurt me

Plagued me all along

As of today

This curse is gone

Remove a Family Curse Spell

Ingredients
- Pen and paper
1. The Devil
2. Queen of Swords sideways
3. Two of Swords
4. King of Swords sideways
5. Ace of Swords reversed
- Chamomile leaves, flowers, or tea

```
        [5]
[2]  [1]  [4]
        [3]
```

Method, Visualization, and Meditation

Have you inherited a family narrative, story, habit, or way of being that is inauthentic to who you are? Free yourself and future generations to write their own stories rather than repeat history. The Devil card represents the inherited curse. The Swords cards are all used as weapons to slice away the curse so that you may be set free. Sprinkled chamomile adds a boundary of protection.

Write down specifically what your "curse" and family story is. Write about how you have unconsciously played this out for yourself and how it is reflected in other family members. Attempt to articulate the curse in a single sentence. After you have composed the sentence, imagine the curse as a tangible symbol, a symbol you can hold and see. See it clearly.

Place the Devil card before you. Ingest the imagery. See the Devil holding the symbol of your family curse. It has been a powerful force in your life but no longer poses any threat. It is about to be dissipated. Bid your curse and the Devil goodbye.

Place the Queen of Swords to the left, her sword piercing into the Devil card. She represents the analytic power and ferocity to deflate the curse. Place the meditative Two of Swords. Her swords both pierce the Devil and the curse on deep, profound levels. Place the King of Swords. He attacks the curse from the east and renders it powerless. To seal your spell, place the Ace of Swords. This sword slices through and dissipates the curse once and for all.

Nature Guide Spell

Ingredients
- Secluded spot in nature
- The Hermit

Method, Visualization, and Meditation

Nature guides are the energies found in the natural landscape. They can be found inside the energy of a creature, animal, rock, or element such as water or wind. You have the power to connect, mingle, and gain insight and wisdom from them.

Go to your favorite secluded spot in nature. It may be beneath a willow tree, inside a grove of trees, or in a meadow. Bring the Hermit card with you. When you are ready, place your awareness inside the card.

See the Hermit lifting his lantern. Move time backwards. See him moving in reverse, climbing down the mountain and going back to his space of solitude. You are surprised to discover he journeys to the very spot in which you sit.

Hold your arm before you and see the imaginary lantern in your hand. The glowing star inside your lantern acts as an attraction element. It is bringing a nature guide close to you. Hold the star until a nature guide makes contact with you.

Once this happens, welcome and communicate with your guide for as long as you like. Thank it when you are finished. Honor the experience by adding images of this spirit in your home, making it offerings and regularly communing with it. You need only raise your glowing lantern to bring it to your side.

Today is Midsummer's Day, the exact middle of summer. Originally a Pagan holiday to mark the mid-season, Christianity took hold and stated this was the night where witches danced and conferred with powerful otherworldly beings. What an excellent excuse to prove them right.

INCANTATION

Nature guide
Where can you be
Make yourself
Available to me
Remind me of mysteries
I've long forgot
And grace me with
The highest thought

King of Swords Connection Ritual

Antoni Gaudí, famed architect of Barcelona, Spain, was born on this day in 1852. His extraordinary architecture defines the very essence of the King of Swords, a personality who can communicate his vision perfectly and has the strength to transform the look of an entire city.

INCANTATION
King of Swords
Wind of thought
Bind me to you
Tie the knot
Protection, fierceness
Strong and fierce
I feel the winds that
Through me pierce

Ingredient
• King of Swords

Method, Visualization, and Meditation
Enter the arcana of the King of Swords.

The north wind begins with his breath. It is he who sends the frost in the air. He who compels pollen to fly. He who cools the slick sweat in the heat of summer with a gentle breeze. He confuses the mind, billows curtains, and gives voice to the trees, whose rustling leaves whisper. While he commands June's tornadoes and cyclones, he intentionally lies dormant and invisible during the long, lazy days of August. He is the breath of the planet.

He sits in the cold and crisp kingdom of the north. Pine and evergreen scrubs quiver in the wind, which rises and falls in the mind of this clever king. The color of his cloak suggests a passionate past tucked away. His solar crown reflects the glory of illumination from above and the wisdom that can be gained only by experience. Though he has the ability to command the wind at will, he allows it to freely flow. He knows things are better left to their own nature and only sometimes encouraged and egged along.

Birds call to each other, daring each other to rise higher. This represents the king's inner thoughts. His sword is crafted from the finest steel; his blade, the sharpest ever made, matches the quality of his wit. His face is serious as he presides over matters of great import.

This king is you and you are this king. You invoke him when you think and speak with authority—when you hold great power but don't necessarily wield it. He is you in your most direct, calculated, and precise moments.

Ace of Wands Connection Ritual

Ingredients
- Ace of Wands
- Fire accessories such as candle, red rocks, red or orange cloth

Method, Visualization, and Meditation

Enter the arcana of the Ace of Wands.

Walk through a warm, lazy summer Tuscan landscape. The heat of summer has begun its sultry dance. It brings the valley to life around you. An ancient rock castle stands in the distance. Delicious hickory smoke catches your attention, and you see a campfire burning. Roasting delicacies turn on a spit over the flames. The fire crackles and pops. You watch as the flames consume the kindling sticks. You place another bunch of kindling on top, and the hungry flames leap to devour them.

You think about the quality of fire as you watch the flames. Fire provides energy to cook food, light the darkness, and generate heat. Consider the heat that rises in your skin when you stand close to a person you are attracted to. Recall the flush of excitement when engaged in a beloved activity.

Clouds build in the sky before you like an oncoming storm. Rain does not fall from these clouds. A giant hand emerges from the cloud and takes up the enormity of the sky. The vision is revealed to you. It is the root of all Fire.

The white, glowing hand is the hand of magic, synchronicity, and mystery. It holds a stick with shedding leaves. As each leaf sheds, a new one grows, repeatedly regenerating itself. You see immediately that this is a magic wand. It holds the power of fire, the energy of passion. Like an engine, the element of fire drives manifestation.

The wand is now yours. What shall you do with it?

As the solstice season approaches, connect with the element of fire with the Ace of Wands.

INCANTATION

Ace of wands
And root of flame
Bring passion
To my life again
I point you like
A laser beam
To manifest
My wildest dream

Helen Keller—activist, author, and the first blind and deaf woman to earn a bachelor's degree—was born on this day in 1880.

INGREDIENTS
- Hard-boiled egg with shell
- Cutting board
- Knife
- Paper towel
- Sriracha or red pepper hot sauce
- Candle
- Emperor card
- Black eyeliner

Spell to See What Others Do Not

Method, Visualization, and Meditation

"Sight" is the esoteric function of the Emperor card as assigned by the Golden Dawn. Primitive magical belief holds that by ingesting an object you will obtain its power. For this spell you shall ingest an egg and gain its symbolic value. You will gain insight and also access the limitless potential that exists inside an unfertilized egg.

Under the blanket of night, collect and prepare all items, including a cutting board, knife and paper towel for your egg. Light the candle and gaze into the Emperor card. Enter the card and become the Emperor. The environment is hot, fiery orange, glowing with the embers of powerful masculinity. He sits atop a throne and surveys his kingdom. His empire was built through victory—some small, some large, but all the sum of his life's work. Recall personal victories, the places you have made yours, both physical and emotional. Let your mind's eye roam to the corners of your known universe. What does your personal kingdom look like? The Emperor sees beyond his boundaries. Push your vision further. Where are your boundaries? See past them.

Crack the shell of the egg. You are cracking through the thin veil of perceived reality. You are cracking your code, breaking down walls so you will see further. Slice the egg in half lengthwise. It looks like two eyes. Place a dot of Sriracha sauce to make a red pupil on the center of each yellow iris/yolk. These are the eyes of the Emperor. Ingest these eyes. Doing so, concentrate on seeing past every boundary, around every curve. Your sight is far reaching.

Meditate as long as you like with your card and candle. Use the eyeliner to draw a black dot on your third eye chakra. Sleep with this. Let it remind you upon waking that you possess the sight of the Emperor.

Find a New Job Spell

Ingredients
1. Seven of Pentacles
2. Eight of Pentacles
3. Nine of Pentacles

Method, Visualization, and Meditation

The makeup of this spell appears like the past-present-future tarot spread. The numerical sequence of seven, eight, and nine contains the luck of the seven, accomplishment of the eight, and the wish fulfillment of the number nine.

Place the Seven of Pentacles before you and observe the abundance below the farmer. His sweat labor has paid off. His crops bloom and burst with life. Each hanging globe represents an accomplishment. You have done the same. Look at your accomplishments. Think of all you have done. Congratulate yourself.

Place the Eight of Pentacles. See yourself happily at work at your new job. You are working with materials you enjoy; your work is on display for others to see. The bench represents the support you are given to do your best. The vest represents the marked difference between your work life and home life. This adds a lovely contrast of pleasure in both sectors.

Place the Nine of Pentacles. See the results of your hard work resulting in the expression of who you are. Your work sets you up for future security and your job feeds your heart and soul. All of these elements add to the happiness of your relationships and home life.

1   2   3

Labor Day became a federal holiday on this day in 1894. It was created to celebrate the economic and social contribution of the American worker.

INCANTATION

Job for me
Open the gate
Let me see
Reveal yourself
Allow me in
Prizes of success
Are mine to win
Do what I love
I do my best
I shine bright
And forget the rest

June • 29

London's Globe Theater burned to the ground on this day in 1613. The Tower card is reflected when unexpected tragedy throws everything into chaos.

INCANTATION

Things destroyed
They break and tear
Something familiar
Is not there
Nothing you see
Is built to last
Just look at history's
Pages past
Embrace and welcome
In the new
Is all that we
Can ever do

Tower Card Connection Ritual

Ingredient
• The Tower

Method, Visualization, and Meditation
Enter the arcana of the Tower.

Night has fallen, and your hair blows wildly about your face. You see the storm coming. The vantage point from high in these mountains affords you a view stretching a hundred miles by the light of day. You cling to the perch you have discovered for fear of the incredible force that might whisk you away.

Sand and rocks slip beneath your feet. A small cavern looms behind you, offering generous shelter. The lightning storm draws closer. The shelter is dark and damp, but you are grateful to sit inside.

Across the craggy ravine a great tower has been constructed, and it reaches toward the sky.

The storm roars in like a freight train, the sound of wind like rusty brakes on frozen rails. White lightning strikes alight the landscape, flashing before your eyes. Raindrops, fat and wet, burst at your feet. You retreat farther inside your cave, not sure if the wetness of your cheeks is the splashing rain or your own tears.

An unfamiliar sound is heard amidst the thunder deafening your eardrums. It is human wailing. Despair and fear echo through the canyon as you see the unturned body of a human falling through the air like a brick. Their garments flap and their cry becomes softer as they fall to the valley below. Another body, and another, until soon there are as many people as raindrops falling from the sky. You dare not look below, where the dark mounds grow higher.

A white streak explodes the top of the distant tower. It crashes down the cliff, shooting showers of sparks as it collides with rock. The storm clouds dissipate as flickering flames lick the top of the tower.

Everything you think you knew no longer exists.

Moon Bewitchment Spell

Ingredients
- Visible moon
- The High Priestess

Today is National Full Moon Day.

Method, Visualization, and Meditation

The High Priestess card is indicative of lunar energy and the synergy of connection to a waxing and waning moon.

On a night where you can spy the moon, remove your High Priestess card from the deck.

Enter the card with your mind's eye. Step before this beautiful moonlit creature. See her luminescent skin, which is lit by the moon from the inside. She resonates with lunar power.

Gaze at her. Know that she reflects the unspoken parts of yourself. Every piece of you is reflected in this card. No one other individual walks on this earth with your particular blend of beauty, knowledge, and mystery. Every unique cell in your body has merged to create you. You are a secret that can never be told. You are a truth that can only be guessed. You are a mystery that can never be unraveled. Communicate with your High Priestess and express to her what quality you desire from the moon.

Stand naked in the moonbeams. Go through the motions of washing oneself in the moon's rays as you would in water. While doing so, absorb all the mystery and moonlight into your skin. Allow her mysterious and beautiful energy to soak into you.

INCANTATION

Glow of moon
Beams of light
Shine beauty across
And inside tonight
My eyes
Are nothing like the sun
The mystery
Has just begun

Two of Cups Connection Ritual

The Two of Cups was called the Lord of Love by the magicians of the Golden Dawn, who assigned it the time period of June 21–July 1.

Ingredient
- Two of Cups

Method, Visualization, and Meditation

Enter the arcana of the Two of Cups.

You have entered the space of division. One has become two. In this space of duality, the Cup has become aware of itself. Context is provided by means of a second. Opposition is born. Oppositional tension creates a new energy.

A man and woman are engaged in a solemn ceremony. Is it a marriage? A promise? A red lion head floating above the couple snarls at you, warning you to stay back. The lion's head is flanked by giant red feathered wings that keep him afloat. Below him two snakes wind themselves around a stake.

Become the woman in the card. Look at the man through her eyes.

You realize she is an actress performing a marriage scene. You see the darkened wings on the stage. A stage manager watches, absentmindedly chewing on a toothpick, waiting for the scene to finish. The director walks up.

"Listen," he says to you. "If you want to get to the heart of this scene, you have to look at him as if he is the love of your life."

You look at the actor. He grimaces at you. His breath smells like dog food. You'd rather run in the other direction.

The director continues. "Have you ever met another person you felt immediately at ease with? So comfortable it's like you've known the person your entire life?"

"Yes," you answer, thinking of your true love.

"Have you ever performed an activity and said, to yourself, 'this is what I am meant to do?'" he asks.

"Yes," you answer, recalling your favorite thing to do.

"That is the heart of this scene, okay?" He looks at you intensely. "Can you do it?"

"Yes," you say.

You begin...

INCANTATION

Two of Cups
Once one, now two
Duality, division
The pairing is new
Clink of cups
Exchange of bliss
Feels free and true
As love's first kiss

Snap Spell to Change a Mood

Ingredients
- The Devil
- Your fingers (which you will snap seven times)
- The World

Method, Visualization, and Meditation

The Devil card represents the dark and tumultuous emotions raging in your psyche. He represents being a slave to your emotions and habits, feeling out of control. Seven is a magical number, representing the days of the week, seven visible planets, seven continents, and seven deadly sins. People asked to choose a number between 1 and 10 usually pick 7; try it. The World card reflects the freedom and grace available in every moment.

This is a quick spell, once mastered. Perform it when you've hit a lull or are suffering through a bad day.

Place the Devil card in front of you. Gaze at his ornery face. Dive deeply into the depths of your bleak mood. Why is he rumbling inside you? Why are you feeling this way? Have you relinquished control like the chained figures? Does your mood give you a false sense of power? Is anger burning like the flames of the Devil's torch? Do tasty treats like the purple grapes on the female's tail seem constantly out of reach? Does it feel like some great force is bearing down upon you? If possible, come to a conclusion regarding the base of your mood before proceeding.

Snap your fingers seven times.

Place the World card over the Devil, completely blocking him out and obliterating him.

Focus on the world dancer's athletic body. She is purity of freedom, form, and spirit. The four creatures in the corner manifest as opportunities in the field of pure potential, appearing when the mind is quieted and the eyes are opened, gazing outwards. The two magical wands in her hands are the mastery of the self, the loss of ego, and freedom from emotion. You have achieved this state. Begin again.

Today marks the exact halfway point of the calendar year. It is the day 183, and there are 183 days until New Year's Eve.

INCANTATION

Seven, seven, magic thing
My snaps the magic
That you bring
My mood is gone
And peace prevails
I move light as the
World dancer's veils
To freedom, peace
And opportunity
Nothing but calm and
Beauty do I see

1 ← 2

INCANTATION

Green, green

Green cash

Credit, mortgage

Financial stash

I am stable

Plant my seed

Have more than

I ever need

Spell for Financial Security

Ingredients
- Yam
- 4 pennies
- Sprig of mint
1. Justice
2. Four of Pentacles
3. Ten of Pentacles
4. The Magician

```
        [ 1 ]

[ 2 ]         [ 3 ]

        [ 4 ]
```

Method, Visualization, and Meditation

Yams are sacred to the Nigerian goddess of protection, Inna. Pennies are the essential denominator of finance, associated with number 1 and the Magician card. Mint brings money. The Justice card's esoteric function is work. The Four of Pentacles reflects financial stability. The Ten of Pentacles represents complete material manifestation. The Magician is an energetic channel.

Wash the yam under running water. Consider its baptismal effect and feel cleansed by this action. Dry the yam. Using a knife, cut four slits in its orange flesh. Across each slit place a mint leaf. Stuff each leaf inside the yam, using a penny. Stuff the entire penny inside the yam.

Place the Justice card. Universal energy works on your behalf. The actions you put out are matched and magnified by the life force. Justice's sword channels high source energy. Her other hand brings it down to you. Place the Four of Pentacles. Consider what you already have. Consider your needs already met. You lay the groundwork for stability.

Place the Ten of Pentacles. Ingest all the riches offered within the framework of this card. Let the pentacles peel away from the card and become affixed to your soul. You will never want for any financial thing. The gentleman on the card is your wisest self. What message does he offer you?

Place the Magician. His posture is akin to Justice. He channels energy into the material world. You attract money without even realizing you are doing so. Bury the penny yam in your yard as a symbol of security. If you have no yard, place in a public park.

Independence Spell

Ingredients
1. Eight of Swords
2. The Fool
3. The World

Independence Day is celebrated today in the United States.

Method, Visualization, and Meditation

Acts of independence can feel uncomfortable, even downright scary. The trick is to let the fear move through you rather than letting the fear move you. Make sense?

The Eight of Swords represents a transformative cocoon. The Fool reflects a new beginning. The World card's nirvana reflects the result of facing a fear and moving through it.

Place the Eight of Swords. Though the figure is comfortable and wrapped, she cannot stay inside of her bondage. Once useful, the white ties are now binding, keeping you from being truly self-sufficient. Unravel them.

Place the Fool. See yourself breaking free. The sky has opened, the sun is bright. You are vulnerable walking as the Fool, but you walk anyway. The dog nips at your heels like resonant fear but you laugh, push away your trepidation, and forge ahead, performing the required actions.

Place the World card. Experience nirvana. You have faced your fears and taken care of yourself. As a result, the world has opened up for you. Possibility manifests everywhere, and you choose the most delightful choices. You hold two powerful wands of magic. You are immersed in the beauty that is the ebb and flow of all creation.

INCANTATION
The Fool, the Fool
To be a Fool
Do not fear
It's super cool
To trod my path
And live my life
Steering away from
Darkness and strife
I will do it!

1   2   3

The bikini made its debut today in 1946 at a fashion show held at the ritzy Molitor Pool in Paris.

Comfortable in My Skin Spell

Ingredients
  1. The Empress
  2. The Star

Method, Visualization, and Meditation

You are the proud owner of your body. You should feel amazing in it and grateful for it. Your body is yours for life.

The Empress reflects your physical body. The Star card reflects what you channel through your body.

Place the Empress card. Move inside the card and take her position. Inhabit her body so it becomes your body. How does it feel to inhabit the Empress's body? How many amazing physical gifts has your body given to the world. How many hugs? How many kisses? How many soft caresses? Has your body created babies? How much physical pleasure has your body provided you? How delicious is the food you enjoy? How delightful is it to listen to your favorite music? How often have you shuddered under your lover's touch? How many landscapes, sunsets, seascapes, snowscapes have made you swoon with delight when your eyes saw them? How many times has your voice served you well? How well have you expressed yourself or sung out loud in delight? How often have you danced with abandon? Your body is your temple of delight and love. It is every way in which you experience the physical world.

Place the Star card before you. Move inside the card and take her position. Inhabit the Star's body so her body becomes yours. Your physical body opens to the metaphysical space above, below, around, and inside. Every molecule in your body hums with the electricity of the stars. You are beautiful. You are luminescent. You are eternal. You are greater than the sum of your physical parts. You are a goddess.

INCANTATION

Place of rest
My bones and skin
My body's the place
I wake up in
I worship you, find delight
Don't hide away; I shine bright
Treat it well
With love and health
Repays me with
Ultimate wealth
I am alive!

French Kiss Spell

Ingredients
- Red lipstick
- Paper and pen
- The Lovers

Method, Visualization, and Meditation

Lips are the gateway of sensuality—the space from which we state our desire, the place where we taste our lover. When we lock lips with a special someone, they send our bodies into overdrive. Lips send a chemical cocktail to the brain that causes surges of excitement and amour.

Apply red lipstick to your lips. Kiss a piece of blank paper once for a clear lip print. Write the name of your lover (or desired lover) inside the lip print.

Place the Lovers card before you. Step inside the body of the woman. Feel the heat of the sun radiate from the card. See your beloved standing across from you. Their eyes move up and down your naked body. Your own eyes return the favor.

Repeat the incantation.

See them walking to you. Feel their embrace.

To close the spell, send this person a message via text, email, telephone, or old-fashioned love letter. Perhaps you find them and whisper a sweet nothing in their ear. If you are drawing a new person or a potential yet unknown lover, write "welcome" on a leaf and release it into the wind.

Want to invoke summer romance? Summer's heat is settling in for the long haul. Make the most of it with a spicy love spell that relishes smoldering energy. Nothing feels, tastes, or looks as good as aligning with summer love energy.

• • • • •

INCANTATION

Lover, lover
Come to me
With my lips
I sing to thee
A song so sweet
You can't deny
In the shadows
Come and lie
Beside me breathing
Naked still
You come to me
It is my will

Harry Houdini performed his first handcuffed escape in New York City on this day in 1912.

. . . . .

INCANTATION

Houdini magic

Escape plan

Away from you

I jumped and ran

Never again

It's finished

I'm done

Freedom's sweetest

When hard won

Houdini's Escape a Bad Situation Spell

Ingredients
1. Eight of Swords
2. Nine of Wands
3. Card representing desired outcome

Method, Visualization, and Meditation

Houdini's trick to escaping straight jackets came from puffing his body up. He expanded himself before he was bound in the straight jacket. He kept his arms crossed rather than folded across his chest. Once upside down, he used gravity and the extra expansion room to free himself.

Give yourself the expansion and room to change a suffocating situation. The Eight of Swords reflects the ties that bind. The Nine of Wands represents a new opportunity. Choose a card describing your ultimate outcome.

Place all three cards facedown before you.

Close your eyes. In your mind's eye expand the energy of your body. Lengthen your spine. Allow your head to float. Plant your feet firmly on the floor. Breathe in deeply. With each breath, expand the boundaries of your body. Perform until you feel you have expanded your body to twice the size.

Reveal the Eight of Swords. Enter the card. Become the figure, experience the heart of your current situation, and feel its binds. See what you have caught. Turn the card upside down. Allow the energy you have built up to release from you. Collapse your physical body in on itself. Wriggle free from the confining binds. Walk away from what trapped you.

Flip the Nine of Wands and see yourself walking through an opened door. The bandage on your head marks the scar of remembrance. You will never repeat a situation like this.

Flip the third card. Embrace your new reality.

| 1 | 2 | 3 |

Success in Business Spell

Ingredients
- 13-inch cord or rope
1. Ace of Wands
2. The Magician
3. Ten of Pentacles

Method, Visualization, and Meditation

The ancient art of knot magic secures your desire. The Ace of Wands represents the genesis of your business. The Magician card represents successful execution. The Ten of Pentacles depicts extraordinary financial abundance empowering you, your employees, and your family.

Place the Ace of Wands before you. Recall your business as you originally conceived it—the brilliant idea you have now made a reality. It blazes with the fire of your originality and passion.

Place the Magician. He holds the Ace of Wands in his left hand, using it to channel energy. You manifest your vision. The tools on his table reflect all the tools you have to make your success a reality. You understand the nature of your desired outcome. It is time to direct your intention. You begin.

Place the Ten of Pentacles below the Magician. Your project is launched. Its effects are far reaching. You see the multiplication of finance; your money grows as time passes. The web of genius is spreading. Your wealth and success affects and empowers all those around you.

Tie nine knots in a thirteen-inch cord while repeating the incantation.

INCANTATION

Knot of one, business begun
Knot of two, this is a coup
Knot of three brings luck to me
Knot of four, prosperity at my door
Knot of five, come alive
Knot of six, strong like bricks
Knot of seven feels like heaven
Knot of eight, reward is great
Knot of nine, success is mine!

1

2

3

197

The first open heart surgery was performed on this day in 1893, without anesthesia. Tarot serves as a reminder that all facets of life are worth living, even the painful ones. Every one of life's events may be used for personal evolution.

INCANTATION

Magic magic
Three, six, and nine
Rejuvination, you are mine
Can't destroy me
I survive still
Nothing breaks my iron will
Three plus three
Is six, then nine
Happiness forever mine

Mend a Broken Heart Spell

Ingredients
1. Three of Swords
2. Six of Swords
3. Nine of Cups
4. The Fool

Method, Visualization, and Meditation

The Three of Swords represents a shattered heart. The Six of Swords represents moving through a painful time. The Nine of Cups is the heart's desire granted. The Fool card reflects new beginnings.

Place the Three of Swords. Enter the card. Open up and allow the feelings of pain to move through you. Let emotion flow freely. Acknowledge the storm clouds and rain. Look at the tender tissues of your heart. Fresh air blows the storm away. In your mind's eye, using both hands, pull the first sword free, placing it next to you. Remove the second sword and the third. Let the heart float away in the wind. The storm is passing. Gather your swords.

Place the Six of Swords. Enter the card. Place your swords in the boat. Carry your lessons with you. The cold steel of the blades did not pierce you in vain. You use them to move forward. Take the helm of the boat and look across the river. See where you are going. Feel the boat beneath you as you push off from shore and head in a brand-new direction. You have secured safe passage.

Place the Nine of Pentacles. You have arrived at your true destination. You are safe in a protected garden where animal totems surround you. Your wounds are healed. You are strong and beautiful for the experience.

Place the Fool across all three cards while uttering the incantation.

Three of Cups Connection Ritual

Ingredient
• Three of Cups

Method, Visualization, and Meditation
Enter the arcana of the Three of Cups.

A new possibility has been born from two. Threes are the sacred triad of manifestation. A third option has emerged. This is the birth of creativity from the tiniest grain of sand to the farthest galaxy in the known universe.

Soft grass tickles your feet. Citrusy lemon, lime, and pomegranate trees scent the air. Three beautiful maidens frolic before you. Their singing and laughing moves through the air like delicate chimes on the breeze. They dance in a vineyard as if it were a grape-crushing festival.

The latent heat of late summer sustains the ripeness of both females and fruit. The girls raise their chalices. Dancing with graceful glee, they move under a blanket of youth, unaware of their beauty, thinking only of their present delight. Wildflowers are woven in their plaited hair, which shines like silk in the afternoon light. Their loose garments burn with the colors of the sun, red and yellow, the color of passionate flames. Soft slippers move in circles across the grass as they dance. Bursting pumpkins and deep purple grapes are clutched by a maiden, signaling there is more wine to come.

The scene echoes the trifold effects of gifts of the heart. Offering oneself to another creates a butterfly effect that ripples beyond what can be imagined. This joyful card reminds us to give to another what we wish to receive for ourselves. The fastest way to experience love and joy is to give to others. Give and you shall receive.

The Three of Cups was called the Lord of Abundance by the magicians of the Golden Dawn, who assigned it the time period of July 2–11.

• • • • • •

INCANTATION
Three of Cups
Dancing girls
There's joy and freedom
In your whirls
Take your cue
Tiptoe with joy
I'll play my life
Like it's a toy

Bringing or Banishing Bridge Spell

The Triborough Bridge, connecting three New York City boroughs, opened on this day in 1936.

Ingredients
- Four of Wands (attract) or
- Five of Cups (banish)

Method, Visualization, and Meditation
We generally take bridges for granted, as we do cars, planes, and many modern conveniences. Imagine traveling two hundred years ago by foot or horse and having to cross a giant river with no bridge in sight.

Bridges are ripe with lore, grumpy old trolls, and billy goats. They can display fabulous feats of engineering. Bridges loom metaphorically in our minds and mark specific places of passage. Trials and tribulations are often implied at bridges. Consider the phrase "We'll cross that bridge when we get to it." Travelers were often ambushed on bridges. What lurks under a bridge is also symbolic.

Attraction Magic
To manifest a desire, stand on the side of the bridge where water rushes toward you. Focus on the Four of Wands (Pamela Colman Smith places a bridge on her card). Feel the card's celebratory nature. Consider the reasons you want to attract this particular thing into your life. Picture it in your mind's eye. See, feel, and hear the roaring water rushing toward you. With every drop plunging in your direction, allow your heart's desire to race toward you.

Banishing Magic
To banish something from your life, stand on the side of the bridge where the water flows away from you. Focus on the Five of Cups (Pamela Colman Smith places a bridge on her card). Feel the sadness of the card. Consider what should be banished from your life. Picture it clearly. See, feel, and hear the roaring waters rushing away from you. With every drop plunging away from you, feel the item in question leaving you.

INCANTATION
Four of Wands and
Rushing stream
See you [state desire]
Grant my dream

Or

Five of Cups
Water wash away
Banish [state desire]
From me today

Death Card Connection Ritual

Ingredient
- Death

Method, Visualization, and Meditation

Enter the arcana of Death.

The familiar image of a white skeleton races across the card. People are terrified; he instills fear as he moves.

"Stop," you yell at him as he approaches a child.

He is shocked to hear your voice. His hollow head turns in your direction, his dark sockets bearing upon you.

"What are you doing?" you ask.

"My job," he replies, taking a step toward you.

"Your job is to kill people?" you ask.

"I kill no one. Nothing lasts forever. I simply remind people of the nature of the physical world. All physical things will cease to inhabit their form."

"What happens to the people inside the bodies?" you ask.

"They move into another state. Released from their physical bonds, they become what they were before they were here. You know this. You simply have chosen to forget."

"Why did I forget?" you ask.

"So you can experience this physical world. You let yourself be fooled. When you see an old man, do you see the infant, the toddler, the teenager he once was? No, you see only his exterior. People are betrayed by their eyes and do not see the truth that is right in front of them."

"What is the truth?"

"That you are all luminous beings. You are all energy. You are all one. I exist to keep your physical world in check so you can learn and relearn this lesson. Please step aside. I have work to do."

Today, Northern Ireland celebrates the 1688 Glorious Revolution in which King James II of England was overthrown. A toppled king is seen upon the Death card, and this day lends itself to close inspection of death.

INCANTATION

Death card, you signal change
And kiss my lips
I tease you with
My supple hips
Angel of Death
To me be true
I promise to embrace
The change of you

July • 13

John Dee, Queen Elizabeth's astrologer and friend, was born on this day in 1527. Dee practiced divination openly during his life. His scrying stone is available for public observation at the British Museum in London.

INCANTATION

Temperance card

And water still

Enhance my vision

Grant my will

See the truth and

Knowledge gain

Images dance across

The reflective plain

Scrying with Temperance

Ingredients

- Temperance
- A pond, lake, or still body of water

Method, Visualization, and Meditation

Scrying is the art of divination upon a smooth and reflective surface. It can be done with mirrors, crystals, or even a bowl of water. The mind is given the freedom to roam across the surface. Messages are often received. Scrying is a subtle art. Never rush a message. It is impossible to know or understand the process fully until you attempt it.

The Temperance card will help you get into the mind space of scrying. The mind space you inhabit when "entering" a tarot card is the same utility with which you will want to scry. You will focus first on the Temperance card, then scry upon your chosen reflective surface.

Enter your Temperance card. Note how the angel channels energy between the two cups. The continuous exchange of energy builds endurance, sharpens skills, and makes something shine with excellence.

Take this angel out of the card. Project the angel above your reflective surface. See and feel the energy of this angel. Thank him for accompanying you. Cast your eyes upon the reflection you have chosen. Keep the energy moving, but now instead of the angel's cups it is the energy exchange between the surface and you. Stay until you have a vision.

Remove Oppression Spell

Ingredients
1. Eight of Swords
2. Knight of Swords
3. The World
- Transplantable flower

Method, Visualization, and Meditation

Oppression can act as a teacher. It shows us that what we rebel against can make us stronger. It may be an unfair decision, imposed rules, or a boss's lousy attitude. Often, we inadvertently oppress ourselves by attracting oppressive things into our life.

You can perform this spell to remove an unwanted thought or attitude. It redirects the energy of the oppressor and allows you to move in a new direction.

Place all three cards facedown in their place on the table before you.

Flip the Eight of Swords. Enter the card. Become the figure. What is binding you? See it visually. What wrapped you up?

See the place you wish to be in your mind's eye. What does your space of freedom look like? What are you doing inside it? In the distance, begin to feel the ground pounding under horse's hooves. Feel the air around you shake.

Flip the Knight of Swords. The knight rushes to your aid. He cuts you free. Feel the oppressiveness slip from your body. The white ties fall to the ground and slither like snakes into the belly of the earth. You are free!

Flip the World card. Feel the freedom of movement you now have. The world is open and available to you. You may go in any direction you choose, making choices that add to your freedom.

Transplant a new flower into your garden or bring a plant into your home to flourish right alongside you.

[1] [2] [3]

On this day in France Bastille Day is celebrated. It marks the beginning of the French Revolution, a revolt against royal tyranny and oppression.

• • • • •

INCANTATION

Binding prison
Bonds of white
You vanish forever
With my knight
Imagined, real
It does not matter
Your strength is gone
Your power scattered
I dance with love
And light and glee
Finally and everlasting
Free to be me

The Rosetta Stone was discovered today in 1759. Scholars, long befuddled by Egyptian hieroglyphs, were finally able to translate them.

INCANTATION

Magcian card

Wisdom of Thoth

Stir a magical

Potent broth

Shed your light

Show me the way

Decide upon

A course today

Wisdom of Thoth Right Study Spell

Ingredients
- The Magician
- Randomly drawn card

Method, Visualization, and Meditation

If you are feeling indecisive regarding a course of study, this spell will help you select the most beneficial option. It leads you in the right direction and the appropriate course of action will become clear.

The Magician card represents the power of Thoth, god of wisdom and the written word.

Place the Magician card in front of you. Focus on him and consider how you act as a magician in your life. You have created every physical manifestation: your home, your friends, the very room you sit in is what you have manifested. Manifestation is expressed by the white lilies and red roses drawn upon the Magician card. Focus on power coursing through you, the energy of your attention, and the amount of energy that shoots out of you when you focus on something. Like a camera's lens, your focus narrows and defines your perspective. You will choose the right course of study.

Begin shuffling your tarot deck. Shuffle with certainty. Fan the cards across the table. Invoke the Magician's power by imitating his posture. Stand up. Point one hand up and let your other hand point down. Let the Magician's pointing finger show you which card to choose. Flip it over. Consider it deeply. This card holds the answer on your course of study. Choose one symbol from the card and let it inform your choice.

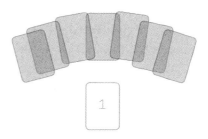

Four of Cups Connection Ritual

Ingredient
- Four of Cups

Method, Visualization, and Meditation

Enter the arcana of the Four of Cups.

Fours represent stability. The arcana of three burst forth creatively. It has evolved into the next stage. A fourth appears. Stability is reached. A square. A home. A haven. The structure is complete. Four seasons. Four directions. Four elements. Four suits of tarot. Reality in the physical world has been achieved.

It is a clear day in July—one of those days that looks like it has been colored in by a child using crayons. The air is calm, the temperature just right. The grass and fields of sweet early hay fill your nose. Sun warms the nape of your neck.

A figure sits beneath a young maple tree. The figure is closed off from the outside world, crossing both his legs and arms. A mysterious hand emerges from a cloud, offering him a cup, yet his eyes are cast downward. It is as if he sees neither the offering nor the three cups spread across the grass in front of him.

The tree at his back holds powerful magic. Its roots reach far beneath the soft earth and reflect the branches that soar above in the daylight breeze. This echoes the human ability to be grounded yet open to inspiration. One foot on the ground, one head in the clouds. The tree is a haven for creatures big and small. An ant crawls between the bark that has been lined with weather and wisdom. A porcupine hides in a branch above, chewing on a leaf. The tree bears fruit, maple sugar generating deep within its trunk.

The figure aligns himself with the energy of the tree. In doing so, he will open his perception to understand more, to see more, to accept more.

When he opens his eyes, he will see the cup.

He will recognize it has been there all along.

He will drink from it.

The Four of Cups was called the Lord of Blended Pleasure by the magicians of the Golden Dawn, who assigned it the time period of July 12–21.

• • • • • •

INCANTATION
Four of Cups
Opportunity unseen
What will it take
To live my dream?
See the choice
And spy the cup
The only place to go
Is up

John Jacob Astor, America's first millionaire, was born on this day in 1763. Channel Astor's unique energy to manifest riches and wealth.

INCANTATION

Lucky, lucky number nine

My dreams are answered

Needs divine

Grant me security

Peace and love

Faithful as the hawk

Upon my glove

Attract the money

Straight to me

Like honey created

By a bee

Bring Money Knot Spell

Ingredients
- Nine of Pentacles
- Your hairbrush

Method, Visualization, and Meditation

Ancient Babylonians developed a system of knot magic. It was thought one could control money, love, health, and well-being through the tying and untying of knots.

Nine is the number of wish fulfillment and getting what you need. The Nine of Pentacles represents personal luxury and delight in the material world.

Lay the Nine of Pentacles before you. Contentment and security fill the card like the nectar of blooming flowers on a late summer day. See the pentacles growing. Know these will be yours. From here on out, each time you spend money, pay a bill, or exchange cash for services, picture the money returning to you threefold.

The universe conspires to aid you at your every turn.

Pick up your hairbrush and brush your hair to a shiny gleam. Pick nine hairs out of the brush. Rub them between your palms, turning them into a string.

Moving from left to right, tie your hair string with nine knots. See the vision of money you need and security sought as you hold and knot the hair.

When the money comes to you, bury the knotted string of hair and return it to the earth with offerings of gratitude.

Increase Confidence Spell

Ingredients
- Journal or paper and pen
1. The Magician
2. The Chariot
3. Nine of Cups

Method, Visualization, and Meditation

What are you building confidence for? Write or journal about what you would like to manifest. Write how you would like to embrace confidence.

Confidence-boosting spells gain extra power when performed during the waxing moon. As the moon grows larger, so does your confidence. Note the bright yellow color on all three cards. The Magician card reflects ultimate confidence and focus. The Chariot brings you to your desire. The Nine of Cups grants it.

Lay the Magician before you. Enter the card. Stand across from this figure. Now move so you are standing next to him. Allow your hand to touch his finger, the one pointing down. Feel his energy channeling into you. It is an electric and dynamic energy, one that fills you from the tips of your toes to the top of your head. He channels confidence into your body.

Place the Chariot card. Feel the forward momentum of your life. The energy coursing through you from the Magician now propels you in new directions. What do you see from inside your chariot seat? What is your view? What lies ahead of you? What do you desire?

Place the Nine of Cups. The genie crosses his arms and grants your wish. Your confidence has brought you the outcome you desire. Feel the delight coursing through your veins. Feel yourself shining with confidence.

[1] [2] [3]

Today is Nelson Mandela's birthday. Confidence is just one of his many admirable qualities.

INCANTATION

Magician's power
Come to me
I live a life
That's wild and free
Chariot wheels
Underneath me turn
While passion and fire
Reveal the burn
The Nine of Cups
Grants my need
But my powers alone
Help me succeed

Caramel Lace for Elegance and Grace Spell

Edward Degas, Impressionist painter of ballerinas, is born on this day in 1834. Ballerinas are among the most graceful creatures on the planet. Perform this tasty spell to assume these gifts in all interactions.

Ingredients
- Three of Cups
- 4 ounces water
- 8 ounces sugar
- Pinch of salt

Method, Visualization, and Meditation

The Three of Cups implies innate gracefulness. As in any cooking spell, let the pleasure of your senses lead your visualization. As you smell the sweetness of the sugar, allow sweetness to soften your situation. The water can dilute any issue that has arisen and caused problems. Allow the salt to purify your intent.

Place the Three of Cups before you and look at this card as if the girls were classically trained dancers moving in sync. See yourself in a future situation handling yourself with excellence.

Place your ingredients into a small saucepan and set to medium flame. Stir until the sugar is dissolved. When the mixture begins to simmer, stop stirring and allow it to take on a rich caramel color. Do not let it burn. Once the color is amber, remove from heat and let it sit for 1-2 minutes.

Using a spoon, drizzle caramel onto parchment paper in delicate lattice designs. Imagine your own gentle footwork as you do so. If beads drop from the spoon, the caramel needs to cool a bit more. Let it completely cool before eating or storing.

Taste your caramel when you need to access the art of delicacy and finesse.

INCANTATION

Elegance and grace

Upon my face

As delicate as lace

I embrace

Actions gentle

Yet strong and bold

This delicate art

I do behold

Small Step Spell

Ingredients
- Page of Swords
- Mint leaves

Method, Visualization, and Meditation

Small steps can be monumental in achieving our hopes, dreams, and desires. Sometimes, what we want is simply too big and scary to face. The most powerful magic can be created in the smallest of space. See the small step you are to take upon the culmination of this spell.

The Page of Swords represents elegant footwork. The hubris of youth makes us brave in completing small steps. Mint leaves put a spring in our step and move us forward.

Focus on the Page of Swords. Think back to when you were about eleven years old. See yourself in your eleven-year-old body. Let the wind blowing through the page's hair remind you of being free on a bike with the wind in your own hair. Recall the fearlessness of youth. Think of how determined you were when you had your sights set on something. You dwelled in the moment rather than thinking ahead or second-guessing yourself. Walk up and ask your eleven-year-old self for a piece of advice toward your small step. Embrace her suggestion.

Sprinkle fresh mint leaves in a pair of shoes while uttering the incantation. Put on your shoes and go for a walk. When you come home, perform one small step in the direction you'd like to go.

Is there something you'd like to change? The most impactful changes often begin with the smallest of steps. Neil Armstrong set foot on the moon today in 1969, declaring, "That's one small step for man, one giant leap for mankind." Small steps turn into giant leaps when we aren't looking.

INCANTATION
Page of Swords
Path of life
I no longer fear
Or avoid the strife
One small step
And then repeat
Life transforms
It's an easy feat

Open Solar Plexus Chakra Energy

At the height of summer we can appreciate the true brilliance that the solar plexus chakra imparts to us. The solar plexus rules physical power and will. It is the part of us that glows when living in our truth. It is your self-esteem and confidence.

INCANTATION

Solar plexus

Shining light

I feel you glow

With all my might

Love to others

Returns to me

Delight in my

Soul's destiny

Ingredient
• The Sun

Method, Visualization, and Meditation

The solar plexus chakra is who you are. When opened, it will enrich your sense of expansiveness and connection as well as your effectiveness in the physical world.

The solar plexus chakra is located in the center of the body. When they work your core in an exercise class, this is the place you are working. It is the core of your body.

Sit on a chair with your feet flat on the floor or sit in yogi position, legs crossed, on the floor. Place the Sun card before you. Focus on the center of your body. Place a palm flat on your chest and the other hand on your back. Feel the energy building between your hands from the center of your body. Imagine it is glowing brilliant yellow, and turn the energy in a circle until it is spinning.

Sit straight and hear the energy, smell it, or maybe taste it. Focus on the Sun card before you and feel the face of the sun in the card upon your chest. Feel the expanse and growth as the energy takes over your entire essence, filling and spilling the entire room with your radiance.

Radiant Child of the Sun Spell

Ingredients
- The Sun
- Fresh lemons

Method, Visualization, and Meditation

This spell invokes solar power across your entire physical and metaphysical body.

Examine the Sun card. Let its image wash over you without judgment or thought. Walk into the card. Move toward the brick wall. Extend your hand to scratch the white horse's chin. His breath is warm in your palm. His coarse tongue licks the salt from your skin. The child looks at you in delight.

Smell the sunflowers, symbols of summer. The wall is warm in front of your body. Heat soaks into your cheeks and forehead. It is the perfect nurturing energy. It fills your body from tip to toe with energy. Radiant health brims. Look at the sun as depicted in the card. The sun's face is also your face. You and the sun are one. You act as a sun to many in your life.

Slice a fresh lemon in half. Gently rub it across your face. Leave on or splash off with water. Rub halves on your elbows and the heels of your feet to smooth. Mix some lemon juice with baking soda and scrub with a cotton swab to whiten your teeth. Apply lemon juice to your hair for sun-kissed highlights. Drink a fresh glass of water with squeezed lemon. Perhaps make a lemon cake.

You are officially a radiant child of the sun.

The longest recorded solar eclipse happened on this day in 2009. Mark this day with a beauty ritual worshipping sun energy at the height of summer. Become as fresh, clean, and exuberant as the child on the card.

INCANTATION

Radiant sun
Help me glow,
Enrich my life
This I know
Source of magic
Truth and light
Bring reflections of beauty
To my sight

Today marks the first day of the astrological sign of Leo. Leos are ruled by the sun; unsurprisingly, they are also assigned to the Strength card. Leos are loyal, creative, disciplined, and self-expressive.

INCANTATION

Strength and self-confidence
Rise like bread
This confusion is
All in my head
I'm strong, I'm brave
Can do anything at all
And while I'm at it
I'll have a ball

Self-Confidence of Leo Salad Spell

Ingredients
- Strength
- Pen and paper
- Fresh baby spinach leaves
- Strawberries, sliced
- Red onion, sliced
- Almonds, diced

Method, Visualization, and Meditation

The Strength card provides self-confidence. Spinach and onions foster strength. Strawberries remind us to be sweet. Almonds invoke healing energies.

Place the Strength card before you. Enter the card and feel the warm sunlight. From this moment forward, when you see or feel sunlight, you will let it fill you with positivity. It will literally zap away the negative thoughts in your head. Look at the lion with gentle eyes and smile at him. Remember to smile at the people in your life. Smile for no particular reason at all.

Make a list of the things you have accomplished.

Place this list where you can see it.

Combine spinach, strawberries, onion, and almonds. Mix with your favorite dressing. While tossing, recite the incantation.

Triple Goddess Spell

Ingredient
- The High Priestess

Method, Visualization, and Meditation

Triad principles exist cross-culturally, from Heaven/Earth/Underworld to Father/Son/Holy Ghost to the idea of Mind/Body/Spirit. The High Priestess card echoes this trinity in her triple moon crown. It reflects the waxing, full, and waning moon. Use the High Priestess as a gateway card.

Mother/Maiden/Crone are especially evocative as they honor the three phases of a woman's life: the joy of childhood, the pleasure of womanhood, and the wisdom of age.

Embrace these sacred parts of yourself, no matter your age. Enter the High Priestess card. Bow before her.

Walk to her left. Find the child version of yourself standing there. Spend time conversing with your seven-year-old self. What does she want to know? What do you want to tell her? What advice might she have for you? Whisper a secret to her.

Walk behind the High Priestess to find your middle-aged self. What does she want to know? What do you want to tell her? What advice might she have for you? Whisper a secret to her.

Walk to the right to discover your crone self. What does she want to know? What do you want to tell her? What advice might she have for you? Whisper a secret to her. Let her whisper a secret back.

The High Priestess combines all phases of life into a single entity. She is your reflection, your subtle mirror. You can communicate with the High Priestess and all three selves. Doing so, you have the power to change the past, present, and future.

Robert Graves, the scholar, writer, and poet who popularized the concept of the Triple Goddess, was born on this day in 1895. The Triple Goddess is the Maiden, Mother, and Crone correlating with the three phases of the moon and other metaphysical triads.

INCANTATION

Triple goddess
All of me
As I embrace you
I am free
Eternal knowledge
Patience, speech
Within my grasp
Within my reach

The Roman festival of Salacia, the female divinity of the sea and Neptune's wife, is celebrated today. This goddess is echoed by the Queen of Cups, who rules the seven seas and the element of water.

INCANTATION

Queen of Cups

Empathy runs deep

Your waves crashing

Eternally in my sleep

Waters dark, purple, and blue

Kindness brings me

Back to you

Queen of Cups Connection Ritual

Ingredient
• Queen of Cups

Method, Visualization, and Meditation

Enter the arcana of the Queen of Cups.

A westward wind has traveled across the expanse of the Atlantic Ocean. It greets your face and blows across your bare shoulders and through your hair. Something sweet cuts through the air's salty brine. You turn, discovering the shocking source. A mermaid leaps from the water with a splash and lands on a throne. Turning herself toward the sun, this glittering vision, scaly and brilliant, transforms into human form.

Her pale blue and silver scales fade into a gown and cape, and her human legs become visible under the sheath of her dress. A human foot slips out upon rocks shimmering like jewels amidst the grainy sand. The tiara on her head grows to a full-size golden crown. She holds a jewel in her hand. It grows into a golden cup, seemingly too big for her delicate hand, yet she gazes into it. Baby mermaids adorn her throne and speak with her in a strange aquatic language. She responds in a murmuring voice and they giggle adoringly at her.

Taking one last long look at her cup, she turns to you. Her otherworldly eyes reflect the clear saline blue of the water. She offers you her cup. You realize you will receive a deep secret of the ocean by accepting it. Thankfully, the heavy-looking cup is light. She nods with a smile. She wants you to look in the cup and discover what lies inside.

You take a deep breath and look down.

What do you discover?

What is the secret?

Five of Wands Connection Ritual

Ingredient
• Five of Wands

Method, Visualization, and Meditation
Enter the arcana of the Five of Wands.

Fives imply challenge. Fives are the halfway point, the turning point, the space in which a new chapter begins. What has manifested up until this point begins to build on itself. This required challenge provides perspective for the ultimate outcome in the finality of the ten. Inside every challenge lies a gift. Can you discover it?

You find yourself standing upon a vast field that spreads to meet the sky. The ground is rocky, covered with moss and grass. You hear scuffling and a commotion, the sound of voices and a wave of activity. Five young men are dressed in colorful clothing. Each bears a giant wand in their hands. The boys wield, lift, and swing the wands easily, though the wands are taller than the boys themselves.

The boys appear agitated, raising their wands in fight or in competition. You peer closer. The two boys in the foreground look deeply into each other's eyes as they measure their sticks up against one another. The boy on the far left of the card raises his stick in jubilation while he looks at a boy who hauls his wand over his shoulder. The fifth boy looks skyward and upward. You realize the boys are not fighting. They are building something.

A great secret of the tarot is revealed to you as you realize the boys are about to create the sign of the pentagram with their wands. The pentagram is the symbol of the witch, the manifestation of earth, air, fire, water, and spirit. When passion meets challenge and ideas, true magic emerges.

Take this symbol back into the world with you. Use as you see fit.

The Five of Wands was called the Lord of Strife by the magicians of the Golden Dawn, who assigned it the time period of July 22–August 1.

• • • • • •

INCANTATION
Five of Wands
Challenge of fire
Channel my energy
Take me higher
The midway point
Brings me further so
Passions manifest
And around me grow

Dream Inspiration Spell

INCANTATION

Star light

Star bright

Shine your sight

In mine tonight

Wish I may

Wish I might

Feel your

Inspirational light

Ingredients
1. The Moon
2. The Star

Method, Visualization, and Meditation

Few things are as exciting as waking from a dream with grand insight or inspiration regarding something in your life. Journaling or meditating about our dreams in waking life causes exciting new effects in our sleeping life. Use night journeys to cultivate important information and take wild rides.

Place the Moon card. Enter the card. Stand between the towers. How is your sense of space larger and expanded in your dreams? How does your body move inside a dream? How do the scenes move in a dream? How far does your vision extend when dreaming, and how are landscapes different? With as much energy as possible, explore the Moon card as if it were a dream rather than a card on the table. Expand the card.

Move to the Star card. Feel the calm and quiet of the landscape compared to the Moon card. Slip yourself, as naked as she is, into the pool of water. Your feet do not touch the bottom. Hold your arms above you and point your toes as you descend deeper and deeper into the cool waters of this card. The water is not dark; it glimmers with incandescent light.

Let the weightlessness of your body pull you back to the surface. Break through to the air and allow her to pour the waters of inspiration all over you.

Utter the incantation.

Place both cards beneath your pillow tonight.

1	2

Spell to Stop Zombies in Their Tracks

Ingredients
1. Five of Wands
2. Nine of Wands
3. Seven of Wands

Method, Visualization, and Meditation

There's nothing wrong with helping loved ones out. But if you feel like you've been giving everything to everyone else and have nothing left for yourself, this spell is for you.

In the movies, characters evade zombies by throwing them off their scent. The same idea exists in this spell. You aren't affecting the people in your life, just sending them in another direction while you take cover.

Use the specific imagery on the cards rather than the meaning behind the arcana to banish your zombies.

Lay the Five of Wands. This card represents the people in your life who are pulling your focus, experiencing drama, and hating on things. Tell them to disperse. Reverse the card.

Place the Nine of Wands. This card represents the person who is most needful of you right now. See the person's face and tell them to look elsewhere for the help they require. Reverse the card.

Place the Seven of Wands. This card represents you. The figure is protecting himself from the people below. See your self doing the same thing. Place an energetic field around you. Visualize white energy swirling around you in a cone pointing upward. Once the cone is erected, you may walk away from the situation.

Blaze this up at any point you need protection in regular life.

White Zombie, the first zombie film ever made, was released on this day in 1932. Real-life zombies are a lot like psychic vampires: people who suck and drain your energy, eat up your brain space, and are always after you for something, be it favors, attention, money, or help.

INCANTATION

Zombies away
You stop, you halt
I was just being nice
It's not my fault
Can't give any more
I am done
Go somewhere else
To have your fun

| 1 | 3 | 2 |

House Hunting Spell

Today is National Tiger Day, honoring the power, prowess, and beauty of these great creatures. Tigers contain amazing hunting energy. Call upon tiger energy when house hunting for yourself and your family.

Ingredients
1. Four of Wands
2. The Hermit
3. The Chariot
• Pen and paper

Method, Visualization, and Meditation

Place the Four of Wands. See the stability of the four wands and the hanging garland suspended between them. Step into the card and stand in the center of the four wands. Become the center of the square. Feel the magic of the space. People murmur in the background, happy voices laughing and celebrating. See the splendor of the castle walls and feel the protection offered by them. Envision the qualities you are seeking in your home. How does it feel, what colors does it have, what is the sunlight like?

Using your pen and paper, describe your dream home. Be detailed. Describe as much as you can. When you are finished, fold it and place beneath the Four of Wands.

Place the Hermit. Focus on the light shining from his lantern. It is a beacon. It will guide you toward the perfect home. What's more, you will know it when you see it. It comes effortlessly.

Place the Chariot. The Chariot's speed, velocity, and certainty directs you toward the home of your dreams. Keep the Chariot available as you search the Internet for properties. Keep the Chariot card with you when you go house hunting.

INCANTATION
Beautiful, cozy
Excellent home
Come to me fast
I do not roam
The price is right
The process fast
The walls I seek
Are built to last

2

1

3

Booming Business Beach Spell

Ingredients
- Ten of Pentacles
- Bare feet
- Sand

Method, Visualization, and Meditation

This spell is best performed at the beach. The beach is a threshold to another reality. The sands of earth meet the cooling waters of emotion while the fire of sun warms the salty air. The Ten of Pentacles reflects booming business.

Focus on the Ten of Pentacles. The figures on the card are the people involved in your business/career: customers, employees, and coworkers. See them intermingling happily. The arched door represents the doorway, the threshold to the possible. The world lies outside the threshold. It knows no boundaries, no limits.

Ten pentacles float in the card. The Kabbalistic Tree of Life represents a tenfold increase in the amount of money you will make. See your bank statements and accounts with extra zeros. What does the electronic balance of your account look like with all those zeros?

Venture to the beach. Let the ocean remind you of the infinite of potential for business growth. Collect ten shells. Dig a hole. Bury the shells, representing your financial stability. Covering the hole, you are essentially burying your treasure.

Trace a giant pentacle in the sand with your toe or a stick. Use your buried treasure as the center point.

Make this pentacle as large as the beach allows. The bigger, the better. Let them see your pentacle from space. Connect the five points with a circle and then stand in the center, over the buried shells. Lie inside, spreading your arms and legs like the Vitruvian Man.

The Small Business Administration was formed today in 1953 and has provided help to small business owners ever since. This spell works to increase your salary or net business earnings. Enjoy the effects long after you return home.

INCANTATION

Salt of air

Sand of earth

At this moment

I give birth

Money, money

Comes to me

Quickly

Swiftly

Effortlessly

Protect Your Relationship Spell

On this day in 1718 an unfortunate pair of lovers, John Hewit and Sarah Dew, were struck dead by lightning in an English field. Ward off unwanted influences with this spell.

Ingredients
1. Card representing you
2. Two of Cups
3. Card representing them
- Three 10-inch lengths of red ribbons

Method, Visualization, and Meditation
This spell works equally well for a romantic relationship or child or friendship relationships.

Place the three cards before you.

Under each card, place a string.

Focus on the card representing yourself. Contemplate why you chose this card.

Focus on the card you chose to represent them. Contemplate your reasons for choosing it.

Focus on the Two of Cups. Meditate on why the two of you are so special together.

Begin to braid all three ribbons, repeating the incantation. Keep the braid in a special place.

INCANTATION
Safe, safe, safe
We are
Negative energy
You stay far
Love and light
Surrounds us two
I dedicate
Myself to you

| 1 | 2 | 3 |

Healthy Birth Spell

Ingredients
1. The Magician
2. The World
3. The Sun

Lammas and Lughnasa, ancient Celtic harvest celebrations, are performed today. The greatest harvest may just be the birthing of a child.

Method, Visualization, and Meditation

Many cultures consider the snake to be a powerful ally to a woman from conception to delivery. While snake imagery may feel counterintuitive to a pregnant woman, it is believed the movement of snakes can teach a woman how to give birth. It is also believed that the unhinging of the snake's jaw is a metaphor for a woman's expanding vagina during childbirth. Images of snakes may be placed around the birthing chamber, and snake jewelry may be worn during the birthing process.

Place all three cards facedown.

Flip the Magician card. Feel his electricity and energy. As you give birth, his conduit of energy moves through you in the pushing process. His snake unclasps from his belt and begins to wriggle. The snake slides into the air before you. It wiggles and moves. You imitate the snake, feeling the undulation of your body pushing out new life.

Flip the World card. See the soul who is about to come through you and into this beautiful world. The green wreath can be viewed as a birth canal. See it expanding in a healthy way, making room for the new child.

Flip the Sun card. See the healthy child come bounding through the card.

Feel this health inside your belly.

INCANTATION

Healthy baby
Healthy me
Deliver this baby
Come with glee
All goes well
All goes right
I deliver you
With all my might

1

2

3

The Fourth of July is the official celebration day for US independence, but the actual signing of the contract occurred today in 1776.

INCANTATION

See what I want

This contract's fair

Wants and needs

Are addressed there

It's soon resolved

Written and signed

Abundance and pleasure

I am to find

Contractual Matters Spell

Ingredients

1. Justice
2. Four of Swords
3. The Emperor
4. Desired outcome card

Method, Visualization, and Meditation

Are you prepping contracts for a marriage, home purchase, new lease, or business? Perform this spell to assure you are covered and receive the best possible deal.

Justice rules over all legal matters. The Four of Swords represents the stability of the contract. The Emperor represents receiving the terms you want. Choose an outcome card that reflects your final desire.

Place Justice before you. Realize you don't have to work on behalf of Justice, whose invisible wheels are already turning for you. Know that if you enter this contract responsibly and with your highest good stated and expressed, you will have satisfactory final terms.

Place the Four of Swords and enjoy the stability and silence of the card. This reflects the final contract.

Place the Emperor. See yourself standing up for exactly what you want. Nothing can sway you from your fair terms.

Place the outcome card you have selected. Envision yourself in your new reality.

Morning Dew Enhance Beauty Spell

Ingredients
- Small bowl
- Vanilla extract
- The Star
- Candle

Method, Visualization, and Meditation

Vanilla is used for attraction beauty. The Star card reflects renewal. Dew will make you as vibrant as a flower.

When the weather is warm and the forecast is fair, dress in your nightgown or a silky slip. Take a bowl and the vanilla out to the woods or your yard. Anoint the bowl with your vanilla while stating aloud how you would like your innate beauty enhanced. Leave the bowl at the base of a tree or in the grass where it will not be touched.

Return to your home.

Light a candle.

Place the Star card before you. Enter the card. Feel the purity of the water the Star pours. Feeling her water, imagine the physical effect you desire. Allow all stress to be washed away. As you sleep tonight, know you slumber beneath the protection of the stars.

At dawn's light, return to the bowl outside and to the morning dew. Anoint yourself with the water, adding and spreading more dew on the places you would most like to effect. Return home and continue with your morning routine refreshed and feeling absolutely gorgeous.

The Aztec goddess Chalchiuhtlicue commanded water, rivers, seas storms, and tempests. Her magic exists in morning dew, which has always been held in esteem for its strength and beauty properties.

INCANTATION

Blazing sun
Morning's light
Prepare my ritual
Well tonight
As tendrils shoot
And flower blooms
I'll prepare
Among my rooms
Freshest drops
I take with joy
Beauty serum
Do deploy

Six of Wands Connection Ritual

The Six of Wands was called the Lord of Victory by the magicians of the Golden Dawn, who assigned it to the time period of August 2–11.

INCANTATION

Six of Wands
Celebration time
Victory march
The ranks you'll climb
But with each step
One more appears
The higher you climb
The wiser your years

Ingredient
• Six of Wands

Method, Visualization, and Meditation
Enter the arcana of the Six of Wands.

Six implies advancement. The challenge of the five has been met. Sixes support forward momentum. A hierarchy is achieved.

Laughter, clapping, and music rises up to the window of your hotel room. You gulp your coffee, push aside the bone-white china cup, and make for the streets downstairs. The electric sound of trumpets fills your ears. Colored flags flap above you in the breeze. Cheers and cries spread around you as the parade commences. People have gathered in the streets as a great procession fills a stonewalled town. You slip through the crowd until you find a spot in front.

You are just in time to see a group of triumphant revelers pass by. They hold red wands that point in the air, bobbing up and down as they walk forward. The main figure, who must be their leader, rides atop a white horse whose hooves clop on the cobblestones with the rhythm of a ticking clock. Flushed with victory, the rider is dressed in the color of flames, red and yellow. A green laurel wreath circles his head and another is fastened to the top of his wand.

You recognize that the circle of victory is complete. The rider won the race he has trained for his whole life. The group of people and wands continues on their route, cheering and optimistic. Strangely, you catch the rider's horse, festooned in celebratory green, casting a look backwards. There is more to come, more to unfold. The victory was not the end but simply a new beginning.

Healing Love Spell

Ingredients
- White candle
- White rose
1. Ace of Cups
2. Two of Cups
3. Six of Cups

Method, Visualization, and Meditation

Roses are sacred to love. White roses represent the purifying love that can wash a soul clean. Choose a white candle for purification and cleansing. The Ace of Cups pours forth love's healing waters. The Two of Cups is love's mirror when we discover what we love in the reflection of the other. The Six of Cups reflects the purposeful act of giving oneself unselfishly to others.

Hold a white rose. Gently remove its petals. Let your defenses down with each pulled petal. Allow yourself to feel vulnerable. With each petal removed, feel a self-imposed layer of protection slip away.

Place the Ace of Cups before the pile of petals. Place the Two of Cups and Six of Cups under the liquid streams pouring from the ace.

The Ace of Cups is a fountain. It pours crystal clear refreshing water into each card. The cards become activated beneath the streams. This is the true nature of love and compassion.

See yourself in each card, giving and receiving healing love. How does it feel to be loved? How does it feel to give love?

Release your flower petals to the wind with a personal message of love. Deliver a message of love to someone you hold dear.

Today is the Roman festival of Salus, goddess of public health. Love has the power to heal all wounds. It soothes and disinfects even those scars that won't disappear. Cast this spell to procure a healing love into your life and imbue yourself with peace.

INCANTATION
Waters of hope and clarity
Bring love of all variety
Let it heal
Let it flow
Give into my heart
And let it go

1

2   3

Lovers Intimacy Spell

Don Juan—*the film with the most recorded onscreen kisses—was released on this day in 1926.*

INCANTATION

Rosemary sprigs
Loyalty true
My love, my soul
I bare to you
You feel my needs
Respond in turn
While Lovers' fire
Within me burns

Ingredients
- The Lovers
- 1 teaspoon orange peel
- 1 teaspoon rose petals
- 1 teaspoon rosemary
- Sheet of paper and envelope
- Champagne or ginger ale

Method, Visualization, and Meditation

This spell may be cast with your partner or alone. In magic, love, and life, you receive what you give. When you seek something from your relationship, freely give what you desire.

The Lovers card reflects the intimacy of amour. Orange peels are used for love. Rose petals echo erotic love. Rosemary refreshes the memory of a lover's first glance. Bubbly drinks tickle the senses.

Place the Lovers card before you. Stand up and slowly take off all of your clothes until you are as naked as the Eve figure on the card. Open your posture like her, feet apart and palms lowered but reaching up. Feel your vulnerability and allow your energy to open completely. Offer yourself to your partner with nothing left hidden.

Write and repeat the words of what you want to experience with your partner. As you do, make a promise to either express this desire to them or tell them what you want. Imagine them doing this for you. Drink your bubbly, imagining the tingles are your lover's fingers tickling you.

Mix your ingredients together on top of the paper. Fold the herbs into the paper and secure in the envelope. Tuck this envelope inside your underwear drawer.

Home Blessing and Connection Spell

Ingredients
1. The High Priestess
2. Four of Pentacles
3. Randomly drawn card
- Four containers of salt

Method, Visualization, and Meditation

Have you recently moved into a new space? Does your living quarters reflect, comfort, and support you in the way it should? Our home is a physical extension of ourselves. This spell is a way to connect to the heart of your home. Cast this spell in the physical spot you consider to be the heart of the house. You will cast and connect from the deepest part of yourself.

The High Priestess reflects the deepest, truest part of your inner self. The Four of Pentacles represents the physical structure of your home.

Place the High Priestess and Four of Pentacles cards. Enter the High Priestess. Embrace the silent, authentic part of yourself that she represents. Listen for the water running behind her; hear the cascading overtures of your soul. Center yourself.

Become the High Priestess. Sit in her throne. Feel her crown. Look through her eyes. Gaze upon the Four of Pentacles. See this figure looming large before you. It is the spirit of your home. Let the vision transform and reveal itself to you. The four pentacles represent the four walls, the wood that absorbs the energy, the foundation upon which your chambers lie.

Shuffle your deck. Ask Spirit how you can best honor them in your home and randomly pick a card. Lay the card sideways between the other two cards. Meditate on the card's message.

Set four containers of salt in the four corners of the home. Leave for twenty-four hours before disposing.

Construction on Florence, Italy's Duomo began on this day in 1420. Thought by many to be the most beautiful cathedral in all of Europe, European cities often have a cathedral or square at the heart of their city.

INCANTATION
Corner crevice
Spaces meet
Hold us tight
Life is sweet
Comfort is our
Permanent guest
As of now
This home is blessed

| 1 | 3 | 2 |

Today is Happiness Happens Day, created by the Secret Society of Happy People.

INCANTATION

Satisfaction in life

Things I love

Intense pleasure

Like a glove

Beauty, luxury

Simple things

For what I need

I have the means

Pleasure in Life Spell

Ingredients
- Dried wisteria petals
- Carrier oil (such as olive or jojoba)
- Yellow candle
- Nine of Pentacles

Method, Visualization, and Meditation

Happiness can feel like a mysterious quality that is seemingly out of reach for many of us. External things and objects—the "pentacle" material world or "wandlike" fame—are thought to provide happiness, but happiness springs from the inside, not the other way around. Change your tack a bit. Rather than focusing on happiness, focus instead on pleasure-producing aspects of life.

Wisteria promotes pleasure and good fortune. Yellow candles promote expansion and creativity. The Nine of Pentacles reflects a fully satisfied, pleased, and pleasured woman.

Inhale the sweetness of your petals. Crush them with your fingers. Blend them into the oil. Dress your yellow candle with the oil and burn. Once your candle's flame has alighted, place the Nine of Pentacles before you in the flickering light.

Enter the card. Stand before this magnificent woman. The two of you inhabit a vineyard, ripe and fertile in the warm harvest sunlight. Bees hum a chorus as they dance between juicy grapes. A snail crawls slowly across the dirt.

The woman holds out her falcon for you to examine. His movement is quick and his ears sharp as he senses your closeness. Put on the musky, thick falconer's leather glove. Reach out to receive the bird. He hops to your hand.

The woman has vanished. You are alone in the vineyard. You have become the Nine of Pentacles. You are surrounded with everything that has ever brought you pleasure: food, people, entertainment, stories, experiences, delights. You recognize now that your five senses are the gateway to pleasure. As you exit the card, you bring the cultivation of sensory pleasure back with you.

Witch's Finger Experiment

Ingredients
- The Magician
- Potted plant or flower

Method, Visualization, and Meditation

Try this experiment to determine how effectively you channel energy. The results may surprise you. A pointed finger, assigned to Jupiter, sends and directs will and intent. It channels energy in a single line like a magic wand—sometimes even more effectively.

The Magician card points his finger to the heavens to channel energy down; he casts it beneath him.

Place the Magician card. Enter the card. Stand as the Magician. You are a powerful conduit of energy. Rather than standing behind the table and acting as the conductor of power channeled from above, find the epicenter of your personal energy. Where does the core of your power reside? Is it inside your belly? Is it at the base of your spine? Every person is built differently. Seek your unique energetic center.

Feel it growing in a ball of yellow, positive energy, matching the color of the card's background. Raise the energy up and feel it moving through your arm. When you feel ready, point the finger at your plant or flower and repeat the incantation.

Perform this act a few times a week. See if there is any noticeable change in your plant. Once you are comfortable channeling energy with your index finger, you never need to be concerned if you leave your magic wand behind.

Michaelangelo's image of God's finger touching Adam's was revealed as the Sistine Chapel in Rome opened on this day in 1483.

• • • • •

INCANTATION
Take my energy
Grow and thrive
With my love
You come alive!

229

Meteor Shower Message of Love Spell

Ingredients
1. Card representing you
2. Card representing them
3. Eight of Wands
- Summer night
- Sparklers

Method, Visualization, and Meditation

Native American tribes once thought shooting stars were made of lunar material and called them "children of the moon."

This spell must be performed at night. You will seal the spell by writing a message in the air with a sparkler.

Lay the cards representing you and them upon the table. Recall the powerful sorceress that you are. Feel the emotion and intention that you are sending. See the other person very clearly in your mind's eye. Lay the Eight of Wands down to direct the path of energy like a road map. Imagine this person—where they are and what they are doing.

Begin rubbing your palms together and feel the friction of energy created. Continue and focus on what you want to send them. When you are ready, pull your hands apart; you will feel the heat and energy. Place this energy over the Eight of Wands and feel it shooting out to them, falling all around them. State your message out loud.

Go outside. Light a sparkler. Write your message to them in the inky black air. When you are done, lie back and look to the sky. Should you see a falling star, know your message of love was delivered.

Today marks the approximate height of the Perseid meteor shower visible across the Northern Hemisphere, making the languid nights of August excellent for shooting-star gazing.

INCANTATION

Across the universe
And night sky
Thoughts to you
From me do fly
Violet night and
Meteors bright
Desire me
And soon reunite

| 1 | 3 | 2 |

Troublesome Guest Cleansing Spell

Ingredients
- Two of Swords
- Sage smudge stick
- Gathered or purchased flowers

Method, Visualization, and Meditation

The Two of Swords breeds peace of mind. Sage clears your mental and physical space. Flowers bring life to a room.

Place the Two of Swords before you. Take a moment to sit, center yourself, and assume the position depicted upon the card, arms crossed protectively in front of your chest. Feel the warmth of your skin through your hands. Feel a soft blindfold upon your eyes. This will block out all distractions. It also protects you from integrating what was seen and heard during the course of your guests' stay.

Embrace your calm, peaceful center. Discover the part of yourself that no person can touch. Sit inside of it. Feel the calmness expand out of your chest so that calm, languid blue surrounds your entire body like an oval ball of energy. Feel it extending further to fill the entire room.

Allow your imaginary blindfold to slip to the ground. Open your eyes. Light the smudge stick. Smudge each and every room in your house, imagining that as the smoke clears, calm blue settles everywhere.

Venture outside. Gather as many flowers, herbs, or ferns as possible to create a fresh vase for as many guests as were in your home. Bring them to your sink and arrange them to your liking. Place the vases in the heart of your home. The vases rebalance the energy of each guest so that the equilibrium of your home is regained.

Summer is high time for entertaining. Sometimes it means having guests who carry negative energy like luggage to your home. Cast this spell the moment their backs are out the door.

INCANTATION

Guests of mine
Family, friends
Your stay has come
To a timely end
I wish you all
The love and light
Peace has now
Consumed my sight

*Today is Helena Blavasky's
birthday. Founder of the
Theosophical Society, she
was a true high priestess.*

INCANTATION
Priestess, come

Impart your wisdom

Take it, learn it

Share my vision

From this moment on

I will be true

Fall into your

Misty blue

High Priestess Authentic Self Spell

Ingredients
- The High Priestess

Method, Visualization, and Meditation

The High Priestess represents our essential true self. She is the receptacle of all true personal knowledge. Whatever issues, decisions, or challenges we are facing, when we act from our authentic self, our highest good is activated.

Enter the arcana of the High Priestess. You are shrouded in velvety darkness. A light pierces the dark like a star twinkling in the night. You focus in on the light and gently fly toward it. The light becomes a cross. This cross is the intersection of the spiritual and the material.

The High Priestess blooms behind the cross that drapes her chest. She is the guardian of knowledge from your true spiritual self. Objects float like mist without physical boundaries. The High Priestess is like a cool fog. Misty tendrils rise from the water surrounding you. You and the priestess are on an island, with only ocean, mist, and moonlight. A sense of peace, a solemn air, pervades. You know this sacred space in churches, temples, mountains, tree groves, waterfalls, and streams.

Stand before the High Priestess. Realize, on the deepest level possible, she is really you: a metaphysical reflection of your soul's essence. The figure seated before you is all you have ever been and will be in eternity. You merge with her, sitting down in your royal seat. Look through the eyes of the High Priestess. What do you see? How does it feel to be inside this astral body, light as a feather? You look down to discover a scroll in your lap. This scroll is the book of your life. Its language becomes decipherable as you live authentically. To live in who you are is to recover the knowledge you have lost. It is your path in this life to reclaim it—to become who you were always meant to be.

Unravel the scroll. Be true to yourself.

Diana's Hunting Charm

Ingredients
- Candle
- Pen and paper
- Page of Swords

Method, Visualization, and Meditation

We are natural hunters and collectors. Not so long ago, we roamed the forests, fields, and beaches to gather from nature. You can charm the Page of Swords, the Nancy Drew of the tarot deck, when hunting for something.

This charm requires absolute specificity.

Light a candle. Write down exactly what you seek, in as much detail as possible.

Place the Page of Swords before you. Enter the card. Feel the rush of alpine wind on your face as you walk to greet the page. She meets you with clever, quick eyes. She is the hunter: analytical, smart, and calculating. Free of responsibility and relationships, she follows only what piques her interest. She is interested in helping you. Tell her what you seek. Birds soar above her. They are her familiars, her lookouts. They act as her eyes, telling her what lies ahead and where to look for what she needs. Her sword points upward to higher realms of crystal-clear thought.

Stand as this page. Look through her eyes. Feel her soft leather boots on your feet and the rocky ground beneath them. See your path as it unfolds before you. Spy your prize in your mind's eye. The object of your desire waits for you and wants for you to claim it.

Place the Page of Swords in your bag and place her image on your electronic devices until you find what you seek.

Ancient Romans celebrated Diana, goddess of the hunt, with a Festival of Torches today, called Nemoralia. Diana, a deity of the moon, communicates with animal and forest realms to locate what is needed.

INCANTATION

Through wild wind
And tangled trees
My gifts have others
On their knees
Track, chase, catch
And then I share
The gift comes with
The speed of air
Page of Swords
Point my way
Find exactly what
I need today

Today is World Lizard Day, celebrating all 6,000 mysterious species of lizard. Lizards and salamanders are fire creatures existing in the sultry domain of Wands.

● ● ● ● ● ●

INCANTATION

Hot grains of sand

Warm beams of sun

Lizard magic

Has begun

Creep and enter

Shadow space

Fire magic fills

Me with grace

Hidden reality

Becomes clear

When experiencing

The lizard sphere

Ritual to Align with Lizard Energy

Ingredient
• King of Wands

Method, Visualization, and Meditation

Are you fascinated by dreamtime, seeking regeneration, or looking for the power to face personal fears? Lizard energy bestows transformational gifts upon you. The King of Wands carries the essence of lizard energy.

Place the King of Wands. Enter the card. Gaze at the lizard at the king's feet. Become the lizard. Look up through the lizard's eyes at the King of Wands. How giant does the king appear from your new perspective? The king gives you a wink. Trace your eyes across the shapes of the desert landscape.

You spy a crevice under the king's throne. This is where you live. Use all four of your legs to move toward the shadow crevice. Feel your belly move across the hot sand.

It is cooler under the throne. A warm nest of eggs is protected from desert scavengers. Turn and place your head at the line where sun meets shadow. You exist between two realities: the wet darkness of the earth's belly and the acrid dryness of the desert air.

You discover a newfound camouflage ability. You transform into any color by standing next to it. You can now melt into any situation and easily avoid danger; when you sense negativity, stand back and let it pass without absorbing it. This power gives you strength. It is the strength of remaining true to yourself. Your tail, like human hair, regenerates itself when broken or cut. It is a reminder to move forward and discard what is no longer needed.

Stay inside lizard energy as long as you wish. Allow it to surprise you. Bring these qualities and visions with you as you exit the card.

Drawing Down the Sun

Ingredients
- Natural sunlight
- Tarot deck

Method, Visualization, and Meditation

Drawing down the power of the sun is a powerful tool to infuse yourself and your tarot deck with solar properties. Decide which aspect of the sun you would like to invoke. Healing and protective properties? Rapid expansion and growth? Warmth and passion?

The sun makes all physical life possible. If you desire growth in any area of life, shine sunlight upon it. Watch as it prospers and grows. Sunday corresponds to the sun, the sign of Leo, and the color gold. Perform on Sunday if possible.

The quality of sunlight is based on the time of year and should be considered. Are you working with the sultry yellow saturation of summer sun or are you working with the white stark sunlight of winter, reflected by snow? Is it the golden and mature, ruddy light of fall or the refreshing and gentle sunlight of spring?

Once you have set your solar intention, sit in the sunlight and mindfully place your deck in order. Begin by ordering the Major Arcana, starting with the Fool and moving through the World. Arrange each suit in numerical order. As you do so, see and feel the sun filling each card. When you have finished ordering, remove the Sun card and place it face up on the top of the deck. Place the deck next to you, using a crystal or rock to keep the cards from flying away if you are outside. Open and relax your posture. Place your palms open to the sun. Absorb the energy into your body. Let it fill you and your deck. Leave the deck to charge under the sun for the remainder of the day. Bring inside as twilight falls.

In 18 BCE Emperor Augustus declared this day would mark Ferragosto, a celebration of the harvest and a rest from the growing season. Mindfully sit back and let the sun fill you with power.

INCANTATION

Rays of light, waves of sun
Your energy around me spun
Solar magic infuses, alights me
Delight abounds for all to see
You are my source
From you I grow
And through your gifts
I do bestow
Into my deck
Spills love and light
I'll use these cards
To my delight

Gain the Edge in Competition Spell

The famed Palio horse race occurs on this day in Sienna, Italy. Call in the frenetic energy of this hallowed event to fill you with power.

Ingredients
1. King of Swords
2. Ace of Swords

Method, Visualization, and Meditation

Use the razor precision of Swords to help you gain the edge in any competition. Focus on the quality you desire for winning. Skill? Speed? Reflex? Knowledge? Charisma? Choose one word describing the competitive edge you require.

Place the King of Swords before you. Enter the card. Look deeply into his steadfast eyes. Feel his resolution as thick and solid as the steel blade in his hand. Make an ally of this king. What would he request of you? What sacrifice or gift might you make to him or to the element of the wind so he will grant you his favor? Ask him. See yourself giving him this gift in your mind's eye. Once you have, make your request. Utter the word you have chosen once.

The moment you say this word, place the Ace of Swords upon the king. Your desire is granted. In your mind's eye take the Ace of Swords in hand. Though the sword is heavy, you command it easily. Pull the sword from its upright position and hold it straight out in front of you. Look down your arm, down the steel of the blade. See your end goal as if through a crosshair. What lies at the center of your aim? What is your focal point? What must you see in your mind's eye to win? This is what you will focus on to give yourself the edge. See this vision clearly and succinctly. Once it is laser focused in your mind, repeat the incantation.

Exit the card. Draw, sketch, or journal what you envisioned to keep it fresh in your mind. Recall this image as a focal point when you compete or when you think about competing.

INCANTATION

I know deeply
Of the reason
That I'm going
To win this season
Quick with speed
I'm ahead, I see
Victory is
Ahead of me

Eucalyptus Banish Bad Habits Spell

Ingredients

- Eucalyptus branch (found in flower shops)
- Pot of water
- Six of Swords
- A warm bath

Method, Visualization, and Meditation

Eucalyptus has been used for centuries by cunning folk and witches, who use it for protection, purification, and health. The Six of Swords helps you banish any bad habit, be it a behavior, a person, or a way of thinking. The Six of Swords reflects moving forward. The suit of Swords represents the mind and the place where habits are formed. The mind is where your synapses fire and create neural pathways of habitual behavior. You have the power to rewire them.

Cut and boil the leaves, bark, and twigs of a eucalyptus branch. Reduce the heat to a simmer for thirty minutes once the water is rolling.

Start your bath.

Place the Six of Swords. Enter the card. Water laps against a dock; silence fills the card. This is a moment of transition. Become the woman on the boat. Step onto the boat, feel it moving with the weight of your body. Find balance in the boat. Cover yourself with a warm scarf. You are safe and secure as the boat moves from the dock. On the damp floor of the boat, your habit lies wrapped in a bundle. Place it in your lap. Thank the habit for the lessons it taught you. You will retain the lessons, but not the habit, in the future. Place the bundle over the side of the boat. Release. Watch it sink to the watery depths below.

Feel the boat reach the distant shore. Exit the card.

Strain the herbs from the liquid on the stove and add the eucalyptus water to your bath. Visualize your new reality while soaking.

On this day in 309, the Emperor Maxentius banished Pope Eusebius to Sicily. Banishing spells, like royal banishing orders, are meant to rid something completely from our life.

INCANTATION

Habit grown like
Wretched weed
Time for you
To go to seed
I'm done with you
Our time is through
Bid you adieu
Time to renew

Today Japanese Buddhists celebrate the Bon Festival to honor ancestor spirits. Lanterns, candles, and luminaries are sent downriver to help spirits find their way to the netherworld.

INCANTATION

Deepest sleep
And waxing moon
I'm blessed to have
You in my room
I feel you close
And love you so
By this candle's
Flickering glow
We can talk and
Laugh and speak
Your wisdom's light
Is what I seek

Dinner with the Departed Ritual and Reading

Ingredients
- Photograph or object of ancestor
- Mindfully prepared meal
- Tarot deck

Method, Visualization, and Meditation

This ritual is a wonderful way to connect with a departed loved one. Performed alone or with a family member or friend, this ritual and reading is best performed for someone existing in your living memory. It is best to perform this ritual for a person you had a deep connection with, rather than a distant ancestor.

Focus on a photograph or object of a departed loved one. Recall their essence. Smell their scent, see their skin, hear their voice. Perhaps you recall a joke or funny mannerism. Take all the time you need to see, feel, and recall them completely.

Once they are in your mind's eye, begin planning a meal consisting of this person's favorite foods, drinks, and desserts. What did they love to cook or eat? Make a shopping list. Imagine they are with you as you shop, looking over your shoulder while you cook. Prepare the meal, allowing the sights, smells, and textures of the food to bring you closer to them. Set the table with their favorite music and flowers—however they enjoyed dinner—and be sure to set out a specific place for them. Place a small bit of food on their plate. Enjoy your meal.

After dinner, communicate with them in proper conversational form through your cards. Take out your tarot deck. Light a candle to represent their spirit. Repeat the incantation. Begin a dialogue of active communication, using the cards as the answering device. Soul communication is delicate, intimate work. It improves with practice. Allow them to speak to you through the cards. Trust your voice and theirs.

Bang for Your Buck Shopping Spell

Ingredients
1. Seven of Swords
2. Nine of Pentacles
3. The Wheel of Fortune

Method, Visualization, and Meditation

This spell assures you will get the best deals and score excellent, drool-worthy items. Perform on the morning of the planned shopping trip. The suit of Swords is used because it is the suit of calculation and observation; Sword instincts serve you well when shopping. The Wheel of Fortune offers supportive energy.

The layout of the spell acts as an energetic pathway, sourcing the power from above down and into your body.

Place the Seven of Swords. Enter the card and become the figure. The swords you escape with are the items you find. Not only do you find precisely what you seek, but all items are heavily discounted.

Place the Nine of Swords. Enter the card and become the figure. You bask in the garden of luxury. Your new items bring you extreme pleasure.

Place the Wheel of Fortune. Watch the card spring to life, revolving and circling. The clouds swirl and all gears, like clockwork, are in full operation. These are the wheels of luck. They churn for you. Thank them and utter the incantation.

1

2

3

Visionary and genius Coco Chanel, who built the famous fashion empire, was born on this day in 1883. Channel Chanel (pun intended).

INCANTATION

Wheel of Fortune
My spinning luck
Assure I get the best
Bang for my buck
Guide me right
To a sale
I'll never have
To pay retail

Embrace My Fear Spell

Ingredients
- Tarot deck
- Celtic Cross spread

Method, Visualization, and Meditation

Our fears offer us many clues to our true nature, and it is often the case that we fear what we want the most. By embracing a fear, facing it, and exploring it, you will emerge transformed.

Perform the Celtic Cross spread for yourself and your life situation. Take careful notes on your reading (sometimes, writing out your reading as if you were speaking to someone will help you become succinct with your answers).

Make special note of card number 9, your hopes and fears. Note also that 9 is the number of wish fulfillment, so keep this card out once all the others are put away.

How is this card emblematic of your deepest fear? How does it also represent your hopes? Are your hopes and fears two sides of the same coin?

Enter this card and embrace it for what it is.

Adopt this card as your talisman, your emblem of action. Decide upon a coarse of action—one single thing you will do to face this fear.

INCANTATION

Swords of action, Wands of fire
Cup's emotion, Pentacle pyre
I face this fear
I will prevail
Through forward channels
I will sail
Fear will always point the way
In one place I will not stay
Transform, change
And then adapt
Victorious life
Become enwrapped

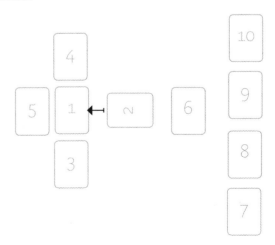

Switch Career Spell

Ingredients
1. Card representing your current career
2. The Hanged Man
3. Card representing what must be released
4. Card representing qualities of your new direction

Method, Visualization, and Meditation

The metaphor of harvesting grains may be used when examining elements of our life that have to do with breadwinning. The selection of cards is as important as the visualization of this spell. Be thoughtful in your selection of card 3. You must release what keeps you bound to your current situation. What is it? Financial security? Stability? Safety? Fear? Expectations?

Place card 1. Focus on the qualities of your current situation. How has it sustained you, defined you, and challenged you?

Place card 2. The wood from which he hangs is a powerful crossroads. You are at an intersection. Enter the card. Stand at the junction.

Place card 3 under the Hanged Man. See the behavior represented by the card leave your body like a ghost. Watch it walking away from you, down the path, becoming smaller, until it disappears. Know this is a dark path you will not follow. You have let part of yourself go; as you venture forward you may feel vulnerable. Vulnerability means you are moving in the right direction.

Place card 4. Walk down the path in this direction full of possibility. See it, feel it, embrace it.

| 1 | 2 | 4 |

| 3 |

Today is the Roman festival honoring Consus, deity of harvest and grain.

• • • • • •

INCANTATION

With these cards
I do brew
A change for something
Shiny, new
All things in time
Come to an end
New opportunity
Is my friend
A turn, a switch
A swap, a shift
The change comes fast
It's very swift

Seven of Wands Connection Ritual

The Seven of Wands was called the Lord of Valor by the magicians of the Golden Dawn, who assigned it the time period of August 12–22.

INCANTATION

Seven of Wands
Passions fight
Lay down your sticks
End this blight
When passion bubbles
To the fore
Time to cool
Not even score
Take a break
Give it a rest
Time will sort out
What is best

Ingredient
• Seven of Wands

Method, Visualization, and Meditation

Enter the arcana of the Seven of Wands.

Seven is a mystical number. Seven is a lucky number. There are seven notes on the musical scale, seven days of the week, seven planets in our solar system besides Earth, seven deadly sins, seven seas, seven colors of the rainbow, seven continents, and seven wonders of the ancient world.

You stand among a crowd in a green field, the sky as blue as if a child had splashed it with tempera paint. Cries and voices fill your ears as the crowd ignores you while jeering and taunting a man. The gentleman stands upon a small hill. The crowd points sticks toward the man, who raises his own staff in defense. You wonder what he could have done to rile everyone up. Gazing at the wand he grips, you note that his tool, an object once used for growth and expansion, has been transformed into a weapon. How could this be?

A grimace of pain and realization fills the man's face. He relinquishes the wand and steps back. He was safe from the crowd all along. He won by not engaging. His power and passion got everyone worked up. The crowd saw something of themselves, something they didn't understand, in this man. Now they would punish him for it. He realizes that the way to win is to not engage. Taking this lesson to heart, he walks out of sight, stick dragging behind him. The crowd disperses, mumbling and disappointed. A single staff lies on the ground. It reverberates with power. Will you pick it up or leave it be?

Knight of Swords Connection Ritual

Ingredient
- Knight of Swords

Method, Visualization, and Meditation
Enter the arcana of the Knight of Swords.

The Knight of Swords contains the expansive energy of a maniacal, focused fury. Small doses of this essence yield quick, direct results.

Step aside. Move quick. Sound and fury surround you. Jagged clouds dart across the sky. Trees succumb to wind gusts that bend them at will. The earth quakes; the ground beneath your feet trembles like a frightened child. You turn to the sound of pounding horse hooves. A knight and horse gallop toward you.

The knight charges forward, his war sword piercing the way, splitting air as he moves. Gleaming silver armor protects his body from attackers. His feet bear razor-sharp points from toe to heel, protecting him from those who approach from the front or back. The knight's cap bears feathers, symbolic of birds; he's decorated with butterflies, emblematic of the flight of the soul and the element of air, from which his temper, vision, and strength were born.

As the knight crosses your field of vision, you note his sturdy horse. The horse is under the knight's command, but he is his own entity. The horse contains his own nature. He moves forward as the knight commands, yet his eyes look back at the knight, questioning the motives of his demanding master. In a flash of insight, you realize the horse represents the choices we make, the actions we take, and the plans we set into place. The horse represents our manipulation of the world and other energies separate from our own.

The pair fade into the distance as the wind dies and the ground becomes stable once again. The time for thinking is over. It is a moment of decisive action.

Scottish hero William Wallace died on this day in 1305. Wallace was the quintessential Knight of Swords: he fought tirelessly for Scottish independence.

INCANTATION
Beware, beware
Blood's in the air
Do not stop
Do not stare
Moving with
A clear directive
The Knight of Swords
Is quite effective
Off he rides
On the breeze, he's gone
Fierce, sharp words
And full of brawn

Today the Roman festival honoring Mania, goddess of spirits, insanity, and madness, was celebrated.

INCANTATION

Insane behavior

You stop now

Banish you far

I don't care how

Frozen, ice bound, frosted

Before you make me

Too exhausted

Leave me in peace

And offer no harm

Your negative power

I do disarm

Stop the Madness Spell

Ingredients
- Slip of paper
1. The Devil
2. Ten of Wands
3. The Star
- Ice cube tray

Method, Visualization, and Meditation

Craft your intention. Write down the behavior and "madness" you wish to terminate. If you wish to stop a behavior stemming from another person, be clear it is the effect of their behavior upon you, not the actual person that you will terminate.

Place the Devil card before you. Contemplate the insanity swirling around you.

Cross it with the Ten of Wands. Feel the dark, destructive energy being blocked by the field of wands. The cycle is over.

Place or roll the paper with your intention inside an ice cube tray or freezable container. Fill with water and place inside your freezer. The mania is stopped.

Place the Star over both cards. Enter the card. Feel the Star's rejuvenation pouring over every aspect of your life.

Veil of Neptune Spell

Ingredients
- Cups court cards (king, queen, knight, page)
- 4 small candles
- Veil, pashmina, or silky scarf
- Seven of Cups

Method, Visualization, and Meditation

Neptune is a dreamy blue planet with five rings and fourteen moons. It rules dreams, subtlety, and the subconscious. This misty, watery planet also oversees witchcraft, sorcery, and mysticism. It is a helpful planet to access when entering a new mystical practice.

Are you looking for privacy in a new metaphysical practice or for work? Are you beginning a yoga practice, a journaling workshop, transcendental meditation, or beginning a creative project requiring solitude? The Veil of Neptune Spell assures you'll receive the privacy needed to conduct your new practice. It assures you spiritual space and the peace needed to perform your work unencumbered.

Begin this spell by staking out new metaphysical space around you. Mark these lines as you would stake property lines. Instead of stakes, you will ground your four corners with the dreamy Cups court cards, who will become your watchtowers and guardians.

Place a candle and the Page of Cups to the east. Repeat the incantation.

Place a candle and the Knight of Cups to the south. Repeat the incantation.

Place a candle and the Queen of Cups to the west. Repeat the incantation.

Place a candle and the King of Cups to the north. Repeat the incantation.

Place the veil or scarf symbolically over your head and focus on the Seven of Cups. Enter the card with your mind's eye and expand the possibilities to include infinite cups spread before you, as far as the eye can see. Stay and meditate with the card on your new practice.

The closest approach to the planet Neptune occurred on this day in 1989 by Voyager 2. Neptune is named for the Roman god of the sea but is undetectable to the naked eye and was unknown to the ancients.

INCANTATION

Veil of Neptune
Claim this space
My work fills up
This special place
Veil of Neptune
Now I'm free
Reveal new things
Unseen by me

Organizing Energy of Virgo Spell

Today is the fourth day of the astrological sign of Virgo, ruled by Mercury. Virgo's attention to detail is second to none. Nothing escapes their watchful and meticulous eye. Virgos are also famous for their caring and compassionate nature.

INCANTATION

Organize, crunch

Edit, throw

If you don't serve me

It's time to go

My energy's quick

I do this fast

My efforts are good

And their effects last

The space is changed

Inside and out

Possibilites around me

Sprout

Ingredient
- The Hermit

Method, Visualization, and Meditation

Cast this spell when it is time for you to power-punch clean, get your office organized, your financial house in order, kick off a healthy eating plan, or clean out your closets. Organizing and cleaning can be a powerful spiritual tool/practice. A skilled practitioner organizes physical space while simultaneously reconstructing metaphysical space. Actions on the physical plane affect the metaphysical plane and vice versa. Remember the Magician's creed: "As above, so below."

The Hermit card is assigned to the sign of Virgo.

Enter the card. You discover yourself inside the dark cave of the Hermit. It is where he was before raising his lantern. A lone candle glows, and by this light you sit and contemplate. See the space you must organize in your mind's eye. What do you want the space to look like? Who or what is the inspiration for setting things straight? What is the implication of getting things straightened out? How does getting rid of the unneeded free you? How have you organized in the past? Do you become distracted, disheartened, or bored? See yourself organizing with crystal-clear vision. What else changes as a result of your organization?

Feel your power and wisdom. Know your vision is unstoppable. You are unstoppable. Blow out the Hermit's candle.

Get to work.

Renewal Spell

Ingredients
- Eucalyptus essential oil
- I cup sea salt
- Fresh lemon, sliced
- Fresh lavender
- Ace of Cups

Today is the Roman festival Volturnalia, honoring Volturnus, god of waters and fountains.

Method, Visualization, and Meditation

Fountains are magical places of renewal, drawing observers like magnets. Mindfully bathing or showering will transform your energy and cleanse your aura. The Ace of Cups, the fountain card, represents the healing essence of a waterfall, the rejuvenating energy of water, and general emotional clearing. Focus on this card while bathing to extract its renewing properties. Eucalyptus and lemons are both associated with the moon, water, and purification. Salt is used for protection, and lavender is used for its healing properties.

Place a few drops of eucalyptus oil into the running water of a bath. Add sea salt, lemon, and lavender. Place the Ace of Cups where you can see it from the tub but where it will not get wet. Hop into the tub as it is filling up. The bath is echoing the properties of a fountain. Focus on the Ace of Cups as the water runs. This ace is the source of the entire suit of Cups. Continue to work with the energy of the card and running water until the bath is full.

Once the tub is full, rub all of your skin with the lemon slices. As you do so, imagine any and all negativity being erased. Feel your stress disappearing. Bask in the water as long as you like. When you are finished, unplug the drain but remain in the tub. Let the water run through the drain. Imagine any residual negative energy being washed down the drain.

Towel off. You are renewed.

• • • • •

INCANTATION

Ace of Cups
Wash and erase
Remove the thoughts
I just can't face
Rinse and down
The drain with you
I'm squeaky clean
And happy too

Today in 1859 a geomagnetic storm caused the northern lights to shine so brightly that they were seen as far as Japan. The term "true north" describes one's internal compass. The magic of the northern lights reminds us to cultivate our own "true north."

INCANTATION

Focus, movement
Getting clear
The time has come
My goal is near
I've dallied now
It's time to run
I see it now
It has begun
Move toward the things
That I must do
To let my hopes and
Dreams come true

Get Back on Track Spell

Ingredients

1. Soul purpose card
2. Instinct card
3. Resource card
4. True north card (where you need to go)

Method, Visualization, and Meditation

This spell snaps you into place and brings clarity when you feel yourself veering off track. Stepping off track can help to reevaluate our situation. This spell helps you hop back on.

Specifically choose four cards.

The spell begins the moment you begin card selection. As each card is chosen, place before you as instructed and enter the card, meditating on each one.

1. Soul purpose card. This card represents the essence of *you*. Why you are here? What is the nature of your soul as best reflected by a tarot image?
2. Instinct card. What do you trust about yourself? What tarot image reflects your best instinct?
3. Resource card. What can you depend on? What represents your support system?
4. True north card. What direction do you want to head in? Where do you deeply desire to go?

Place cards 1, 2, and 3 in place, and set card 4 randomly outside of the triangle. Because this is representing the track you are getting on, move all the cards in the triangle to face that card.

Once the cards have been selected and worked with, turn cards 1, 2, and 3 to face card 4. This channels all efforts toward your true north.

248

Lampadomancy

Ingredients
- Kerosene or hurricane lamp
- Tarot deck
- Question

Method, Visualization, and Meditation

Lampadomancy is a form of divination using the wick of a lamp. The practice dates back to ancient Egypt and Mesopotamia. Ancient lamps were formed with terra cotta, filled with thick oils, and cotton string served as a wick. Diviners observed, interpreted, and divined the dancing flames and wick. You can do the same.

Clear your space. Formulate a excellent question. Take your time observing the lamp; consider the oil, and examine the wick. Align your energy with the lamp. Ask your question out loud when you light the wick. Align your energy with the flame. Can you make the flame rise by asking? Will it dance for you? Where does the flame end and the air begin?

Watch the wick carefully to read its signs. Is it an explosive or calm flame? Does it extinguish quickly or dance happily? Is it giving off smoke or burning cleanly?

When you feel you have found guidance to your question or topic, shuffle and randomly pull a few cards from your tarot deck for further clarification.

Charitable donors in ancient England provided funds for candles, wicks, and lanterns to shed light for travelers on dark nights. On this date in 1656 John Wardall gave the sizable bequest of four English pounds to churchwardens for an evening glass lantern to hang in their vicinity.

• • • • • •

INCANTATION
Whispering crickets
Dancing flame
My questioning heart
Comes again
Burning energy matches
My heart's desire
I often feel
Consumed by fire
Need to know
What to do next
In your flicker
My truth reflects

INCANTATION

Eight of Pentacles

Artisanal card

Reminds me loving

Work's not hard

I'm paid well and

Time, it flies

With gorgeous work

Before my eyes

Happy to indulge

My day

In doing work

That feels like play

Eight of Pentacles Connection Ritual

Ingredients
- Eight of Pentacles

Method, Visualization, and Meditation

Enter the arcana of the Eight of Pentacles.

A knock, knock, knocking is heard. Your attention is drawn to a man who whittles away on a wooden bench. The scent of cedar and pine hangs in the heady, sweet air inside a woodworking chamber. The item upon which he works is not wood but a yellow stone. He chips away at the stone, wiping the granules to the floor. They fall at his feet like snow. He wipes sweat from his brow as he works. He has displayed previous examples of work in a neat vertical line.

His feet are covered with crimson slippers, his legs by red tights, and a tunic of sea blue is covered by a craftsman's apron. His hair turns in sweet curls, and a look of pleasure plays across his face and gentle lips.

The artisan is the bridge between the invisible world of the imagination and thought and the physical world of manifestation. His image, this card, reflects personal energy, emotion, and intention used to create a new form of matter. This craftsman manipulates the physical world, crafting it in his vision. He is using the gifts he was born with to create. You are free to do the same at any moment. You hold his power in your hands. You manipulate energy with everything you do and create butterfly effects in the world with thoughts and actions.

Bring a Long-Distance Lover Close to You Spell

Ingredients
1. King of Cups
2. Eight of Wands
3. The Chariot
4. Queen of Cups
- Pinch of cinnamon

Method, Visualization, and Meditation

The King of Cups and the Queen of Cups represent the two of you. Select more suitable cards to represent each of you if you prefer. The Eight of Wands spurs action because it contains the essence of combustion set free. The Chariot directs them to you in the quickest possible way. Cinnamon is used for attraction magic.

Place the King of Cups before you. In your mind's eye imagine your lover sitting in their throne, eyes cast in your direction. Feel their love and attention being placed on you. See yourself in their eyes.

Place the Eight of Wands, the card of travel and speed. Feel unseen forces kicking into action. The wheels are greased; the way has been paved.

Place the Chariot card, the vehicle bringing them to you. See them leaving and setting off for you.

Place the Queen of Cups, the card of full female reception. She waits patiently. She knows things always unfold as they should and in the right time. See your lover walking through your door and into your arms.

Finish the spell by sprinkling a pinch of cinnamon at your front door.

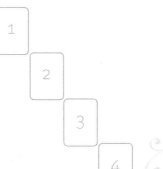

The Flaming Fireball Festival is held today in El Salvador. Men dressed as skeletons divide into teams and hurl flaming gasoline-soaked rag balls at one another.

INCANTATION

Lover, lover come to me
Cross the oceans, part the sea
Smell you, see you, need you near
In my ears your voice I hear
Your breath is warm
Your touch so soft
You send my aching heart aloft
I can't wait
Must see you soon
Embark your journey
By the light of the moon

Today is the earliest day on which Labor Day can fall. What better time to reach for the stars and take control of your professional life?

Labor Day Next Level Career Spell

Ingredients
- Felt-tip pen
- Sharp pin
- Egg
- The Tower
- Almonds

Method, Visualization, and Meditation

A clear intention energizes this spell. The Tower card provides an additional power, boosting you to the next level.

Wash a raw egg with soap and water. To blow the yolk and white from the egg, push the pin into the egg's tip. Pierce the other end of the egg, hold the egg over a bowl, and begin to blow out the yolk and white. Blow the egg hollow and imagine you are cleansing your life, pushing away unneeded qualities, emptying stress, and blowing out the need, worry, and want. Let each breath of air come from deep in your belly.

Once the egg is hollow, use your felt-tip pen to write what you want on the egg. What is your next level? Be specific. Be precise. Write as many applicable words as possible upon your eggshell.

Gaze into the Tower card. Normally this card is feared, but here, now, you fearlessly venture inside to harness the power of a breakthrough. Smell the electricity, the brimstone, in the card. See the card as it is the moment before the lightning strikes. Feel the power gathering in the storm clouds above you. Repeat the incantation. Smash the egg (either in your yard or into a garbage can) on the final word, "year," of the incantation. You have unleashed the power of the Tower card. Eat a handful of almonds to keep yourself grounded.

INCANTATION
Tower card
Spark of light
Open new paths
For me tonight
Tear the ether open
Wide and clear
Life transforms for
Me this year!

Chariot Card's Take Action Spell

Ingredients
- The Chariot
- Ginger tea
- Bread
- Peanut butter
- Honey bear

Method, Visualization, and Meditation

Ginger contains the sacred power root of fire and energy. Honey attracts good things, and peanut butter is grounding and will keep you steady as you fly. The Chariot card places you directly into the driver's seat, a place of power.

Decide what you want to take action on. What will your first step be? When these two things are clearly determined and set in your mind like cement, set bread in the toaster and the tea water to boil. Pull your Chariot card. Look at the city behind the charioteer; this is what he leaves behind. Imagine yourself pulling away from your old reality. The freedom of the open road represents the space you are creating inside yourself. Feel leather straps in the palm of your hands, the movement of the carriage beneath you, and the slow and steady clopping of hooves and the whir of wheels. See clearly where you are going as you take this step.

Spread the peanut butter on your toast. With a honey bear, write in honey a word which describes the action you are about to take. Eat the toast, sip your tea, and perform this task. Keep the Chariot card in sight all day, if possible. Invoke the Chariot and "see" your destination when you are in your car, in any form of transit, or walking.

Today Greeks celebrate Nike, goddess of speed, strength, and victory. Nike is often depicted as the charioteer who flies across battlefields awarding fame and glory to the victors. She and the Chariot card will get you moving.

INCANTATION
Chariot card
Goddess of speed
Transform within
Follow my need
Direct and fast
My action's swift
And with my deed
The results lift
Me high and up
Above the fray
My course will change
Upon this day

September • 3

INCANTATION

Hanged man
Place of change
Alter your view
But don't derange
Morphed perceptions
Help to see
Opportunities right
In front of me

Hanged Man Card Connection Ritual

Ingredient
• The Hanged Man

Method, Visualization, and Meditation
Enter the Hanged Man card.

You aren't quite sure how long you've been walking now. The dirt road sends up little dust puffs at every step. You are approaching a three-way intersection and stop to scratch your head. You aren't sure whether you should turn left or right. You see a signpost and approach in hopes of directions or guidance. Instead of a sign, you discover a man hanging upside down. He seems quite content as he dangles from one foot tied with a yellow rope.

"Do you need help?" you ask.

"Oh, no. I am just where I am meant to be," he answers.

One leg crosses the other deliberately as if holding a ballet pose, and his arms are hidden behind his back.

"How long have you been here?" you ask.

"Long enough," he answers.

Fresh green leaves sprout from the wood he is hanging from.

"Which way do you think I should go?" you ask, pointing to the crossroads.

"It depends on where you are going," he replies. "Where are you going?"

His head takes on an otherworldly yellow glow.

"I don't know," you reply.

"In that case, stay here with me until you spy something new," he replies.

And you do.

Winning Spell

Ingredients
1. Five of Wands
2. The Wheel of Fortune
3. Six of Wands

Method, Visualization, and Meditation

Place the Five of Wands before you and observe the card. Watch the youths come alive before you and hear their cries of effort and their scuffling feet. Think about the situation you are attempting to win. It seems you are all fighting for the same thing, doesn't it?

Observe the youths again, only this time, rather than fighting, see them working together. Positioning their sticks in synchronization, they form a five-pointed star, the symbol of magic. Know on the deepest, most profound level that there is enough victory to go around—more than enough prizes for everyone. Victory for you does not mean someone else loses out. In fact, your victory makes the world a far richer, better place.

Place the Wheel of Fortune card over the Five of Wands. The ticking of the wheel spins like a beach boardwalk or carnival wheel game. See the name or a picture of the prize you desire spinning round and round on the wheel. Slow the wheel down until it stops perfectly on your prize.

Place the Six of Wands beneath the Wheel of Fortune. Review what you want. Feel the accolades of the people around you. Feel the buoyancy that comes along with winning. What are you looking forward to? What will you enjoy from your win? How has your life changed?

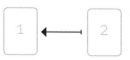

Today marked the beginning of ancient Roman Games that entertained the public with gladiators, chariot races, and highly theatrical events.

INCANTATION

A win for you is a win for me
Encourage each other
Unconditionally
Life's a game
It's all fair play
I'll enjoy a win today

Find a Mentor Spell

Today is Teachers' Day in India, a day celebrated in many countries recognizing and honoring the role of educators and mentors.

Ingredients
1. Page of Pentacles
2. The Hermit
• Green apple

Method, Visualization, and Meditation

Mentors and teachers encourage and champion your talents and goals. They might show you how certain things are done or serve as an example of what is possible. Mentors come in all shapes and sizes. Do not make the mistake of predetermining who or what your mentor should look like or be. Set your intention. Let the universe take care of the rest.

The Hermit card represents the mentor. The Page of Pentacles is the student card. The hermit shines his light of personal knowledge on the student, who soaks it up.

Place the Page of Pentacles. Enter the card. Become the young figure. Stand on the edge of rolling farmland, rich and fertile. The breeze carries the gentle hum of distant tractors who turn over the soft ground, preparing the earth for planting. You know you are at the precipice of learning. You balance a globe upon your nimble fingers. Inside the ball, you see all of the things you wish to accomplish. Take your time. See this quite clearly.

The pentacle glows like a spark or searchlight. Place the Hermit card before you. Note how the page and the hermit mirror each other. The hermit's star is six-pointed due to the nature of his experience. The hermit and page act as a yin and yang for each other, exchanging energy. Feel energy radiating outward from your body into the subtle world, acting like strings attracting the right mentor into your life.

Walk to a favorite place in nature and leave the apple as an offering to your future mentor while reciting the incantation.

INCANTATION

Pentacle of power

Light my way

Bring a teacher

Toward me today

Passion and yearning

Fill me so

In all the ways

I wish to grow

Guide me, teach me

Show me how

Hear my call

Greet me now

1   2

Accepting Loss Spell

Ingredients
• Queen of Pentacles

Method, Visualization, and Meditation

The five stages of grieving claim acceptance as the last and final stage. The process of grieving the loss of anything is highly personal and completely subjective. Nothing prepares us for deep, unexpected loss. Finding acceptance will make the process more bearable to move through.

Place the Queen of Pentacles. Enter the card. She sits in the garden of paradise. It is wild and overgrown, saturated with blooming red roses, honeysuckle, and jasmine. Her clothing is as rich and colorful as her landscape. Every blade of tender green grass quivers with her breath, the air that caresses the landscape. Her eyes bring this beauty to life. Her touch brings fat bunnies to her feet. Her ears bring the whistles of birds from treetops.

The queen looks quietly at the pentacle on her lap. She is the queen of the material world. She has manifested the glorious bounty that surrounds her. Yet she knows, she deeply understands, that the rich landscape will cool and grow silent as winter approaches. She gazes at the pentacle as if into a crystal ball, knowing that the perfection of this moment will disappear and transform into something else. She knows that nothing remains, that all life is constant motion, flux. Knowing this brings her sadness and melancholia. She doesn't fight it. She allows it to wash over her. She has found acceptance; it does not sweeten her sorrow, but she understands it is the way of life.

Diana Spencer, Princess of Wales, was laid to rest on this day in 1997.

INCANTATION
Nothing stops
The pain inside
Feels like my soul's
Been broken wide
But nothing's lost
It's just transformed
And soon enough
Will be reborn.
I'll feel it all
Push no feeling away
And wake to see
Another day

A solar eclipse on this day in 1251 marked the birth of Greek Heracles, whose Roman equivalent is Hercules.

Grant Me the Strength Spell

Ingredients
1. Strength
2. Ace of Wands
3. Ace of Pentacles
4. Ace of Swords
5. Ace of Cups

Method, Visualization, and Meditation

This spell marks the gentle, strong tendon and muscle building in the mind and body. It is not a burst of strength that pops once like a balloon. The invoked power remains.

Place the Strength card before you. Enter the card. Embody the figure. Place one of your hands upon the lion's head while your other hand supports his jaw. Feel the strength he possesses, though he does not snap his sharp teeth. Let yourself be filled with the lion's energy. Feel his muscles, his speed, his hunger. Feel the lion's pleasure in himself for yourself. Feel the stability that four legs bring. Apply all this strength to the situation you face and the strength required. Know you have this.

Place the Ace of Wands and feel the burst of fire and passion supporting you. Place the Ace of Pentacles and feel the gift of receiving what you need when you need it. Place the Ace of Swords and feel the steel of protection and the quickness of thought. Place the Ace of Cups and feel the life-sustaining waters of emotion filling you.

Focus on this mandala for as long as needed.

INCANTATION

Passion of fire
Life-changing seed
Steel of thought
Emotion I need
Strength is mine
Resolution strong
Nothing and no one
Can do me wrong

Wildest Dream Spell

Ingredients

- Paper and pen
- Candle

1. Tarot card representing what you need to make it happen
2. Tarot card representing you living your dream

Method, Visualization, and Meditation

Life-changing dreams don't occur when outside circumstances change. They occur when your inside circumstances change. Transform the inner to transform the outer. The process becomes simplified with the use of tarot images.

Light your candle.

Using paper and pen, write out your wildest dream. Have fun and do not hold back. Once you have described every single aspect of the dream, reduce it to its simplest and most powerful denominator. Write your dream in one sentence.

Place card 1 before you. Enter the card. Imagine the phone calls, the actions, the steps you can take in order for you to manifest your wildest desire.

Place card 2 before you. Enter the card. Inhabit the figure or place inside the card. See yourself very clearly doing what you dream of. What has changed? Can you figure out what inner quality needed to change in order to live this dream? How does it feel? How does it smell? How does it look? How is your perspective different?

State your wish out loud. Blow out your candle like it's your birthday.

Consider magic. Consider that you could actually manifest, have, and create your wildest dream. This very moment, this spell is an opportunity for you to cast for it. The biggest life-altering dream come true begins here and now. Are you ready?

INCANTATION

Wildest dream
I'm courting you
I know together
We'll come true
I see you
And you see me
Together use the skeleton key
Soar to unimaginable heights
Embrace new worlds
Of delights

The Nine of Pentacles was called the Lord of Material Gain by the magicians of the Golden Dawn, who assigned it the time period of September 2–11.

INCANTATION

Secret gardens, flowers

Bountiful herb

Enter this space

Do not disturb

Ancient vines

And walls of stone

This stands for me

And me alone

An inner wealth

Reflects around

This sacred space

That I have found

Nine of Pentacles Connection Ritual

Ingredient
- Nine of Pentacles

Method, Visualization, and Meditation

Enter the arcana of the Nine of Pentacles.

You feel summer's grip on shortening days as you stand amidst the lush warmth of early September. Beaujolais grapes burst with ripeness, fat apples pull their tree branches low to the ground, and raspberries ooze with juice and attract bees and butterflies. Rambling ivy and tangled grapevines run along ancient stone walls. You see no exit, no gate. A castle stands in the distance.

Secret gardens are not easily discovered, yet you have found your way inside of one. Its sacred nature tucks you away from the ordinary world.

You are startled by the appearance of a regal-looking woman. She looks through you as if you were a ghost. You relax when you realize she cannot see you. She is magnificently dressed in a sumptuous gown with silken slippers. The red velvet of her fine cloak plays off the creaminess of her skin, luminescent and lovely. She wears a falconer's glove, and her bird of prey perches on her hand with its razor-sharp talons.

This woman has a powerful ally. Her raptor would hunt and kill any creature for her, yet, like the female on the Strength card, she restrains his wild nature. He waits for her command. In polar opposition to her fierce bird, a snail glides across the ground. The snail leaves a glistening trail of slime behind its slowly moving, spongy body.

The woman's outward reality reflects her inner mastery. She maintains the polarity of speed and patience, of strength and vulnerability. She has matriculated inside the animal and vegetable world. A rose woven labyrinth winds around her, hiding her from the pressures of "reality" she has left behind. Time ceases to exist. Now that you have found this space, you may enter whenever you desire.

Tarot Gris Gris Bag

Ingredients
- 2 x 3-inch bag
- Candle corresponding to your goal
- Incense corresponding to your goal
- Tarot card corresponding to your goal
- Gem or stone corresponding to your goal
- Fingernail clippings
- Pinch of your hair
- Paper with your signature
- Corresponding charms
- Corresponding flower petals and herbs
- Lucky token
- Roots and shells
- Runes and sigils
- Pen and paper

Method, Visualization, and Meditation

Gris gris, both a noun and a verb, originates from a West African term. Originally referring to dolls, it can be used interchangeably with the terms mojo bags, conjure, or charms. It is said a gris gris bag should always contain an odd number of items: it should have no less than three and no more than thirteen items inside.

The creation of a gris gris bag is highly intuitive. Each item should have meaning for you. The ingredients are suggestions.

Enter your selected tarot card with your mind's eye. Gather what you will need from inside the card. How does this card help you to manifest your desire?

Sketch a miniature version of the card for inclusion in your gris gris. Doing so, contemplate the card and its qualities in relation to your desire. As you finish, pass the paper through the incense and fold, placing it into the bag.

Smudge each item by passing through incense smoke before placing into the bag. Pass the finished bag through the incense.

Today is the birthday of New Orleans Voodoo queen Marie Laveau, who literally put Voodoo culture on the map. She read minds, created protective amulets, cast fortunes, and invited the public to view her rituals.

INCANTATION

Write a personal incantation. Whisper it as you smudge your ingredients. Your words should be simple, powerful, and direct.

Thoth Writing Spell

Today is the first day of Thoth on the Egyptian calendar. Thoth is the god of knowledge, secrets, writing, and scribes. Call upon Thoth's energies for inspiration and clarity of the written word.

Ingredient
- The Magician

Method, Visualization, and Meditation

Thoth is such an ancient deity that Egyptians claim he predates the world's very creation and inhabits multiple realms simultaneously. Call to him for inspiration from dark, hidden places within yourself and for inspiration from above. Call to him when you want to surprise yourself. This small spell will work wonders.

Place the Magician card upon the computer or the blank paper you are to write on. Place your mind's eye inside the card. You discover that this magician stands inside a pyramid of Egypt. Feel the hollow of this temple of Thoth. The heat and sand of the desert are held back by thick walls of stone. Torches flicker and cast yellow light upon the sunken chamber. The room is filled with the thick, sweet scent of blooming rose and vegetation, though there is no sun. The magician channels the energy to inspire these flowers to grow.

The table before you, your writing table, becomes the magician's table. Let the card and your reality merge so you see the magician's room inside your room. Your tablet is set with a glowing wand, gleaming sword, golden cup, and sparkling pentacle, just like the magician. The tools of magic rest at your fingertips. They are ready for your use whenever you need them.

Stand up. Take the posture of the Magician. Point your right hand to the sky and your left hand toward the writing device you are using. Utter the incantation while holding this posture. Feel yourself channeling pure, direct energy from above, down into the place you shall write.

INCANTATION

Hermes Trismegistus

Hermes Trismegistus

Hermes Trismegistus

Fill my words

And make them right

Evoke the genius

Tonight, tonight

Your eloquence falls

On me like rain

As I work on

The writing plane

Spell to Conceive a Baby

Ingredients
1. The Wheel of Fortune
2. The Sun
3. The Empress

Method, Visualization, and Meditation

The Wheel of Fortune represents the force of destiny in action. It propels the events of our life and orders them in a linear fashion. The Sun represents life expansion and a healthy baby and mother. The Empress reflects pregnancy and fruitfulness of all life as she reigns from a field of wheat. Three is the number of cards in this spell and the number of creativity and new life.

Place the Wheel of Fortune before you. See the wheel spinning. Allow yourself to become hypnotized by it. It is a circle, the essential shape of all life. Our solar system, our planet, our cells. See the wheel as an ovary, an egg. It is healthy and soft yet strong. See the snake on the card as it slithers down the curve of the wheel. Invite the snake inside the warm, dark center. The snake enters. Life ignites; cell division begins.

Place the Sun card. Feel the solar energy fill the wheel. The cells divide inside the wheel. See the formation of a child from a clump of cells. Feel the warmth of the sunlight on your body. Feel the heat on your skin. Feel the warmth inside of you. Move the warmth to your belly and feel it there.

Place the Empress card before you. Enter the card and become the Empress. Imagine the baby inside you, warm and snug. You are safe and comfortable The baby is happy and growing. Know this will happen in the right way and in the right time.

Today Russians celebrate a Day of Conception or Procreation Day. Russia found itself in demographic crisis. To ease the situation, couples who deliver a child by June 12 are rewarded by the government.

INCANTATION

Wheel of life, revolving fast
In this life, the good will last
Invite a life to join my own
I give their soul a loving home
Love and nurture
Feed and care
When they need me
I'll be there
Because my heart
Is wise and sound
In your reflection
I am found

1

2   3

September • 13

Have you noticed that triple deities are found cross-culturally? Think of the Father/Son/Holy Spirit or Maiden/Mother/Crone or even Mind/ Body/Spirit. Today was the Roman feast day of the Capitoline Triad of Jupiter, Juno, and Minerva.

INCANTATION
Tarot triad
Point of three
Feel your power
Energize me
Imprint upon me
All day long
Feel you, need you
Keep me strong
Work your magic
Three levels deep
Inside me all your
Secrets keep

Tarot Triad Ritual

Ingredients
- Three cards of choice
- Candle
- Your favorite incense

> ```
> [ 1 ]
> [ 2 ]   [ 3 ]
> ```

Method, Visualization, and Meditation

Create a personal tarot triple deity. Create sacred space inside your triple deity.

Choose three cards and archetypes who you genuinely love, admire, and wish to embrace. You may choose a power triad of three cards that will inspire you to a series of actions. For a female power triad you could choose the World, the Empress, and the High Priestess. For a spiritual mystery power triad, choose the High Priestess, the Hierophant, and Justice, who, with their pillars and veiled secrets, represent the unspeakable. For a love power triad, you might choose the Star, the Lovers, and the World.

Choose the three cards with whom you would like to create a triad. Light your candle and incense. Clear your space and place the cards before you.

Contemplate each card individually.

Contemplate each card in relation to the other.

See a direct line of open, coursing energy between two cards and then three.

Place the cards in a wide triangle on the floor and then sit in the center. Bring the coursing energy of the three into a cone of energy above you, creating a 3D energetic cone with you at the center. Alternatively, you may sit above the triangle of cards and imagine the three cards coming together to form a line of energy that is directed straight into your body.

When you discover a triad you enjoy working with, keep them with you. Imagine the cards imprinted on your back. Keep one at your third eye and two at your ears or shoulders. Create art, a mandala, or jewelry to keep them close.

Finding Time Spell

Ingredients
1. Temperance
2. Ace of Cups
3. The Wheel of Fortune
4. The Sun

Method, Visualization, and Meditation

Take a good look at the time budget of your day. Have you replaced TV with Internet? Could your commute be put to better use? Cut obvious time suckers and perform this spell.

Place the Temperance card before you. Imagine you are the angel. Feel the dampness of the pond beneath your bare feet, the silken fabric of your white gown, and the weight of red wings supporting you. You combine energy between two golden cups. The energetic flow is the essence of what you are making time for. See yourself doing what you want with your time. Pour this energy into the right cup.

Lay the Ace of Cups to the left of Temperance. See your cup overflowing with all the energy and enthusiasm you have placed inside. For something this rich, the world will rearrange itself to make room.

Place the Wheel of Fortune, the master of time flowing, sideways, beneath the ace. See the liquid of your desire spill from the golden chalice and fall into the gears of your life, as spun by the Wheel of Fortune. As an extra flower grows in a crowded garden, so do your life and schedule make room for your desire.

Place the Sun card beneath the wheel. Feel the heat of the new space you have created. As the child moves forth, so do you into your new time zone. You have cleared a path. Take the first step.

2	1

3

4

The British Empire adopted the Gregorian calendar on this day in 1752. It skipped ahead eleven days and ushered in the solar calendar still used in the Western world.

INCANTATION
Wheel of time
Hustle and flow
Round and round
And round you go
Adjust the clock
Fix that gear
New time opens
For me this year

Today is Free Money Day. People give money freely and without obligation during this global event. It promotes sharing and passing on wealth to others. Invoke wealth for yourself on this day, and be sure to pay it forward.

INCANTATION
Money magic
Financial charm
Fantastic wealth
Does me no harm
I'll save and spend
Give some away
Give thanks to fortune
Every day

Financial Oil

Ingredients
- Ace of Pentacles
- Equal parts angelica root, bay laurel leaf, and clove
- Cinnamon extract, 3 drops
- Vanilla extract, 6 drops
- Jojoba oil

Method, Visualization, and Meditation

Ritual dressings and spirit oils are a cross-cultural phenomena, from Catholic sacramental oils to the conjure oils of Hoodoo. Money oil can be utilized in a variety of ways. Dab on your wrists and behind the ears when you seek well-paying work. Massage into the palms of your hands to attract money with handiwork. Dab on your feet for financial stability. Use for anointing magical candles, add to money sachets, incorporate into crafts, or use as an offering to your god of choice.

Assemble all your ingredients so they are in hand's reach. Place the Ace of Pentacles before you. Enter the card. This is the garden of manifestation. Honeysuckle grows, wisteria creeps, and seeds flourish and sprout as life takes shape. This sacred space is the pure source of all abundance, financial and otherwise.

A pentacle, the seed of growth, is extended. The orb glows with life in the palm of a ghostly pale white hand. Bring the pentacle closer to your perspective. It grows bigger as you bring it even closer. Draw it toward you until you are surrounded by the yellow orb. You can reach out your arms and legs. You can hit the five points of the star inside the pentacle with your hands, feet, and head. You are the star. You are magic. You are attraction. You are a magnet for what you require and desire.

Mix the ingredients into the oil while repeating the incantation.

Outside Your Comfort Zone Spell

Ingredients
1. Strength
2. The Tower
3. The Fool

Method, Visualization, and Meditation

This spell provides the courage to do something challenging for yourself. Perhaps you are moving, reemerging on the dating scene, or seeking a job in a field that intimidates you. Often the things we desire most fill us with fear. This spell will help you get closer to what you want so that you can put yourself out on a limb and feel vulnerable.

Imagine your comfort zone. See yourself doing the things that bring you comfort. Imagine very clearly exactly what lies outside this zone. What makes you nervous? What do you want to do?

Place the Strength card before you. Focus on the lion. The lion is calling for you. He represents everything outside your comfort zone. He wants you to put yourself out there. He wants you to take control.

Become the woman on the card. Place your hand around the lion. You are controlling the situation. The situation does not control you. Imagine your single biggest fear. See the fear taking shape as a tower.

Place the Tower card on top of Strength. Watch your fear explode into a million shards of debris. Smell the sulphur and smoke. Watch the flames burn away any residual misgivings. Now you have been cleared.

Place the Fool card on top of the Tower. See yourself walking past your comfort zone. Put yourself out there, tall and proud. As feelings of fear or vulnerability arise, simply feel the feelings, knowing they can't hurt you, and keep on moving.

Today the Mayflower set sail from Plymouth, England, in 1620. Imagine the strength and guts it took for the voyagers who set sail that day. They faced sea storms, uncharted territory, and an unsettled distant land. Let their strength inspire you.

INCANTATION

Fool, essential card
You've got my back
Extend myself
I'll never lack
Expand boundaries
Stretch and grow
Within my heart
I deeply know
I'm safe, protected
Have no fear
My path extends
And it is clear

September • 17

The Library at Alexandria was destroyed today in 642, an incalculable loss of priceless books and manuscripts.

INCANTATION

On and up
Forward move
Nothing's lost
Universal groove
Embrace, transform
And transcend
Old habits and patterns
Come to an end

Spell to Move Forward Without Resentment

Ingredients
1. Strength
2. Six of Cups
3. Eight of Cups
4. The World

Method, Visualization, and Meditation

Are you ready to say goodbye and move forward? You can either let it go or live in the loss. Moving forward without resentment assures the situation will not repeat itself.

Place the Strength card. Enter the card. Stroke the lion's fur. Feel his mane between your fingers. His breath is hot and wet on your hand. You feel his power. He represents the fiercest part of yourself. You possessed power and control all along. This power leads you to the next card.

Place the Six of Cups. Enter the card. Become the taller figure. You have retained the power, control, and posture from the Strength card. The smaller figure represents what you are leaving behind. You are offering this behavior/person/situation love. You are leaving because it is what is best for you. You release anger, cruelty, and any other bitter feelings. Acknowledge the good and the lessons this brought to your life.

Place the Eight of Cups. Stand in the mysterious energy of a solar eclipse. Look at the new path stretching out before you. The path moves up a mountain, higher, until you can no longer see it. Set foot on this path. Move forward freely.

Place the World card. Dancing and spinning, things you want and need are available to you. The love you offered in the Six of Cups has come back to you because everything is connected. You are radiating with magic. You are glowing. It is here you stand, basking in the glory of what you have been able to effectively put behind you. The view is immense. You are infinite.

| 1 | 2 | 3 | 4 |

268

Ten of Pentacles Connection Ritual

Ingredient
- Ten of Pentacles

Method, Visualization, and Meditation
Enter the arcana of the Ten of Pentacles.

It is the one and only tarot card reflecting a threshold into the heart of a city. The cards you've encountered before took place either inside city walls or outside. The Ten of Pentacles is the gateway to a new reality. Docile twin dogs, unlike the harried beasts met in previous cards, nuzzle an older man, licking his palm and wagging their tails. The man's hair has grown white with wisdom and the passing years. Across from the grandfather appears his grandchild, whose cheeks are rosy and plump with youth. The child begins his life while the old man reaches the culmination of his. The mother and father stand tall between them, etching the middle arch of life.

Pamela Colman Smith's card reflects the exterior of the fortress appearing in stark black and white. Tapestries with bare lunar landscapes of the imagination, towers, and balancing scales decorate the wall. The black-and-white images are ghostly compared to the sunny inner courtyard beyond the gate. Inside the arch of the city, the interior is lush with Technicolor.

You walk under the arch and can feel the difference between the inner and outer walls. You realize that your entire life is brighter, richer, and more beautiful now that you have stepped inside your cards. To experience the tarot you must step into the cards as you have done. Move past the family and look up. You see, like a giant hologram, ten pentacles hanging in the formation of the Tree of Life. You have been given the key. You have moved past the visible and into the invisible.

You now understand that the Ten of Pentacles is the gateway to the metaphysical world. It is the very space where these two realities meet and mingle.

The Ten of Pentacles was called the Lord of Wealth by the magicians of the Golden Dawn, who assigned it the time period of September 12–22.

INCANTATION

Ten of Pentacles
Foundation gate
Hurry through
It's not too late
Step through, pass over
Enter quick
Destinies change
Like a magic trick
The place where visible
And invisible meet
New realities
You will greet

Soften the Edges Artichoke Spell

This spell is like a loofah sponge for your psyche. Artichokes, derived from the thistle family and eaten since antiquity, are in season right now.

Ingredients
- Eight of Swords
- Artichoke
- Bay leaf
- Lemon slice
- Mayonnaise

Method, Visualization, and Meditation

Feeling brittle or on edge? Are you being short with yourself or the people you love? We all build up walls and develop sharp, pointy edges that serve to protect us. Protective edges can remain, like dead skin cells, long after they are useful. This spell helps you to release what is no longer needed.

Artichokes are plants of personal protection, bay leaves are symbols of victory, and lemons contain life-sustaining solar energy.

Focus on the Eight of Swords. Make a mental swoop of the recent decisions you have made about the world and about others. Think of how you act as a harsh critic toward yourself and others. Does thinking this way make you feel powerful? These old ideas and harsh judgments are holding you hostage.

Snip off the sharp points of each artichoke leaf with scissors. Start at the bottom and work your way around the globe. As you do so, quite literally imagine you are cutting off the sharp points of yourself. Place the artichoke in a saucepan with a few inches of water, lemon, and a bay leaf. Cover and cook (checking to add water if needed) for about 30 minutes or until artichoke is tender.

Dip the bottom of each leaf in mayo or your favorite sauce as you work your way to the center of the flower. Imagine the binds of the Eight of Swords coming loose as you eat more and more leaves. Should you devour the heart, make it symbolic of the change you are undertaking.

INCANTATION

Nasty thoughts
Feel really bad
Critiquing others
Is simply sad
End behavior
I deplore
And darkness will
Choke me no more
What I put forth
Comes back to me
By the ancient
Law of Three

Keep a Secret Spell

Ingredients
- The High Priestess
- Lip gloss

Method, Visualization, and Meditation

Sometimes keeping a secret is the hardest thing in the world—even secrets about ourselves. It can feel so good, so tasty and delicious, to confide in someone, even when we know we are acting against our better judgment. Cast this spell when you know ahead of time when you need to keep your mouth shut.

Light a candle and gaze at the High Priestess. Silence is the providence of the High Priestess. The High Priestess transcends the physical world; indeed, she transcends time and space and exists in the realm in which we dwelled before arriving here. She is the knowing place we return when we leave. The High Priestess contains *all* secrets.

Language is a recent human convention. Spoken words are a flawed way to express the true self. The High Priestess represents what is felt—information conveyed wordlessly in a glance. She is the gray area. When you read in between the lines, this is the High Priestess communicating. When language falls short it is she who intervenes. The High Priestess is all realities at once. Before you articulate anything, she has conveyed it.

Operating from the High Priestess, you are as close to your authentic self as you will ever be. She has no need to confess, and neither do you.

Look deeply into the card. You need say nothing.

Apply a coat of lip gloss as a reminder to keep your lips sealed.

Today marks the seventh day of the Eleusinian Mysteries. Elusive, secret initiatory ceremonies were held by the women of ancient Greece for the cults of Demeter and Persephone.

• • • • •

INCANTATION

Dark as night
Words see no light
Secret safe
Or lips will chafe
Have a special
Secret shield
This mouth is safe
And knowledge sealed

Celtic Mabon falls on this day, coinciding with the autumnal equinox, which falls on the modern calendar near September 20. The word equinox is derived from the root "equal." There is an equal number of day and night hours during an equinox.

INCANTATION

Season of fall
Harvest nights
Evening's dark
Turn on the lights
Ghosts a-wandering
Spirits fly
Bring on the night
Moon in your eye

Ritual to Align with Fall

Ingredients
- The Moon
- Favorite fall items and symbols

Method, Visualization, and Meditation

Balancing spells are extra powerful during the spring and fall equinox. Working with seasonal energy is like working within the moon's phases. A season's energy surrounds us. We need only to open ourselves in order to access its gifts. Gather seasonal energy like a weaver gathering her silken strands. Crispy nights, plump tree fruits, summer's final harvest, and purple sunsets support you and your magical intent.

The energetic qualities of autumn are wisdom, ripeness, harvest, knowledge, and preparation.

Gather your favorite fall objects. You might select Halloween candy, apples, leaves, woolen socks, glittered skulls, or Indian corn. Place all items around the Moon card.

The nights grow longer and more of the moon's landscape is available to us. How is knowledge born in darkness? Now that winter is ahead of you, what preparations are taken? How does cool, crisp air help you dive into inner wisdom?

Enter the Moon card. See only the darkness at first. Allow the moon's glow to soften the edges of what you can see. Bring the towers into focus. Hear the yelping of the dogs, the scurry of the crawfish. Who is hidden inside the shadows? What guides appear with information for you? What lies beyond the borders of this card? What is hidden in the moon of your subconscious?

Explore into the card as far as you can go on your own.

Ace of Cups Connection Ritual

Ingredient
- Ace of Cups

Method, Visualization, and Meditation
Enter the arcana of the Ace of Cups.

You are seated cross-legged on a green lily pad. The lilies and delicate pink lotus flowers bob in a gentle inlet. A vast ocean spreads before you. The water is teeming with life; glittering fish dart in and around the coral beneath. Though you are on the surface, you see what dances, dips, and swims beneath you. Your connection to this place is strong. Dip your hand in the sparkling water. It feels cool and fresh. You scoop a palm of water and splash it on your cheeks.

Feathers rustle and you look up. A white dove with a sacramental wafer secured in its beak descends into a baptismal font. The metaphor is complete. Water is rejuvenation and life. The symbol transforms before your eyes, and you see the Fountain of Youth, the Holy Grail, and other symbols.

You realize this ace connects to your emotional state as well as health. Emotions move like water, passing across your consciousness. You will continue to allow yourself to feel your emotions without necessarily acting out of reaction to them.

You dive from the lily pad into the water. The coolness invigorates your skin. Swimming beneath the fountain, you let the waters splash down upon your head. Float here as long as you like. Rejuvenate and come to these springs whenever you need refreshment.

You see a white, glowing hand above you. It is the hand of magic, synchronicity, and mystery. It hands you the cup.

The cup is now yours.

Fall equinox is the best time of year to connect to the Ace of Cups, a card that accesses the entire realm of emotions and feelings.

• • • • • •

INCANTATION
Water sprung from
Wells dug deep
Flow when waking
And asleep
The source of life
From where we spring
Natural rejuvenation
Is what you bring
The cup stays open
Emotions flow
It's good to feel
This I know

Today is the first day of Libra. With scales as Libra's symbol, it is no wonder they adore balance, tend to be poised, and share a deep love of inner and outer harmony.

INCANTATION
Pieces of life
Align, align
Balance and harmony
You are mine

Libra Balancing Act Spell

Ingredients
• Pen and paper
1. Justice
2. Six of Pentacles

Method, Visualization, and Meditation

Life can be hectic. To access the balancing energy of Libra, perform this mindful meditation spell.

Think about how you spend your energetic reserves. What fills most of your day? Work? Family? Relationship? Internet? Passionate pursuits? Chores? Commute? Write all the responsibilities, behaviors, and activities that take up time in your day on a piece of paper. Don't forget to include the things, issues, and people you spend time thinking about or dealing with. Include the things you do to relax and rejuvenate.

Leave space in between each listed item. At the bottom of the page write something important you should do for yourself but don't. When you are finished, cut each item out. Look carefully at all the things you put your attention on.

Separate your items by the time they take. What activities do you enjoy? What do you do because other people expect you to? Which items do you not enjoy? Which items take the bulk of your time? What are the time suckers?

Find the responsibility that is least important or unnecessary. Select, crumple, and toss into your garbage can. Do not concern yourself with this item. It has thrown your scales out of whack.

Place the Justice card and the Six of Pentacles before you. Observe the scales on each card. Arrange your items above each card as if you are balancing them on a scale.

Continue to arrange your items as a mindful meditation. Remember as you arrange that balance means living in the full emotional spectrum. Allow things to be in flux. As you balance the items above your cards, see yourself finding a sense of balance in daily life as well.

Lawsuit Spell

Ingredients
1. King of Swords
2. Justice
3. The Wheel of Fortune
• Bay leaves

The United States Supreme Court was created today in 1789.

Method, Visualization, and Meditation

The King of Swords represents an excellent orator, the Justice card ensures that justice is actually served, and the Wheel of Fortune spins destiny in your favor. The cards are arranged in a straight line, a conduit of inspiration and energy.

Place the King of Swords before you and enter the card. Stand before this king and look into his steadfast eyes, feeling his strength and keen intellectuality. Step toward the king and sit in his throne, becoming him. Feel the sword in your hand. Look through his eyes as if they were your own. From this moment forth, your self-expression finds its peak. Your personal communications with all people connected to your case is swift, clear, and to the point.

Place the Justice card before you. Enter the card and stand before her. See yourself reflected in her eyes. Justice represents outer and inner justice. This situation is part of your soul's learning process. Why has this happened? What have you learned? What is your lesson? What is your takeaway from the experience?

Place the Wheel of Fortune. See it spinning. There are ups and downs in the process. Look at the center of the wheel. This is where you go to find your centeredness.

What is the outcome you desire? See the outcome spinning on the wheel. Slow the wheel down so it stops with your desired outcome at the top of the wheel.

Hang a sprig or individual bunch of bay leaves above the inside of your front door to ensure victory.

INCANTATION

Sword of Justice
Work for me
Argue, bargain
Freedom plea
What's fair is fair
And comes to pass
What's meant to be
Is built to last

England and Scotland signed the Treaty of York today in 1237. It marked the official boundary line between the two countries.

INCANTATION

Boundaries strong

The lines are set

My space is claimed

And peace I get

Setting Boundaries Spell

Ingredients
- Sea salt with mortar and pestle
- Pen and paper
- Lighter and ashtray
1. Page of Swords
2. King of Swords
3. Queen of Swords
4. Two of Swords

Method, Visualization, and Meditation

Hoodoo traditions make use of magical powders. Traditional botanicals and roots are ground. The grinding process creates charged powders that can be sprinkled, drawn, or blown. For this spell protective salt is used. A mandala of cards is created so you can focus on creating some boundaries and, in doing so, place a wall of protection around you.

Place your intention of protection into the sea salt as you grind it into smaller particles. Make a list of all the things you are not willing to do anymore. List the ways you have given yourself away to people, things you have done so people like you, things you agreed to that were not authentic to your personal truth. When you are finished, draw a circle around this list and place aside.

Place the Page of Swords. See that she looks out for you, protecting your back and the places you cannot see. Place the King of Swords. He looks straight at you and encourages you to mark your ground. Place the Queen of Swords. She sets future boundaries. Place the Two of Swords. She protects the part of you that needs the most nurturing. Your true guardian, she harbors what is most special about you.

Go outside. Using the salt, sprinkle a protective circle around you. Place the ashtray outside of your circle. Light your list on fire. Let it burn away.

Open Heart Chakra Energy

Ingredient
- Ace of Cups

Method, Visualization, and Meditation

Love and beauty are the essential emotional functions of the human heart. The heart chakra, the fourth chakra, is the part of ourselves that experiences our interconnectedness with other living things. The heart chakra feels and expresses warmth and delight, compassion and joy. Through love we grow and flourish; we transform the world and ourselves. The act of loving can be understood as the very root of magic. We focus, protect, and cherish what we love. Love's nature helps us to realize that there is no line between ourself and the other. Love helps us to see how all things are connected.

The heart chakra is located between the breasts, in the center of the breastbone, between and below the shoulder blades. The heart chakra's traditionally assigned color is green.

Sit in a chair with your feet flat on the floor or sit in traditional yogi position, legs crossed, on the floor. Focus on the space behind your breasts. Feel the energetic center warm and glow. Turn the color to emerald green. You can try spinning the green color to make it more energetic. Perhaps you hear the energy, smell it, or even taste it.

Place the Ace of Cups card before you while maintaining the energy in your chest. See and hear the water spilling out of the cup. Pour your heart energy into the water. Feel it flowing back toward you. The water fills you up and flows back out. Move the energy between your heart and the Ace of Cups. Each breath fills you with more love. Feel the connection of divine tenderness. Feel a ball of energy rise through your spine. It fills your entire essence with love; it spills across your skin, your face, and even the top of your head. You are a glowing, divine creature of love.

Julius Caesar dedicated a temple to Venus, goddess of love and beauty, on this day in 46 BCE.

INCANTATION

Ace of Cups
And heart aglow
Love's the answer
This I know
Give love freely
And I see
Ecstasy thrives
In front of me

Invoke Travel Spell

Today is World Tourism Day, a day to open to the possibilities of world travel.

INCANTATION

Travel far and wide

New realities

Transform me

Deep inside

The spell is cast

The deed is done

This trip will happen

I will have fun

Ingredients
- Yellow candle
- 4 bat nuts
- Page of Wands

Method, Visualization, and Meditation

This spell opens channels of traveling energy for yourself. Have a specific destination you would love to visit? Cast the Manifest a Trip Spell on page 94 too.

Trapa bicornis is a Chinese ling nut or horn nut. The shell resembles a bat, and they are sometimes called a devil pod or a bat nut. They may be purchased online or found in large cities. Place a bat nut above your door to ward off evil.

Light the candle. Place the Page of Wands before you. Place a bat nut in each direction surrounding the card. Begin with the east and move clockwise toward the north.

Turn your attention to the Page of Wands and focus on your desire for travel and discovery. Imagine yourself grabbing your passport, packing your bags, and visiting the far corners of the world.

Look specifically at the tip of the wand on this card and allow it to glow with your desire, red hot like a flame or burning ember. Push this desire out toward the four bat nuts. Imagine each of them flying away with your desire. They will clear the way for you.

Seal your spell by visiting a place—a store or restaurant, park or part of town—you have heard about but never visited before.

When the spell is complete, place these bats, your spirit allies, where you can see them.

Chi Energy Tarot Deck Charging Spell

Ingredients
- Sunrise
- Tarot deck

Method, Visualization, and Meditation

Sunrises and sunsets echo beginnings and endings, births and deaths, youth and wisdom, and they tend to mark the most spiritual and revered moments of the day. Worldwide, people marvel at this transition, whether it be for the deeper metaphor or for the sheer beauty of the symphony of light. Of course, the subtle world is readily available to any of us all the time, yet the subtle reality is easier for human senses to grasp as the veil pulls back and morning light appears over the horizon or as the veil of twilight descends in the evening.

This spell will bind you to your deck. Check your local sunrise time and set your alarm. Wake up early enough to be fully conscious as the sun rises. You will want to access full, present, and gentle energy and attention for this process.

Sit in a comfortable place, outside if possible. Keep your tarot deck in hand. Observe the darkness. How is the darkness like sleep? What creative potential exists here? How comfortable do you feel in darkness? How far does the darkness extend? Do you sense anything there that wants to see the light of day? Do you feel anything wanting to surface?

Watch the sky. Observe the rising sun as it transforms the sky. Feel the life energy coursing through your body. Consciously transfer the energy between you and your tarot deck. Blur the line between your physical body and your tarot deck, imbuing yourself and the deck with life-giving energy. Feel the sun's energy from the center of our solar system. It moves through outer space, through the earth's atmosphere, into you and into your deck.

End when you feel energized. Repeat every season if possible.

The Wisdom of Confucius Day is celebrated today in Taiwan. Celebrations begin as early as 6 am, as it is believed that qi or chi, universal energy, is strongest when night's curtain is pulled back and morning emerges.

INCANTATION
Sacred tarot
Is an extension
Of me, myself
My soul's intention
Source of life
Gorgeous sun
This tarot deck and I
Are one

The Two of Swords was called the Lord of Peace Restored by the magicians of the Golden Dawn, who assigned it the time period of September 23–October 2.

INCANTATION

Two of Swords

Peace of mind

Security and answers

You will find

Cut out distraction

Noise and vice

Meditative recluse

It is quite nice

Two of Swords Connection Ritual

Ingredient
• Two of Swords

Method, Visualization, and Meditation

Enter the arcana of the Two of Swords.

You have entered the space of division. One has become two. In this space of duality the sword has become aware of itself. Context is provided by means of a second. An opposition is born. Oppositional tension creates a new energy.

A woman sits in ceremonial garb. You are close enough to the ocean to hear waves lapping against mossy green stones. The woman is blindfolded as if for an initiation ceremony. Solemnness and seriousness pervade the air. You look left and right to see if there are other people here, perhaps her coven or sorority, but it is just the two of you.

Two long swords are in her grasp. She sweeps them up in a protective stance. You know this woman is inside a deep trance and nothing will break her from it. She has descended down a labyrinth into her own inner world, into the depths of her subconscious.

She travels alone in the highways and byways of her mind, shamanlike, looking for the thoughts and the information she needs. Does she journey to her High Priestess?

She journeys to the place where the mind is allowed to wander freely—it is the deep recess of the self, that place which no one can interfere with. It is the closest waking space to sleep and the place where truth is discerned and uncovered. She has moved there willingly. If you search yourself, you will discover you have been to this place too.

This is the place of decision. This is the place where a story becomes real for the individual. It is the card of discernment.

Never Again Lover Spell

Ingredients
- 12 walnuts
- Ten of Swords
- Ten of Wands

Method, Visualization, and Meditation

This spell has been crafted for when you are ready to end a relationship. However, you must be absolutely steadfast and vow never to sleep with this person ever again. Walnuts have the power to strip away negativity and banish the unwanted. The Ten of Swords marks the end of mental ties, while the Ten of Wands marks the culmination of passion.

Place the walnuts in a pot of water on gentle simmer for three hours, then let the water come to room temperature. Remove the walnuts.

Prepare a bath and pour the walnut water into your bath.

Remove your clothes. Place the Ten of Swords before you. Enter the card and contemplate the finality of it. The figure on the card represents the way your lover makes you feel. Any pain you feel is about to end. You are stopping this.

Place the Ten of Wands before you. Feel the fire and passion you felt for this person. Know you will feel this again for someone else—someone who is worthy of you. This passion has been transformed into a heavy weight upon your back. It is time to release this burden.

Bathe. Contemplate what new potentials will open up as you release this lover from your psyche and your life.

Remain in the tub as you let the water drain and feel all psychic ties slip down the drain.

Today marks the last day of the month and signals a time of endings. Use this energy to find the strength to walk away from an addictive or toxic sexual relationship once and for all.

INCANTATION

Lover, lover
Let me be
You cease to have
A hold on me
Our time is over
Relationship's done
No more battles
Lost or won
I wish you the best
I let you go
New potential
Begins to grow

Today is the first day of October, marking the true season of the witch. This power breakfast, a mindful meal, is a simple way to connect with your inner power.

INCANTATION

Witching season
Time has come
Magic thrives
Webs I've spun
Orange sky
Bone-chilling breeze
Enchantments cast
Manifest with ease

Witch's Power Breakfast

Ingredients
- Apple
- Instant oatmeal (organic if possible)
- Cranberries
- Flax, chia and additional seeds.
- Walnuts, almonds, etc.
- Randomly pulled tarot card

Method, Visualization, and Meditation

Apples are the witch's fruit. Oatmeal is used for bathing and as a medicinal remedy for sunburn and poison ivy. Cranberries, which grow in bogs, are associated with emotion and passion due to their color. Chia seeds belong to the mint family and attract wealth, while flax seeds are featured in Ayurvedic tradition. Eating tree nuts connects us to the power of that tree.

Place your kettle to boil. Slice an apple in half horizontally. Let the five-pointed star inside remind you of the magical power thriving inside you. Remove and keep all of the apple seeds. Dice the apple. Add to your oatmeal with all other fruits, seeds, nuts, and boiling water.

Eat mindfully. Taste each flavor and consider the energy of the foods you are consuming. When you are finished, pull a tarot card randomly from your deck. This card is your personal message of the day.

Take the apple seeds in hand and go outside. Under the changing leaves, toss each seed while you name aloud something you are grateful for.

Give thanks that you have fed yourself well, received a message, and spread gratitude around you. Enjoy your day!

No More Waiting Spell

Arthur Edward Waite, occult writer and creator of the Rider Waite Smith tarot deck, was born on this day in 1857.

Ingredients
1. Card representing your desire
2. The Sun
3. The Chariot

Method, Visualization, and Meditation

How much in your life gets pushed aside? You tell yourself you'll get around to it someday. Don't push your hopes, dreams, and desires into the back drawer like a bundle of mismatched socks.

For this spell, choose one thing you've been putting off. It could be an action, a journey, a practice, a habit, a class, an indulgence, or something that you want. You will shower your desire with light from the Sun card, and the Chariot card will bring it to you. The "Waite" is over.

Decide specifically what you are taking action on. Once you have it firmly in mind, choose a tarot card to represent it. Place this card before you. Imagine yourself doing it or having it. What does it sound like when you are doing it? How does it make you feel? How do you look while doing it?

Place the Sun card above it. Feel the heat of the sun growing and expanding your action. Each flower on the card sends waves of potent, expansive energy to your desire.

Place the Chariot. Enter the card, step into the cart, and become the charioteer. See your final destination. Feel yourself being pulled toward your goal. Direct yourself there in the quickest way. See yourself through the eyes of your desired thing. What do you look like? Imagine yourself in its crosshairs; see yourself becoming larger in its view. It comes closer and closer until the two of you are joined.

INCANTATION
The wait is over
The time is now
Take my desire
Don't ask how
The speed of light
Is quick and fast
And in my life
Good things, they last

2

1

3

Paul Foster Case was born on this day in 1884. Case was an occultist, author, and creator of BOTA, an authentic Western Mystery School offering an intricate and elaborate tarot correspondence course.

INCANTATION

As above

So below

This truth is held

I deeply know

What is imagined

Comes to be

Great power lies

Inside of me

As Above, So Below Ritual

Ingredient
- The Magician

Method, Visualization, and Meditation

This ritual gives us a chance to reflect on the nature of magic.

The Magician's pointed fingers echo the occultist sentiment of "as above, so below." The essence of this statement expresses that what exists inside of you also exists on every other level, seen and unseen. Because of the interconnectedness of all things, to bring about change in your life, one must imagine it first, then work to bring it to existence in the material world.

Place the Magician card before you. Enter the card. Step into the magician's shoes. Feel the energy thriving within you. Where is your body's energy most concentrated?

What you are drawn to naturally? What sort of magic works best for you? How are you connected to the tree outside your window or the cloud passing in the sky?

Consider your imaginative landscape. Where does your mind wander during the day? Where do you journey in your nighttime dreamscapes? What themes tend to pop from your subconscious? What do you desire at the deepest level of your soul? How have you manifested it in your life?

How do you connect the seen and the unseen?

How much of the world actually exists inside your head?

What stories do you tell yourself about the world around you? About your life?

If all worlds are interconnected, how does inner peace and calm make the world a better place? Where is peace most easily cultivated? In the imagination? In your work? In your daily life?

Discover something in your imaginative landscape—something you would like; something good. Picture it completely and fully for what it is. Bring it to your world by drawing a simple sketch of it.

Gravitate Toward Me Spell

Ingredients
1. Significator card (representing you)
2. Card representing what you want
3. The Moon

Earth's first satellite was launched into orbit on this day in 1957.

Method, Visualization, and Meditation

Our bodies are our center, and the life we have imagined and created for ourselves orbits around us. You exert your own gravitational pull. How often do the same type of situations, people, and experiences occur repeatedly in your life?

Choose a card reflecting what you want to attract. For example, for travel opportunities, choose the Eight of Wands. New friends? Choose the Three of Cups. Financial opportunities? Choose the Ace of Pentacles.

Place cards 1 and 2 next to each other. See yourself inside the cards, experiencing them. For instance, if you chose travel opportunities, see your packed suitcase, feel crisp, cool hotel sheets, hear the sound of a soda can popping above the hum of an airplane's engine, experience the weight of a time zone change on your muscles. Find and feel the small details enveloped inside your desire.

Place the Moon card. Enter the card. Stand between the two towers and feel the gravitational pull of the moon. The moon circles the body and planet. Feel the lines of energetic connection between your body and the moon. The lines pull thin when the moon is farthest away but, like a retractable leash, they become taut and strong as the moon comes closer to you. The same thing happens as the moon waxes and wanes. Imagine the same lines of gravitational pull between you and your desire.

Using your finger, circle the Moon card counterclockwise around cards 1 and 2, sealing you and your desire, while repeating the incantation.

INCANTATION
Silver strands of moon
Light of sky
Seal me to things
I want to try

October • 5

On this day in 1789, the Woman's March on Versailles occurred. The riot quickly spread to the palace as these women said, "No more!" The French king and his family were forced to flee to Paris.

INCANTATION

Here is where

I draw the line

Energy's precious

This life is mine

From now on

Move with the flow

And enjoy the power

To say no

Power of "No" Spell

Ingredients
1. Six of Cups
2. Page of Swords
3. Nine of Pentacles

Method, Visualization, and Meditation

We often say yes to others because we want to be liked, avoid conflict, genuinely want to help, or fear being rude. Sometimes, saying no to others means saying yes to yourself. This spell gives you the power of no. It may be the beginning of a personal revolution.

Place the Six of Cups. Enter the card. See yourself in the warm town square. Become the boy in the red hood. You hold a golden cup bursting with flowers you have planted and cultivated. A small girl looks up at you, her face shining with excitement. She wants your flowers. Behind her is a second small girl, a third and fourth—you see hundreds of figures standing in line. They wait to take what you happily hand over. You see, the more you give, the more is taken. It is an endless cycle and everlasting line.

Place the Page of Swords. She lowers her sword and walks into the Six of Cups card. She steps next to you, gently grasps your hand, and pulls you away from the line of children. Using her sword, she draws a line in the soft ground. "This is your personal boundary," she says. "You can say no. No one will be angry with you. This is your space now."

You look and discover all the children have wandered toward someone else who gives out cups.

Place the Nine of Pentacles. She has the power to say yes or no as she likes. Become the figure on the card, relishing her personal space. Focus your attention on yourself, your interests, your own personal pursuits.

| 1 | 2 | 3 |

Mother/Daughter Contemplation

Ingredients
1. The Empress
2. Page of choice
3. Two of Cups

Today the Greek festival of Stenia was celebrated, honoring Demeter and Persephone, the central figures of the Eleusinian Mysteries.

Method, Visualization, and Meditation

This contemplation can be performed to strengthen the bond between yourself and your mother or yourself and your daughter. No matter the nature of your relationship with your mother and/or daughter, a bond exists; this can be performed even if one person has passed to the other side or is not physically present.

The Two of Cups represents the happy union of souls and the magic of their integral connection and reflection. The Empress represents the archetypal essence of motherhood. Pages represent young female energy. Select the appropriate page to represent either yourself or your daughter.

Place the Empress before you. Enter the card and contemplate the qualities of motherhood. How do you experience the physical presence of your mother? What does she feel like? How do you feel? What did you desire from your mother? How do you desire motherhood yourself?

Place the page before you. Enter the card and contemplate the qualities of childhood. How does it feel to be a child? How does it feel to be a small person with a big spirit?

Place the Two of Cups. Consider the energetic connection between mother and child. What do they reflect to each other? What do they teach each other? How are you alike? How are you different? What has grown as a result of your intermingling energy? How does it feel to look at each other? How does it feel to hold each other? How does it feel to laugh together? What does it take to support each other?

What one thing can you do to strengthen or honor the connection between you? Commit to doing this today.

• • • • •

INCANTATION

Mother of earth
Child of light
Our synergy climbs
To a new height
Love and female
Friendship grows
Affection between us
Overflows
Our outer selves
Slip away
As our souls
Reflect and play

| 1 | 3 | 2 |

Jung described the shadow aspect in people. His Red Book, *published today in 2009, reflected images from his own shadow psyche. The shadow is an unconscious and unexpressed aspect of our personality that harbors both positive and negative connotations.*

● ● ● ● ● ●

INCANTATION

Shadow's dimness

Dark as night

Embrace your presence

Hold you tight

Integrate your gifts

And charm

Finding you

Does no one harm

Makes complete

My fractured soul

Complete expression

Is my goal

Shadow Self Integration

Ingredients
- Pen and paper
- The Moon

Method, Visualization, and Meditation

Uncovering aspects of your shadow self is a fascinating exercise in personal archeology whereby you unearth hidden aspects of yourself. The shadow self is anything relevant in your psyche living outside of your awareness or "light." It is not necessarily bad or wrong, but it may be something you deny or suppress because you are afraid of it or don't like it.

We often project shadow qualities onto other people. A simple way to detect your shadow self is to examine your reaction to other people.

With pen and paper, write a complete list of qualities of people you know that cause extremely strong emotional reactions in you. This should include people you know, people who are close to you. Your reactions may include envy, jealousy, anger, resentment, annoyance, or even obsession. The list may be in the form of sentences, single words, or essays.

Make a parallel list of how you personally express these exact same qualities. If you wrote, "Sarah drives me crazy because she is inauthentic and selfish," examine your personal expression of authenticity and selfishness. Perhaps your shadow is a selfish fiend who expresses herself with no self-restraint; that's why Sarah strikes a chord in you and why she has appeared in your life.

Place the Moon card and enter it. Feel yourself moving amidst the watery shadows. Focus on the long and winding road before you, leading to the mountains. A familiar black silhouette moves toward you. You recognize this figure as your shadow self. What does she look and sound like? What does she want to do? What does she say?

Write or sketch out a short story about your shadow self.

Three of Swords Connection Ritual

Ingredient
• Three of Swords

Method, Visualization, and Meditation
Enter the arcana of the Three of Swords.

A new possibility has been born from two. Threes are the sacred triad of manifestation. A third option has emerged. This is the birth of creativity from the tiniest grain of sand to the farthest galaxy in the known universe.

Wet winds hit your cheeks; your lips dampen with raindrops. A searing flash of lightning momentarily robs you of sight, and a rumble of thunder shocks your heart, making it beat faster. The air is pungent with electricity. Gaseous clouds morph and swirl in the storm.

A red valentine heart appears, bulging with blood and spider veins. It bobs up and down like a balloon in the storm wind. Three swords pierce the heart with exact precision as if the heart was a tattoo. A nightmare vision hovers before you.

What causes you pain? What makes your heart ache? What is the most painful event you have ever experienced?

What has heart pain taught you about how to live your life? What have you done to avoid or embrace pain?

How have these experiences defined the way in which you think and formulate your world? Swords are the suit of the mind, and this image reflects the way in which we intellectualize pain and betrayal.

Why does it hurt to be a third wheel? Is the third always the outsider?

What happens if you use your clever hands to remove the swords? Grasp the icy cold handle and pull the sword out of the heart. As you hold the sword, it speaks to you. What does it say? Remove the second sword. What does it say? Remove the third and final sword. What does that sword say to you?

The deflated heart blows away on the winds, and the storm passes.

The Three of Swords was called the Lord of Sorrow by the magicians of the Golden Dawn, who assigned it the time period of October 3–12.

• • • • •

INCANTATION
Three of Swords
Strife, pain, and fear
Embrace your blades
Cold and clear
Free the heart
To stop the pain
Slowly ebbing
Springtime rain
Swordlike words strike
Harsh and fast
Remove dangerous piercings
So love will last

October • 9

INCANTATION

Supernova of light
And tower of power
Bring energy to
My goal this hour
Expand, grow
Move with speed
Tower energy fills
My every deed!

Supernova Power Boost Spell

Ingredients
- Warm can of soda
- Sharpie
- The Tower

Method, Visualization, and Meditation

Are you beginning a new creative venture or business or do you simply have a new goal? If you want to place explosive energy behind it, use this power boost spell when you want an idea or creative project to "blow up."

Using the Sharpie, write your intention, goal, or idea all over the warm can of soda. The more precise, the better. You may write your goal on paper and tape it over the can.

Place the Tower card in front of you. Enter the card. Imagine yourself inside and at the bottom of the tower. You look at the spiral staircase as it winds above you into the tower's rafters. Hold your intention in hand. Walk up the stairs. Hear the rumble of distant thunder and see cracks of lightning shoot across the sky as you climb up. When you reach the top of the tower, place your intention at the stone landing.

Descend the stairs until you have made your way to safety outside the tower. Exit the card.

Take the can of soda in your hand—and be sure you are wearing clothes that can get dirty or wet. Bring the can outside and to a safe place. Begin to shake the can while repeating the incantation. Crack open the can at the last line to release the power.

Anti-Anxiety Spell

Ingredients
1. The Devil
2. Temperance
3. The Magician

National Mental Health Day is celebrated today internationally. Applaud the effort by clearing your psyche.

Method, Visualization, and Meditation

Anxiety disorder is a serious affliction requiring professional help. If you suffer from severe anxiety, find professional help. Otherwise, this spell will help you integrate and rid the general stress.

The Devil represents anxiety. Temperance reflects you gaining control over your feelings. The Magician reflects you taking powerful and specific action.

Place the Devil card before you. Enter the dark cave of this card and examine the devil in his darkest capacity, as captor and controller. Your nerves have taken control. They have formed into the image of the devil. You are a chained figure beneath. The devil releases a rip of comic book laughter. Stop him now. Allow the fear and nervousness you have been experiencing to come out of your chest and form a ball of energy in front of your belly. It is blue and glowing. Grasp it. Throw it at the devil. Next take the cold chain from your neck and pull it over your head. The devil has vanished from his post. Climb up to where he was sitting. Perch upon his spot. You have the power now.

Place the Temperance card before you. Enter the card and become the figure. The nervous anxiety has become a beautiful blue ball of energy. Feel a cup in each hand. Blend the blue energy rhythmically. You are harnessing the energy and power, refining it and making it stronger for when you need to access it.

Place the Magician card before you. You are now free of your nerves and in control. Access the powerful blue energy when you need an extra jolt of personal power.

INCANTATION

Nervous ticks
Release your hold
It's my life
I will be bold
Embrace the joy
Release the fear
I move forward
Now I'm clear

1   2   3

Open Throat Chakra Energy

Eleanor Roosevelt—a vibrant speaker, a beautiful orator, and one of the most quoted women in the world—celebrates her birthday today.

INCANTATION

Speak my peace
Words are kind
Wonderful willing ears
They find
Whispered truth
Uttered love
Inspiration fills me
From above

Ingredient
• The Empress

Method, Visualization, and Meditation

The throat chakra is the energetic center of our communication and creativity. Perform this exercise to open and expand your expressive energy.

The throat chakra is located at the base of your neck, in the hollow of your collarbone. Feel this delicate yet powerful area with your fingertips.

Sit on a chair with your feet flat on the floor or sit in yogi position, legs crossed on the floor. Sit straight. Place the Empress card before you. Focus on the space inside your throat. Feel the energy there from the front, back, and side of your neck. Let it extend in all directions. Warm and glow the energy. Imagine the energy is pale blue, like placid Caribbean waters. You might even begin to spin the chakra's energy clockwise and then counterclockwise. Perhaps you hear the energy, smell it, or even taste it.

Allow the circle of energy to open like a budding flower.

Focus on the Empress card before you. Feel the connection of divine love. Let the blue energy move from your neck to the throat of the Empress and back again.

The Empress is filled with personal authenticity. Your words are full of compassion and creativity; they make the world a more interesting place. Your unique points of view and talents blossom and grow. Inspiration finds itself inside your vocal cords. Your voice has the power to transform your world.

Move the ball of energy around. Let it rise through your spine, filling your entire essence with expression.

The Power and Expression of Crowley Spell

Ingredients
1. The Hierophant
2. The Magician
3. Judgement

Method, Visualization, and Meditation

This spell operates on three levels: the spiritual (Hierophant), the physical (Magician), and the unconscious (Judgement).

Place the Hierophant before you. Enter the hallowed halls of your highest spiritual self. Become the Hierophant and sit on the throne of your spirit center. This is the holy chamber of your spiritual self. It is furnished with the flowers of Babylon. What do they smell like? What fills your cathedral? You look out to see that you are above the highest mountains, above the clouds, above the atmosphere. You have extended past the physical world into a direct line with spirit.

Place the Magician before you. Channel the divine Hierophant light and energy down through your body and onto the physical plane where you move on a day-to-day basis. You control the direction of this energy with your attention.

What do you care most about? People? A set of ideas? A beloved hobby or pastime? A passion? Place these things upon your magician table. Focus all of your energy, will, and attention on them.

Place the Judgement card before you. Feel the doors of your subconscious opening up, shining divine light down into the deepest realms of yourself. What you have repressed opens and comes to life. You shine your light on them. See them coming up and out of the figures from the coffins.

The things you have thrust away are now given love and light. As a result, your life is transformed.

Occultist and mystic Aleister Crowley was born on this day in 1875. His possession of power and expression cannot be denied. What would happen in our own life if we expressed ourselves powerfully as Crowley, the ultimate magician?

INCANTATION

Power from
The heart of me
Moving wildly
Now it's free
Nothing's held back
In my groove
Expression fills
My every move

October • 13

INCANTATION

Fire and passion
Clear the way
Bring on the change
Today's the day
Explosive energy
Is the key
I can finally
Be free

Energize Your Career Mars Spell

Ingredients
1. Two of Wands
2. The Tower
3. The World

Method, Visualization, and Meditation

The Two of Wands represents a career holding pattern. The Tower card is ruled by Mars. The World reflects you in full empowerment at work, being in the moment and doing what you were born to do.

You will be asked to destroy the behavior that is keeping you in a holding pattern. Please note: this destruction, like the power of the Tower card and Mars, makes way for new growth.

Place the Two of Wands. Enter the card. Become the figure holding the globe. Transform the globe into a shiny crystal ball. Watch as the globe transforms. Discover a figure inside the globe. Looking closer, you realize it is you. You are at work in your holding pattern. See yourself going about your tasks. What do you look like from an outside perspective? What are you doing? How are you doing it? What needs to change in order to set you in a new direction, shake things up, and free you? See this very specifically. Once you see this, raise the ball above your head and send it crashing down over the wall.

Place the Tower card before you. The collected energy of the Tower's explosion is bright enough to send you literally flying in a new direction. Hear the crash, thunder, and din.

Place the World card over the Tower. You have unleashed enough energy to completely change your direction. You may now walk forward into a new situation. Doors will open. Change is at hand. See yourself as you'd like to be.

With renewed energy, go get 'em.

Four of Swords Connection Ritual

Ingredient
• Four of Swords

Method, Visualization, and Meditation
Enter the arcana of the Four of Swords.

Fours represent stability. The arcana of three burst forth creatively and has evolved into the next stage. A fourth appears. Stability is reached. A square. A home. A haven. The structure is complete. Four seasons. Four directions. Four elements. Four suits of tarot. Reality in the physical world has been achieved.

You have been traveling by foot all day in the October Tuscan sun. A castle appears. Isn't that the way with traveling? Unexpected corners yield surprise and delight.

Leaving the wildness of lavender moors and dense forest borders, you enter the castle. The cooling darkness of the five-hundred-year-old structure feels welcome. You wander through dozens of halls and rooms until stepping into a chapel. Stained-glass-colored light fills the chamber. The antique glass depicts a woman with the word PAX over her head, the kiss of peace at a mass. She embraces a young child.

Oleander and citrus mixed with earthy thyme and basil spill from ceramic mugs. A tapestry reflects the heroic deeds of a knight. His effigy lies before you, hands engaged in pious prayer, but his dusty bones and dancing teeth whisper secrets to you. They jiggle and clink from their dusty box. There is something more ancient than Christianity in this place. This chapel, as sacred spaces often are, is built upon the space of a maiden cult. Their priestess is buried beneath the knight. Ancient grain gods lie beneath her.

Sanctuary for all. Whisper your secrets to the knight's bones. Mindful stability and balance lead to peaceful rest, blooming creativity, and solace. This sacred chamber is yours. To find it, merely flip the card and enter.

The Four of Swords was called the Lord of Rest from Strife by the magicians of the Golden Dawn, who assigned it the time period of October 13–22.

INCANTATION
Four of Swords
A rest from strife
Bring stability
To my life
Solid, substantial thoughts
Reign strong
Never dwell
In places wrong

The first hot air balloon was launched on this day back in 1783.

INCANTATION

Queen of Swords

Goddess of Air

Alight my dreams

Take me there

Your winds blow strong

Clean and true

A part of me

Thrives in you

My manifest is

Concise, clear

Bring my desire

Close and near

Queen of Swords Balloon Spell

Ingredients
- Biodegradable helium balloon*
- Sharpie
- Queen of Swords

Method, Visualization, and Meditation

Balloons are magical in nature, whether transporting Dorothy back to Kansas or marking a birthday celebration. Skybound objects, birds, butterflies, balloons, or lanterns express contact with the divine spiritual realm existing above humankind.

This spell sends a message to the Queen of Swords, who will grant your wish from her airy throne. If possible, choose a balloon whose color matches your intention: green for money, red for romantic love, yellow for creativity, blue for expansion, purple for intuition, white for protection.

Requests to the Queen of Swords should be simple and concise. She responds in the same manner. Gently write your desire on the balloon, being sure not to pop it. Decorate your balloon with symbols, sigils, your astrological symbols, your name. Anything you might engrave on a candle can be drawn upon a balloon.

When you are finished decorating your balloon, place the Queen of Swords before you. In your mind's eye enter her blustery kingdom. Imagine that you stand before her, balloon in hand. Looking directly in her piercing eyes, tell her exactly what you want. Remember, the Queen of Swords respects articulation. The clearer you are, the quicker she will grant you your desire.

When you have finished, go outside and release the balloon to the wind. Watch as it disappears from sight.

*If you don't wish to release a balloon or are unable to find biodegradable balloons, blow the fluff of a dandelion or scatter flower petals at the point where you would release the balloon.

Get Exactly What You Want Spell

Ingredients
- Queen of Swords
- Pen
- Paper
- Envelope

Method, Visualization, and Meditation

The Queen of Swords knows what she wants, when she wants it, and how to receive it. Her left hand, traditionally the passive and receiving hand, is extended to accept what she has asked for. The Golden Dawn has bestowed the title of Decisiveness of Cardinal Air upon this queen. This reflects the fresh, swift action of air and thought.

Place the Queen of Swords before you. Enter the card in your mind's eye and feel the cool air circulating around her. See the clouds blossoming in the distance and smell the clean alpine landscape. She sits in profile on a concrete throne and you can feel her power humming like an engine. She turns to look at you. Serious, stark, she speaks in a singsongy, otherworldly voice. "Everything you want and desire is available to you, child. You must only ask for it." She turns back to her profile.

Take your pen and paper and begin writing the queen a letter or poem. Write specifically and exactly what it is you want. Write why you want it. Write what happens once you obtain it.

When you are finished, place it in the envelope and address it to the Queen of Swords, with no return address. Take this letter (without postage) and deposit it in a mailbox.

Utter the incantation as you place it in the mailbox. Offer the Queen of Swords thanks by opening your window and playing beautiful music in the evening breeze.

Jadwiga was crowned King of Poland on this day in 1384. Why so special? Jadwiga was a woman. It was highly unusual to have a female reining monarch, let alone a female crowned as king.

INCANTATION
Queen of Swords
Heed my call
Hear my desire
I want it all

Paris's Chartres Cathedral, whose floor still bears an ancient labyrinth for walking meditation and contemplation, was consecrated on this day by King Saint Louis in 1260.

INCANTATION

Walking path
Stones and rock
With every step
I unlock
Connections to
The sacred earth
New potentials
Are given birth

Walking Spell for Connection

Ingredients
- Eight of Cups
- The World
- 30 minutes or more set aside to walk

Method, Visualization, and Meditation

It is easy to feel disjointed in the modern world. Fast-paced lifestyles, technology, and gadgets convince us that we are separate from the swirling, glittering universe around us.

That is not the case. Cast this spell to reconnect and feel the world around you.

Get your walking shoes ready and have a path planned in advance. If you are taking a walk in the woods or a place you need to drive to, take the cards along with you. Perform this spell right before you set out on your journey.

Place the Eight of Cups before you. This is a card of transformation. The walker moves to a new state of consciousness. You are moving to a new state of mindfulness, just like the traveler on the card. The eclipse signifies the uniqueness of this moment and marks the beginning of your journey.

Place the World card over the Eight of Cups. The dancer is naked save for her scarves. As her feet dance and move, she moves with the flow of the world. Hear the breeze around you. Listen to the trees, the buzzing bees, even passing cars. Every sound is a connection to the world. Smell the freshness of the earth and sweet green leaves. Your five senses are your gateway to the physical world.

Let all defenses and responsibilities drop away. Magic thrives when you move in step with the world. Take the first step of your journey. Move with the essence found within yourself. Bring the World card along with you. Turn every bit of your awareness outside of yourself. Lose yourself in your walk.

Future Lover Visioning Spell

Ingredients
- Seven of Cups
- ¼ can pumpkin
- 1 tablespoon honey
- Scant teaspoon cinnamon
- Scant teaspoon nutmeg

Method, Visualization, and Meditation

The Seven of Cups is the visioning card. Pumpkins are sacred to the moon and are used for divination and healing. Cinnamon and nutmeg will draw suitors to your door.

Arrange all of your ingredients. Focus on the Seven of Cups card. Imagine the dreams to unfold this evening. Become the figure in the card. See yourself in a smoky movie theater. The film projector purrs behind you like the engine of possibility. Multiple scenarios are displayed for your viewing pleasure. Focus on the cup bearing a castle built on a mountaintop. Behind the dark window of the tallest tower awaits your future lover.

Place the pumpkin in a small saucepan, add the honey and sprinkle the spices as you combine them, creating a delicious aroma. Allow the mixture to cool (outside and under the moon if weather allows).

Once cool, spread the mixture upon your face. Close your eyes, sit back, and relax for ten minutes before washing it off.

Remove the mask, look in the mirror, and recite the incantation. Tonight your future lover will visit you in your dreams.

Today St. Luke's Day is celebrated in Great Britain. Girls divine their future marriage prospects by placing a mixture of honey, spices, and vinegar upon their face. Before hopping into bed they recite, "St. Luke, St. Luke, be kind to me; in dreams let me my true love see."

INCANTATION

Seven of Cups
Be kind to me
In dreams let me
My true love see

Today marks Armilstrium, the Roman festival honoring Mars, god of war. Soldiers were glorified during this festival and their weapons ritually purified.

Ingredients
- Four of Swords
- All four knights

Method, Visualization, and Meditation

The Four of Swords represents peace of mind. Knights are the protectors, soldiers, and warriors of the tarot deck. Each of the tarot knights carries the unique elemental gift of his suit: the Knight of Swords has strength of mind and word; the Knight of Cups, strength of emotion and poetry; the Knight of Wands, strength of passion and fire; Knight of Pentacles, the strength of earth and brawn.

Place the Four of Swords card before you. Enter the card. Feel the security, protection, and safety inside this card.

Shuffle the four knights. Place them facedown on each side of the Four of Swords.

Repeat the incantation.

Select one card and flip it over to reveal your protector knight!

Contemplate your knight. Enter the card. Talk to him and offer him welcome. Perhaps he tells you his name and whispers his secret abilities, wisdom, or advice to you. Discover his favorite food or flower. Make him offerings to keep his energy strong. Project his image upon your front door, over your bed, at your workplace, in your car, or any space needing protection. Connect with him when you need help, defense, or armor.

INCANTATION

Four of knights
Power of four
One of you
Come to my fore
Protect my space
Let nothing through
I give eternal
Thanks to you

Spell to Scare Away Monsters

Ingredient
- Queen of Wands

Method, Visualization, and Meditation

The Queen of Wands is a powerful elemental icon with the ability to banish any monster with the wave of her wand. This spell calms the nerves of children and adults who fear monsters under the bed, inside the closet, or behind the shower curtain.

Place the Queen of Wands before you. Enter the card. Walk to her and sit down in her golden throne. Embody her. Feel the heat rise within you as you become the queen of fire. Look down at your vibrant dress that harnesses the energy of the desert sun in its magical fibers. Your legs are spread apart, feet firmly planted on the ground, while your spine lines up straight and tall. A shiny black feline sits at your feet, licking her lips with a tiny red tongue.

Flat desert landscape lies before you. This valley of fire extends to a bountiful oases of palm, distant seas, and rising cliffs. Wild animals scavenge for food while caravans of men snake across golden sands transporting goods. Dunes rise and fall like ocean waves, undulating and drifting in the blowing winds, shapeshifting from one day to the next.

You know you have nothing to fear. The power of the sun and desert is yours to direct as you like. You have the power to cleanse any space.

Walk as the Queen of Wands into the room with the supposed monster.

Flick the light switch on and off thirteen times while reciting the incantation.

Actor Bela Lugosi, famous for his role of Count Dracula and other terrifying monsters, was born on this day in 1882.

INCANTATION

Beasts of wild
Monsters beware
I banish you
Don't harm a hair
Vanish your power
You aren't even here
By my word
This room is clear!

The UK celebrates Apple Day today. Apples represent love and adoration, while an apple's darkest shadow aspect inspires seduction and trickery.

INCANTATION

I love you

You love me

Happy feelings

Meant to be

Love and Good Feelings Warm Apple Spell

Ingredients

- Two of Cups
- 2 apples, peeled, cored, and chopped
- Pat of butter
- Splash of liquid (apple juice, cider, or water)
- Sprinkle of brown sugar
- Sprinkle of cardamom
- ½ teaspoon cinnamon

Method, Visualization, and Meditation

Apples are in season, sweet and crisp at this time of year. Simmering apples and spices warms the home and the heart.

The Two of Cups represents love, sweet feelings, and affection. Cinnamon, sometime called sweet wood, carries attracting energy and is used in love and money spells. Cardamom is utilized for fidelity.

This is a luscious, intuitive recipe. Add or subtract ingredients as you see fit. Serve over oatmeal, waffles, or pancakes in the morning or in the evening as dessert, alone or beside ice cream or cake.

Place the Two of Cups in your kitchen. Enter the card. Become one of the figures. See the object of love in your mind's eye (it may be more than one person). Extend a cup of love toward them. Accept their gift back to you.

Make the recipe. As you prepare the apples, focus on qualities of love and devotion.

Place all ingredients in a heavy bottomed pot and simmer until soft while repeating the incantation.

Lick the Wound Spell

Ingredients
- Ace of Cups
- Aloe vera leaf or gel

Method, Visualization, and Meditation

How can we heal from personal destruction without building walls and becoming bitter? This spell heals the pain of personal destruction without becoming brittle.

The aloe plant, used for healing topical wounds and burns, was sacred to Egyptians and called the plant of immortality. The Ace of Cups reflects healing waters of love and light, hope and rejuvenation.

Think about the pain you have been caused. Allow your feelings to surface.

Place the Ace of Cups before you. Enter the card with all the feelings of betrayal, embarrassment, or pain. Find yourself in the waters beneath the cup. The water is up to your neck. Your body is immersed in the warm and healing waters of the card. Gravity has disappeared, and you are weightless. The cup pours water like a fountain before you. Falling drops and streams of water splash your face and dance musically in your ears.

Allow the water to wash away your sorrow. Take as long as you need inside the card.

When you are ready, bring your awareness back to where you are.

Recite the incantation.

Break apart the aloe vera leaf to remove the gel. Spread a thin layer of the magical elixir on your hands and arms, allowing it to soak into your skin.

The Greek Temple of Apollo, god of art and knowledge, was destroyed on this day in 362.

INCANTATION
Wounds and pain
You are no more
I let you go
Cast to the floor
Absorb, return
To earth once again
Heal my shattered
Feelings and skin

October • 23

Scorpio Regeneration Spell

Today is the third day of the astrological sign of Scorpio. Scorpio magic is all about regeneration. It helps you come back better than ever. Call upon Scorpio's energy when physical, spiritual, or financial transformation is your goal.

INCANTATION

Darkness caress my gentle soul
Regeneration is my goal
Spin, spin, spin in my cocoon
Changing faster than the moon
Self-direct with will of steel
Fool's dog nipping at my heel
Old ways of life are gone and past
New incarnation stays, will last
World watch what happens when
Transform, transform, I rise again

Ingredients
1. Ace of Wands
2. Death
3. Eight of Swords
4. Judgement
5. Card representing what you are generating into

Method, Visualization, and Meditation

Place and enter the Ace of Wands. It carries sacred fire that burns what must be destroyed. Think of what must be cast aside. What is to be discarded from your life? What is no longer essential? Hold this before the ace. Touch this with the wand and watch it dissolve into cinders and fly away on the wind.

Place and enter the Death card, which is ruled by Scorpio. Amidst this darkness you will be reborn. Let Death's horse march over you. Hear his clopping hooves. Feel the winds of change driving the horse. Death's evocative blackness swaddles and protects you. Move deeper within the embryo of yourself.

Place and enter the Eight of Swords. You are like a cocoon spinning in darkness: compact and dense, you can't become any smaller. Binds support you and lift you off the ground. Hover in the air. Old ways of being disappear as you regenerate in this cocoon. When the blindfold is removed, you see your reality with a new set of eyes.

Place and enter Judgement. Feel yourself awaken like a newly made vampire. Rise from the grave, seeing the world as you are born again.

Place and enter your final card. Welcome to the new incarnation of yourself. Enter your new state of being.

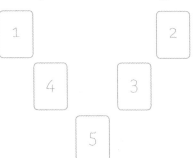

Wedding Planning Spell

Ingredients
- The Empress
- Fresh lilies

Method, Visualization, and Meditation

Planning a wedding should be as joyful and pleasurable as the wedding day itself. Perform this spell to ensure stress be kept to a minimum, discover creative solutions to any sticky issue, and find unique and beautiful vendors and venues for your special day.

Etruscan goddess Juno is the matron of females and marriage. June, the most popular wedding month, is named in her honor. Juno was originally named Uni, the root of the modern words "unify" and "unity," meaning to blend and create harmony.

Call upon Juno's powers to assist you while wedding planning through the Empress card, who represents creativity and effectiveness in all things. Thank Juno by making an offering of her sacred flower, the lily.

Place the Empress card before you. Enter the card. Look to discover the most creative aspect of the Empress. It rests inside her glittering crown, which reflects dazzling light in its effervescent stars. The scattered light refracts and extends beyond you. It shines light on the people who will aid you in your wedding. Dress designers, caterers, printers, planners, and every single person who crosses your path during the planning of this wedding are subtly being alerted to your presence now. When they sense your sparkling light, they will help you as best they can. Your family acts with charm and grace in all the ways you need their support. Envision the light of the Empress's crown reflecting on everyone you know. The path is now clear.

Thank Juno (and the Empress) by placing a bouquet of lilies in sight. Keep this bouquet where you perform most of your planning. Add lilies to your wedding bouquet or flower arrangements.

The oldest surviving tarot deck, the Visconti-Sforza deck, was commissioned as a wedding gift. It celebrated the marriage of Francesco Sforza and Bianca Maria Visconti on this day in 1441.

INCANTATION

Empress Juno
Love and light
Feel your strength
Harness your might
Thank you for
Your gifts and charms
Embrace you with
My bridal arms

October • 25

Renowned painter Pablo Picasso was born on this day in 1881. Call on this Spaniard's delicious energy when seeking ideas for any project, from what to cook for dinner to what to do with your life.

INCANTATION

Stars of night
Beauty's sight
With the words
That I recite
Book of life
Is mine to write
My soul's truth
Alights tonight

Inspiration Spell

Ingredient
• The Star

Method, Visualization, and Meditation

The root of inspiration comes from the Latin *spirare*, which means to breathe. The Latin *spiritus* means spirit. When we are filled with excitement and inspiration, we feel full and buoyant like a balloon.

The Star card reflects muse communication and being open to spirit. A breathing exercise will calm, relax, and open you to inspiration.

Sit with your feet firmly on the floor, body open and relaxed, spine straight. Mentally scan yourself. Breathing deeply, move from the top of your head and relax inch by inch down to the soles of your feet.

Once you have reached physical relaxation, place the Star card before you. Enter the card.

The pre-dawn pastoral landscape glitters under the luminescent sky. The summer herbs mint, marjoram, and sage tickle your nose. Their green leaves are heavy with the weight of morning dew. The air is wet and rich with a gentle humidity. A woman before you pours water onto land and onto a glistening pool. The figure is the engine of your creative being that you use in all aspects. Inspiration is yours.

Bring your awareness back to your body. Close your eyes. Breathe deeply. Inhale for four counts and exhale for four counts. Do this until you are able to maintain a steady rhythm.

Imagine the Star card before you. Inhale the scene; inhale the image of the card into your body. Breathe in herbs, water, starlight, the female figure.

When you are ready, bring your awareness back to the present room.

Inspiration is now yours.

Banish a Bad Habit Necromancy Spell

Ingredients
- Death
- Pen and paper
- Graveyard dust
- Small bottle with lid
- Candle

Today marks the feast day for Saint Quadragesimus, the Italian shepard who, in the sixth century, brought a dead man back to life.

Method, Visualization, and Meditation

Graveyard dust contains magical properties depending on your spiritual and cultural relationship to death. It is traditionally gathered from graveyards. Hoodoo tradition retrieves graveyard dust by scooping three handfuls from a grave, one from above the corpse's head, one from their heart, and one from below their feet. Other traditions will remove a handful of dust from within cemetery walls or swept off a tomb. Some practitioners abandon graveyards altogether and blend a homemade herbal mixture into graveyard dust.

Gather all your items. Set the Death card before you. See the card in motion; feel the motion of the horse. Feel the power it contains to destroy anything. Consider the habit that needs to be removed from your life. Write the habit on a piece of paper.

Roll the paper up and place it inside the bottle, closing tightly. Seal the cap with hot candle wax. To banish the habit, take the bottle outside. Dig a hole and bury the bottle, covering it with dirt. When you have finished, spit on the site three times. Scatter the graveyard dirt across the bottle site while chanting the incantation.

INCANTATION

You are done

Return to sleep

Bury you

Nice and deep

Habit, habit

Dead to me

Away with

Necromancy

Knight of Wands Connection Ritual

On this night in 312 the Emperor Constantine prepared for battle and received an impassioned vision of the Cross. Visions and battles are all aspected by the fiery, spiritual suit of Wands. The Knight of Wands is the most explosive and passionate knight of the tarot deck.

INCANTATION

Knight of Wands
Rush of passion
Get worked up
It's his fashion
Leap, fly, and
Forge ahead
By determination
His passion's led

Ingredient
• Knight of Wands

Method, Visualization, and Meditation

Enter the arcana of the Knight of Wands.

Hot desert sand blows in your face. You lift your hand to shield your vision from stark sunlight. A creature advances toward you. It is a knight on a horse. An acacia tree is growing close to where you stand. Its thorns match the sharp look on the knight's face. His fiery stallion rears up on his back legs at your presence.

You jump aside to avoid the horse's kicking hooves. The soldier pulls his reins, barely able to control his steed. You note how the knight is adorned in fiery yellow and burnt orange. His fabric matches the glowing shade of his own hair and the hair of his horse. Circular salamanders, representing eternity, decorate the knight's tunic, which rests over a fine suit of shiny armor. The feathers on the knight's helmet leap like flames. He brandishes a red, glowing stick that sprouts green leaves.

The ancient pyramids of Giza beckon in the distance, pointing skyward. You can see the knight yearns to go in the opposite direction. He is caught for a moment between the pyramids and your presence. You feel the energy of connection as his eyes lock with yours. You see a fire burning in his soul that can only be quenched by adventure and exploration. It seems an eternity that he looks at you, taking you in. Your body wells with heat, and you realize you are absorbing the knight's intense energy. You are filled with a sudden longing to see, feel, and explore.

As fast as he arrived, he departs. Your skin cools as you watch him ride to where sand meets sky. Heat waves wiggle and shimmy. You watch his figure until he merges in the landscape and you are left alone once more.

King of Pentacles Connection Ritual

Ingredient
• King of Pentacles

Method, Visualization, and Meditation

Place the King of Pentacles card. Enter the card. The air carries the scent of sun-warmed pears. Buzzing bees collect pollen from bursting flowers as they move through the soft, warm air. Rich, fertile ground is firm under your feet. Spongy ink mushrooms, shiny grapevines, and heavy clumps of grapes grow so thickly that you almost miss the man who sits amidst the foliage and greenery. He is right in front of you in a throne.

It is almost impossible to see where the king stops and the garden begins. It is as if he has sprung from the very earth himself and grown from a vine. His hair curls like the tendrils of a vine; his skin is the ruddy red and brown color of earth. He moves with a slow, deliberate grace, and the vegetation around him quivers as he moves, responding in turn.

In the distance a bustling city contains the yelps of children, calling mothers, and laughing people. The king sits in solitude, apart from the crowds, preferring to contemplate the pentacle resting between his left hand and knee. He is connecting to the pure energy of growth and expansion. In doing so, he removes himself from the bustle of everyday life. He makes this sacrifice so life can thrive around him.

Beneath his cloak he wears a coat of armor, symbolic of battles fought and won. His foot peeks out. You realize he may be the most protected figure in the deck. He is the root of physical manifestation.

Bill Gates was born today in 1955 and was named the wealthiest man in the world by Forbes Magazine *in 2015. The King of Pentacles archetype is typically the wealthy businessman who has perfected mastery over his physical world.*

INCANTATION

King of Pentacles
Man of earth
Call for grace
You'll both give birth
To all things physical
Meaningful, real
Be true to nature
You will heal

Today is National Cat Day. How appropriate that the witch's favorite familiar is honored on a day falling so close to All Hallows Eve. They say a cat has nine lives; many people believe in nine or more past, future, or parallel lives that have come besides this one.

INCANTATION

Of all the roads
I've walked before
I come to knock
On memory's door
Open wide and
I'll slip through
Discover wisdom and
Truth from you

Past Lives Exercise

Ingredients
- Petrified wood
- Wisteria branch
- Tarot deck

Method, Visualization, and Meditation

Petrified wood is said to contain memory. It can be used to access the secrets buried deep within you. Retrieve the secrets you have forgotten. Petrified wood can be found online and in gem stores. It is said wisteria connects one to the past. Tarot can be used to tell any and every story.

Hang a wisteria branch over your bed.

Keep a piece of petrified wood close to you or carry it with you.

For nine consecutive nights, contemplate your past lives. Open yourself up to the sensitivity of emotion within you. Consider places, people, and things you felt you have known before. What feels most familiar? To what do you have a natural affinity? If there is a single lesson to learn in this lifetime, what do you think it is?

On the ninth night, at the stroke of midnight, perform a tarot reading by the light of a single candle.

Use the Celtic Cross spread. This is the reading of your former self. Be sure to record aloud your observations or journal it meticulously for future reference. Pull additional cards as needed.

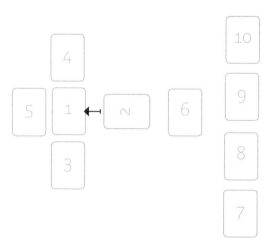

Mischief Night's Loosen Up Spell

Ingredients
- The Devil
- Radish

Method, Visualization, and Meditation

One of the perils of growing up is losing touch with the inner self who was just discovering the boundaries of her world. Senses of adventure can be dampened by responsibilities, burdens, and the pressure to be a grown up. What better night than Halloween eve to get in touch with the deviant side of yourself?

Spicy radishes are ruled by Mars, the creator of strife and the perfect symbol for mischief night. The Devil represents your shadow self, your repressed desires.

Slice the radish. Place the Devil card before you. Eat the radish as you contemplate the Devil card.

- What do you want that you aren't allowing yourself to have?
- What experience do you crave?
- What would make you feel alive?
- If you were set free in the darkness, where would you go?
- What would you do?

Formulate a plan for harmless mischief—perhaps a moon-lit picnic with your beloved and an elicit outdoor tumble in the weeds. Perhaps it's a 2 AM drive to a diner or underground club. Perhaps you throw a hedonistic party where all guests wear masks and keep their identity hidden. You are limited only by your imagination. Act upon your decision immediately, putting it into action.

Hidden by darkness, the world opened up and anything seemed possible, didn't it? Mischief makers roam the shadows and scurry through neighborhoods performing pranks tonight. Cars are soaped; trees and homes are strewn with white toilet paper.

INCANTATION

Mischief night
And Devil card
I'd forgotten that
Once I played hard
I'll run and play
And have some fun
By the light of the moon
This spell is done

Contemplate Death Ritual

Today is Halloween and Samhain. It marks the beginning of fall, Persephone's return to the underworld, and a time to turn inward. We can choose to become more reflective as the nights grow longer and the earth prepares for sleep.

INCANTATION

Death and life

Intertwined

Like a vine around me

You wind

Some say ticking clock

Our time will come

I say life's a game

And I've won

Not because I'll

Outlive everyone

But because my life

Has just begun

Ingredients
- Halloween objects
- Death (multiple versions)

Method, Visualization, and Meditation

It is said that one who catches a falling leaf on Halloween shall have all her wishes granted within the next year.

On Halloween the veil between the world of the dead and the living is at its thinnest. It is believed ghosts and spirits cross the veil on this night. Halloween calls out each day as twilight descends, a reminder of the journey of souls crossing into and out of life.

Gather Halloween objects around you. Place them in front of the Death card. Gather as many Death cards from as many decks as you have. Perform this ritual on Halloween night or at twilight or daybreak.

Light a candle and contemplate the card using the following questions as prompts:

- How is your consciousness altered when someone close to you departs to the other world?
- Where does the realm of Death exist?
- Where were you before you were born?
- What do you envision the state of death to be like?
- Are you able to communicate with consciousness that has passed over?
- How does it feel to inhabit a borrowed body?
- What does death teach us about living?

Release Psychic Ties Spell

Ingredients
- Ten of Swords
- Necktie
- Fabric shears
- Black candle

Method, Visualization, and Meditation

Are you obsessed or consumed by the past? Even if the person or situation is no longer physically present in your life, you may be psychically tied to them if they remain a constant fixture in your thoughts. This spell releases psychic ties so you can invite fresh possibility to your reality.

The Ten of Swords represents endings. A necktie may be picked up in a thrift store. Be very clear that you are cutting psychic ties, not imposing physical harm on anyone. The color black represents death. It absorbs all energies.

Gather all ingredients. Place the Ten of Swords. Enter the card. Consider the figure lying on the ground. The body represents your good/bad/indifferent feelings in regard to your situation. Ten silver swords align the body's spine. Grab hold of the first sword, feeling the cold steel in your hand. Bring up an emotion you feel when you think of this situation. With all your strength, grind the sword deeper into the body. When the sword won't go any deeper, pull the sword out. Throw it off the cliff. You have just severed a tie. Continue doing so with the remaining nine swords, finding a different emotion or attachment with each.

After the tenth sword has been removed, look toward the yellow dawn rising in the distance. Feel the tangerine light on your skin. Allow yourself to bask in freedom.

Take the tie in hand. Cut into ten pieces using your shears. Bury the pieces in the earth.

Light the black candle. Utter the incantation.

Leaving a person or situation can be understood as a metaphor for death. The Day of the Dead is celebrated in Mexico and other Latin cultures today. Skulls, skeletons, and roses are symbolic of this celebration that pays homage to the dead.

INCANTATION
Past is finished
What's done is done
There's nothing to be
Lost or won
It's severed and
The cord is cut
I'm free and light
No nagging gut
Found my truth
Learned my lesson
Welcome freedom
Release all tension

Five of Cups Connection Ritual

The Five of Cups was called the Lord of Loss of Pleasure by the magicians of the Golden Dawn, who assigned it the time period of October 23–November 2.

INCANTATION

Five of Cups

Empty loss

What to do

Which river to cross?

Turn around

And drink some more?

Or stand there

Looking at the floor?

Ingredient
- Five of Cups

Method, Visualization, and Meditation

Enter the arcana of the Five of Cups.

Fives imply challenge. Fives are the halfway point, the turning point, the space in which a new chapter begins. What has manifested up until this point begins to build on itself. This required challenge provides perspective for the ultimate outcome in the finality of the ten. Inside every challenge lies a gift. Can you discover it?

A dark-cloaked figure stands across from you, oblivious to your presence. His head is bent. It is unclear what he is doing with his hands. What would his face look like if he turned to you? Is it ravaged by time or the desperate look of youthful ignorance? You assume he is male, but perhaps it is a cloaked female? Step back.

Three golden chalices are knocked on their sides. Green and red liquid oozes from the cups. Two cups remain upright.

The figure might drink out of the remaining cups, thereby continuing their current path. They might cross the stone arch bridge, pass over the river, and enter into the distant reality of a small fortress surrounded by cypress trees. Or they can remain immobile, making no decision at all.

The air of expectation hangs. Consider the nature of emotional cups themselves. Emotions act as filters to the physical world around you. The fives of tarot ask for us to give something of ourselves so that we may grow. It is the toughest cards that invite evolution, change, and growth.

You walk forward and select a cup while the figure remains impassive. Inside is an emotional attachment. Inside is an illusion you can release. Look inside the cup. What is there? Once you see it clearly, walk to the river and pour it in.

Watch the waters dissolve it. You are now free.

Block Unwanted Sexual Advances Spell

Ingredients

1. Ace of Wands reversed
2. The Lovers reversed
3. Nine of Cups reversed
- Turnip

Method, Visualization, and Meditation

Is someone getting a little too close for comfort? Are you routinely bothered by snide sexual comments and inappropriate men? Sick of cat calls? Cast this spell to make it stop.

A reversed Ace of Wands extinguishes passion's fire. Reversed Lovers severs romantic ties. A reversed Nine of Cups extinguishes all hope. Ozark folklore states that turnips act as illusion breakers. The triangle of cards is used to form a cone of energy.

Sit on the floor and place the cards in a triangle formation. Face the Ace of Wands. Imagine the hand holding the wand is floating before you. See the flaming wand turn over. It is ground out like a cigarette in an ashtray on the floor in front of you.

Face the Lovers. Imagine shadowy figures of leeches and sexual predators walking away from you. Face the Nine of Cups. Imagine a table with nine cups sitting on a blue tablecloth before you. Walk up to the table. Knock each cup over, spilling the liquid and dashing any hopes.

Turn away from the cards and focus on yourself and the triangle of energy you have raised. How does it feel? What color has it taken on? Make a mental note of exactly how it feels. In daily life, place this cone of protection around you to protect you from unwanted advances.

Imagine unwanted energy dissipating as you scrub and clean the turnip. Place the turnip in your handbag for extra sexual repellent.

Today is Saint Winifred's feast day. Winifred had decided to enter a convent. Her suitor become so enraged, he cut off her head. It rolled to the bottom of a hill, a healing spring appeared, her head reattached, and she came back to life. Her suitor was swallowed up by the earth.

INCANTATION

Begone with you
Away, away
Nasty come-ons
Don't haunt my day
Focus elsewhere
Offer respect
My beautiful body
I protect

1

3   2

King of Wands Connection Ritual

INCANTATION

King of Wands
Man of fire
See me, bless me
Forge desire
Hot to touch
Skin like flame
Your burning heat
Will never tame

Ingredient
• King of Wands

Method, Visualization, and Meditation
Enter the arcana of the King of Wands.

Heat—immense, dry desert heat—seeps through every inch of your skin. Your sandaled feet step over grainy sand. Palm trees offer generous shade from the noonday sun. Heat waves appear on the horizon.

A salamander slips over his desert domain. His rosy body moves from dark depths to the light. His eyes gleam with intelligence and wisdom, and he moves as a cohesive unit.

You follow the salamander and he leads you to a figure seated on a golden throne. Rosy red flames lick; a crackling sound is heard. The flames of hunger are never satisfied. They will devour everything in their wake. Cleansing and purifying heat enters you. Everything is taken from your body, moved out with sweat, and dried upon the hot air.

The king commands the rays of the sun, bringing life to the world and passion to lovers. He is on fire. The king's throne is engraved with lions and salamanders devouring their own tails, symbols of eternity. His right hand holds the wand of transformation. Salamander rings decorate his cape, yellow like his throne; his gown imitates the orange, fiery pallor of the sun.

His eyes, focused on the dry horizon, turn toward you. You find yourself unable to move as they devour you. His predatory nature consumes you. Should you step forward and embody the nature of this king, there is nothing you would not have, nothing that you could not own, no desire that would not be granted, and no passion forbidden.

But like Icarus, who lost his wings when he flew too close to the sun, what could melt away if you gave yourself entirely to the flames of passion and desire?

Attract Positive Energy Spell

Ingredients
  • Triple wick candle
  1. The Moon
  2. Ace of Wands
  3. Eight of Wands
  4. Three of Wands

Bonfire Night is celebrated tonight in Britain, marking Guy Fawkes Day with massive bonfires, feasting, and fireworks.

Method, Visualization, and Meditation

This spell creates a glow of positive energy around you. Positive energy can be stoked and fed like a fire; like attracts like.

The triple wick candle is a miniature version of a bonfire. The Moon card offers the magnetic pull of gravitation. The Ace of Wands represents a fresh primal spark. The Eight of Wands represents the manifestation of the energy of attraction, while the Three of Wands marks its return.

Light the candle's wicks. Focus on the flames as beings of light. You are about to send a message to the universe. Contemplate the flames while you consider everything you are grateful for. You may make a handwritten list of gratitude if you like.

When you are filled like a helium balloon with as much pleasure and happiness as possible, send it into the flames. Watch it rise through the light and smoke. Your intention of positivity has been sent to the world.

Place the Moon card before you. Enter the card and feel the magnetic attraction pulling positivity back toward you. In your mind's eye find the actual moon's position in relation to where you sit. Glow as white as the moon and feel your gravitational pull.

Place the Ace of Wands under the Moon card as an image of your spark of gratitude. Place the Eight of Wands next to the ace. Feel your positive energy moving out and around you from every possible direction. Place the Three of Wands. Feel the energy you put out being returned in the form of energy, people, and opportunity.

INCANTATION

Fire's passion

Flames that lick

Bring the light

Let it stick

Darkness seeps

Like water to well

As I craft

This lovely spell

Plutonium, an ingredient used in the atomic bomb, was first produced on this day in 1944.

INCANTATION

Round and round

Our life does turn

Fate's fingers like

To mix and churn

No victim, I stand

Strong and true

It's my life

Time to undo

I switch and alter

Now reverse

And as I do

I lift this curse

Hanged Man Reverse the Situation Spell

Ingredients
1. Eight of Wands
2. The Hanged Man
3. The Tower

Method, Visualization, and Meditation

There are so many things we may wish to undo. While we can't always change the past, we can reverse our experience of it. The Eight of Wands gathers and directs energy. The Hanged Man represents being hostage to a particular situation. The Tower is used as an explosive blast of energy to reverse a situation.

Place the Eight of Wands. Enter the card. Feel each wand and the momentum they carry as they fly toward their target. Place the Hanged Man where the eight wands are headed. See the hanged man as he sways back and forth. Can you hear the creak of his rope? He swings like a pendulum, caught like an insect in a spider's web. Let the halo surrounding his head remind you of the power he contains to free himself. All hope is not lost.

Envision the situation you wish to escape. Enter the philosophical side of the Hanged Man. Realize what you have learned by being held in this situation. What new lesson have you learned? This predicament has taught you to look at life from a new perspective, like the Hanged Man. Once you have grasped your lesson, you are ready to exit.

Place the Tower card beneath the Hanged Man. Watch the wild energy travel up the tower, shaking its base. A lightning bolt strikes the top, releasing the crown, causing a huge, hot, thundering explosion. It reverberates through you, your table, your entire space. With the force of this blow, take the Hanged Man card and physically reverse him.

Your situation has now changed. Look through the Hanged Man's eyes as he looks ahead with new vision.

You are now free.

Tarot's Shamanic Art Exercise

Ingredients
- Art museum/gallery/piece of art
- Tarot deck

Method, Visualization, and Meditation

Art is the mystical and invisible made physical and visible.

It is extremely pleasurable to enter a painting. You can inter-mingle with the brushstrokes, experience the painting though the artist's eyes, or even experience the painting as others have while observing it. Each journey is different.

Journey inside a painting the same way you might journey into a tarot card. There is, however, one important difference. Unless your tarot deck is handmade, tarot cards are printed on comput-ers and covered with a thin plastic veneer. Paintings and sculp-tures bear a tactile history that bear the hands of the artist and carry a strong life of their own, especially when on view to the public.

A painting emerged from the brushstrokes of the artist who breathed, made love, smoked cigarettes, ate fruit, and drank cof-fee in front of it. Who knows where the painting has hung or what it has seen? You can dive into the art (and perhaps the artist as well) and discover previous owners, those who have gazed and lived their lives in front of and around it.

What secrets would your personal art collection whisper about the things you have done in front of them?

Find a museum or gallery where you can sit comfortably and observe a painting for at least thirty minutes.

Set the timer on your phone (quietly) and observe the paint-ing, allowing yourself to fall inside of it.

When you are finished, pull a random tarot card as a message from this piece of art.

Journal and record your thoughts.

New York City's Museum of Modern Art opened on this day in 1929.

INCANTATION

Artist's brushstrokes
Shadows and light
Reveal your secrets
To my sight
Give me a message
Let me see
Story unravel
In front of me

INCANTATION

High Priestess

The silence inside

To you I'm true

Will never hide

Authenticity flows

With your water

I am bound

Your faithful daughter

High Priestess Card Connection Ritual

Ingredient
• The High Priestess

Method, Visualization, and Meditation

Enter the arcana of the High Priestess. The holiest of incense, frankincense, myrrh, and sandalwood mix with saline ocean air. She sits perfectly still in inky blue darkness, illuminated by flickering torches, the fire of eternity.

She sits, the center pillar between the B and J pillars. Move close to her. Touch her robes. Their silk has been spun by silk worms who glow with the luminescent power of the moon.

Her silence is deafening. It is part of every sacred tradition. Profound mysteries are brought forward by her stillness. The High Priestess's silence roars against words that seek to define, yet fail. Words came to be after the silence. Her antiquity predates language. The High Priestess moves through what cannot be contained, uttered, or stated. She simply knows, as do you.

She need not speak because she understands in a glance. She knows the most important things are not spoken. They are understood and inferred.

The gentle lap of water breaks below the two of you. The water meanders, knowing it will get to its destination with no rush. The water enjoys reflecting the stars like the High Priestess enjoys being reflected by you.

Her crown moves. Like the moon it waxes and wanes, the ever-moving cycle of the tides matching your heart's beating.

The scroll upon her lap is the story of your life—secrets of your soul scratched across crisp parchment. You can't read this language but simply know the story is there. The scroll extends; you write the story with each passing moment of your life.

Skull Transformation Ritual

Ingredients
- Incense
- Candles
- Skull jewelry or item
- Death

Method, Visualization, and Meditation

Near La Paz, Bolivia, the witch's market is found. Small shops and street carts sell charms, talismans, and potions to ward off evil and attract good fortune. Burning a dried starfish is said to bring luck. Small llama corpses are procured and buried to bless a home. Fortunetellers divine by scattered cocoa leaves and owl feathers. Mother/daughter witches cast spells of any sort—for the right price.

Open the energy of your space by lighting your candles and incense. Place the Death card before you. Enter the card. Cast your eyes to the fiery sun rising between the two towers above the cardinal's head. Contemplate how death, like the morning sunlight, transforms the darkness of night with its glowing, crystalline, ruby-red light.

The wheels of death, like that of transformation and transmutation, are simply the transfer of one state into another. The more you embrace your fears, the more you love, the more you let go, the more transformed you will discover yourself to be.

The skeleton of this card and the skull on your table, though frightening to some, are stark reminders that the physical nature of the world is temporary. This skull will inspire you toward action, and through action you will find yourself transformed. Through your transformation, you transform the world.

Pass the skull through your incense to bless it. Place on your body or in your home. Every time you notice this skull, let it remind you that you are an evolutionary creature whose journey will never end.

The Day of the Skulls is celebrated today in Bolivia. Similar to the Day of the Dead, the skulls of ancestors are honored, blessed, and bestowed with flowers. Select a personal skull decoration or jewelry. This ritual provokes the wheels of transformation within you.

INCANTATION

Skull of bone
Card of Death
I honor you with
Every breath
Your lesson lives
I do not fear
Miraculous transformations
Will appear

Six of Cups Connection Ritual

The Six of Cups was called the Lord of Pleasure by the magicians of the Golden Dawn, who assigned it the time period of November 3–12.

INCANTATION

Six of Cups

Heart-centered place

This card is full

Of love and grace

Gifts of the heart

Are always free

Love others freely

Peace returns to me

Ingredient
- Six of Cups

Method, Visualization, and Meditation

Enter the arcana of the Six of Cups.

Six implies advancement. The challenge of the five has been met. Allies support forward momentum. A hierarchy is achieved.

Fresh orchids, flowering cactus, and star flower scents fill the air. An ancient medieval town surrounds you. Stone towers and edifices rise in a fortress that has offered protection to its residents for hundreds of years. Six cups stand before you. Unlike other Cups cards, these cups do not contain drinks or liquid. Rich vegetation, flowers, and lush green leaves spring from the cups, the manifestation of love.

Hot summer sun beats down on top of your head and fills the courtyard with yellow light. A boy wearing a red hat hands a delicious cup of blooms to a young girl. She is tiny, compact, and smiling. Dressed in a peasant costume, she accepts the gift graciously.

You note a similarity between the postures of the figures and the six of wands, swords, and pentacles. In each six card one figure towers over another, implying rank. Each card relates actions of giving and reception. Somewhere in the back of your mind, you recall the number six relates to the heart on the Tree of Life.

Their exchange of love is apparent. In the distance a soldier figure walks away. He carries a staff, implying his role as a guard or soldier. The children are free and safe to express themselves now that he has left them in peace. Their gifts of love have elevated them past the need for protection or rules, for love is the highest emotion, greatest gift, and loftiest joy.

Compassionate Divorce Spell

Ingredients
1. The Lovers reversed
2. Two of Cups
3. The Star

Method, Visualization, and Meditation

This spell has been created to move forward through the process of divorce with compassion for your former partner and for yourself.

The reversed Lovers card implies your current situation and the split between the two of you. The Two of Cups implies partnership. The Star card carries rejuvenation and new inspiration.

Place the reversed Lovers card before you. Enter the card. Allow yourself to feel every emotion that bubbles up for the situation at hand. Look at the reversed figures. Imagine you and your spouse as you once were. See yourselves at your best. See yourselves at your worst. Allow any and all feelings to seep through. Emotions cannot hurt you, no matter how intensely they are felt. Experience your emotional spectrum. Love yourself for feeling it so deeply.

Place the Two of Cups beneath the Lovers. See the couple coming together in complete peace. You and your spouse came together to learn essential lessons from one another. Goodness and decency still exists. You can't fault someone for being essentially who they are, nor can you fault yourself for being who you truly are. Look to discover the common ground between the two of you.

Place the Star card at the top of the cards. Allow the Star's healing waters to wash over you. Forgive yourself. Find forgiveness for your partner.

You can face this situation with compassion and caring. You got this.

Today is Armistice Day, celebrating the official end of World War I. It is marked by two minutes of silence on the eleventh hour of the eleventh day of November.

INCANTATION

Stars of night
Heal this blight
Dry my tears
Release my fears
Compassion come
Marriage undone
I am free
Peace fills me

3

1

2

Marty McFly returns to this date in 1955 in the classic 80s flick Back to the Future. *The best time travel machine is our own consciousness.*

INCANTATION

Time's an illusion

The present's here

Yet inside

I move to any year

Travel freely

Greet my past

So the present's

Peace will last

Time Traveling Journey

Ingredients
- Personal effects
- Rosemary crackers
1. The Chariot
2. Ace of Swords
3. Card representing the place you will travel to

Method, Visualization, and Meditation

Decide what time period, place, or person you would like to visit. Your senses will be your gateway for this journey. Think of how you are transported by a whiff of perfume or the scent of your favorite childhood food, a song, or an old friend. Find music, movies, toys, places, scents, food, clothing, and pictures that remind you of the place you'd like to go. Pinterest boards can serve as excellent inspiration for past decades.

Rosemary is used for remembrance. The spell effectively begins the moment you begin collecting things of the past.

Go to the physical place you have chosen to perform the journey. Nibble on a rosemary cracker. Place the Chariot before you. Enter the card. Take the reins and journey to the place you wish to go.

Place the Ace of Swords to direct you to that place. Look down the blade of the sword to see your final destination. Place the card representing where you are traveling to. Do you wish you had said something or done something different? Do you need to discover information or talk to your younger self? Would you like to give or take advice from your former self? Perform the actions you desire in this place.

Meditate on this as long as you like.

Reverse all actions to come back to the present.

3   2   1

Friday the 13th Good Luck Spell

Ingredients
- The Wheel of Fortune
- 1 penny

Method, Visualization, and Meditation

You've heard the old saying, "Find a penny, pick it up; all day long you'll have good luck." The Wheel of Fortune represents a change in one's luck for the better.

Place the Wheel of Fortune before you. Enter the card, hearing the spin of the wheel. Does it sound like a wheel at a country fair? Does it sound like an electronic slot machine? See the wheel spinning and recognize the forces of fate surrounding you at all times. Contemplate the figures in each corner of the card. These are your spirit guides and guardian angels. Thank them for looking out for you.

Contemplate the sphinx at the top of the wheel who holds the secrets of the universe. Feel the wind of destiny blowing through the card. Feel the wind at your back, nudging you where you need to go. You don't need to know where. It is enough to trust.

Pick up the penny. Shine it with your thumb. This penny is the beginning of material abundance—the pure symbol of luck. Place the penny inside the Wheel of Fortune card and inside the wheel. To persevere the winds of fate, stay centered on the wheel, just like this penny.

Leave this card and penny in sight until night falls. When evening blankets the earth, your spell is complete.

To seal this charm, take the penny with you tomorrow and flick it on the sidewalk or a heavily trafficked place. Share the wealth and luck of the penny with others to make it grow.

The oldest reference to the bad luck of Friday the thirteenth was documented on this day in 1868.

INCANTATION
Craft my penny
Pick it up
All day long
I'll have good luck
Share to others
Fortune found
Great luck is spread
All around

The Seven of Cups was called the Lord of Illusionary Success by the magicians of the Golden Dawn, who assigned it the time period of November 13–22.

INCANTATION

Seven of cups
Options aglow
Some bring happiness
This I know
If what I want
Is best for me
As time unfolds
I suppose we'll see

Seven of Cups Connection Ritual

Ingredient
• Seven of Cups

Method, Visualization, and Meditation

Enter the arcana of the Seven of Cups.

Seven is a mystical number, a lucky number. There are seven notes on the musical scale, seven days of the week, seven planets in our solar system besides Earth, seven deadly sins, seven seas, seven colors of the rainbow, seven continents, and seven wonders of the ancient world.

The scent of fresh popcorn mixes with recycled air as you stand in the dark. Your feet are sticking on the floor. The ceiling is high, and the spread of seats suggests you stand in a movie theater. The whir of a projector sounds behind you. A blue screen alights. A dazzling array of golden cups appear before you.

A gentleman jumps to his feet, excited by the images. He reaches for the selections, as beguiling as they are intriguing. A snake flicks his tongue and descends from a golden palace. Next to him, a ghostlike figure covered in gauze opens her palms to the sky. The third cup displays a sweet, carved face of youth and tender beauty. Beneath this cup, glorious towers extend from a cup and reach toward the sky. It sits next to a cup flowing with jewels; you almost shield your eyes from the sparkling gem glory. A victory bay wreath escapes another cup. A mysterious dragon crouches from the final cup.

More cups crowd the sky. There is an infinite amount of cups, as the choices you can make are as infinite and as varied as the people who make them.

Which cup would you choose? How will you know what is right?

Choose from within. Choose from your deepest desire. Choose as many as you like. Life is for the living.

Greater Mysteries Meditation

Ingredients
1. The Hierophant
2. The Hermit
3. The High Priestess

Method, Visualization, and Meditation

Perform this when you seek a deeper meaning of your chosen spirituality. Expect messages via dreams, experiences, and divinations following this meditation.

This spell calls for the wisdom of the big three Hs of tarot. The Hierophant represents the gatekeeper to higher mysteries of collected human consciousness, the Hermit is the shaman who travels highways of imagination and the occult, and the High Priestess is the gatekeeper to personal mystery.

Lay the Hierophant. Enter the card. Smell the burning incense as the chanting of monks rises among the pews. You have entered sacred space. It is the space of worship every human being has entered. Transcending cathedrals, this space exists in nature, mountains, and people. The Hierophant's crossed keys rise up before you. They glimmer in a golden glow, becoming larger, until they have passed right through your skin and are absorbed by your body.

Place the Hermit card. Enter the card. Feel the cold blast of air and see the gold keys reflected in the lantern's light. You are pulled at the speed of light, the molecules of your body rearranged. Travel on this highway of space and time. Absorb ancient knowledge.

Place the High Priestess. Enter the card. Her cool, lapping waters carry you off the astral path and back to earthy reality. She floats in and out of focus as you move forward to embody her. You take a seat between the pillars, secure in the knowledge of who you are and why you are here. Time, space, and swirling lights collect around you. You are the center of your universe. You are the conduit. You have awoken the mystery of yourself. Contemplate this knowledge for as long as you like.

Two Spanish ships land off Easter Island on this day in 1770 and discover over 900 monolithic statues. How they were moved and why the island was deforested remains a mystery.

INCANTATION
Powerful answers
Are always right there
Handle the knowledge
With great love and care
These cards with the combined
Magic of three
Relinquish their secrets
And hand them to me

Hecate's Shamanic Meditation

Tonight is sacred to Hecate, the goddess/witch of magic, witchcraft, and necromancy. Hecate connects to many Western shamanistic practitioners because she moves through the darkness of the lower worlds.

Ingredients

1. The World
2. Ten of Pentacles
3. The Moon

Method, Visualization, and Meditation

Modern shamans travel to the upper, lower, and middle worlds. The traveler usually imagines a great tree, staircase, or ladder connecting all three worlds inside the tree. In this meditation you will construct gateways to these worlds and enter them using three tarot cards.

The World card represents the upper world. As you might suspect, it is the dwelling space of the celestial beings, angels, and spiritual wisdom. The Ten of Pentacles represents the middle world. This is the world we live in, but shamanically it is the subtle world that mirrors the actual world we live in. It is also the ego and our conscious self. The Moon card reflects the lower world. It contains the essence of organic matter, plant energy, animal spirits, darker goddess archetypes, guides, our own subconscious, and creativity.

Music can be a powerful link for shamanic travel. Play drumming, chant, or singing bowl music if you like as you perform this exercise.

Pick your entry point and enter the tarot as if through a gate.

Allow Hecate to present herself to you inside the Moon card. She will have a message for you. What is it?

INCANTATION

Hecate, crossroads

Lower gate

Burrow deep

And excavate

Guide me deeper

With precision

Grant me with

A brand-new vision

1

2

3

Courage and Charisma Public Speaking Spell

Ingredients
- Queen of Wands
- Cardamom
- Almonds, crushed
- Vanilla ice cream

Method, Visualization, and Meditation

Cast this spell for courage and charisma for any public speaking engagement. Perform this spell after you have created, written, and researched your topic. Cast within a few days of delivering.

The Queen of Wands is the most charismatic card of the deck. Cardamom is used for eloquence and to charm a crowd. Almonds carry a masculine energy, sacred to Mercury, which clears succinct speech. Vanilla ice cream is moon food. It connects to a balancing feminine energy.

Sprinkle cardamom and crushed almonds over a scoop of vanilla ice cream. Allow the ice cream to melt as you place the Queen of Wands before you.

Enter the card. Feel the hot desert wind and walk toward her. Reach down to pet the warm black fur of her cat, who purrs pleasantly at your touch. Stand before this radiant queen, tan and golden. She may have been carved from gilded gold. Her radiance makes every grain of sand sparkle. She exudes the fire of the sun, her aura completely electric. It reaches to the far boundaries of her kingdom.

Sit down in her throne. Become this queen; look through her eyes. What do you see before you? Feel your energy reaching the boundaries of your kingdom. How does it feel to have your fiery energy reach that far? Feel the inner glow bursting through your skin. Feel a wand in your right hand, a sunflower in the other.

When you give your speech, speak it as the Queen of Wands.

Look at the melting ice cream before you. When it is completely melted it will be putty in your hands, like the audience. Scoop it up and devour it.

Today is Accession Day, a series of feasts and festivities marking the day in which Queen Elizabeth ascended the throne in 1558.

INCANTATION
Spark of fire
And delight
Fill my words
And face with light
Queen of Wands
Your siren call
Brings together
One and all
As words pass
Across my tongue
The audience listens
And I've won

*Today is Occult Day.
It recognizes all occult groups,
aims, and practices. The word
occult means "hidden" and is
derived from the Latin occulere,
which means "to hide from
view" and "to conceal."*

INCANTATION

Devil's darkness

Priestess light

Reveal truth

By moon's light

Reveal Hidden Truth Meditation

Ingredients
  1. The Devil
  2. The High Priestess

Method, Visualization, and Meditation

This meditation is meant to reveal a hidden truth. What covers these truths? Your own perceptions. To cultivate a new hidden truth, you must open your perception. Dispense with hallucinatory drugs; a tarot deck will suffice.

The Devil is the trickster who veils and confuses truth and information inside his darkness. The High Priestess represents all inner truth. The key to this meditation is what happens after it is performed.

Place the Devil before you. Enter his dungeon realm. Molten lava reflects in the caverns behind you. Moans and cries of the cursed echo as you stand before the great beast. He waves to you and smiles. You grin with the knowledge of a shared inside joke. You know he is not the scapegoat the world has chosen to project their fears onto. You know he is the essence of power and control inside each person, including yourself. With all this power, he reaches toward you, taps you on the head, and pulls a dark veil from your head.

Place the High Priestess card over the Devil and watch the entire scene transform into her shadowy realm. The book of secrets on her lap contains a hidden truth that will be revealed to you, but lean closer—she has a message:

"You with the eyes of a child—do not look at things as you have been taught to see them. See them as they really are. Disregard labels, names, and words. Find your eyes. Observe the world, and then you will find a profound truth."

With her words comes a sound like the tinkling of chimes in the wind. Exit the card and explore your new reality.

Star Card Connection Ritual

Ingredient
• The Star

Method, Visualization, and Meditation
Enter the arcana of the Star.

The landscape is illuminated as if a million candles burned at once and reflected the soft earth around you. Sweet purple clover and hay fill the air. A flaxen-haired woman hovers above the ground before you. Her soft, creamy flesh is uncovered by clothing. She pours two jugs of liquid. One stream pours into a blue pool of water. Cascading circles echo the circular path of the planets, each revolving around the star of their solar system.

You realize in this moment she is the source of magic, energy, and fire that ignites the life of a star, but she is also you. You understand that you contain the same combustible energy. Your life is a solar system revolving around you.

She pours an essence onto the earth that fuels manifestation in the material; it is how she feeds the conscious.

The sky is so black that it's blue. A blanket of diamonds dots the sky. The stars twinkle to remind you of the infinite possibility of their light. They brim with inspiration and ideas, and you carry the ability to channel them.

A single star chooses you. She is your guide. Think of her brilliance and feel her light to communicate with her.

How can a star differ from a sun if stars are, in fact, suns? Perspective is your answer. Remember, things can be spotted easily at a distance. Some things are so close you can't see them, but with distance comes perspective.

The Star card offers you a quiet spot of reflection. This sacred pool is yours and yours alone.

A high, beautiful song escapes the bird who sits in the tree. She sings to remind you of your connection to the natural world.

You are made of star stuff.

Jodie Foster, Meg Ryan, Calvin Klein, Ted Turner, and Indira Gandhi all share a birthday today.

INCANTATION
Star of light
Star of night
Fill my heart
Embrace my sight
Pastoral, sweet
And feeling free
The essence of you
Lives in me

Today is Universal Children's Day.

Happy Children Cupcake Spell

Ingredients
- Your favorite cupcake recipe
- Cherries

1. Ten of Cups
2. Page of Wands
3. Page of Cups
4. Page of Swords
5. Page of Pentacles

```
        [ 2 ]
[ 5 ] [ 1 ] [ 3 ]
        [ 4 ]
```

Method, Visualization, and Meditation

Prepare your favorite cupcake recipe. Pop them in the oven, and as the scent of sugar, butter, and sweetness envelops your kitchen, create a mandala with your cards.

Place the Ten of Cups. This is the place you create. You set the tone and the energy people discover in your home. You lead by example, exuding happiness and security. It teaches the children around you to cultivate their own happiness and security.

Place the Page of Wands. Consider how passionate your children are with every single day—how excitable and how much energy they contain and express. Think of these gifts in your life.

Place the Page of Cups. Meditate on the qualities of emotion your children exhibit. Hear their laughter in your ears.

Place the Page of Swords. Reflect on how clever your children are. Are they adventurous like this page? Do they find unique ways of doing things you never would have thought of?

Place the Page of Pentacles. Consider how your children learn, study, and read. When was the last time you read like an eleven-year-old?

Ice your cupcakes. Pop one cherry on top of each one, whispering a wish to the cherry.

Optimism of Sagittarius Spell

Ingredients
1. Ace of Cups
2. Two of Pentacles
3. Ten of Cups

Method, Visualization, and Meditation

The Ace of Cups represents renewed optimism. The Two of Pentacles reminds us that every action we take is a choice we make. The Ten of Cups represents the ultimate happy ending.

The card's layout should be placed like the archer's arrow, pointing toward the sky.

Place the reversed Ace of Cups before you. Look at all the water draining away. Turn your card right-side up, repeating three times:

"My cup is full."

Place the Two of Pentacles before you. Watch as the figure juggles his pentacles back and forth, repeating three times:

"I have a choice."

Place the Ten of Cups before you. Lay your dream at the end of the rainbow, repeating three times:

"Follow my heart."

Perform any small act encompassing personal happiness. Step toward it by watching a movie, drawing, or journaling about it.

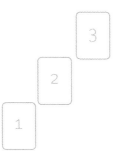

Today is the first day of the astrological sign of Sagittarius, the archer and adventurer. Ruled by Jupiter, generous, and intelligent, Sagittarius's lucky day is Thursday and lucky color is intuitive purple.

· · · · ·

INCANTATION

Divine joy
Fill up my cup
Inhale life
I drink it up
The cup runs over
Life's a gift
Enjoyment fills
My spirits lift

In 498 the Roman papacy was up in arms. The previous pope died. Two different popes were elected by opposing factions, setting off a dramatic series of events leading to one pope fasting himself to death.

INCANTATION

Pontiff, preacher

Vicar man

I'm in the space

Your presence spans

Higher secrets

Dwell in me

I don't need

The priest to see

Divine nature

Belongs to all

Passions, potentials

Are my call

Hierophant Card Connection Ritual

Ingredient
- The Hierophant

Method, Visualization, and Meditation

Enter the arcana of the Hierophant, which was called the Pope in early tarot decks. Enter the card and cross the threshold into sacred space. Hundreds of men—monks by the look of their red caps—span the pews of this great temple. A massive Hierophant towers over this divine place. You move before an ancient priest who sits high on a throne. All known religion and dogma is left behind. Myrtle and mugwort incense burn, their smoky tendrils winding and climbing through the air, moving along the columns into the highest reaches of this temple. Beings populate the darkness and look down from above, their watchful eyes upon you.

A humming grows in your ears. It is the call and response of monks in prayer. Their voices echo through the great chamber, opening a vibrational channel within you.

You step forward to the center aisle. The monks to your right are adorned by gowns covered in white lilies. Sweet white blooms have been placed in jugs and vases filling the space as far as the eye can see. The monks to your left bear cloaks of red roses. Their side of the temple is filled with the fragrant red flowers. You stand in the intersection of passion and potential.

Passion and potential are the keys crossed at the Hierophant's feet. He sends these keys to you, one representing the lily of pure white potential, the other, the red rose of passion.

This combination unlocks the Hierophant.

He sees that you hold the keys. He stands up and vacates his throne. The throne slides back; his pillars part. You are invited to take your passion and potential and walk straight into the heart of the Divine.

Will you proceed?

Banish Loneliness Spell

Ingredients
1. Five of Cups
2. Ace of Cups
3. The World
• Black candle

Method, Visualization, and Meditation

Black candles absorb negative energies. The Five of Cups reflects desolation of spirit. The Ace of Cups inspires rejuvenation. The World card reflects integration.

Light the black candle. Allow it to absorb your loneliness.

Place the Five of Cups before you. Enter the card. Become the figure in black. Allow yourself to feel the dark, scary, and negative feelings. Dwell in the darkness. You may feel fear, sadness, lack of connection, or any variety of uncomfortable feelings. Acknowledge them. Feel them. Allow them to move through you.

Turn around. Notice two cups are standing behind you. Reach down and pick up one cup. Allow healing waters to flow out, falling over your hand and across your arm, filling you with warm light.

Place the Ace of Cups over the Five of Cups. Enter the card. Healing waters wash away what is left of sadness. Know that emotions can't hurt you. Sit with them. Let them pass like water; you can move through them. Let sadness wash away.

Place the World card over the Ace of Cups. Enter the card. Observe the environment. You are part of the world, and the world is part of you. There is no separation. All is one. The separation of your ego is but an illusion. Focus on the World card to remember this truth.

Select one thing that brings you joy.

Do it.

A boat steward named Poon Lim went overboard on this day in 1942. He survived 133 days alone at sea in the South Atlantic and inadvertently set a world record. His loneliness and pain can only be imagined.

INCANTATION

Waters wash my
Tears away
In your space
Good feelings lay
Loneliness gone
Goodbye, so long
A new life
Begins to dawn

Romans greeted winter's long nights with the festival of Brumalia celebrated on this day. Drinking and merriment honoring Saturn, Ceres, and Bacchus brought life to the lengthening nights.

INCANTATION

Doors spring open
Welcome guest
Giddiness spills
Across my chest
Extend my magic
What's mine is yours
And giggle behind
The closed doors

Queen of Pentacles Domestic Goddess Spell

Ingredients
1. Queen of Pentacles
2. The Emperor
3. Six of Wands
4. Nine of Pentacles

Method, Visualization, and Meditation

Cast this spell when you are expecting guests, a date, or visitors to your home. It should be performed before you begin cleaning, shopping, cooking, or preparing for their arrival.

Place the Queen of Pentacles before you. Enter the card. Sweet, fertile earth richness fills the air. Flowers and tart little berries pepper the card. Sit in her throne. Feel the richness of her garments, the silk of her sleeves, the heavy velvet of her red dress, the dazzling, heavy weight of her crown. Fields and lush forests fill your vision, their bounty awaiting your expert touch. You are the queen of your realm, and everything is at your disposal.

Place the Emperor at her feet. Slip into his card. Note the care and order that he brings to the Queen of Pentacles' universe. He is activated and ready. His organizing energy fills you; no detail is overlooked.

Place the Six of Wands. Hear the crowds roar in appreciation and excitement. This will be the feeling your guests emulate when they connect to your generosity and bounty.

Place the Nine of Pentacles. Everything you craft, cook, and create for others feeds your own soul. Let the female inside the vineyard remind you to stop when you are tired, pause when you need rest, and realize when it is time to say no and retreat into a cocoon of comfort for yourself.

1

2   3

4

Empower/Mentor Another Spell

Ingredients
1. The Hierophant
2. The Sun

Method, Visualization, and Meditation

Mentoring and empowering another person is satisfying and builds rich relationships. It also extends an energy to the universe in ways you might not comprehend or expect. Cast this spell when you've made the decision to mentor and attract the right "mentee" into your life.

The Hierophant is the ultimate mentor. The Sun represents a young person with the glorious solar energy of expansion.

Place the Hierophant before you. Enter the card. Stand between his two priests. Streams of sunlight move the air, which is thick with myrrh and copal incense. The light filters through a rose stained-glass window above the Hierophant.

Standing at the foot of the Hierophant, consider your life. Consider the knowledge you possess and have accumulated through the years. Think about the people who helped you along the way. How did they open doors for you? Who revealed possibilities? How did they change your life?

Step up and take the Hierophant's seat.

Place the Sun card in front of you. From the Hierophant's throne see the child and horse moving toward you. The brilliance of the sun shines behind them, outlining their figures. Welcome the student into your life.

1   2

International Day for the Elimination of Violence Against Women is celebrated worldwide today. The fastest way to end violence or oppression is to empower people.

INCANTATION
Cards of knowledge
Bringer of light
Someone's close
Who needs insight
Share the wealth
Shed my grace
Transform the world
To a better place

Attitude of Gratitude Ritual

George Washington was responsible for the first American Thanksgiving. It was celebrated on this day in 1789.

Ingredients

1. Knight of Cups
2. Page of Cups
3. Ace of Cups
4. Card representing you
• Paper and pen

Method, Visualization, and Meditation

Place the Knight of Cups. Think about all the glorious gifts that have been given to you by others. This is the poetic knight. What has the gift of romance brought to you? What physical gift have you recently received? What beautiful emails, texts, phone calls, or words have you recently heard?

Place the Page of Cups. What talents do you possess? What gifts has your magical practice brought to your life? What gifts of nature have you received? How does art make your world a better place?

Place the Ace of Cups. Feel gratitude filling you, spilling from you. Look closely as the abundance of your life is reflected in the crystal-clear waters of this iridescent card. Feel the waters of generosity and abundance falling all over you.

Place the card representing you. What about yourself are you grateful for? Why are you thankful for your body?

Take your paper and pen and list your gratitude for as long as you like.

You could take this gratitude practice a step further and make it an excellent way to start your day. Select a like-minded friend and commit to writing a morning email to one another with a list of reasons you are grateful.

INCANTATION

Ace of Cups

Water of light
I shine with abundance
And gratitude tonight
My well flows over
Good people are near
I'm thankful for each and
Every gift this year

1   3   2

4

Inherit the Good Stuff Spell

Ingredients
- Photograph of departed
- Cards representing their qualities

Method, Visualization, and Meditation

Do you have the strength or inclination to change your family bloodline? Did you know you can alter the lives of those who live before and after you? This can be accomplished by living a life that is truly authentic to who you are.

Our families form and shape every aspect of us, from the financial space to the angles of our face and luster of our eyes. Inherited qualities do not negate the unique individual and separate qualities we are born with.

Teen years give us the courage to break away from our familial identity. Growing older, it is easy to spot themes and narratives playing out in our lives that are a direct result of our connection to those who came before us.

To focus on the extraordinary qualities of your family, select a relative who has passed on. Find a photograph of them or an object they owned. Make a list of the qualities you admire in them. Choose corresponding tarot cards that embody these qualities: Star card for glamour, Wheel of Fortune for success, Ace of Cups for compassion, etc.

Place the photo before you. One by one, place the cards that match their qualities. Meditate on each card. As you place each card, consider how the family member embodied the energy of each arcana. Consider how you can do the same. Move clockwise until you have moved through your cards.

To perform this spell for a living family member, make a date to take them to lunch. Luxuriate in their wonderful qualities, ask them for advice, and open your energy so that you may absorb as much of them as possible. Perform the card meditation when you come home.

On this day in 176 Roman Emperor Marcus Aurelius bestowed the rank of Supreme Commander to his son, Commodus, granting him command over all Roman Legions.

. . . . .

INCANTATION

[Name],
I love you much
Today I hope
Your soul I touch
Thank you for
Your gifts and love
Together we fit
Like hand in glove

Right Job for Me Spell

The Secret, *the book companion to the film of the same name, was released on this day in 2006. It became an instant bestseller by explaining the law of attraction.*

Ingredients
- Pen and paper
1. Two of Cups
2. Two of Wands
3. Eight of Pentacles

Method, Visualization, and Meditation

The law of attraction is the same as the Hermetic doctrine of "as above, so below." This spell attracts the job of your dreams. Don't know what that job might be? Befuddled by what field you should be working in? No worries. Focus on the qualities you desire, the broad strokes of a life you want to live, then let your magic take care of the rest. The key is to believe. Keep your mind open to unexpected possibility.

Twos in tarot imply duality and a coming together. The Eight of Pentacles is happiness in work.

Make a list of all the qualities you seek: hours, atmosphere, salary, vacation time, what sort of people you want to work with. List every single quality. The more specific, the stronger your spell will be.

Place the Two of Cups. Recall the last time you felt a perfect fit and a swell of recognition with something. Imagine a job, a work situation, that is a perfect fit for you. Imagine this takes shape as the male figure in the card. Walk up and bid him hello.

Place the Two of Wands. Feel the energetic ties of passion bringing you closer to the right situation. See it coming to you inside the globe as if it were a crystal ball.

Place the Eight of Pentacles. Feel the pleasure of work done well. Enjoy the satisfaction and accomplishment washing over you. Meditate on the mandala of cards until you feel ready to repeat the incantation.

3

1   2

Eloquence Spell

Ingredients
  1. King of Cups
  2. Queen of Swords

Method, Visualization, and Meditation

The art of self-expression may always be refined. Like the Temperance card, we can work on it, making it better, clearer, and more precise. Doing so, we can express ourselves in simple and true ways.

The King of Cups is the master of the imagination. The Queen of Swords is also the goddess of articulation and expression. These two cards will guarantee your personal expression is inspired, succinct, and to the point.

Enter the King of Cups. Feel the rolling expansiveness of the ocean. The card is wet, deep, and brimming with life and ideas, just like your brain. The king sits on his throne and prevails over the seascape. He controls what comes to the surface. By the time an idea appears, it is inspired. Feel the thoughts, rich and rolling in your subconscious. He is bubbling with creativity, and so are you. Sit on his throne. Look at the world through his eyes.

Enter the Queen of Swords. She directs and commands her outward expression. Her hand is open, happy to receive information that aids her. Her sword points upward to the space of inspiration. Her cape matches the sky. She drapes herself in expansiveness. Through her, you cultivate what you need to say. Thoughts form quickly on your tongue. You are not afraid to speak your mind from your heart. Sit on her throne. Look at the world through her eyes.

Louisa May Alcott was born on this day in 1832. Alcott gained fame for many books, including the classic Little Women.

INCANTATION

King and Queen
My perfect pair
He controls water
She commands air
Within my soul
You both live
Manifest through me
Like a sieve

Romans set aside two feast days for Hecate, ancient goddess of magic, witchcraft, the moon, and necromancy. Today is one of them.

INCANTATION

Power of Hecate

Hear my plea

Change is what

I want to see

Help me, power me

Share your spark

As I bestow gifts

In the dark

Hecate Crossroads Power Spell

Ingredients
- The Hanged Man
- Bulb of garlic (an offering sacred to Hecate)
- Sea salt
- Wine or cider

Method, Visualization, and Meditation

Hecate is the goddess of the three-way crossroads. Crossroads are potent thresholds of magic where paths intervene and choices are made. Opposites collide and power converges at a crossroads. Said to be the gateway to the underworld, crossing roads were thought to be the place a person could sell their soul to the devil, and ancient criminal and suicide corpses were disposed there.

The Hanged Man is representative of the three-way crossroad, as seen on his hanging post. He is often a signpost of change. This spell should be performed after midnight.

Place the Hanged Man before you. Enter the card. Bring your attention to his hanging foot. Shrink yourself so you are the size of an ant. Stand above his toe and survey the road of your life. Look back at how you've moved and traveled. See the crossroads. What new opportunities do you want to usher in? What powerful, life-changing magic would you like to make use of? Say it out loud; state it to the Hanged Man. He glows in response to the knowledge of your intention.

Take the Hanged Man, garlic, sea salt, and wine/cider to the closest crossroads. Repeat your desire aloud. Leave the garlic, sprinkle the salt, and pour the wine/cider into the ground as an offering to Hecate.

Holiday Magic Spell

Ingredients
- The Star
- Glass of water
- Ace of Wands

Method, Visualization, and Meditation

The Star card reflects sacred illumination, and the Ace of Wands is the spark of passion.

Place the Star card before you. Enter the card. You stand naked with your bare feet on warm grass, looking up. A shining night sky glimmers above you. The universe is ablaze with points of light. Move toward a glistening pool of water. It reflects the night sky like a mirror. A cup is next to your feet. Kneel to scoop up the star water, sending little waves as you do. Drink the star water (your physical glass of water), feeling it cleanse and electrify you.

Place the Ace of Wands. See yourself bringing this wand of fire into the Star card with you. Hold the wand firmly in both hands. It warms your body, yet it does not burn. Your skin reflects the powerful red glow. Internal warmth creeps through your body. It moves through your arms, up your spine, and spreads to your head and down to your feet. It is the warmth of love and generosity.

You spy a village below. It is a snug little town with snow-encrusted roofs and white lights. You walk toward it and peek into homes, seeing roaring fireplaces and tables set with sumptuous food and drink. Shiny gifts peek from beneath evergreens. Children's laughter floats through the air. A bonfire is alight in the town square, and people are dancing and singing.

All this happiness and celebration resides in your heart. The bonfire is the warmth of your spirit.

December's holidays celebrate light in the darkness. We gather with loved ones, indulge in hearty foods, and celebrate the year's closing. Amidst the flurry, keep your heart warm and your spirits high by inviting the magic to glow inside of you. Become the light in the darkness.

INCANTATION

White lights aglow
Warmth of night
Speed of fairy
Spirits alight
Filled with love
Tinsle in hand
Sparkle through
Holiday land

The Eight of Wands was called the Lord of Swiftness by the magicians of the Golden Dawn, who assigned it the time period of November 23–December 2.

INCANTATION

Eight of Wands
Passion in flight
Streaks across the sky
Heart's delight
A plan in motion
No stopping now
When you see the result
The response is wow!

Eight of Wands Connection Ritual

Ingredient
- Eight of Wands

Method, Visualization, and Meditation
Enter the arcana of the Eight of Wands.

Fields of green spread around you as far as your eye can see. Fertile hills slope in the distance and settlements lie beyond a lazy, winding river that meanders like a blue path through the countryside.

The sky's blue is reflected in the cool water that runs its course in its own perfect time, bouncing and babbling over stones and rocks. A far-off sound, the spring of a catapult is heard. As quick as the sky was empty, it is now full of flying wands, like shooting stars, moving at incredible speed. Your hair flies up and around your face as eight wands come flying past you. You crouch to avoid being knocked back by one of them. They are precise, not randomly flung, but moving with specificity and elegance. Someone unknown to you launched them with intention and knows exactly where they aim.

Tiny sprouts of vegetation spring from each wand. They grow, like seedling transplants, in mid air. There is nothing you could do to stop this energy in motion. Their course is set.

Deep down, you know their energy is harnessable. The only things needed to launch these wands of change are passion, poise, and a plan.

What shall you set in motion?

Bona Dea Personal Healing Spell

Ingredient
• The Sun

Method, Visualization, and Meditation

The Sun card represents perfect health. Perform this healing spell in conjunction with other medical or holistic treatments.

Scan your body to discover the areas requiring healing. If you are suffering from congestion, focus on the nose or lungs; if you are suffering foot pain, focus on the feet. Remain open to discover any surprising and unexpected spots.

Place the Sun card before you. Allow the warm exuberance of the sunshine to envelop you. It is the gentle, early warmth of summer. This is the healing energy that entices the world to wake up, quiver, and expand.

Feel the spot in your body awakening. Feel and focus on the sun's energy as if it were raindrops of light.

Place the Sun card on that part of your body. Feel the warmth on the top of your skin. Let it saturate and move through your layers of skin, into the blood and flesh beneath. Bring the heat between your skin and bone so that everything between sucks in the Sun's healing warmth. Your cells soak and receive the yellow sunlight. Each molecule of your body glows with health, becoming plump and rosy.

Blanket your cells in warm, healing light. Let the energy in a ball glow with healing, pulsating light. Any darkness or decay, any sickness, becomes dispersed and inoculated with white light. Allow the energy ball to grow large enough to encompass your entire body.

The Festival of Bona Dea was held today in Rome. This "Good Goddess" was sacred to women and healing. No man was allowed to speak or utter her name. Her rituals were known as the "secret sacrifice," and men were banned from her ceremonies.

INCANTATION

Health of sun
Warmth of one
Heal this body
Return to fun
Strength and health
Physical wealth
Come to me
So mote it be

December • 4

Get It Together Jupiter Pasta Spell

*Pioneer 10 reached
Jupiter on this day
in 1973.*

Ingredients
- The Wheel of Fortune
- 4 sage leaves
- 2 tablespoons butter
- Single serving pasta or pumpkin/butternut squash ravioli

Method, Visualization, and Meditation
Jupiter rules luck, growth, enthusiasm, and expansion. The Wheel of Fortune and hearty sage leaves are both ruled by Jupiter. Sage offers strength and calm for any situation.

Place the Wheel of Fortune card before you. See the elements on the card spinning just like our solar system's planets. Which part of the card stays still?

The only way you aren't going to spin out of control is to find the exact center of the wheel.

Find your personal center inside your body. Breathe deeply to fill this centered place with warmth and light. This marks the ultimate center of your universe.

Move to the stove and to your frying pan. See the Wheel of Fortune's circle inside the pan. Place over a low flame and add the butter. As the butter melts, feel your stress melting away. As the aroma fills your kitchen, allow the sweetness to calm you down. As the butter browns, toss in the sage leaves. Allow the sage to brown (not burn).

Toss over prepared pasta or ravioli with fresh cheese and enjoy. You have found your grounding and thereby gained control over your situation. You are ready to face anything.

INCANTATION
Spinning planet
Globe revolve
Gather together
Problem solve
Equilibrium gained
Balance back
Now I'm feeling
Back on track

Venus Spell to Stop Being So Hard on Yourself

Ingredients
- The Empress
- Sprig of holly
- Soft piece of fabric
- Wooden box

Pioneer Venus 1 began to orbit Venus on this day in 1978. Venus represents the epitome of love.

Method, Visualization, and Meditation

Do you brush off compliments? Do you make excuses for your talents and gifts? Do you put yourself down? This is not kind, nor is it productive. If this sounds like you, perform this spell to stop being so hard on yourself. Replace the inner critic with Venus, planet and goddess of love.

The Empress is ruled by Venus. Ancient Druid priests utilized mistletoe for fertility rituals.

Place the Empress card before you. Enter the card. Stand in the Empress's wheat fields. See the person you love most in the world standing in the fields of gold. What do you say to them? How do you act toward them? How do you encourage them? What is your general feeling toward them? Reach forward to embrace them. Smell the nape of their neck and their hair. Feel love emanating.

Let them go and discover it is *you* you have been hugging. Feel all those feelings of love for yourself.

Walk to the Empress. She is the essence of love. Feel her capacity of love coming toward you. Exit the card.

Take the holly in hand. Gently trace the outside of the leaves with your finger, feel the sharpness but don't poke yourself. These poking edges represent the words and thoughts you have used against yourself. Make a solemn promise you will never do this again.

Wrap the holly up in the fabric while whispering the incantation.

Place inside the box for safekeeping. Use the holly for future self-protection spells.

INCANTATION

Sharp words, piercing thoughts
Bring forth blood
Transform to kindness
And forge bloom to bud
Love myself in
Kind, gentle ways
Away my weapons
Goodness stays

Psychic Self-Defense Spell

Dion Fortune, the author of Psychic Self-Defense, *was born today in 1890.*

Ingredients
1. The Moon
2. Page of Cups
3. All four knights

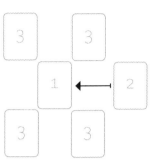

Method, Visualization, and Meditation

The Moon card is associated with the color of silver and represents the subtle psychic landscape. The Page of Cups is the most impressionable card of the deck. The knights offer their protective energies.

You will create a mirrored bubble surrounding your entire body. The reflective surface will bounce all unwanted energy away from you.

Lay the Moon card. Enter its vague shadows. Walking toward the mountains, note how different everything looks in the moonlight. You walk past the towers. This psychic landscape is the place of the mythic and the imagination. Honor and validate the psychic power you possess.

Lay the Page of Cups over the Moon card. Hold the cup in your hand, as pictured on the card. Watch carefully as something emerges from the cup. A water creature pokes his head at you. To your surprise and delight, you notice he is blowing a bubble. The clear bubble is blossoming, becoming so large you put the cup on the floor. Step back as the fish continues to blow and release the bubble.

The bubble is now large enough for you to step inside of it. You pass through its membrane. It encloses you perfectly. You are able to see the room around you with perfect clarity, yet the shimmering bubble protects you. It bounces and refracts all energies and emotions back to the people who created them. At any point in your life when you need to activate this bubble, imagine it around you. You will be sealed and protected.

Place the knights at the four corners of the Moon card for protection.

INCANTATION

Reflective bubble
Bounce, refract
To others
I will not react
Deflect their energy
Duck and pass
This spell will be
Sure to last

Attract Positive People Spell

Ingredients
- 2 cups chamomile tea
- Honey
- Three of Cups

Method, Visualization, and Meditation

Sticky honey is used in drawing and attraction spells. Its sweetness brings things we desire to us. Chamomile, a sacred Druid herb, is a bright and cheerful flower containing the qualities of people you'd like to attract. Jupiter, the planet of luck and expansion, also helps attract upbeat people into your life.

Prepare two cups of infused tea. Add honey. Take one cup for yourself and place one at the seat next to you. This is an offering to your future friends.

Place the Three of Cups card before you. Enter the card. Feel the warmth of good feelings surrounding you. Feel the celebration and camaraderie of being among people who make you feel good. See their cups lifted in the air and then feel how high other people can bring you when they shine the light on your positive qualities. Return the love.

The three figures inside the card are like flowers in a garden. Each carries unique beauty and talent. They inspire one another to do better, be greater. Each member of the circle is better for knowing the others. Friends with warm hearts and good intentions are heading toward you as you work this spell.

Contemplate the card as you finish your tea, taking your time and enjoying the space of friendship. When your cup is empty, take the second cup and pour as a libation outside of your home while repeating the incantation.

Galileo Spacecraft went into orbit around Jupiter on this day in 1995.

INCANTATION

Three of Cups
With love and light
Bring wonderful people
to my sight
My circle surrounds me
Honest and true
A sweet, delightful
Witch's brew
Friends come to me
Come quick, come soon
Find you by the
Light of the moon

Today is Bodhi Day. According to Japanese tradition, Buddha became enlightened on this day as he sat under a tree and meditated until he found the root of all suffering.

INCANTATION

Opportunies thrive

Discover you now

Marvelous things in life

I do allow

Perception opens

To include

Things that foster

A good mood

Four of Cups Unseen Opportunities Spell

Ingredients
- Pen and paper
- Four of Cups
- Dried figs
- Goat cheese
- Honey

Method, Visualization, and Meditation

The figure on the Four of Cups is often associated with the sitting Buddha. How often have we missed opportunities and not even realized we didn't see them? Our brain/eye connection to the world filters portions of perception; otherwise, we would be inundated with too much information at once. Cast this spell to hone your perception and allow the most useful, positive, and uplifting opportunities and people to be noticed. You may also perform this spell when you are searching for something in particular, such as a new home, a new lover, or a new perspective.

Figs are sacred to the Bodhi tree. Goat cheese connects to lunar energy. Write down the opportunities or types of people you would like to notice, attract, and cultivate in your life. Hone your list into a series of simple descriptive words.

Take the seated position of the Four of Cups. Place the Four of Cups before you. Enter the card, becoming the figure under the tree. Feel the tree bark against your spine. Look out at the three cups before you. These cups represent your current state of being and seeing. State each item of your list out loud, ending with "I see you now." Repeat each item on the list three times.

Exit the card.

Place goat cheese on figs, drizzle with honey, and enjoy your sweet, rich new reality.

Releasing Stress/Invoking Peace Spell

Ingredients
  1. Nine of Swords
  2. Ace of Swords
  3. The High Priestess

Method, Visualization, and Meditation

Swords represent the mind, thoughts, and calculations. The Nine of Swords represents a stressful state of mind. The Ace of Swords will be used as a tool to remove stress triggers. The High Priestess represents your natural state of calm and peace.

Place the Nine of Swords. Enter the card. Embody the woman in bed. The springs of the mattress support you. The nightgown's soft cotton folds caress your shoulders and waist. Your head is in your hands with emotional despair. Remove your hands from your eyes. Look at the wall next to you. Each sword represents a trigger to stressful thinking. You have the power to change your thoughts. Grasp one sword by its cold steel handle. Use it to strike the other swords from the wall.

Place the Ace of Swords over the Nine of Swords. You have harnessed the power of thought. The strength of the sword reverberates in your hand, up your arm, and through your whole body with a gentle hum. You have command of your thoughts. If a stressful thought enters your consciousness, notice it and let it pass.

Turn both cards sideways so the sword faces right. Place the High Priestess to the right of the sword. You now direct all your mental energy to the calm resting place of your natural intuition. Moonlight filters the card. The gentle waves break behind her. Your sleeping gown has become regal robes whose silken fabric shimmers with the moon's luminescence. Each fiber of her gown carries the vibrancy of a moonbeam. You sit in her chair, at perfect peace. This is your natural state.

You are perfection.

The holidays are gearing up, expectations abound, and there's a good chance you are feeling overloaded with responsibility. Cast this spell to free yourself.

INCANTATION

Release the stress
Invoke the calm
Tonight I am
Safe and warm
Night fades softly
And I see
A peaceful
Calm reality

Have a million things to manage and accomplish? This spell acts like a power boost to help you blow through your day with ease. It aids in productivity, ensuring things run smoothly and your work is effective and quick.

INCANTATION

Spinning wheel
Glowing wands
Energetic release
Of my bonds
Move with grace
I'm free and clear
The wheels turn
A clock's clever gear
They spin, revolve
And circle so
My life moves
With perfect flow

Increase Productivity Spell

Ingredients
- List of things to accomplish
1. Five of Wands
2. The Wheel of Fortune
- Mint gum

Method, Visualization, and Meditation

The fives in tarot's minor suits represent the friction that keeps the momentum going through each suit as it grows toward the ten. The Wheel of Fortune, bearing an old, iconic image, keeps energy moving. It ensures things get done. Mint enlivens the senses and increases memory recall so you are faster and more effective.

Place the Five of Wands before you. See the energy that the five characters are generating from their heat and play. Do not move too close. Stay at the outskirts. Simply observe their momentum and exertion.

Place the Wheel of Fortune above the Five of Wands. In your mind's eye see the wheel spinning. Listen to the whir as it speeds up faster and faster. As the wheel revolves, look at your to-do list. See the first item, pull it toward you off the list, and throw it toward the wheel. It happens effortlessly, pleasantly. Continue down the list until all items have been thrown into the wheel.

Pop a stick of mint gum in your mouth. Get to work on your list, and enjoy your productivity.

2

1

Nine of Wands Connection Ritual

Ingredient
- Nine of Wands

Method, Visualization, and Meditation
Enter the arcana of the Nine of Wands.

Nines in tarot reflect the closing of a cycle. Nines are akin to standing at the front of a long line, knowing you are next to be called. Nines provide what is wanted: wishes are granted, actions have culminated, the experience of manifestation is at hand. In the best cases, we sit on cloud nine.

A beaten and bruised actor stands before you. Turning his head cautiously left and right, a fence of upright wands stands behind him. He grasps a single wand in his hand. He has taken this wand from the fence. Doing so opens a new door for himself. He steps onto a virgin path.

You have seen this moment in films and plays. It never ceases to thrill you. The character you've been rooting for breaks through their barriers. Moving past self-imposed walls, they enter new territory.

The figure's fear and uncertainty do not cause him to retrace his steps and return to the field of comfort. He has come too far. The drama unfolds before you like a tasty meal.

But long after red velvet curtains drape across the stage in finality, after the actors have finished their post-show cocktails, after the torchlights are snuffed out, after you've returned home, paid the babysitter, brushed your teeth, and gone to bed, how does the story resonate in your dreams? Has the hero taught you how to move past your comfort zone? Was it merely entertainment?

When will you supersede your barriers? When will you break the bonds that hold you? When will you pick up your wand and open a doorway to a new reality?

The Nine of Wands was called the Lord of Great Strength by the magicians of the Golden Dawn, who assigned it the time period of December 3–December 12.

INCANTATION
Nine of Wands
Passions fight
Move, evolve
Break forth tonight
Seek the dark
Untrodden lands
Cause the future
In my hands

There are a lucky thirteen days left until Christmas Day. That means if you are shopping for gifts, you have less than two weeks to get it done. Perform this quick spell before shopping for any type of gift any time of the year.

INCANTATION

Perfect present

Find you soon

Come to me quick

Make them swoon

A gift to others

Is a gift to me

Abundance abounding

Is what I see

Shop with ease

And fun and flair

By end of day

All gifts are there

Perfect Gift Spell

Ingredients
1. Ace of Pentacles
2. Seven of Swords

Method, Visualization, and Meditation

All aces in tarot represent the gift of their suit. The Ace of Pentacles is the gift of earth, which reflects things we can see, hold, smell, and touch. These are physical gifts. The Seven of Swords is the selection and editing card. Harness the Seven of Swords card to gain the power of quick decisions and see with clarity.

Bring to mind the person or people for whom you are shopping.

Place the Ace of Pentacles. See yourself giving your gifts. Experience the delightful look of surprise on their face when they open it. How does this make you feel?

Place the Seven of Swords over the ace.

See yourself shopping. The figure selects carefully, taking only what is needed. This is the card of curation, discrimination, and speed. See yourself shopping quickly, speedily, and being directed exactly toward the item that will make your giftee's heart glow. Become the Seven of Swords as you shop, picking and selecting only what you need, leaving the rest behind.

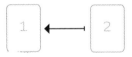

Page of Pentacles Connection Ritual

Ingredient
• Page of Pentacles

Method, Visualization, and Meditation

Enter the arcana of the Page of Pentacles, the perpetual student who is fascinated by the very process of learning and the physical world around her. The Apennine Mountains reach toward the sky in the distance, and cheerful spring poppies dance in the breeze. A grove of cherry laurel trees offers shade from the vibrant sun. The hum of tractors plays over the landscape as they turn the soft earth up to receive seeds.

A young person stands before you with a golden disk balanced in her fingertips. She is absorbed by the globe's complexity and refracted, vibrating light. She memorizes its every detail, including the five-pointed star at the very center. The star rotates, whirring with energy. She and you realize at the same moment that the power inside the pentacle is magic. It is magic that, when imbued with solar energy or intention, creates growth. When fed by the sun, it germinates a seed. It is the spark of physical magic. It propels the growth of everything, from individual molecules to the expansive solar system. All retain the shape of the pentacle.

The student recognizes that the circular, global nature of the pentacle lends itself not only to the molecule, our planet and solar system, but also to the nature of time, the scope and range of personal emotion, and even a human life span. Even tarot's journey is circular in its narrative pattern, though it deceives the reader as a rectangular stack of cards. The Fool moves through the majors to the World, only to begin again. The minor arcana's ace appears, grows, and blooms to the tenth card, only to return again in ace form.

The Page's hat is red, the color of creation; her tunic is green, the color of manifestation.

What will this pentacle become when you plant it?

The Ivy League's Dartmouth College, one of only nine colleges founded before the American Revolution, broke ground on this day in 1769.

INCANTATION

Page of Pentacles
Study is play
What should I
Grow today?
Plant the seed
Of learning now,
Future brilliance
I will plow

Abundance in All Things Garland

One of the best ways to manifest abundance is to offer it up. Winter creatures such as birds and squirrels will quiver with excitement when you make an offering of a popcorn and cranberry garland. This is an excellent spell to perform with children.

INCANTATION
Tie the knot
Fast and tight
[Insert desire] comes
It feels right

Ingredients
- Ten of Pentacles
- Bag of fresh cranberries
- Bowl of popcorn (homemade or bought)
- Strong waxed thread
- Needle

Method, Visualization, and Meditation

The Ten of Pentacles represents complete material abundance that encompasses everything touchable, from people to objects to finance. Cranberries are ruled by the element of water and offer protective qualities. Corn is a symbol of prosperity and is ruled by fire; it is useful for abundance spells.

Refine your intention before casting this spell. Are you seeking general abundance or something more specific? See clearly in your mind's eye what you would like to attract.

Place the Ten of Pentacles before you. Enter the card. Stand under the threshold of physical manifestation. This is the arched doorway to the city. Look toward the inside of the city. See what you have already manifested in your life within the city walls. See the things you own, the people you know, the items you currently have.

Turn and look outside the city to what is available to you in the outside world. The possibilities are infinite. See very clearly what you would like to bring to your world. Invite it in.

Begin the garland's construction by creating a knot at the end of the string. While knotting, repeat the incantation. String the cranberries and popcorn alternately until you have finished. Fasten a new knot at the other end and repeat the incantation over the knot. Make as many as you like.

Hang your garland outside in the trees when you are finished.

Ten of Wands Connection Ritual

Ingredient
- Ten of Wands

Method, Visualization, and Meditation
Enter the arcana of the Ten of Wands.

You are in a theater. The thunderous sound of clapping fills your ears. The audience is on their feet cheering, hooting, and stomping.

A man walks across the stage carrying a mysterious bundle of wands that have been fashioned together like a bundle of corn stalks. His clothing matches the color of the sticks.

Tears stream down the plump cheeks of the woman sitting next to you. "Bravo! Bravo!" calls the tuxedoed gentleman behind you. One couple rushes out of their seats to avoid the crush of people. The red curtains above descend across the stage as the crowd roars louder. The play is over. The drama is done. The passion and energy has come to its logical yet surprising conclusion.

Actors line up in the wings, getting ready to come out for their bow, each in the order of their character's importance. Producers nod to themselves, satisfied with the evening's receipts and the audience reaction. Bow-tied ushers stand straighter and ready themselves to fling open the doors.

The pub next door readies itself for the influx of customers, the bartender inhaling one last drag of his cigarette in the alley. A single-file line of black taxis waits at the curb outside the theater.

The passion play is over. Out of a playwright's single flame came a fire. It is now extinguished. But as easily as night has fallen, a new day soon begins. With the new day comes new fires, new passions, and different stories.

This is the rhythm and flow of our life.

The Ten of Wands was called the Lord of Oppression by the magicians of the Golden Dawn, who assigned it the time period of December 13–21.

INCANTATION
Ten of Wands
Passion spent
It's curious to discover
Where time went
Kindle again
A new day will rise
And with it comes
A delightful surprise

Go Away Head Cold Roasted Garlic Spell

Drippy noses and congested heads are the last thing you need in the bustling holiday season. Cast this spell as a preventative measure or when you feel run down or when you've got a touch of the sniffles.

INCANTATION
Knight of Swords
Lord of air
Keep my health
Hear my prayer

Ingredients
- Large bulb of garlic
- Olive oil, salt, and pepper
- Knight of Swords

Method, Visualization, and Meditation

Garlic is known to ward off those pesky, blood-sucking vampires, but it's also a treasure trove of antibacterial and health-inducing properties. No wonder garlic picked up a protective reputation. Garlic undergoes a magical transmutation when it roasts. Its spiciness and bite become mellow and sweet.

The Knight of Swords is also known as the Knight of Air. He will combat airborne sickness for you and keep enemies and germs at bay.

Focus on the Knight of Swords. Feel his protective properties surrounding you. In your mind's eye allow him to hand you his sword. Feel it heavy in your hand. Use the sword to create a protective barrier around your entire body. Draw a protective barrier in the air around you and the ground before you. Stand inside and light the barrier with protective white light. Repeat the incantation.

Preheat your oven to 350 degrees. Slice the pointy head of the garlic off so each clove is exposed. Rub exposed cloves with olive oil and sprinkle fresh pepper and salt on top. Wrap in tin foil, place in oven, and roast for one hour, letting the aromatic smell entice you.

Remove from oven when the garlic is soft and spreadable.

Spread across hearty toasted bread with cheese or whisk into soups, stews, sauces, or pastas.

Let Go of Old Behavior Spell

Ingredients
1. Ten of Wands
2. Ace of Swords
3. The Star

Method, Visualization, and Meditation

The Ten of Wands represents endings and the finality of passion, effort, and energy. The Ace of Swords is the tool used to cut away what is not needed. The Star card represents an open soul, ready for nourishment that is blessed by the celestial realm.

Place the Ten of Wands. Note the figure in the card and what he carries. What are you carrying? What do you want to rid yourself of? Filter through your thoughts. Choose one particular thing—the most annoying, plaguing issue. Become the figure on the card holding ten wands in your arms. This is the issue at hand. Stand up. Release the wands. They scatter before you like pick-up sticks.

Place the Ace of Swords. Enter the card. Grasp the cold steel of the sword. It glitters in the December sun, reflecting the cold light of truth. Use your blade to mark the ground in front of you. Mark a line in the dirt that separates you from the wands. The wands disintegrate before your eyes.

Place the Star card. Feel her freedom and vulnerability. The weight of the wands has been replaced by the weightless light of inspiration. It is energized. The starlight comes from millions of miles across the galaxy, but you can travel there in a thought. A seed of brilliance has been planted where old blocks once stood. You are free and clear.

[1]   [2]   [3]

The darkest night of the year draws close. Now is the time to extinguish old habits, disruptive thought patterns, and lingering strange emotions for good. As psychic ties to behaviors, people, or habits are officially released, new growth occurs. New potentials and possibilities will emerge.

INCANTATION
Dark of night
End of year
Release behaviors
That aren't dear
You depart
Are left behind
Embrace the new
Possibility I find

December • 18

The time period near a solstice is a good time to connect with elemental energy.

INCANTATION

Ace of Pentacles

Root of earth

All around me

Life gives birth

I take this energy

Spend it well

And honor the place

Where I do dwell

Ace of Pentacles Connection Ritual

Ingredient
- Ace of Pentacles

Method, Visualization, and Meditation

Place the Ace of Pentacles. Enter the card. You are standing amidst a lush garden. Foxglove reaches for the sun as bees bounce from flower to flower collecting nectar. Crickets chirp in symphony around you.

Lie on the soft green grass. Feel the weight of your entire body supported by the earth. Garden beds have been churned. The earth waits for seeds bursting with life energy. Fat earthworms burrow down, and spiders scurry from the sunlight, finding refuge amidst tender green shadows.

You see the sprig of green and tug on it. A carrot slips from the ground. You brush off the dirt and taste the crunchy, sweet orange flesh. Press your fingers into the earth. Feel the warm, crumbly, mossy dirt fall between your fingers. Anything planted in this garden will bloom.

A mysterious hand extends before you from a swirling cloud. It is the hand of magic, synchronicity, and mystery. A pentacle rests on its palm. The pentacle transforms into an atom, a nucleus surrounded by a cloud of electrons. It transforms again, now into a seed, then a shiny golden coin, a planet, a witch's pentagram, a sequence of DNA yet to be unraveled. In a flash you see the entire life span of a human, wobbly infant to old man and back to atom. The entire physical world is contained in a ball.

The pentacle belongs to you. It always has. It always will.

Emerald ivy dappled with red berries covers the fence. An opening invites you out of the garden and down a new path. Mountains rise up to the sky's embrace in the distance.

Will you walk through?

Embrace the Darkness Spell

Ingredients
1. Four of Swords
2. Eight of Cups
3. The High Priestess

Method, Visualization, and Meditation

The Four of Swords reflects deep slumber. The Eight of Cups shows a willingness to take a road less traveled. The High Priestess is personal authenticity.

The longest night of the year is upon us. It is human nature to be afraid of the dark. Animals and danger lurked there for ancient man. Modernity brings us electricity, safety, and the knowledge that inside darkness, true birth occurs.

Lay the Four of Swords. Enter the card and become the sleeping knight. How deep you sleep! Feel the darkness behind your eyelids. You know you are safe to wander, dream, and invent.

Lay the Eight of Cups. Rise from your slumber. Begin an upward trek. Feel the moonlight around you, lighting your way. Stand at the foot of a hill. At the summit is an answer, a solution, a new way of being. It is a new evolution and manifestation of your deepest personal self. It is a part of yourself that has always wanted to surface. Step toward this.

Lay the High Priestess card. She sits on a throne at the top of the hill. The waters flow around you both. You move toward her and touch her glowing, pale skin. Your fingers move right through her; she is pure spirit—not of the physical realm. You heed her silent invitation to sit down on her throne. You are her. On this deepest night, she fills you with knowledge. Look through the High Priestess's eyes. What do you see? What do you now know? What will you do?

Dark, chilly mornings beg for extra sleep and five more minutes under the covers. Honor this special time of year. Allow gloomy nights to lead to the manifestation of your heart's desire, creativity fulfilled, and authentic manifestation that will blossom and emerge with clarity in the new year.

INCANTATION

Pregnant, fecund
Darkest night
Deepest slumber
Brings new sight

1	2	3

INCANTATION

Page of Wands
Excited fire
Magic wands
Youths never tire
Point the wand
Where shall you go?
Once you get there
You will know

Page of Wands Connection Ritual

Ingredient
- Page of Wands

Method, Visualization, and Meditation

Enter the arcana of the Page of Wands.

The dry sands of the desert blow past your shoulders and through your hair. The fiery orange landscape rises to meet the expansive blanket of blue sky distance like a woman leaning back to receive her lover's body. Aromatic sagebrush, acacia, and tamarisk shrubs bearing pink flowers dot the scene. Salamanders scurry at the sound of your footsteps. A darting antelope catches your eye in the distance.

A spark, an ember of a girl, stands before you. She is costumed in vibrant orange and yellow as if leaping flames of desert fire had transformed into clothing. A single flame of red feather extends from her hat. A sense of déjà vu washes across your psyche. It feels like a ghost skipped over your grave, but then you realize where you have seen the feather before. The Fool, the Sun, and the Death card wear the same red feather on their heads.

This golden girl with locks of pure sunlight holds a wand in her hand. She is captivated by its tip. Cool green leaves shoot out. She realizes the power of attraction something can hold. The magic she makes with this wand is the ability to follow the flame of passion. It is the journey from point A to point B. Her wand will transport her anywhere.

Where shall you journey? The world is waiting.

Goal-Setting Capricorn Spell

Ingredients
- Pen, paper, and scissors
1. The Devil
2. Eight of Cups

Method, Visualization, and Meditation

The sign of Capricorn is assigned to the Devil card. The Devil can represent a person rooted in the material who is ever thirsty for more. It is Capricorn's steady nature that makes Capricorn's dreams and reality. The Eight of Cups represents the journey toward the manifestation of desire.

Make a list of the goals you would like to achieve.

Lay the Devil before you. Stand before the great beast. Feel how his energy has been operating through you, keeping you stuck in habits that are comfortable yet no longer useful. Walk over to the two nude figures. Lift their chains above their heads. They exclaim with excitement and run off. The Devil turns his eyes to you, but his energy is different now. You are no longer enslaved. You are now empowered.

Pick up the scissors and cut out each goal. Arrange the goals in order of ease and short term to more difficult and long term.

Place the Eight of Cups. Place the simplest goal at the top right corner of the card. See yourself setting off in a new direction. Move the card past it, to the top right side of the goal. Place a new goal at the top right side of the card. See yourself moving toward it. Repeat with all goals.

Today marks the first day of the astrological sign of Capricorn, the pragmatist. Capricorn's Saturn energy is steady, sure, and always operates with the end goal in mind.

INCANTATION

List of goals
Get me straight
Bring what I need
To my plate
I reach, I strive
I get it done
The battle's over
And I've won

Ritual to Align with Winter

Winter solstice is upon us. It marks the shortest day of the year and the longest number of nighttime hours. Creativity and rumination spells are well cast at this time of year. Winter energy aligns with the new moon, a return to sleep and rest, pregnancy and potency.

INCANTATION

Season of winter
Bright, white light
Lays in opposition to
Long, dark night
Snowflake crystals
Are very clear
What will I
Create this year?

Ingredients
- Death
- Favorite winter items and symbols

Method, Visualization, and Meditation

Working with seasonal energy is like working within the moon's phases. The energy surrounds us; we need only to be open to it in order to access its gifts. The energetic qualities of winter include rest, sleep, silence, stillness, pause, stark clarity, and focus.

Gather seasonal energy like a weaver gathering silken strands. Cold nights, frosty air, falling snow, bare trees, bubbling stews, roasting vegetables, and white winter light support you and your magical intent.

Gather your favorite winter objects to place around the Death card. You might select mistletoe, pine cones, holiday chocolates, fairy lights, or garlands.

Enter the Death card.

Watch as Death marches across the card. As he moves, he leaves silence and stillness in his wake. A fresh, blank slate is left in his wake, as fresh as newly fallen snow. Death clears the space for us so we have room to blossom, grow, and expand. This season brings rest to our bodies so, come springtime, we can burst with fullness.

What do the qualities of dreamtime mean to you? What is changing in your life along with the Death card, quietly, under the surface, where no one else sees? What are the realms you visit when you slumber? What do you fill your mind with? What visions appear on snowscapes? How does the quiet feed you?

Explore into the card as far as you can go on your own.

Holiday House of Spirits Spell

Ingredients
- Photographs of the departed
- Nine of Pentacles
- Six of Cups
- Four of Wands
- Small chocolate offering

Method, Visualization, and Meditation

Bring family close together and draw the departed closer to you with this spell.

Ancient Romans used Lares to represent ancestors, but you can use photographs. It is best if the photo is inside a frame and can freely stand on an altar or table. The Nine of Pentacles represents our family tree connection through the familial castle and vineyard. The Six of Cups reflects emotional attributes that are passed down to us. The Four of Wands reflects happiness and stability in the hearth and home.

Place the family photographs before you. Lay the Nine of Pentacles. Enter the card. Smell the vineyard's fertile earth. Consider those spirits who lived before you. They are as old as the grapevines surrounding you. They are as loyal as the falcon. These spirits wrote their story and passed their themes and qualities down to you.

Place the Six of Cups. Think of the emotional gifts that have been passed to you. How does the sense of humor thrive within you? What is your relationship to art? How do the issues of love and support play out in your family? Think of positive emotional qualities and thank them for it.

Place the Four of Wands. Feel the stability of the ground you walk upon. The house your family has built, the support you stand upon that was created by those who came before. They can feel your warmth and thanks, and they will feed you through the coming year in invisible ways. Place an offering of chocolate before each photograph while repeating the incantation.

Today was Larentalia, the Roman festival honoring ancestors and blessing the home with joy. Prayers were offered to Lares, small figures displayed in the home. The Lares represented ancestor spirits who watched over the welfare of each family.

INCANTATION

Happy home
Family tree
I accept the gifts
You offer me
Gratias tibi ago
(Latin for "thank you")

It is Christmas Eve. Children and adults will soon eagerly tear apart wrapping paper and open gifts. Perform this spell for the gift you most desire. It doesn't matter if you celebrate Christmas or not.

Gift for Me Spell

Ingredients
- Tarot cards representing what you want
- Gift for someone else
- Wrapping items

Method, Visualization, and Meditation

Choose the cards that express your desire. If you want a trip to Aruba, you might choose the Eight of Wands and the Sun card together. For heightened creativity, choose the Empress; for a financial windfall, choose the Nine and Ten of Pentacles. The sky is the limit. Ask for anything your heart desires.

Place the cards before you. Walk away from your table. Return to peruse them with a fresh set of eyes. See yourself unwrapping the gift you desire. Imagine yourself doing, enjoying, and basking in it.

Now that you have enjoyed receiving, pick up the gift you have selected for another.

Wrap it carefully. Imagining their joy opening it.

While uttering the incantation, place it in a unique and surprising place where they will discover it upon waking up.

INCANTATION

By the holiday lights
Hanging bright
My wish is coming
True tonight

Open Third Eye Chakra Energy

Ingredient
• The High Priestess

Method, Visualization, and Meditation

The third eye chakra is located in the center of your forehead, between and slightly above your eyebrows.

Sit on a chair with your feet flat on the floor or sit on the floor in yogi position, legs crossed.

Place the High Priestess card before you. Focus on the third eye space on your forehead. Feel the energy there begin to warm and glow. Imagine it is colored indigo or royal blue. You might even begin to spin the chakra's energy, revolving it in a whir of color. Sit straight. Perhaps you hear the energy, smell it, or even taste it.

Focus on the High Priestess while spinning the energy in your third eye. Connect your eyes with hers. Drink her essence in through your eyes. Note the full moon on her crown. It matches your third eye chakra.

Feel the connection of divine love. Let the indigo energy move from yourself to the High Priestess and back again. Feel the ball of energy fall through your body and move up your spine. It fills your entire essence with divine vision.

Give yourself the greatest gift today by opening your third eye chakra energy. The third eye is the seat of your intuition and the base of spiritual knowledge. Access this to open yourself to giant leaps of awareness and connections regarding your life.

INCANTATION

Third eye truth
The second sight
Glow within me
On this night
I look, I see
The truth reveal
Use this knowledge
To help and heal

Two of Pentacles Connection Ritual

The Two of Pentacles was called the Lord of Harmonious Change by the magicians of the Golden Dawn, who assigned it the time period of December 22–30.

Ingredient
- Two of Pentacles

Method, Visualization, and Meditation

Enter the arcana of the Two of Pentacles.

You have entered the space of division. One has become two. In this space of duality, the pentacle has become aware of itself. Context is provided by means of a second. Opposition is born. Oppositional tension creates a new energy.

Bring your mind's eye inside the card and smell the fresh sawdust and wood of a stage. You are standing in an outdoor theater. You stand opposite a curly haired performer who is dressed in a colorful costume. Painted ships traverse rolling waves behind him. The performer hops from one slippered foot to the next. He is passing two yellow balls across the front of his chest. The balls move in tandem with an odd green band of energy in the symbol of infinity, the figure eight. He doesn't stop to look at you but remains absorbed in his work.

Choices, choices, this card reflects choices. It holds a deeper truth as well. It is the nature of life that every single thing is in motion. Your table, chair, glass of water, and even the tarot card you gaze upon is alive and in motion. This energy is reflected inside this card. It is the energy of division, motion, attraction, and reaction. Everything you do creates an effect on the world.

And like a mini Wheel of Fortune, which echoes the movement and passing of time, this performer shows you how to dance and leap and stay fluid. He also reminds you to take your time. Never rush. Let the situation unfold.

Hold the tension of opposites. If you do so long enough, a third option will emerge.

INCANTATION

Two of Pentacles
Endless dance
Life moves quick
Strut and prance
Stay nimble and quick
Upon my feet
When destiny knocks
How will I greet?

Destroy Fear Spell

Ingredients
1. Card representing your fear
2. The Tower

Method, Visualization, and Meditation

The implicit destruction observed within the Tower card can be used to your advantage. Use the power of the Tower card to transform a tightly grasped fear into a positive association. Your fear also may be something causing you extreme stress.

Choose a card representing your fear. We often fear the very thing we desire. Consider the Celtic Cross spread's position 9; hopes/fears are represented by the same card. If we fear what we desire, this is often why we don't have it yet. Discover and visualize the underlying emotional reaction that blooms when you are close to getting what you want. Choose an appropriate tarot card to represent your fear or stress.

Place your chosen card in front of you. Enter the card. Face your fear. What does it look like? Select a piece, an aspect, a visual from the card to embody your fear. Allow your fear to become the tangible form inside the card. Discover a zipper running vertically up and down this embodiment.

Walk closer to your fear and unzip it.

Place the Tower card above your chosen card. Hear the crack of thunder, feel the heat of the lightning, and smell the smoke of the explosion.

Your fear is turned inside out. Gaze at what lies on the opposite side of your fear. What is there? What does it look like?

Your fear is now the opposite state. Walk into that state. Dwell inside it.

You are now free.

Use this time to your best advantage. The week between Christmas and New Years Eve holds a succinct and particular magical quality. The year is winding down; we rest from holiday madness and plot and plan for what's to come in the year ahead.

INCANTATION

Fear and joy
A coin of two sides
Pull out the stress
From my insides
Cleanse me, clear me
Awake, anew
Pure joy is now what
Will run through

2

1

Spell to Stop People Pleasing

It's a crazy time of year and demands run high. Cast this spell when you find yourself running ragged trying to please everyone and find yourself getting lost in the mix.

Ingredients
  1. Seven of Wands
  2. Eight of Cups
  3. The Hanged Man reversed

Method, Visualization, and Meditation

The Seven of Wands represents your current state of people pleasing. The Eight of Cups marks the transition to a new reality. The reversed Hanged Man reflects a new and settled reality.

Place the Seven of Wands. Enter the card with your mind's eye. See yourself standing on the rocks' edge. All of the demands and needs are placed on you by others who hold the wands. See each person or situation holding a wand upward demanding your attention. See yourself for a moment in a frantic effort to satisfy them all. Stop. Stand back. Thank each and every one of them for being in your life. Tell them it is time for you to go. Put down the wand and walk away.

Place the Eight of Cups. Enter the card. Become the figure walking up the mountain. You have entered a quiet, solitary space of twilight. The cups behind you represent your old way of life. Reach the top of the mountain. An infinite ocean expands before you. Place the reversed Hanged Man. The glow around his head represents the new reality of headspace you have entered. You do not shun your responsibilities to others, but you put yourself first. Doing so, you become more helpful and vivacious to the people in your life than ever before.

INCANTATION

Magic flickering

In the card

Change my ways

It's not hard

My boundaries set

My mind is staid

I no longer please like

The scullery maid

Weird Witches of Macbeth Power Spell

Ingredients
1. Three of Cups
2. Page of Wands
3. Queen of Wands
4. Strength
• Ginger tea

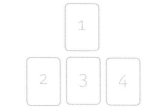

London's Lyceum Theater hosted its first production of Macbeth *today in 1888. Raise energy and send it toward your desired goal in this spell inspired by the Bard's famous witches.*

Method, Visualization, and Meditation

Increase your own power by performing this spell when you need more energy and desire to become more effective, proactive, and powerful.

The Three of Cups represents the three witches and the Maiden/Mother/Crone energy. The Page of Wands represents youthful passion (Maiden). The Queen reflects mature passion (Mother). The Strength card is the mastery of personal power (Crone). You will call to the three archetypes using Shakespeare's powerful speech.

Place the Three of Cups before you. Focus on the power of the triad, the power of three, and see the cone of energy these dancers create by coming together.

Place the Page of Wands and chant:

Double, double, toil and trouble
As I speak, my powers double

Place the Queen of Wands and chant:

Fillet of a penny snake
With this spell its power I take

Place the Strength card and chant:

Eye of newt and toe of frog
Power fills my monologue

INCANTATION
Wool of bat
And tongue of dog
Adder's fork and
Blind-worm's sting
Lizard's leg
And owlet's wing
For a charm
Of powerful trouble
Like a hell-broth
Boil and bubble

Feel the power generated by your words and the cards. See your ultimate goal, and send all this raised energy toward it. Sip the ginger tea to kindle your growing power.

Fabulous Party Spell

An unforgettable evening can be as mysterious as the nature of magic itself. It is almost that celebrated night of the year. Help the stars align with memories that will last a lifetime and be talked about for years to come.

Ingredients
- Oregano (fresh or dried)
1. Queen of Wands
2. Queen of Pentacles
3. Queen of Swords
4. Queen of Cups
5. Three of Cups

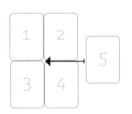

INCANTATION
Party night
Shining bright
Fabulous party
Disco light
Wicked fun
With harm to none
I do declare
This spell is done

Method, Visualization, and Meditation

Oregano is ruled by Venus and used for happiness, luck, and protection. The four queens represent the stability of planning and effort. The Three of Cups reflects the creativity abounding as everyone draws together. If possible, leave this mandala out for the duration of your planning stages and up till the event itself to connect you with party creativity and good ideas.

The Queen of Wands (fire) connects to charisma and the Egyptian cat goddess Bast. The Queen of Pentacles (earth) relates to food, decorations, and comfort. The Queen of Swords (air) relates to guest selection and conversation. The Queen of Cups (water) represents the emotional levels of guests and good feelings.

Lay the Queen of Wands. Feel her warmth radiating. You absorb her sparkling party hostess personality. Stroke the cat's soft black fur. Her purring hums under your palm and fills you with wicked delight. Lay the Queen of Pentacles. Smell the richness and luxury, the scent of good food and festive decor. Lay the Queen of Swords. The wind whistles as she calls forth electric people and stirs the energy of your party with exciting conversation and exchanges of clever wit. Lay the Queen of Cups, who guarantees that each guest feels welcome in your space. Lay the Three of Cups, representing the party itself; it pulls the creativity of each queen in the center of the mandala.

When you are finished, take your oregano and walk clockwise around your house or block while sprinkling it for the love and protection of all who enter.

World Card's Fabulous New Year Spell

Ingredients

1. The World
2. Ten of Swords
3. Ace of Swords
4. Ten of Wands
5. Ace of Wands
6. Ten of Pentacles
7. Ace of Pentacles
8. Ten of Cups
9. Ace of Cups

It's the last day of the year. Time to say goodbye to the past and walk through the gate of the world dancer into a new year of wonders.

Method, Visualization, and Meditation

Nine is the number of wish fulfillment. Nine cards are used for this spell.

Place the World card before you. Enter the card. Allow yourself to become the world dancer. Feel the energy of the past year swirling around you like warm and cleansing ocean waters. Float in the middle of her nebula. Recall a way of thinking that you ended this year or a decision you made that put an end to something negative. State out loud what you decided or did as you lay down your Ten of Swords card. Focus on this card and honor yourself for removing what was no longer needed. What new decision have you made? State it aloud and place your Ace of Swords to the left of the ten.

Think of a work or passion project you completed this past year. Say it aloud as you place the Ten of Wands. Where and what new project will you focus your attention on? Say it as you place the Ace of Wands below the Ten of Wands.

Think of the material things you manifested into existence this year: the money you've acquired, the people you've attracted, the food you've cooked, the environments you've created. Say out loud the thing you are proudest of manifesting as you lay the

Ten of Pentacles. What new thing do you want to bring into existence? Say it aloud as you lay the Ace of Pentacles.

Think what you've felt good about in the past year, especially relationships with others, as you lay the Ten of Cups above the World. What new emotional opening do you desire? Say it aloud as you place the Ace of Cups.

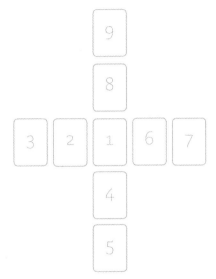

INCANTATION
The end of year
Time is here
Goodye to old
Usher in the new
Acknowledge everything
I've been through

Astrological Spells

Aquarius Outside-the-Box Originality Spell   JANUARY 20

Mystical Visionary Pisces Spell   FEBRUARY 19

Action of Aries Spell   MARCH 21

Sensual Pleasure of Taurus Spell   APRIL 20

Gemini Lighten Up Spell   MAY 21

Invoke Empathy for an Annoying Person Spell   JUNE 21

Self-Confidence of Leo Salad Spell   JULY 23

Veil of Neptune Spell   AUGUST 25

Organizing Energy of Virgo Spell   AUGUST 26

Libra Balancing Act Spell   SEPTEMBER 23

Scorpio Regeneration Spell   OCTOBER 23

Optimism of Sagittarius Spell   NOVEMBER 21

Goal-Setting Capricorn Spell   DECEMBER 21

Banishing

Give It Up Spell   APRIL 24

Halt the Haters Spell   JUNE 3

Stop Nasty Gossip Spell   JUNE 11

Remove a Family Curse Spell   JUNE 23

Bringing or Banishing Bridge Spell   JULY 11

Banish Loneliness Spell   NOVEMBER 23

Astrological Spells, 375

Banishing, 375

Career & Work Life, 376

Chakra Opening, 376

Creativity, 377

Education, 377

Family, House & Home, 377

Finance & Money Matters, 378

General, 379

Health, Beauty & Wellness, 379

Justice, 380

Letting Go, 380

Love, 381

Luck, Be a Lady, 382

Magical Oils, 382

Moody Spells, 382

Nature, 383

Personal Power, 384

Power Planet Spells, 386

Protection, 386

Recipe Spells, 387

Seasonal, 387

Sleepy Spells, 388

Tarot Cards, 388

Tarot-Specific Spells
& Rituals, 391

Travel, 392

Witchy Enchantments, 392

Career & Work Life

Boost Your Business Spell   JANUARY 16

Finish a Project Spell   APRIL 26

Leadership and Inspiration Spell   MAY 30

Peace in the Workplace Spell   JUNE 10

Find a New Job Spell   JUNE 28

Success in Business Spell   JULY 8

Booming Business Beach Spell   JULY 30

Switch Career Spell   AUGUST 21

Labor Day Next Level Career Spell   SEPTEMBER 1

Find a Mentor Spell   SEPTEMBER 5

Energize Your Career Mars Spell   OCTOBER 13

Courage and Charisma Public Speaking Spell   NOVEMBER 17

Right Job for Me Spell   NOVEMBER 28

Increase Productivity Spell   DECEMBER 10

Chakra Opening

Open Kundalini Root Chakra Energy   JANUARY 18

Open Sacral Chakra Energy   FEBRUARY 21

Activate Crown Chakra Energy   APRIL 9

Open Solar Plexus Chakra Energy   JULY 21

Open Heart Chakra Energy   SEPTEMBER 26

Open Throat Chakra Energy   OCTOBER 11

Open Third Eye Chakra Energy   DECEMBER 25

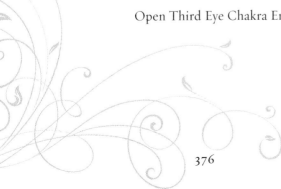

Creativity

Activate the Muse Spell   JANUARY 10

Creative Project Spell   JANUARY 31

Creative Boost Spell   MARCH 6

Permission to Explore My Creativity Spell   MARCH 28

Inspiration Spell   OCTOBER 25

Tarot's Shamanic Art Exercise   NOVEMBER 7

Education

School Admission Spell   FEBRUARY 1

Ace the Exam Spell   FEBRUARY 25

Wisdom of Thoth Right Study Spell   JULY 15

Find a Mentor Spell   SEPTEMBER 5

Family, House & Home

Honor Your Ancestors Spell   JANUARY 2

Spell to Reconnect with Personal Magic   JANUARY 6

Postpartum Ritual for Peace   JANUARY 11

Healthy Pregnancy Spell   JANUARY 15

Spell for Peace in the Home   JANUARY 28

Banish Negativity from the Home   FEBRUARY 3

Fertility Spell   FEBRUARY 13

Peaceful Homecoming Spell   APRIL 5

Mother's Day Meditation   MAY 12

Home Protection Spell   MAY 19

Evil Eye Protective Charm   JUNE 2

Sell a House Spell   JUNE 7

Father's Day Spell   JUNE 19

House Hunting Spell   JULY 29

Healthy Birth Spell   AUGUST 1

Home Blessing and Connection Spell   AUGUST 7

Troublesome Guest Cleansing Spell   AUGUST 11

Dinner with the Departed Ritual and Reading   AUGUST 18

Spell to Conceive a Baby   SEPTEMBER 12

Mother/Daughter Contemplation   OCTOBER 6

Happy Children Cupcake Spell   NOVEMBER 20

Queen of Pentacles Domestic Goddess Spell   NOVEMBER 24

Inherit the Good Stuff Spell   NOVEMBER 27

Holiday House of Spirits Spell   DECEMBER 23

Fabulous Party Spell   DECEMBER 30

. . . .

Finance & Money Matters

Get Out of Debt Spell   JANUARY 8

Financial Manifestation Spell   MARCH 3

St. Patrick Money Spell   MARCH 17

Pentacle Pomander for Financial Wealth Spell   APRIL 3

Grow My Money Spell   APRIL 17

Spell for Financial Security   JULY 3

Bring Money Knot Spell   JULY 17

Financial Oil   SEPTEMBER 15

General

The Fool's Fresh Start Spell   JANUARY 1

Fairy-Tale Magic Spell   JANUARY 4

Invoke Kindness Spell   FEBRUARY 17

Honor Personal Magic Spell   MARCH 8

Four Directions Spell   MAY 3

Witch's Finger Experiment   AUGUST 9

Diana's Hunting Charm   AUGUST 13

Winning Spell   SEPTEMBER 4

Perfect Gift Spell   DECEMBER 12

Abundance in All Things Garland   DECEMBER 14

Health, Beauty & Wellness

Weight-Loss Spell   JANUARY 7

Aphrodite's "Face the World" Spell   FEBRUARY 6

Love Your Body, Respect Yourself Spell   FEBRUARY 11

Send Healing Energy Spell   MARCH 18

Ensure Good Health Kale Charm   MARCH 30

Inner Beauty Salt Bath Spell   APRIL 18

Glamour Jewelry Spell   MAY 16

Mesmerizing Spell   MAY 23

Picnic Spell for Excellent Health   JUNE 18

Moon Bewitchment Spell   JUNE 30

Comfortable in My Skin Spell   JULY 5

Caramel Lace for Elegance and Grace Spell   JULY 19

Radiant Child of the Sun Spell   JULY 22

Morning Dew Enhance Beauty Spell   AUGUST 3

Bona Dea Personal Healing Spell   DECEMBER 3

Go Away Head Cold Roasted Garlic Spell   DECEMBER 16

Justice

Marie Laveau Lawsuit Spell   MAY 7

Contractual Matters Spell   AUGUST 2

Lawsuit Spell   SEPTEMBER 24

Letting Go

Give It Up Spell   APRIL 24

Accepting Loss Spell   SEPTEMBER 6

Outside Your Comfort Zone Spell   SEPTEMBER 16

Banish Loneliness Spell   NOVEMBER 23

Let Go of Old Behavior Spell   DECEMBER 17

Spell to Stop People Pleasing   DECEMBER 28

Love

Spell to Attract a Lover   JANUARY 19

Rejuvenate Love and Tender Feelings Spell   JANUARY 21

Send Love to a Crush Spell   FEBRUARY 14

Attract Best Possible Relationship Spell   MARCH 10

I Want You in My Bed Sweet Apple Spell   MARCH 11

Entice a New Lover Spell   MARCH 14

Vampire Regeneration Love Spell   APRIL 12

Hot Date Spell   APRIL 14

Happy Marriage Spell   APRIL 29

Mexican Chocolate Love Truffles   MAY 5

Stop Obsessing Over Someone Spell   MAY 13

Lodestone Attraction Spell   JUNE 1

Love Yourself Spell   JUNE 5

Get Lucky Tonight Cleopatra Spell   JUNE 9

Sensitive Breakup Spell   JUNE 22

French Kiss Spell   JULY 6

Houdini's Escape a Bad Situation Spell   JULY 7

Mend a Broken Heart Spell   JULY 9

Protect Your Relationships Spell   JULY 31

Healing Love Spell   AUGUST 5

Lovers Intimacy Spell   AUGUST 6

Meteor Shower Message of Love Spell   AUGUST 10

Bring a Long-Distance Lover Close to You Spell   AUGUST 31

Never Again Lover Spell   SEPTEMBER 30

Gravitate Toward Me Spell   OCTOBER 4

Future Lover Visioning Spell   OCTOBER 18

Love and Good Feelings Warm Apple Spell   OCTOBER 21

Wedding Planning Spell   OCTOBER 24

Block Unwanted Sexual Advances Spell   NOVEMBER 3

Compassionate Divorce Spell   NOVEMBER 11

Luck, Be a Lady

Gain the Edge in Competition Spell   AUGUST 16

Bang for Your Buck Shopping Spell   AUGUST 19

Gift for Me Spell   DECEMBER 24

Magical Oils

Car Safety Oil   FEBRUARY 26

Night Visions Oil   MAY 25

Financial Oil   SEPTEMBER 15

Moody Spells

Invoke Internal Peace Spell   JANUARY 30

Path of Forgiveness Spell   FEBRUARY 20

Wrong Side of the Bed Spell   FEBRUARY 22

Release Sadness Beach Spell   JUNE 8

Snap Spell to Change a Mood   JULY 2

Increase Confidence Spell   JULY 18

Stop the Madness Spell   AUGUST 24

Renewal Spell   AUGUST 27

Soften the Edges Artichoke Spell   SEPTEMBER 19

Anti-Anxiety Spell   OCTOBER 10

Lick the Wound Spell   OCTOBER 22

Mischief Night's Loosen Up Spell   OCTOBER 30

Attract Positive Energy Spell   NOVEMBER 5

Attract Positive People Spell   DECEMBER 7

Four of Cups Unseen Opportunities Spell   DECEMBER 8

Releasing Stress/Invoking Peace Spell   DECEMBER 9

Nature

Whisper the Wind Weather Spell   FEBRUARY 5

Connect to the Elements Spell   FEBRUARY 9

Bountiful Garden Spell   MARCH 12

Raise the Wind and Your Energy Spell   APRIL 2

Tree Journey with the Four of Cups   APRIL 10

Primrose Hidden Treasure of the Soul Spell   APRIL 19

Totem Animal Discovery   APRIL 28

Financial Nest Egg Spell   MAY 4

White Lotus Meditation   MAY 8

Nature Guide Spell   JUNE 24

Walking Spell for Connection   OCTOBER 17

Personal Power

Spell to Reconnect with Personal Magic   JANUARY 6

Mermaid Magic Bath Spell   JANUARY 9

X-Ray Vision Spell   JANUARY 12

Open Kundalini Root Chakra Energy   JANUARY 18

Cleopatra's Power Spell   JANUARY 22

Release Obsessive Thoughts Spell   JANUARY 24

Face Your Fears Spell   JANUARY 26

Extinguish Jealousy Spell   FEBRUARY 4

Make the Right Decision Spell   FEBRUARY 15

Path of Forgiveness Spell   FEBRUARY 20

Masonic Stability Contemplation   FEBRUARY 23

Leap Day Soul Realignment Spell   FEBRUARY 29

Stop Procrastinating Spell   MARCH 1

Envy Banishing Powder Spell   MARCH 4

Honor Personal Magic Spell   MARCH 8

Alchemy Spell for Self-Transformation   MARCH 9

Spell to Unleash Magic in Your Day   MARCH 16

Wash Away Past Pain Spell   APRIL 13

Da Vinci Follow Your Passion Spell   APRIL 15

Charm to Gain Your Heart's Desire   APRIL 30

May Day Grounding Spell   MAY 1

Birthday Wish Spell   MAY 24

Fly Your Freak Flag Solar Eclipse Spell   MAY 28

Spell to See What Others Do Not   JUNE 27

Independence Spell   JULY 4

Small Step Spell   JULY 20

Pleasure in Life Spell   AUGUST 8

High Priestess Authentic Self Spell   AUGUST 12

Gain the Edge in Competition Spell   AUGUST 16

Eucalyptus Banish Bad Habits Spell   AUGUST 17

Bang for Your Buck Shopping Spell   AUGUST 19

Embrace My Fear Spell   AUGUST 20

Get Back on Track Spell   AUGUST 28

Grant Me the Strength Spell   SEPTEMBER 7

Wildest Dream Spell   SEPTEMBER 8

Finding Time Spell   SEPTEMBER 14

Spell to Move Forward Without Resentment   SEPTEMBER 17

Keep a Secret Spell   SEPTEMBER 20

Setting Boundaries Spell   SEPTEMBER 25

No More Waiting Spell   OCTOBER 2

Power of "No" Spell   OCTOBER 5

Shadow Self Integration   OCTOBER 7

The Power and Expression of Crowley Spell   OCTOBER 12

Queen of Swords Balloon Spell   OCTOBER 15

Get Exactly What You Want Spell   OCTOBER 16

Banish a Bad Habit Necromancy Spell   OCTOBER 26

Release Psychic Ties Spell   NOVEMBER 1

Hanged Man Reverse the Situation Spell   NOVEMBER 6

Empower/Mentor Another Spell   NOVEMBER 25

Attitude of Gratitude Ritual   NOVEMBER 26

Eloquence Spell   NOVEMBER 29

Perfect Gift Spell   DECEMBER 12

Let Go of Old Behavior Spell   DECEMBER 17

World Card's Fabulous New Year Spell   DECEMBER 31

. . . .

Power Planet Spells

Uranus Technology Spell   MARCH 13

Mercury Retrograde Protection Bag   MAY 15

Fly Your Freak Flag Solar Eclipse Spell   MAY 28

Veil of Neptune Spell   AUGUST 25

Supernova Power Boost Spell   OCTOBER 9

Energize Your Career Mars Spell   OCTOBER 13

Get It Together Jupiter Pasta Spell   DECEMBER 4

Venus Spell to Stop Being So Hard on Yourself   DECEMBER 5

. . . .

Protection

Personal Protection Spell   JANUARY 3

Banish Negativity Spell   MARCH 19

Keep Enemies at Bay Spell   JUNE 16

Remove Oppression Spell   JULY 14

Grant Me the Strength Spell   SEPTEMBER 7

Keep a Secret Spell   SEPTEMBER 20

Setting Boundaries Spell   SEPTEMBER 25

Invoke a Knight's Protection   OCTOBER 19

Spell to Scare Away Monsters   OCTOBER 20

Psychic Self-Defense Spell   DECEMBER 6

Destroy Fear Spell   DECEMBER 27

. . . .

Recipe Spells

Venetial Shadows and Mist Hot Chocolate Spell   MARCH 25

Ensure Good Health Kale Charm   MARCH 30

Irresistibility Empress Tea Spell   APRIL 8

Mexican Love Truffles   MAY 5

Caramel Lace for Elegance and Grace Spell   JULY 19

Self-Confidence of Leo Salad Spell   JULY 23

Soften the Edges Artichoke Spell   SEPTEMBER 19

Witch's Power Breakfast   OCTOBER 1

Happy Children Cupcake Spell   NOVEMBER 20

Get It Together Jupiter Pasta Spell   DECEMBER 4

Four of Cups Unseen Opportunities Spell (Figs, Goat Cheese, and
    Honey)   DECEMBER 8

Go Away Head Cold Roasted Garlic Spell   DECEMBER 16

. . . .

Seasonal

Brighten Winter Doldrums Spell   JANUARY 25

Ritual to Align with Spring   MARCH 22

Ritual to Connect with Summer   JUNE 20

Ritual to Align with Fall   SEPTEMBER 21

Holiday Magic Spell   DECEMBER 1

Ritual to Align with Winter   DECEMBER 22

. . . .

Sleepy Spells

Enchanting Dream Spell   JANUARY 27

Sound Sleep Spell   JANUARY 29

Banish Nightmares Spell   MARCH 15

Dream Inspiration Spell   JULY 27

. . . .

Tarot Cards

Fool Card Connection Ritual   APRIL 1

Magician Card Connection Ritual   FEBRUARY 8

High Priestess Card Connection Ritual   NOVEMBER 8

Empress Card Connection Ritual   APRIL 7

Emperor Card Connection Ritual   JUNE 4

Hierophant Card Connection Ritual   NOVEMBER 22

Lovers Card Connection Ritual   MARCH 2

Chariot Card Connection Ritual   APRIL 21

Strength Card Connection Ritual   MAY 6

Hermit Card Connection Ritual   MAY 22

Wheel of Fortune Card Connection Ritual   MAY 31

Justice Card Connection Ritual   MARCH 5

Hanged Man Card Connection Ritual   SEPTEMBER 3

Death Card Connection Ritual   JULY 12

Temperance Card Connection Ritual   JUNE 13

Devil Card Connection Ritual   JANUARY 17

Tower Card Connection Ritual   JUNE 29

Star Card Connection Ritual   NOVEMBER 19

Moon Card Connection Ritual   MARCH 31

Sun Card Connection Ritual   MAY 10

Judgement Card Connection Ritual   MARCH 24

World Card Connection Ritual   APRIL 22

Ace of Pentacles Connection Ritual   DECEMBER 18

Two of Pentacles Connection Ritual   DECEMBER 26

Three of Pentacles Connection Ritual   JANUARY 5

Four of Pentacles Connection Ritual   JANUARY 14

Five of Pentacles Connection Ritual   APRIL 27

Six of Pentacles Connection Ritual   MAY 9

Seven of Pentacles Connection Ritual   MAY 14

Eight of Pentacles Connection Ritual   AUGUST 30

Nine of Pentacles Connection Ritual   SEPTEMBER 9

Ten of Pentacles Connection Ritual   SEPTEMBER 18

Page of Pentacles Connection Ritual   DECEMBER 13

Knight of Pentacles Connection Ritual   JANUARY 13

Queen of Pentacles Connection Ritual   MAY 18

King of Pentacles Connection Ritual   OCTOBER 28

Ace of Swords Connection Ritual   MARCH 26

Two of Swords Connection Ritual   SEPTEMBER 29

Three of Swords Connection Ritual   OCTOBER 8

Four of Swords Connection Ritual   OCTOBER 14

Five of Swords Connection Ritual   JANUARY 23

Six of Swords Connection Ritual   FEBRUARY 7

Seven of Swords Connection Ritual   FEBRUARY 10

Eight of Swords Connection Ritual   MAY 29

Nine of Swords Connection Ritual   JUNE 6

Ten of Swords Connection Ritual   JUNE 17

Page of Swords Connection Ritual   FEBRUARY 18

Knight of Swords Connection Ritual   AUGUST 23

Queen of Swords Connection Ritual   MAY 2

King of Swords Connection Ritual   JUNE 25

Ace of Wands Connection Ritual   JUNE 26

Two of Wands Connection Ritual   MARCH 23

Three of Wands Connection Ritual   APRIL 4

Four of Wands Connection Ritual   APRIL 16

Five of Wands Connection Ritual   JULY 26

Six of Wands Connection Ritual   AUGUST 4

Seven of Wands Connection Ritual   AUGUST 22

Eight of Wands Connection Ritual   DECEMBER 2

Nine of Wands Connection Ritual   DECEMBER 11

Ten of Wands Connection Ritual   DECEMBER 15

Page of Wands Connection Ritual   DECEMBER 20

Knight of Wands Connection Ritual   OCTOBER 27

Queen of Wands Connection Ritual   FEBRUARY 12

King of Wands Connection Ritual   NOVEMBER 4

Ace of Cups Connection Ritual   SEPTEMBER 22

Two of Cups Connection Ritual   JULY 1

Three of Cups Connection Ritual   JULY 10

Four of Cups Connection Ritual   JULY 16

Five of Cups Connection Ritual   NOVEMBER 2

Six of Cups Connection Ritual   NOVEMBER 10

Seven of Cups Connection Ritual   NOVEMBER 14

Eight of Cups Connection Ritual   FEBRUARY 24

Nine of Cups Connection Ritual   MARCH 7

Ten of Cups Connection Ritual   MARCH 20

Page of Cups Connection Ritual   MAY 27

Knight of Cups Connection Ritual   MARCH 29

Queen of Cups Connection Ritual   JULY 25

King of Cups Connection Ritual   APRIL 25

Tarot-Specific Spells & Rituals

Tarot Candle Spell   FEBRUARY 2

Lunar Ritual to Connect with Your Tarot Deck   FEBRUARY 16

Powers of Prophecy Tarot Reading Ritual   APRIL 6

Ace of Wands Cloud Divination   APRIL 11

Necromantic Tarot Reading   JUNE 15

Chariot Card's Take Action Spell   SEPTEMBER 2

Chi Energy Tarot Deck Charging Spell   SEPTEMBER 28

Hanged Man Reverse the Situation Spell   NOVEMBER 6

Tarot's Shamanic Art Exercise   NOVEMBER 7

Travel

Car Safety Oil   FEBRUARY 26

Safe Crossings Travel Spell   FEBRUARY 27

Manifest a Trip Spell   MARCH 27

Ease of Travel Spell   MAY 20

Invoke Travel Spell   SEPTEMBER 27

Witchy Enchantments

Open Sacral Chakra Energy   FEBRUARY 21

Clairvoyance Exercise   FEBRUARY 28

Alchemy Spell for Self-Transformation   MARCH 9

Venetian Shadows and Mist Hot Chocolate Spell   MARCH 25

Powers of Prophecy Tarot Reading Ritual   APRIL 6

Ace of Wands Cloud Divination   APRIL 11

Charmed Grimoire Spell   APRIL 23

Four Directions Spell   MAY 3

Banish a Ghost Spell   MAY 11

Powered-Up Pendulum Charm   MAY 17

Psychic Vampires Begone Energy Shield   MAY 26

Outdoor Sigil Magic   JUNE 12

Third Eye Diamond Spell   JUNE 14

Necromantic Tarot Reading   JUNE 15

Scrying with Temperance   JULY 13

Triple Goddess Spell   JULY 24

Spell to Stop Zombies in Their Tracks   JULY 28

Diana's Hunting Charm   AUGUST 13

Ritual to Align with Lizard Energy   AUGUST 14

Drawing Down the Sun   AUGUST 15

Dinner with the Departed Ritual and Reading   AUGUST 18

Lampadomancy   AUGUST 29

Tarot Gris Gris Bag   SEPTEMBER 10

Thoth Writing Spell   SEPTEMBER 11

Tarot Triad Ritual   SEPTEMBER 13

Witch's Power Breakfast   OCTOBER 1

As Above, So Below Ritual   OCTOBER 3

Past Lives Exercise   OCTOBER 29

Contemplate Death Ritual   OCTOBER 31

Skull Transformation Ritual   NOVEMBER 9

Time Traveling Journey   NOVEMBER 12

Friday the 13th Good Luck Spell   NOVEMBER 13

Greater Mysteries Meditation   NOVEMBER 15

Hecate's Shamanic Meditation   NOVEMBER 16

Reveal Hidden Truth Meditation   NOVEMBER 18

Hecate Crossroads Power Spell   NOVEMBER 30

Embrace the Darkness Spell   DECEMBER 19

Weird Witches of Macbeth Power Spell   DECEMBER 29

Fool   8, 31, 80, 99, 154, 193, 198, 235, 267, 304, 355, 362

Magician   13, 14, 22, 46, 80, 106, 134, 192, 197, 204, 207, 221, 229, 246, 262, 284, 291, 293

High Priestess   44, 67, 75, 90, 111, 116, 130, 145, 154, 163, 164, 189, 213, 227, 232, 264, 271, 280, 320, 327, 330, 351, 361, 367

Empress   7, 22, 26, 38, 44, 51, 75, 105, 106, 119, 138, 140, 144, 163, 164, 194, 263, 264, 287, 292, 305, 347, 366

Emperor   38, 68, 88, 163, 178, 186, 222, 235, 237, 308, 336, 339

Hierophant   7, 90, 118, 137, 156, 264, 293, 327, 334, 337

Lovers   51, 59, 69, 77, 78, 81, 82, 110, 112, 127, 149, 195, 226, 264, 315, 323

Chariot   64, 88, 119, 160, 180, 207, 218, 251, 253, 283, 324

Strength   29, 30, 32, 33, 102, 125, 134, 158, 184, 203, 212, 223, 253, 258, 267, 268, 281, 305, 345, 353, 371

Hermit   150, 158, 160, 183, 218, 246, 256, 327

Wheel of Fortune   80, 109, 135, 159, 239, 255, 263, 265, 275, 325, 339, 346, 352, 368

Justice   72, 90, 135, 175, 192, 222, 264, 274, 275

Hanged Man   19, 53, 107, 151, 241, 254, 318, 342, 370

Death   2, 8, 128, 136, 160, 201, 304, 307, 312, 321, 334, 362, 364

Temperance   42, 67, 72, 76, 129, 135, 172, 178, 202, 265, 291, 341

Devil   24, 82, 182, 191, 244, 278, 291, 311, 330, 342, 363

Tower   27, 29, 92, 157, 188, 252, 267, 290, 294, 299, 318, 369

Star   14, 17, 18, 27, 41, 65, 67, 77, 86, 95, 111, 126, 153, 156, 194, 216, 223, 244, 264, 306, 323, 331, 339, 343, 359

Moon   57, 79, 92, 98, 110, 130, 145, 150, 153, 207, 216, 230, 247, 272, 285, 288, 299, 317, 320, 328, 348, 351, 367

Sun   14, 19, 22, 32, 51, 79, 85, 94, 97, 113, 138, 179, 210, 211, 221, 235, 263, 265, 283, 337, 345, 362, 366

Judgement   91, 293, 304

World   38, 49, 75, 107, 109, 120, 124, 140, 143, 191, 193, 203, 221, 235, 264, 268, 294, 298, 328, 335, 355, 373, 374

Ace of Cups   26, 28, 47, 55, 85, 110, 111, 121, 131, 136, 168, 225, 247, 258, 265, 273, 277, 303, 333, 335, 338, 339, 373, 374

Ace of Pentacles   38, 47, 58, 84, 95, 121, 131, 258, 266, 285, 354, 360, 373, 374

Ace of Swords   10, 27, 47, 60, 64, 93, 121, 131, 141, 182, 236, 258, 324, 351, 359, 373

Ace of Wands   26, 42, 47, 51, 73, 89, 95, 109, 121, 131, 133, 158, 168, 185, 197, 258, 304, 315, 317, 343, 373

Two of Cups   28, 55, 77, 85, 127, 140, 190, 220, 225, 287, 302, 323, 340

Two of Pentacles   53, 333, 368

Two of Swords   10, 37, 182, 231, 276, 280

Two of Wands   90, 294, 340

Three of Cups   17, 55, 199, 208, 285, 349, 371, 372

Three of Pentacles   12, 61

Three of Swords   111, 198, 289

Three of Wands   102, 317

Four of Cups   108, 205, 350

Four of Pentacles   21, 192, 227

Four of Swords   34, 36, 222, 295, 300, 361

Four of Wands   9, 114, 127, 139, 140, 200, 218, 365

Five of Cups   200, 314, 335

Five of Pentacles   125

Five of Swords   30

Five of Wands   215, 217, 255, 352

Six of Cups   9, 55, 140, 225, 268, 286, 322, 365

Six of Pentacles   137, 274

Six of Swords   45, 65, 94, 139, 162, 198, 237

Six of Wands   224, 255, 322, 336

Seven of Cups   34, 66, 117, 245, 299, 326

Seven of Pentacles   115, 142, 187

Seven of Swords   48, 239, 354

Seven of Wands   217, 242, 370

Eight of Cups   33, 62, 103, 154, 156, 268, 298, 361, 363, 370

Eight of Pentacles   61, 187, 250, 340

Eight of Swords   19, 31, 122, 157, 170, 193, 196, 203, 270, 304

Eight of Wands   52, 68, 71, 85, 124, 230, 251, 285, 317, 318, 344, 366

Nine of Cups   11, 74, 83, 128, 198, 207, 315

Nine of Pentacles   9, 79, 122, 126, 132, 187, 198, 206, 228, 239, 260, 286, 336, 365

Nine of Swords   60, 141, 165, 239, 351

Nine of Wands   161, 196, 217, 353

Ten of Cups   35, 87, 124, 169, 332, 333, 373, 374

Ten of Pentacles   23, 39, 70, 103, 124, 166, 192, 197, 219, 269, 328, 356, 366, 373, 374

Ten of Swords   124, 176, 281, 313, 373

Ten of Wands   15, 124, 244, 281, 357, 359, 373

Knight of Cups   65, 96, 148, 160, 245, 300, 338

Knight of Pentacles   15, 20, 79, 300

Knight of Swords   10, 65, 203, 243, 300, 358

Knight of Wands   13, 181, 300, 308

Page of Cups   66, 149, 155, 245, 332, 338, 348

Page of Pentacles   39, 115, 181, 256, 332, 355

Page of Swords   56, 158, 209, 233, 276, 286, 332

Page of Wands   13, 94, 278, 332, 362, 371

Queen of Cups   7, 16, 66, 104, 149, 167, 173, 214, 245, 251, 372

Queen of Pentacles   146, 257, 336, 372

Queen of Swords   10, 100, 130, 141, 182, 276, 296, 297, 341, 372

Queen of Wands   3, 13, 23, 25, 50, 112, 151, 301, 329, 371, 372

King of Cups   57, 73, 123, 147, 245, 251, 341

King of Pentacles   3, 15, 101, 147, 309

King of Swords   10, 63, 147, 182, 184, 236, 275, 276

King of Wands   13, 23, 112, 147, 234, 316

To Write to the Author

If you wish to contact the author or would like more information about this book, please write to the author in care of Llewellyn Worldwide and we will forward your request. Both the author and the publisher appreciate hearing from you and learning of your enjoyment of this book and how it has helped you. Llewellyn Worldwide cannot guarantee that every letter written to the author can be answered, but all will be forwarded. Please write to:

Sasha Graham
c/o Llewellyn Worldwide
2143 Wooddale Drive
Woodbury, MN 55125-2989

Please enclose a self-addressed stamped envelope for reply
or $1.00 to cover costs. If outside the USA, enclose
an international postal reply coupon.

Many of Llewellyn's authors have websites with additional information and resources. For more information, please visit our website:

www.llewellyn.com